A NEW BOOK OF COOKERY

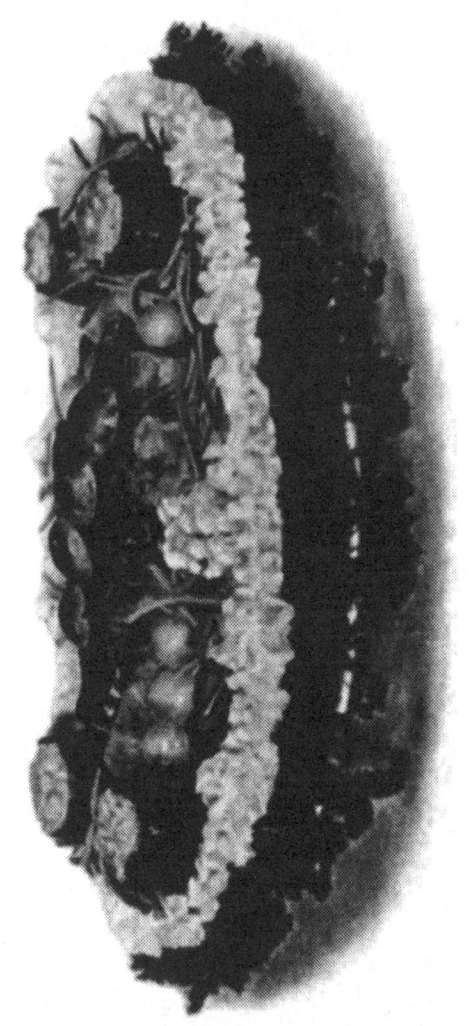

PLANKED RUMP STEAK. *Frontispiece.* See Page 108

A NEW BOOK OF COOKERY

BY

FANNIE MERRITT FARMER

Of Miss Farmer's School of Cookery

AUTHOR OF "THE BOSTON COOKING-SCHOOL COOK BOOK"
"FOOD AND COOKERY FOR THE SICK AND CONVALESCENT," AND "CHAFING-DISH POSSIBILITIES"

EIGHT HUNDRED AND SIXTY RECIPES, COVERING THE WHOLE RANGE OF COOKERY, EIGHT COLORED PLATES, AND TWO HUNDRED AND TWENTY-SIX HALF-TONE ILLUSTRATIONS

Creative Cookbooks
Monterey, California

A New Book of Cookery

by
Fannie Merritt Farmer

ISBN: 1-4101-0372-2

Copyright © 2003 by Fredonia Books

Reprinted from the 1917 edition

Creative Cookbooks
An Imprint of Fredonia Books
Monterey, California
http://www.creativecookbooks.com

All rights reserved, including the right to reproduce this book, or portions thereof, in any form.

In order to make original editions of historical works available to scholars at an economical price, this facsimile of the original edition of 1917 is reproduced from the best available copy and has been digitally enhanced to improve legibility, but the text remains unaltered to retain historical authenticity.

"*The art of cookery, when not allied with a degenerate taste or with gluttony, is one of the criteria of a people's civilization.*"

"*We grow like what we eat;*
  Bad food depresses, good food exalts us like an inspiration."

PREFACE

WITH the advancement of the art of cookery, it has become impossible to compress within the limits of a single volume the wealth of material which is at hand. It is now seventeen years since The Boston Cooking-School Cook Book was first published. Since that time it has been frequently revised and a large number of new recipes added, first in the form of an appendix and addenda, later incorporated in logical order throughout the volume. But the results of the labors and experiments of the last seven years have, I believe, justified the publication of an entirely new work. It will be understood that this new work is in no sense a substitute for my earlier one, but rather a sequel. It is, let me repeat, a comprehensive survey of the progress of the last few years and contains recipes economical and simple as well as expensive and elaborate, covering the whole range of cookery.

My earnest hope is that the book will fulfil a real and vital need. I cannot send it forth without an expression of sincere appreciation for the kindly aid of enthusiastic pupils and devoted teachers.

F. M. F.

BOSTON, September, 1912.

TABLE OF CONTENTS

Chapter		Page
I	How to Measure and Combine Ingredients	1
II	Beverages	5
III	Raised Bread Mixtures	14
IV	Quick Breads, Muffins, and Doughnuts	25
V	Cereal, Cheese, and Vegetarian Dishes	38
VI	Eggs	53
VII	Soups and Soup Accompaniments	64
VIII	Fish	79
IX	Beef	107
X	Lamb and Mutton	120
XI	Veal and Sweetbreads	125
XII	Pork	132
XIII	Poultry	139
XIV	Game	146
XV	Stuffings for Game and Poultry	151
XVI	Meat and Fish Sauces	154
XVII	Vegetables	161
XVIII	Potatoes	182
XIX	Salads	194
XX	Salad Dressings	212

TABLE OF CONTENTS

Chapter		Page
XXI	Entrées	219
XXII	Hot Puddings	245
XXIII	Pudding Sauces	257
XXIV	Cold Desserts	265
XXV	Frozen Desserts	281
XXVI	Pastry and Pies	304
XXVII	Pastry Desserts	312
XXVIII	Gingerbreads, Cookies, and Wafers	319
XXIX	Cake	328
XXX	Cake Fillings and Frostings	345
XXXI	Confections	355
XXXII	Hors-d'Œuvres	372
XXXIII	Sandwiches	381
XXXIV	Fruits: Fresh, Preserved, and Canned	391
XXXV	Pickling	401
XXXVI	Suitable Combinations for Serving	411
	Index	421

ILLUSTRATIONS

Planked Rump Steak. *In Color* . . . . *Frontispiece*	
	FACING PAGE
Necessary Utensils for Correct Measurements .	2
Five O'Clock Tea Tray	3
Accompaniments to the Five O'Clock Cup of Tea	3
Luncheon Coffee	8
Swedish Nut Wafers, Marguerite Squares, Peanut Wafers	8
Marshmallow Chocolate	9
Iced Fruit Juice	9
Moette Punch	12
Fruit Punch with Whipped Cream	12
Ginger Ale Cup	13
Claret Cup	13
Currant Loaf	16
Cincinnati Coffee Bread	16
The Method of Rasping	17
Rasped Rolls	17
The Shaping of Crossett Rolls	20
Crossett Rolls	20
Butterfly Rolls	21
Moravian Bread ready for the Oven	21
Fried Bread	24
Raised Doughnuts	24
The Shaping of Holland Brioche Cakes	25
Holland Brioche Cakes	25
Hot Cross Buns	30
Swedish Wreaths	30
Cream Wafers	31

ILLUSTRATIONS

	FACING PAGE
Afternoon Tea Doughnuts	31
Fried Rice	40
Little Brahmins	40
Little Ducklings	41
Shapleigh Luncheon Cheese	41
Pimiento Cheese Wafers	46
Walnut Deceits	46
Piquante Cheese Crackers	47
Mock Sausages with Fried Apple Rings	52
A Group of Dishes for Eggs, Vegetables and Entrées	53
Windsor Eggs	62
Jellied French Poached Eggs	62
Bouillon Cups	63
Toasted Triangles	63
Mock Cassava Bread in the Making	76
Mock Cassava Bread	76
Pulled Bread	77
Hominy Croûtons	77
Scallop Cocktail	84
Sardine Cocktail	84
Broiled Pompano, Cucumber Hollandaise	85
Shattuck Halibut	85
The Preparing of Stuffed Turbans of Flounder	94
Stuffed Turbans of Flounder	94
Fillet of Flounder in Paper Cover ready for Oven	95
Fillet of Flounder in Paper Cover	95
Petite Halibut, Lobster Sauce	98
Moulded Rolled Fillet of Halibut	98
Iroquois Steak	99
Tournadoes of Beef	99
Planked Sirloin Steak	108
The Larding of a Fillet of Beef	109

ILLUSTRATIONS

xiii

FACING PAGE

Cold Roast Beef à la Shapleigh	109
Lamb Chops à la Rector	122
Tournadoes of Lamb ready for Cooking	122
Mutton Duck ready for Oven	123
Mutton Duck Garnished for Serving	123
Loin of Veal Allemande ready for Oven	128
Loin of Veal Allemande	128
Kernels of Pork	129
Roast Crown of Pork	129
Frosted Ham. *In color*	136
Little Roast Pig	140
Moulded Jellied Chicken	140
Canadian Meat Pie	141
Chicken Pie, Country Style	141
Planked Boned Chicken	144
Ambassadrice Capon	144
Knickerbocker Suprême of Chicken	145
Chicken à la Cadillac	145
Larded Breasts of Guinea Chicken	148
Squabs en Casserole	148
French Artichoke, Vinaigrette Sauce	163
Peppers Stuffed with Fresh Green Corn	163
Arlington Asparagus	164
Asparagus, Mousselaine Sauce	164
Moulded Spinach	173
Moulded Spinach on Artichoke Bottoms	173
Radishes Cut for Garnishing	174
Delmonico Tomatoes	174
Jellied Vegetable Ring	184
Vegetable Panachée	184
Potatoes à la Suisse	185
Lorrette Potatoes	185
Nut and Potato Croquettes	192
Piedmont Potato Croquettes	192
Rector Salad	193

ILLUSTRATIONS

	FACING PAGE
Carlton Salad	193
Indian Salad. *In Color*	196
Spring Salad. *In Color*	196
German Tomato Salad	198
Huntington Salad	198
Celery Salad Bonne Femme	199
Flemish Beauty Salad	199
Asparagus Salad, I. *In Color*	200
Easter Salad. *In Color*	200
Parisian Grape Fruit Salad	202
Touraine Grape Fruit Salad	202
Cherry Nut Salad	203
Campestris Salad	203
Grape Fruit Jelly Salad	206
Banana Salad	206
Ginger Ale Salad	207
Los Angeles Fruit Salad	207
Scallops en Brochette	220
Cutlets of Ham Alexandria	220
Chicken à la King	221
Chicken and Mushroom Timbales	221
Lining of Mould for Traymore Timbales	224
Traymore Timbales	224
Lobster Boats	225
Crab and Mushroom Vol-au-Vent	225
Sweetbreads à la Root	228
Sweetbreads Monroe	228
Pear Condé, Compote of Rice	229
Waldorf Sweetbreads	229
Macedoine in Aspic. *In Color*	234
Moulded Fish in Aspic	238
Dressed Cucumber	238
Preparation of Stuffed Smoked Tongue	239
Sliced Stuffed Smoked Tongue	239
Boned Turkey	242

ILLUSTRATIONS

FACING PAGE

Slices of Boned Turkey and Cubes of Garnished Aspic	242
Snow Eggs	254
Sterling Fruit Pudding	254
Irish Plum Pudding	255
Irish Plum Pudding steamed in Ring Mould and garnished for Christmas	255
Fancy Cutters, Pans and Moulds	260
Charlotte Russe in the Making	261
Charlotte Russe	261
Jelly Panachée	272
Cold Pineapple Soufflé	272
Macedoine of Fruit	273
Jellied Fruit, Moulded	273
Utensils for Freezing	282
Standish Pudding	283
St. Valentine's Pudding	283
Montrose Pudding	286
Strawberry Ice Cream en Surprise	286
Lighted Ice Cream	287
Macaroon Basket filled with Ice Cream	287
Grape Fruit Cocktail with Mint Balls	294
Coupe Caruso	295
Parfait Amour	298
Cognac Pear Coupe	298
A Tray of Pastry Novelties	299
Devonshire Pie	316
Mont Blanc	316
Keswick Gingerbread	317

ILLUSTRATIONS

	FACING PAGE
Nut Oatmeal Cookies	317
Peanut Bars	320
Peanut Macaroons	320
Marshmallow Teas ready for Oven	321
Marshmallow Teas	321
Chocolate Walnut Wafers	324
Peanut Wafers	324
The Rolling of Swedish Nut Wafers	325
Swedish Nut Wafers	325
Gratan Mocha	328
Vienna Cake	328
Birthday Cake for a Three-Year-Old	329
Raised Loaf Cake	332
Devil's Food Cake	332
Lady Baltimore Cake	333
Lord Baltimore Cake	333
Butterfly Cake. *In Color*	336
Anniversary Cake	338
Christmas Cakes	339
Ornamented Wedding Cake	339
Anniversary Cake. *In Color*	342
The Salting of Filberts	356
Chapin Chocolate Caramels	356
Raisin Opera Caramels	357
Fudge	357
After Dinner Mints	362
Turkish Mint Paste	362
Marshmallow Mint Bonbons with a Variety of Garnishings	363
Dipped Cream Mints in the Making	366
Dipped Cream Mints	366
Candy Basket filled with Glacéd Strawberries	367
A Basket of Home Made Sweets for Christmas	367
Crystal Cups in the Making	370
Crystal Cups	370

ILLUSTRATIONS xvii

FACING PAGE

Cinkites	371
Chocolate Dipped Candied Orange Peel	371
Allen Canapé. St. Valentine's Canapé. Dexter Canapé	374
Smoked Fish Canapé	375
Fish Canapé	375
Horn of Plenty Canapé	378
Butterfly Canapé	378
Kindergarten Sandwiches in the Making	379
Kindergarten Sandwiches	379
Mosaic Sandwiches	382
Honor Sandwiches	382
Horseradish Sandwiches	383
Dream Sandwiches	383
Fairmont Sandwiches	386
Egg and Potato Salad	386
Belmont Baked Apples ready for the Oven	387
Belmont Baked Apples	387
Grape Fruit à la Russe	390
Rector Leaf	390
Canteloupe Suprême	391
Lenox Strawberries	391
Pastry Boats filled with Fresh Fruit	394
Rhubarb Conserve in the Making	394
Home Made Jelly Bags	395
Lemons cut for Garnishings. *In Color*	396
Cranberry Jelly with Celery	398
Mint Jelly, Corn Relish and Peach Conserve	398
Table laid for Breakfast	410
Table laid for Luncheon	411
Table laid for Dinner	414
Table laid for Luncheon Buffet	415
Table laid for Afternoon Tea	418
Table laid for Sunday Night or After Theatre Supper	419

A New Book of Cookery

CHAPTER I

HOW TO MEASURE AND COMBINE INGREDIENTS

THERE is nothing which has done so much to place cookery on an improved basis as the almost universal introduction of accurate methods in measuring. A generation or two ago each household had its favorite cups and spoons of varying sizes which helped as guides in measuring. It was in these days that one often heard the statement, "Cooks are born, not made." Good judgment coupled with experience taught some to measure by sight, which was a step towards good results, but the vast majority needed definite guides. Thus arose the necessity of uniform measuring cups and spoons which are an essential in every kitchen.

Measuring cups (holding one-half pint), divided into quarters or thirds, are made of tin, graniteware, or glass and may be bought of any dealer in kitchen furnishings or at large department stores. Measuring spoons come in two sizes, the smaller of which is called a teaspoon, the larger a tablespoon. Mixing spoons, which are somewhat larger than tablespoons, should not be confounded with them. A case knife, which is used for levelling as well as dividing ingredients, is also necessary to make measuring as accurate as is possible.

All ingredients are measured level.
A cupful is measured level.
A tablespoonful is measured level.
A teaspoonful is measured level.

TO MEASURE DRY INGREDIENTS

I. *By cupfuls.*

Put in the ingredient to be measured by spoonfuls or from a scoop, round slightly and level with a case knife for a cupful. For fractions of cupfuls fill in like manner to correct division line indicated in cup. Never shake the cup while filling.

II. *By teaspoonfuls or tablespoonfuls.*

Dip spoon in ingredient, fill, lift, and level with a case knife having the sharp edge of knife towards tip of spoon. Divide with a case knife lengthwise of spoon for a half spoonful. Divide halves crosswise for quarters, and quarters crosswise for eighths. Less than one-eighth teaspoonful is called a few grains.

TO MEASURE BUTTER, LARD, AND OTHER SOLID FATS

I. *By cupfuls.*

Pack solidly into cup and level with a case knife for a cupful. For fractions of cupfuls pack in like manner to correct division line indicated in cup.

Necessary Utensils for Correct Measurements.

Five O'Clock Tea Tray.

Accompaniments to the Five O'Clock Cup of Tea

II. *By teaspoonfuls or tablespoonfuls.*

Pack solidly into spoon and level with a case knife. Divide with a case knife lengthwise of spoon for a half spoonful. Divide halves crosswise for quarters, and quarters crosswise for eighths.

TO MEASURE LIQUIDS

I. *By cupfuls.*

Pour liquid to be measured into cup and fill to very top for cupfuls. A cupful of liquid is all that the cup will hold and cannot be easily moved from one place to another without overflowing. For fractions of cupfuls fill in like manner to correct division line indicated in cup.

II. *By teaspoonfuls or tablespoonfuls.*

Dip spoon in liquid, fill and lift, taking up all the spoon will hold. When dry ingredients, liquids, and fats are all called for in the same recipe, measure in the order given, thereby using but one cup.

HOW TO COMBINE INGREDIENTS

Next to measuring comes care in combining, — a fact not always recognized by the inexperienced. Three ways are considered, — stirring, beating, and cutting and folding.

To stir, mix by using circular motion, widening the circles until all is blended. Stirring is the motion ordinarily employed in all cookery, alone or in combination with beating.

To beat, turn ingredient or ingredients over and over, continually bringing the under part to the surface, thus allowing the utensil used for beating to be constantly brought in contact with bottom of the dish and throughout the mixture.

To cut and fold, introduce one ingredient into another ingredient or mixture by two motions: with a spoon, a repeated vertical downward motion, known as cutting, and a turning over and over of mixture, allowing bowl of spoon each time to come in contact with bottom of dish, is called folding. These repeated motions are alternated until thorough blending is accomplished.

By stirring, ingredients are mixed; *by beating*, a large amount of air is inclosed; *by cutting and folding*, air already introduced is prevented from escaping.

CHAPTER II

BEVERAGES

Hawaiian Five o'Clock Tea

ALLOW to each cup of five o'clock tea three cubes prepared pineapple cubes and sugar to taste. For pineapple cubes, put one-half cup syrup drained from canned pineapple in small saucepan, add two tablespoons sugar and one-half cup canned sliced pineapple, cut in half-inch cubes. Bring to the boiling point, and let simmer until syrup has been almost absorbed by fruit.

Lemon Cut Sugar

Rub entire surface of blocks of domino sugar over the rind of a lemon which has been washed and wiped until dry. Store in a glass jar, and use to sweeten and flavor five o'clock tea.

Orange Cut Sugar

Rub entire surface of blocks of domino sugar over the rind of an orange which has been washed and wiped until dry. Store in a glass jar, and use to sweeten and flavor five o'clock tea.

Syracuse Five o'Clock Tea

Sweeten five o'clock tea with white or red rock candy.

Jamaica Five o'Clock Tea

Allow to each cup of five o'clock tea from one-half to one teaspoon rum.

Luncheon Coffee

Strain coffee remaining from breakfast, sweeten to taste and chill. Dilute with cream and pour into a glass pitcher. Serve in tall glasses, allowing two tablespoons vanilla ice cream to each glass.

Chocolate Syrup

4 squares Baker's chocolate	⅛ teaspoon salt
1¾ cups sugar	1½ cups boiling water

Melt chocolate in saucepan placed in a larger saucepan of boiling water, add sugar and salt and stir until well mixed; then pour on gradually, while stirring constantly, boiling water. Stir until smooth, bring to the boiling point and let boil five minutes. Cool, turn into a jar and keep in ice box or cold place.

Chocolate Egg and Milk Shake

2 tablespoons finely crushed ice	1 egg
2½ tablespoons chocolate syrup	⅜ cup milk

Put ingredients in glass and shake thoroughly (using one of the shakers that may be bought at any kitchen-furnishing store), and strain into another glass for serving. A few gratings nutmeg or a few grains cinnamon may be sprinkled on top. The ice may be omitted if the ingredients have been thoroughly chilled in the ice box.

Chocolate Ice Cream Soda

3 tablespoons chocolate syrup 2 tablespoons vanilla
Soda water   ice cream

Put syrup in tall glass, add vanilla ice cream, and fill glass with soda water drawn from siphon. Stir thoroughly and serve.

Siphons of soda may be bought of any druggist or first-class city grocer.

Hot Marshmallow Chocolate

4 cups milk   Few grains salt
2½ ounces vanilla chocolate   Sugar
                   Marshmallows

Put milk and chocolate in double boiler, and when scalding point is reached add salt and sugar to taste. Beat two minutes, using a Dover egg beater. Put two marshmallows in each chocolate cup and fill cups two-thirds full of hot chocolate. Use the inexpensive kind of marshmallows, as they melt more quickly.

Cocoa Egg Nog

White 1 egg   1 teaspoon breakfast cocoa
1 teaspoon sugar   Few grains salt
                   ¾ cup cold milk

Beat egg white until stiff and add gradually, while beating constantly, sugar, cocoa, and salt. Add to one-half the mixture, while beating constantly, cold milk. Turn into a glass and pile remaining egg mixture on top.

Iced Fruit Juice

Arrange fresh mint leaves, lengthwise, at equal distances in frappé glasses, allowing four to each glass. Put in finely crushed ice to three-fourths depth of glasses, and pour over to fill glass fresh fruit juice, sweetened to taste, using grape juice, fresh raspberry juice, fresh strawberry juice or fresh pineapple juice. Arrange glasses on small plates covered with doilies, and accompany each with a teaspoon.

Serve as a first course at a ladies' luncheon. Mint leaves may be omitted.

Card Punch

Mix one pint bottle grape juice and two pint bottles ginger ale. Have glasses half full of finely crushed ice and fill with mixture.

Luncheon Punch

1 quart Apollinaris   1 quart White Grape Juice

Pack bottled ingredients in salt and ice and let stand until thoroughly chilled. Just before serving mix and pour into a chilled pitcher.

LUNCHEON COFFEE. — *Page 6.*

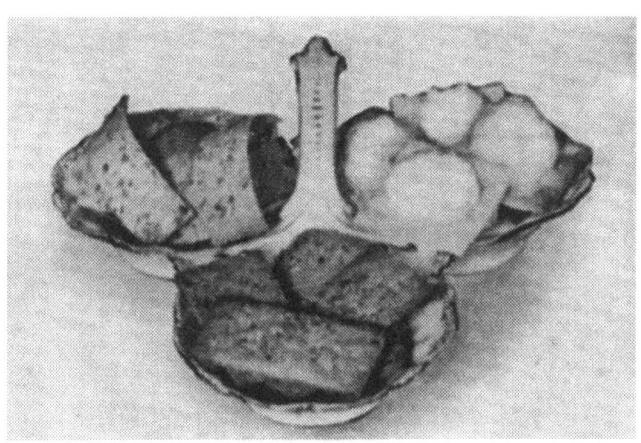

SWEDISH NUT WAFERS. MARGUERITE SQUARES
PEANUT WAFERS.

MARSHMALLOW CHOCOLATE.—*Page* 7

ICED FRUIT JUICE.— *Page* 8.

Moette Punch

1 cup pineapple syrup
1¼ cups white grape juice
1 pint Apollinaris
Sugar

Mix fruit juices, add Apollinaris and sweeten to taste. Pour into punch bowl and add one quart raspberry ice moulded in five round moulds.

German Punch

1 cup grape juice
1 cup cider
½ cup grape fruit juice
2 bottles Lithia water
Sugar

Mix first four ingredients and sweeten to taste. Pour into a punch bowl over a large cake of ice.

Oriental Punch

1 cup sugar
1 cup water
6 cloves
1 inch stick cinnamon
½ tablespoon chopped Canton ginger
Juice 2 lemons
Juice 3 oranges
1 drop oil of peppermint
Green coloring
Mint leaves

Make a syrup by boiling sugar and water six minutes. Add cloves, cinnamon, and ginger; cover and let stand until cold. Add fruit juices, strain, color green, and add peppermint. Let stand one hour and pour into punch bowl over a cake of ice. Garnish with fresh mint leaves.

Fruit Punch with Whipped Cream

1 pint bottle grape juice	Zest 1 orange
3 tablespoons lemon juice	4 sprigs fresh mint
⅛ cup orange juice	Few grains salt
1 cup fresh pineapple pulp with juice	Few gratings nutmeg
	Crushed ice
¾ cup domino sugar	1 pint bottle soda water
Zest 1 lemon	Whipped cream

Mix fruits and add sugar, which has been rubbed over lemon and orange to remove zest; then add mint, salt, and nutmeg. Cover, and let stand in ice-box one hour to ripen. Pour over crushed ice, add soda water, and serve in tall glasses with whipped cream on top. Garnish with mint leaves.

Pineapple Julep

1 quart canned pineapple	½ cup raspberry syrup
Juice 2 lemons	¼ cup brandy
Juice 2 oranges	2 tablespoons gin
1 cup sugar	1 pint Moselle wine
½ cup water	1 pint Apollinaris water

Cut pineapple in small pieces and add lemon juice, orange juice, sugar, and water. Bring to the boiling point and let boil seven minutes. Add remaining ingredients, cool, and strain into a punch bowl over a large cake of ice.

Siberian Punch

2 cups sugar	¼ cup brandy
1 cup orange juice	Few grains salt
1 cup lemon juice	Pink coloring
1 cup pineapple juice	Block of ice
¼ cup rum	1 quart Apollinaris

Pour fruit juices over sugar, cover and let stand until sugar has dissolved. Add rum, brandy, and salt, and color pink. Pour over ice in punch bowl, and just before serving add Apollinaris. Garnish with four thin slices of lemon (from which seeds have been removed), five thin slices of banana cut crosswise, and eight strawberries cut in halves lengthwise.

Alumni Punch

3 pounds sugar	1 quart bottle Sauterne
Grated rind 3 lemons	1 cup crême de menthe
1 quart water	Green coloring
Juice 1½ doz. lemons	Ice
1 pint pineapple juice	2 quarts Apollinaris water
1 cup Malaga grapes	

Make a syrup by boiling sugar, grated rind, and water fifteen minutes. Strain, cool, and add lemon juice, pineapple juice, Sauterne, and crême de menthe. Color green and pour over a large piece of ice in punch bowl. Add more sugar if necessary, and just before serving, Apollinaris water, and grapes, skinned, seeded, and cut in halves.

Ginger Ale Cup

2½ tablespoons Maraschino	1 quart bottle ginger ale
2½ tablespoons Benedictine	Chopped ice
1 tablespoon lime juice	1 slice lemon
2½ teaspoons powdered sugar	2 slices oranges
2 thin slices cucumber rind	Few sprigs fresh mint

Mix first six ingredients and pour into pitcher one-third full of chopped ice. Garnish with thin slice of lemon from which seeds have been removed, cut in halves; orange slices from which seeds have been removed, and a few large sprigs fresh mint leaves, sprinkled with powdered sugar.

Claret Cup

- 2½ tablespoons Benedictine
- 2½ tablespoons Maraschino
- 2½ tablespoons Yellow Chartreuse
- 1 tablespoon lemon juice
- 2½ teaspoons powdered sugar
- Chopped ice
- 6 strawberries
- 2 slices orange
- 2 strips cucumber rind
- 3 sprigs fresh mint
- 1 quart bottle claret

Mix first five ingredients, shake thoroughly, and strain into a pitcher containing chopped ice. Add strawberries, cut in halves, slices of orange (from which seeds have been removed), cucumber rind, and claret. Garnish with sprigs of mint, the leaves of which have been sprinkled with powdered sugar.

Sauterne Cup

Make same as Claret Cup, using Sauterne in place of claret.

Champagne Cup

Make same as Claret Cup, using "Great Western" Champagne in place of claret.

MOETTE PUNCH. — *Page 9.*

FRUIT PUNCH WITH WHIPPED CREAM. — *Page 10*

Ginger Ale Cup. — *Page* 11

Claret Cup. — *Page* 12.

Champagne Punch

1 quart "Great Western" Champagne   3 pints orange sherbet

Put sherbet in punch bowl and pour over Champagne. When sherbet is nearly melted serve in sauterne glasses.

A luncheon **beverage.**

CHAPTER III

RAISED BREAD MIXTURES

Family White Loaf
[Made of Condensed Milk]

1 tablespoon lard	¼ cup condensed milk
1 tablespoon butter	1 yeast cake
2 teaspoons salt	¼ cup lukewarm water
1¾ cups boiling water	6 cups sifted flour

Put lard, butter, and salt in bread mixer or bowl without a lip; pour on boiling water and condensed milk, and, when lukewarm, add yeast cake, broken in pieces and dissolved in lukewarm water, and five cups flour. Stir until thoroughly mixed, add remaining flour, toss on a slightly floured board and knead until mixture is smooth. Return to bowl and cover with a clean cloth and board or tin cover. Let rise at a temperature of 65° F. until mixture has doubled its bulk, the time required being about three hours. Cut down, toss on a slightly floured board, shape into two double loaves and put in buttered pans. Cover, again let rise, and bake in a hot oven fifty-five minutes.

Currant Loaf

Use same recipe as for Family White Loaf. When shaping into loaves, knead in one-third cup cleaned dried currants.

Graham Raised Loaf

2 cups milk
6 tablespoons molasses
1½ teaspoons salt
⅛ yeast cake
¼ cup lukewarm water
2 cups sifted Graham flour
½ cup Graham bran
Flour

Scald milk and add molasses and salt. When lukewarm, add yeast cake dissolved in water, Graham flour and Graham bran, and white flour to knead. Cover, let rise, shape into loaves, again let rise, and bake in a hot oven.

German Caraway Bread

2 cups scalded milk
2 tablespoons sugar
2 tablespoons butter
1 teaspoon salt
1 yeast cake
½ cup lukewarm water
2 tablespoons caraway seeds
6 cups rye flour
1½ cups entire wheat flour

Add sugar, butter, and salt to scalded milk. When mixture is lukewarm add yeast cake dissolved in lukewarm water, caraway seeds, and rye flour. Turn on a board and knead, while incorporating entire wheat flour. Return to bowl, cover and let rise until mixture has doubled its bulk. Shape into loaves, put in buttered bread pans, again cover, let rise, and bake in a hot oven.

Reception Rolls

1 cup scalded milk
1½ tablespoons sugar
1 teaspoon salt
¼ cup shortening
1 yeast cake
¼ cup lukewarm water
White 1 egg
3½ cups flour

Put sugar, salt, and shortening (using one-half butter and one-half lard) in a bowl, pour over milk, and when mixture is lukewarm, add yeast cake, dissolved in lukewarm water, white of egg beaten until stiff, and flour. Toss on a slightly floured board and knead. Return to bowl, cover and let rise until mixture has doubled its bulk. Again toss on a slightly floured board, shape, place in buttered pan, cover, again let rise, and bake in a hot oven twenty minutes.

Rasped Rolls

1½ cups scalded milk	¾ teaspoon salt
2 tablespoons butter	1 yeast cake
½ tablespoon sugar	2 tablespoons lukewarm water
3½ cups flour	

Add butter, sugar, and salt to milk, and when lukewarm add yeast cake dissolved in water, and three cups flour. Beat five minutes, cover and let rise until mixture has doubled its bulk. Cut down, add remaining flour and beat five minutes. Cover and again let rise. Toss on a slightly floured board and knead thoroughly. Shape in biscuits, then roll from centres, using the hands, forming rolls four inches long and pointed at ends, arrange on a buttered sheet, cover, let rise, and bake in a hot oven. Cool slightly, remove outside crust with grater, return to oven and bake five minutes.

Currant Loaf. — *Page* 14.

Cincinnati Coffee Bread. — *Page* 19

THE METHOD OF RASPING. — *Page* 16

RASPED ROLLS. — *Page* 16.

Crossett Rolls

Scald one cup milk, turn into mixing bowl (without a lip), and add one tablespoon, each, lard and sugar, and three-fourths teaspoon salt. When lukewarm, add one yeast cake, dissolved in one-fourth cup lukewarm water, and flour to knead, the amount required being about two and one-half cups. Toss on a slightly floured cloth, knead, return to bowl, cover and let rise until mixture has doubled its bulk. Put in ice box and let stand until chilled. Toss on a floured cloth, pat and roll into a long rectangle one-fourth inch in thickness. Dot over with four tablespoons butter and fold from ends towards centre, making three layers. Turn half-way around, pat, roll out as before and dot over with butter; repeat twice. Put in ice box and let chill for two hours. Toss on a floured cloth, pat and roll as thin as possible. Cut in four-inch squares and squares in halves on the diagonal, using a sharp knife. Roll, beginning on the diagonal (as shown in illustration), and shape in crescent fashion. Place on buttered sheet, again chill in ice box twenty minutes and bake in a hot oven.

Butterfly Rolls

½ cup butter	2 eggs
1 cup boiling water	1 teaspoon salt
⅔ cup sugar	2 teaspoons lemon extract
½ yeast cake	4½ cups flour
Sugar and cinnamon	

Put butter and sugar in bowl, pour on boiling water and when lukewarm, add yeast cake, broken in pieces. Add eggs, unbeaten, salt, and lemon extract; then add flour gradually, while beating constantly, using the hand. Cover and let rise. When mixture has doubled its bulk, knead and again let rise. Toss on a floured cloth, pat with rolling pin to one-fourth inch in thickness and roll in rectangular shape. Brush over with melted butter, sprinkle with sugar and cinnamon and roll like a jelly roll. Cut crosswise in one-inch pieces; then each piece nearly in halves, crosswise, and turn over in such a way as to leave a surface of layers on top. Shape, using fingers, to represent a butterfly. Insert two currants in each, place on a buttered sheet, cover, and again let rise. Brush over with milk or yolk of egg diluted with water, and bake in a hot oven. The sprinkling of sugar and cinnamon may be omitted.

Cream Bread Fingers

½ cup heavy cream
2 tablespoons sugar
¼ tablespoon salt

1 yeast cake
¼ cup lukewarm water
1½ cups flour

Scald cream, and add sugar and salt; when lukewarm, add yeast cake dissolved in lukewarm water and flour. Toss on a slightly floured board and knead. Return to bowl, cover, let rise, toss on a slightly floured board, and pat and roll to one-fourth inch in thickness. Shape with a lady finger cutter, first dipped in flour, arrange on a buttered tin sheet, cover, again let rise, and bake in a moderate oven. Brush over with two tablespoons milk, mixed with one tablespoon sugar, and return to oven to glaze.

Moravian Bread

1 yeast cake	1 egg
¼ cup lukewarm water	¾ cup shortening
1 cup hot mashed potatoes	1 cup sugar
2 cups scalded milk	2 teaspoons salt
2½ cups flour	2¾ cups flour

Dissolve yeast cake in lukewarm water and add potatoes, scalded milk, which has become lukewarm, and two and one-half cups flour. Cover and let rise until light; then add egg, well beaten, shortening, using equal parts of lard and butter, sugar, salt, and remaining flour. Turn into a buttered dripping pan and spread evenly. Cover and again let rise until light. Brush over with melted butter and at two-inch intervals make parallel rows of three-fourths inch depressions, using the forefinger. In depressions thus made put a bit of butter and fill with brown sugar. Sprinkle with two tablespoons brown sugar mixed with one teaspoon cinnamon and bake in a moderate oven thirty-five minutes.

Cincinnati Coffee Bread

Put one-third cup sugar, one-third cup butter, and one-half teaspoon salt in bowl, and pour over one cup scalded milk. When lukewarm, add one yeast cake, dissolved in one-fourth cup lukewarm water, two eggs, slightly beaten, and enough flour to make a stiff batter. Cover and let rise until mixture has doubled its bulk. Cut down, beat thoroughly and spread evenly in two buttered, round layer cake tins. Sprinkle with Nut Mixture, let rise and bake in a hot oven forty minutes.

Nut Mixture — Mix two tablespoons sugar and three-fourths teaspoon cinnamon and add three-fourths cup soft, stale bread crumbs, two tablespoons melted butter, and three tablespoons chopped, blanched Jordan almonds.

Fried Bread

Toss a piece of raised bread dough on a floured cloth and pat and roll to one-eighth inch in thickness. Cut in strips two and one-half inches wide and cut strips in squares or diamond-shaped pieces. Cover and let stand from ten to fifteen minutes. Fry in deep fat until well puffed and delicately browned; drain on brown paper and serve with maple syrup.

Holland Brioche Cakes

1 cup scalded milk	$\frac{1}{8}$ cup melted butter
$\frac{1}{8}$ cup sugar	$\frac{1}{4}$ teaspoon salt
$\frac{1}{8}$ yeast cake	Grated rind $\frac{1}{2}$ lemon
$1\frac{1}{2}$ cups flour	Juice $\frac{1}{2}$ lemon
2 eggs	$1\frac{1}{2}$ cups flour

Add sugar to milk, and when mixture is lukewarm, add yeast cake broken in pieces, and when yeast cake is dissolved, add flour, cover and let rise

THE SHAPING OF CROSSETT ROLLS. — *Page* 17

CROSSETT ROLLS. — *Page* 17.

BUTTERFLY ROLLS. — *Page 17.*

MORAVIAN BREAD READY FOR THE OVEN. — *Page* 19

until full of bubbles. Add eggs, well beaten, and remaining ingredients. Cover and again let rise. Toss on a slightly floured board, pat and roll in long rectangular piece one-fourth inch thick; spread with softened butter and fold from sides towards centre to make three layers. Cut off pieces three-fourths inch wide; cover and let rise. Take each piece separately in hands and twist from ends in opposite directions, coil and bring ends together at top of cake. Let rise in pans and bake twenty minutes in a moderate oven; cool and brush over with confectioners' sugar, moistened with boiling water to spread and flavored with vanilla.

Tea Cakes

1 cup scalded milk	1 yeast cake
4 tablespoons butter	2 tablespoons milk
2 tablespoons sugar	1 egg
1 teaspoon salt	3 cups flour

Add butter, sugar, and salt to scalded milk. When mixture is lukewarm, add yeast cake dissolved in two tablespoons milk, egg slightly beaten, and flour. Cover and let rise until mixture has doubled its bulk. Cut down and fill buttered muffin tins two-thirds full. Cover, again let rise, and bake in a moderate oven.

Flume Flannel Cakes

1½ cups milk	½ teaspoon salt
¼ cup sugar	½ yeast cake
⅓ cup butter	4 cups flour

Whites 2 eggs

Scald milk and add sugar, butter, and salt; when lukewarm, add yeast cake and when yeast cake is dissolved flour. Mix thoroughly and add egg whites beaten until stiff. Cover and let rise over night, in the morning cut down, turn into buttered iron gem pans, having pans one-half full of mixture. Let rise, and bake in a hot oven twenty minutes.

Sally Lunn Tea Cakes

2 tablespoons butter	½ yeast cake
2 tablespoons sugar	¼ cup lukewarm water
½ teaspoon salt	3 eggs
1 cup scalded milk	Flour

Put butter and sugar and salt in bowl, pour over scalded milk, and when lukewarm, add yeast cake dissolved in lukewarm water, eggs well beaten, and enough flour to make a stiff batter. Cover and let rise until very light. Fill buttered muffin tins (set in buttered dripping pan) one-half full of mixture; cover, again let rise, and bake in a hot oven.

Russell Buns

1¼ cups scalded milk	1 teaspoon cinnamon
1 yeast cake	1 teaspoon salt
¼ cup lukewarm water	2 eggs
3¾ cups flour	1 tablespoon butter
½ cup sugar	1 tablespoon lard
½ cup currants	

Break yeast cake in pieces, dissolve in water and add milk after it has become lukewarm. Add three cups flour, cover and let rise until mixture is light.

Add remaining flour with other ingredients, except currants, cover and again let rise until mixture has doubled its bulk. Turn on a floured cloth and knead in the currants. Shape in the form of biscuits, place in buttered pan close together, cover and let rise. Brush tops with milk and bake in a hot oven twenty-five minutes. Take from oven, brush over with melted butter and sprinkle with powdered sugar.

Hot Cross Buns

1 cup scalded milk	¼ cup butter
1 tablespoon sugar	1 tablespoon lard
1 yeast cake	¼ cup sugar
1 cup flour	Grated rind ½ lemon
⅔ teaspoon salt	½ cup raisins or currants

Flour

Add sugar to milk, and when lukewarm, add yeast cake, broken in small pieces. Cover and let stand twenty minutes; then add one cup flour, and salt; cover and let rise until light. Work butter and lard until creamy and add sugar, gradually, and lemon rind. Combine mixtures and add flour to make a stiff batter (the amount required being about one and one-half cups). Cover, again let rise, add raisins (seeded and cut in pieces) or currants, and enough more flour to make a soft dough. Cover, again let rise, shape in the form of large biscuits, arrange on buttered tin sheet one inch apart, cover, let rise, brush over with yolk of egg diluted with one teaspoon cold water, and bake in a hot oven twenty-five minutes. Remove from oven and garnish top of each with cross made of ornamental frosting forced through a pastry bag and tube.

Swedish Wreaths

Work into one cup bread dough one-half cup butter and one-fourth cup lard, using the hands. When thoroughly blended toss on a floured board and knead, using just enough flour to prevent sticking. Cut off pieces and roll same as very small bread sticks; then shape into rings. Dip upper surface in Jordan almonds, blanched, chopped, and seasoned with salt. Arrange on buttered baking sheet and bake in a hot oven until delicately browned. A delicious accompaniment to afternoon tea or a dinner salad.

FRIED BREAD. — *Page* 20.

RAISED DOUGHNUTS. — *Page* 36

THE SHAPING OF HOLLAND BRIOCHE CAKES. — *Page* 20

HOLLAND BRIOCHE CAKES. — *Page* 20.

CHAPTER IV

QUICK BREADS, MUFFINS, AND DOUGHNUTS

Emergency Drop Muffins

1½ cups pastry flour	3 tablespoons lard
3½ teaspoons baking powder	⅛ cup milk
¾ teaspoon salt	⅛ cup water

MIX and sift flour, baking powder, and salt. Work in lard, using the tips of the fingers; then add milk and water, mixing quickly. Drop by spoonfuls into buttered, hot iron gem pans and bake in a hot oven fifteen minutes.

Manhattan Muffins

¼ cup butter	1 cup milk
¼ cup sugar	2 cups bread flour
1 egg	½ teaspoon salt
5 teaspoons baking powder	

Cream butter, and add gradually, while beating constantly, sugar; then add egg well beaten, milk, and flour mixed and sifted with salt and baking powder. Beat thoroughly and bake in buttered gem pans in a hot oven twenty-five minutes.

Tea Muffins

3 tablespoons butter	1 cup milk
½ cup sugar	2 cups flour
1 egg	2 teaspoons cream of tartar
1 teaspoon soda	1 teaspoon salt

Cream butter, add sugar, gradually, and egg, well beaten; then add milk, alternately, with flour mixed and sifted with remaining ingredients. Turn into buttered gem pans and bake in a moderate oven from twenty to twenty-five minutes.

Rye Breakfast Gems

1 cup rye flour
1 cup bread flour
½ teaspoon salt
5 teaspoons baking powder
2 eggs
1 cup milk
2 tablespoons molasses

Mix and sift flour, salt, and baking powder; then add eggs, well beaten, milk, and molasses. Beat thoroughly and bake in buttered gem pans in a hot oven twenty-five minutes.

Oatmeal Muffins

2 cups rolled oats
1½ cups sour milk
¼ cup melted butter
⅛ cup sugar
1 egg, well beaten
1 teaspoon soda
½ teaspoon salt
1 cup flour

Soak rolled oats in sour milk over night. In the morning add remaining ingredients; fill buttered iron gem pans with mixture and bake in a hot oven twenty minutes.

Virginia Corn Cake

1 cup corn meal
½ cup flour
2 tablespoons baking powder
¾ teaspoon salt
1 egg
¼ cup sugar
½ cup milk
2 tablespoons melted butter

Mix and sift corn meal, flour, baking powder, and salt. Beat egg and add sugar. Combine mixtures and add milk and butter. Turn into a buttered pan and bake in a hot oven twenty minutes.

Corn Meal Crisps

7/8 cup corn meal
1 cup boiling water
2½ tablespoons melted butter
½ teaspoon salt

Add corn meal gradually to boiling water and when smooth add butter and salt. Spread evenly on a buttered inverted dripping pan to one-eighth inch in thickness, using a long broad-bladed knife. Bake in a moderate oven until well browned. Cut in two and one-half inch squares, remove from pan and serve at once.

Forest Hall Corn Sticks

1 cup corn meal
¾ cup flour
3 teaspoons baking powder
½ teaspoon salt
½ cup hot, boiled hominy
¼ cup butter
1 cup milk
1 egg

Sift together corn meal, flour, baking powder, and salt; then add hominy, to which have been added butter, milk, and egg well beaten. Turn into buttered bread stick pans and bake in a moderate oven twenty minutes.

Southern Spoon Corn Bread

2 cups white corn meal
2½ cups boiling water
1½ tablespoons melted butter
1½ teaspoons salt
Yolks 2 eggs
1½ cups buttermilk
1 teaspoon soda
Whites 2 eggs

Add corn meal gradually to boiling water and let stand until cool. Then add butter, salt, egg yolks, slightly beaten, and buttermilk mixed with soda. Beat two minutes and add whites of eggs beaten until stiff. Turn into a buttered pudding dish and bake in a hot oven forty minutes.

Littleton Spider Corn Cake

1⅛ cups corn meal	2 eggs
⅛ cup flour	2 cups sweet milk
1 cup sour milk	¼ cup sugar
1 teaspoon soda [scant]	½ teaspoon salt
1½ tablespoons butter	

Mix and sift corn meal and flour and add sour milk mixed with soda, eggs, well beaten, one-half the sweet milk, sugar, and salt. Heat an iron frying-pan, add butter, and, when melted, turn in mixture. Pour over remaining milk and bake in a hot oven. Cut in pie-shaped pieces for serving.

Southern Pone

1 pint milk	3 tablespoons butter
1 cup granulated Indian meal	2 eggs
1 teaspoon salt	1 teaspoon baking powder

Scald milk and add gradually Indian meal, salt, and butter. Cool slightly and add eggs, well beaten, and baking powder. Turn into a buttered earthen dish and bake in a moderate oven thirty-five minutes. Cut in pie-shaped pieces for serving.

Bran Muffins

1 cup flour	2 cups bran
1 teaspoon soda	1¼ cups milk
1 teaspoon salt	½ cup molasses
1 egg	

Mix and sift flour, soda and salt. Add bran, milk, molasses and egg, well beaten. Bake in buttered individual tins. The egg may be omitted and the result will be satisfactory.

Rye Popovers

⅔ cup rye meal	1 cup milk
⅛ cup flour	2 eggs
¼ teaspoon salt	1 teaspoon melted butter

Mix and sift dry ingredients, add milk gradually, eggs, well beaten, and butter. Beat two minutes, using an egg beater. Turn into hissing hot buttered iron gem pans and bake in a hot oven from thirty-five to forty minutes.

Sultana Biscuits

2 cups flour	3 tablespoons lard
4 teaspoons baking powder	2 tablespoons butter
1 teaspoon salt	¾ cup milk
¼ cup Sultana raisins	

Mix and sift flour, baking powder, and salt. Work in lard and butter, using a case knife or tips of fingers; then add milk and raisins. Toss on a slightly floured board, pat and roll to one-third inch in thickness and shape with a very small round cutter, first dipped in flour. Put close together in a buttered pan and bake seven minutes in a hot oven. Split and spread with butter. Pile on a plate covered with a doily and serve with afternoon tea.

Sardine Biscuits

Make same as Sultana Biscuits omitting raisins. Split while hot, spread under parts with sardines (from which skin and bones have been removed) flaked, seasoned with salt and moistened with sardine oil. Put on tops and pile on a plate covered with a lace paper doily. An afternoon tea novelty.

Cheese Biscuits

1 cup bread flour	½ tablespoon butter
2½ teaspoons baking powder	⅜ cup milk and water
½ teaspoon salt	in equal parts
½ tablespoon lard	½ cup grated cheese

Mix and sift dry ingredients. Work in lard and butter with tips of fingers and add liquid gradually; then add cheese. Toss on a floured board and pat and roll to one-third inch in thickness, shape with a small round cutter, first dipped in flour, place in a buttered pan and bake in a hot oven ten minutes. Serve hot as an accompaniment to a dinner salad.

Afternoon Tea Crackers

2 cups bread flour	2 teaspoons baking powder
1 cup butter	½ teaspoon salt
	Milk

HOT CROSS BUNS. — *Page* 23.

SWEDISH WREATHS. — *Page* 24

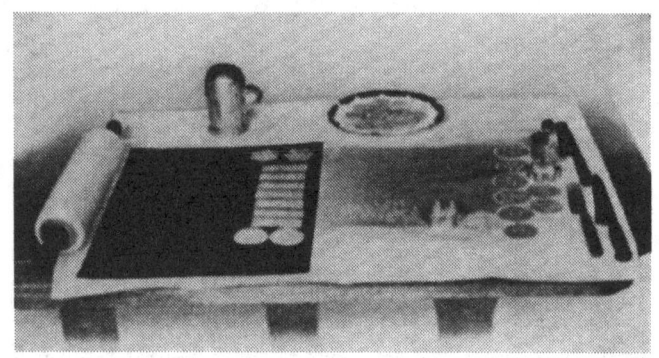

CREAM WAFERS. — *Page* 31.

AFTERNOON TEA DOUGHNUTS. — *Page* 37

Mix and sift dry ingredients and work in butter, using the tips of the fingers. Add milk to make a stiff dough, toss on a floured board and pat and roll to one-fourth inch in thickness. Shape with a round cutter (one and three-fourths inches in diameter) first dipped in flour, arrange on buttered sheet and bake in a hot oven ten minutes. Split, while hot, return to oven and bake until a golden brown. These crackers will keep for weeks without crumbling.

Cream Wafers

Mix and sift one and one-half cups pastry flour and one teaspoon salt. Add, gradually, heavy cream to make a dough, the quantity required being a scant half-cup. Toss on a slightly floured cloth and knead until smooth. Pat and roll as thin as possible. Prick with a fork and shape with a small round or fancy cutter, first dipped in flour. Arrange on a buttered sheet and bake in a moderate oven until delicately browned. Serve with salad course, or as an accompaniment to five o'clock tea.

Quick Graham Bread

2 cups Graham flour	1 teaspoon salt
½ cup white flour	4 tablespoons melted lard
⅛ cup sugar	1½ cups sour milk
1 tablespoon baking powder	1 teaspoon soda

Mix and sift flour, sugar, baking powder, and salt; then add lard and sour milk mixed with soda. Turn into a buttered bread pan and bake from forty-five to fifty minutes.

Quick Nut Loaf

2 cups bread flour
½ cup sugar
4 teaspoons baking powder
1 teaspoon salt
3 tablespoons butter
2 tablespoons lard
1 egg
Yolk 1 egg
1 cup milk
½ cup English walnut meats

Mix and sift flour, sugar, baking powder, and salt. Work in butter and lard, using the tips of the fingers; then add egg and egg yolk well beaten, milk, and walnut meats, broken in pieces. Beat thoroughly and turn into a buttered bread pan. Let stand twenty minutes; then bake in a moderate oven forty minutes. A delicious bread for sandwiches.

Quick Pecan Nut Bread

2 cups unsifted Graham flour
1 cup pastry flour
⅜ cup brown sugar
1 teaspoon salt
3 teaspoons baking powder
2 cups buttermilk
1⅛ teaspoons soda
1 cup pecan nut meats, finely cut

To Graham flour add pastry flour, sugar, salt, and baking powder. When thoroughly mixed add remaining ingredients. Turn into a buttered bread pan, cover and let stand twenty minutes. Bake in a moderate oven forty-five minutes.

Luncheon Caraway Bread

¼ cup butter
¾ cup sugar
1 egg
1⅔ cups flour
1 tablespoon baking powder
¾ cup milk
1 tablespoon carraway seeds
¾ teaspoon vanilla
¼ teaspoon salt

Cream butter and add sugar gradually and egg well beaten. Mix and sift flour and baking powder, and add alternately with milk to first mixture; then add caraway seeds, vanilla, and salt. Turn into a buttered and floured cake pan, sprinkle with sugar, and bake in a moderate oven thirty-five minutes. Remove from pan, cut in squares, and serve hot.

Cinnamon Toast

Cut stale bread in one-fourth inch slices, remove crusts, and cut in three pieces, crosswise. Toast, spread with butter and sprinkle with sugar, mixed with cinnamon, using three parts sugar to one part cinnamon.

English Dumplings

¼ pound beef suet	½ teaspoon pepper
1¼ cups flour	1 teaspoon minced parsley
3 teaspoons baking powder	½ teaspoon onion juice
1 teaspoon salt	⅛ cup cold water

Force suet through meat chopper. Mix and sift flour, baking powder, salt, and pepper, and work in suet, using the fingers; then add parsley and onion juice, and moisten to a dough with water. Drop by spoonfuls into buttered timbale moulds, having moulds two-thirds full. Cover with buttered paper and steam one hour.

Sweet Potato Waffles

1 cup mashed sweet potato	½ cup melted butter
1 cup bread flour	1 cup milk
¼ cup sugar	1 egg

Mix first five ingredients in the order given; then add egg yolk, beaten until thick, and egg white beaten until stiff. Cook in greased waffle iron over a hot fire.

Buttermilk Griddle Cakes

1 cup buttermilk	½ teaspoon salt
½ cup sweet milk	1 tablespoon melted butter
1 egg, well beaten	2 tablespoons granulated
1 teaspoon soda	corn meal
2 cups flour	

Mix ingredients in order given. Drop by spoonfuls on a greased hot griddle. Cook on one side; when puffed, full of bubbles and cooked on edges, turn and cook other side.

Serve with butter and maple syrup.

Cheap Doughnuts (without Shortening)

4 cups flour	1 teaspoon salt
1 cup sugar	½ nutmeg, grated
2 teaspoons cream-of-tartar	2 eggs
1 teaspoon soda	Milk

Mix and sift dry ingredients, add eggs, well beaten, and milk, the amount required being about three-fourths cup, sometimes more but never as much as a cup. Toss on a slightly floured board, pat, roll, shape, and fry. Remove from fat, using a two-tined fork, and pass quickly through water kept at the boiling point. The fork must be wiped each time before putting into fat.

Sour-milk Doughnuts

1 egg	4 cups flour
1 cup sugar	1¾ teaspoons soda
1 cup sour milk	1¾ teaspoons cream-of-
1½ tablespoons melted	tartar
lard	1½ teaspoons salt
1 teaspoon grated nutmeg	

Beat egg until light and add sugar, milk, and lard. Mix and sift flour with remaining ingredients and add to first mixture. Toss on a floured cloth, knead slightly, pat and roll to one-fourth inch in thickness, shape with a doughnut cutter, first dipped in flour, fry in deep fat, take up on a skewer, and drain on brown paper.

Chocolate Doughnuts

¼ cup butter	4 cups flour
1¼ cups sugar	1 teaspoon soda
2 eggs	1 teaspoon cinnamon
1½ squares melted chocolate	¼ teaspoon salt
1 cup sour milk	1½ teaspoons vanilla

Cream butter and add sugar gradually, while beating constantly; then add eggs, well beaten, melted chocolate, sour milk, and flour, mixed and sifted with soda, cinnamon, and salt. Add vanilla, and enough more flour to handle the mixture. Toss on a slightly floured cloth, knead slightly, pat and roll to one-fourth inch in thickness, shape with a doughnut cutter, first dipped in flour, fry in deep fat and drain on brown paper.

Raised Doughnuts

3½ tablespoons sugar	½ yeast cake
1 teaspoon salt	2 tablespoons lukewarm
1 cup scalded milk	water
2 tablespoons lard	3 cups flour

Mix sugar and salt, pour over scalded milk, and add lard. When mixture is lukewarm, add yeast cake dissolved in lukewarm water, and one cup flour. Cover, let rise until light, and add two cups flour. Toss on a slightly floured board and knead. Cover, again let rise and knead; repeat. Pat and roll to one-half inch in thickness, and cut in strips eight inches long by three-fourths inch wide. Put on board, cover and let rise. Twist several times, pinch ends together, drop into hot deep fat, fry until delicately browned and drain on brown paper.

Health Food Doughnuts

⅛ cup sugar	1 cup sour milk
⅛ cup molasses	1 teaspoon soda
⅜ cup hot mashed potatoes	1½ teaspoons salt
	¾ teaspoon grated nutmeg
1 egg	2 cups entire wheat flour

Mix sugar, molasses, potatoes, and egg well beaten; then add sour milk and flour mixed and sifted with soda, salt, and nutmeg. Toss on a floured cloth, knead slightly, pat, and roll to one-fourth inch in thickness. Shape with a doughnut cutter, first dipped in flour, fry in deep fat and drain on brown paper. Sprinkle with powdered sugar.

Afternoon Tea Doughnuts

1 egg	1 tablespoon melted
2 tablespoons sugar	shortening
½ teaspoon salt	1 cup flour
3 tablespoons milk	2 teaspoons baking powder

Beat egg until light, and add sugar, salt, and shortening. Mix and sift flour and baking powder and add to first mixture. Force through a pastry bag and tube (using a small lady finger tube) into hot deep fat, and fry until browned. Drain on brown paper and sprinkle with powdered sugar. Serve with Julienne-shaped pieces of American factory cheese as an accompaniment to five o'clock tea.

CHAPTER V

CEREAL, CHEESE, AND VEGETARIAN DISHES

Samp

½ cup samp
Cold water

2½ cups boiling water
1 teaspoon salt

COVER samp with cold water, and let stand five or six hours. Drain, put in double boiler and add boiling water and salt. Bring to boiling point, place over under part of double boiler (containing boiling water) and let steam four or five hours, or cook in fireless cooker over night.

Parched Rice with Tomato Sauce

Pick over three-fourths cup rice and add slowly to two quarts boiling water, to which is added one tablespoon salt. Let boil twenty-five minutes, or until kernels are soft. Drain, and pour over one quart hot water; return to kettle in which it was cooked, and let stand until cool and dry, when kernels will be distinct. Heat an iron frying pan very hot, add two tablespoons butter, and when melted, add rice, and cook until rice is slightly browned, stirring lightly with a fork. Put in a hot serving dish, pour over one cup hot tomato sauce and sprinkle with one-half cup grated cheese, lifting rice with fork, that sauce and cheese may coat each kernel.

Tomato Sauce

2 tablespoons butter	1 cup stewed and strained
1 slice onion	tomatoes
2½ tablespoons flour	¼ teaspoon salt
Few grains paprika	

Cook butter with onion until slightly browned, add flour, and when well browned, pour on, gradually, while stirring constantly, tomatoes. Bring to the boiling point, add seasonings, and strain.

Fried Rice

Pick over and wash one-half cup rice. Cook in double boiler with one-half cup boiling water, until rice has absorbed water. Add one cup scalded milk or boiling water and three-fourths teaspoon salt, and continue the cooking until rice is soft, adding more liquid if necessary. Turn into a dish and let stand until cold. Shape into balls one inch in diameter and plunge into deep fat; fry until delicately browned and drain on brown paper. Serve as a substitute for potatoes, or as an entrée with fruit sauce.

Rice Croquettes, Cheese Sauce

½ cup rice	2 tablespoons chopped canned
½ cup boiling water	pimientos
1¼ cups milk	½ teaspoon salt
¼ cup cream	Few grains cayenne

Soak rice over night in cold water to cover. Drain, add boiling water, and cook in double boiler until rice has absorbed water; then add milk and cook until rice has absorbed milk. Add cream, pimientos chopped and drained, and salt and cayenne. Spread in plate, cool, shape, dip in flour, egg and crumbs, fry in deep fat and drain on brown paper. Pile on serving dish, pour around Cheese Sauce and garnish with parsley.

Cheese Sauce. — Melt three tablespoons butter, add three tablespoons flour, and stir until well blended; then pour on gradually, while stirring constantly, one and one-half cups milk. Bring to the boiling point, and add one-half teaspoon salt, one-eighth teaspoon pepper, and one cup mild cheese, grated or cut in small cubes.

Little Brahmins

½ cup rice
½ cup boiling water
½ teaspoon salt
1¼ cups scalded milk

Yolks 2 eggs
1 tablespoon butter
⅛ teaspoon paprika
1 tablespoon tomato catsup

Wash rice, put in double boiler, add boiling water and salt, and cook until rice has absorbed water; then add milk and cook until rice is soft. Add remaining ingredients and spread on a plate to cool. Shape in the form of chickens; dip in crumbs, egg and crumbs, fry in deep fat and drain on brown paper. Insert pepper-corns or

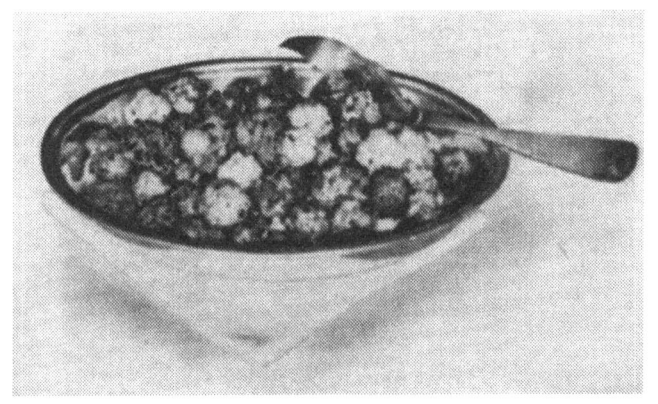

FRIED RICE. — *Page 39.*

LITTLE BRAHMINS. — *Page* 40

LITTLE DUCKLINGS. — *Page* 41.

SHAPLEIGH LUNCHEON CHEESE. — *Page* 48

CEREAL, CHEESE, AND VEGETARIAN DISHES 41

allspice berries to represent eyes, and arrange on a hot platter.

Little Ducklings

Use same mixture as for Little Brahmins. Shape in the form of little ducklings. Dip in crumbs, egg and crumbs, fry in deep fat and drain on brown paper. Insert allspice berries to represent eyes.

Baked Hominy, Southern Style

¾ cup fine hominy	¼ cup butter
1 teaspoon salt	1 tablespoon sugar
1 cup boiling water	1 egg
2 cups milk	

Mix water and salt and add gradually, while stirring constantly, hominy. Bring to the boiling point and let boil two minutes. Then cook in double boiler until water is absorbed. Add one cup milk, stirring thoroughly, and cook one hour. Remove from range and add butter, sugar, egg slightly beaten, and remaining milk. Turn into a buttered dish and bake in a slow oven one hour.

Hominy and Horseradish Croquettes

¼ cup hominy	2 tablespoons butter
½ cup boiling water	3½ teaspoons grated horse-
½ teaspoon salt	radish root
¾ cup scalded milk	

Steam hominy with water until water is absorbed; then add milk and steam until tender. Add butter and horseradish and salt. Cool, shape, dip in flour, egg and crumbs, fry in deep fat and drain on brown paper.

Macaroni, Virginia Style

1½ cups macaroni
2 tablespoons butter
1 teaspoon mustard
½ cup grated cheese
1¼ cups white sauce
3 tablespoons dried bread crumbs

Break macaroni in one-inch pieces and cook in boiling, salted water twenty minutes or until soft; drain in colander and pour over one quart cold water. Put half in buttered baking dish, dot over with one-fourth the butter and sprinkle with one-half the mustard and cheese; repeat, pour over white sauce, cover with dried bread crumbs mixed with remaining butter and bake in a hot oven until crumbs are brown.

White Sauce. — Melt three-fourths tablespoon butter, add three-fourths tablespoon flour and stir until blended; then pour on gradually, while stirring constantly, one and one-fourth cups milk. Bring to the boiling point and add one-half teaspoon salt.

Baked Macaroni with Chipped Beef

Break macaroni in one-inch pieces (there should be three-fourths cup) and cook in boiling, salted water until soft; drain and pour over one quart cold water. Remove skin from one-fourth pound thinly sliced smoked dried beef and separate in pieces. Cover with hot water, let stand ten minutes, and drain. Arrange in buttered baking dish alternate layers of macaroni and dried beef, having two of each. Pour over two cups white sauce, cover with three-fourths cup buttered cracker crumbs and bake in hot oven until crumbs are brown. For the *White Sauce*, melt four tablespoons butter, add three tablespoons flour and stir until well blended, then pour on gradually, while stirring constantly, two cups milk. Bring to the boiling point and add one-half teaspoon salt and one-eighth teaspoon pepper.

Baked Macaroni with Peanut Butter

1 cup macaroni, broken in 1-inch pieces	3½ tablespoons peanut butter
2 cups milk	1 teaspoon salt
¾ cup buttered bread crumbs	

Cook macaroni in boiling salted water twenty minutes, or until soft, drain in strainer, and pour over one quart cold water to prevent pieces from adhering; then put in buttered baking dish. Heat milk in double boiler, and add gradually to peanut butter. Pour over macaroni, cover and bake in a slow oven forty minutes. Remove cover, sprinkle with crumbs, and bake until crumbs are brown.

Italian Spaghetti

Take one-fourth pound spaghetti in hand and dip ends in boiling, salted water. As spaghetti softens it will bend easily, when it may be coiled under the boiling water. Let boil twenty minutes or until soft; drain in a colander and pour over one quart cold water. Arrange on a hot platter, over which have been poured two tablespoons olive oil, and pour over the following sauce: Remove fat and meat from three pork chops and cut in pieces. Put in saucepan with one small onion, peeled and sliced, and cook, stirring frequently until well browned, then add one quart can tomatoes, one-half teaspoon salt, and one-eighth teaspoon paprika. Bring to the boiling point and let simmer very slowly two and one-half hours. Force through a purée strainer.

Napoli Spaghetti

4 slices bacon	⅛ teaspoon pepper
1 sliced onion	¼ teaspoon allspice
½ can tomatoes	¼ teaspoon mace
½ box Italian tomato paste	Few grains cayenne
½ teaspoon salt	Bit of bay leaf

Hot, boiled spaghetti

Cut bacon in small pieces and try out. Add remaining ingredients, except spaghetti, bring gradually to the boiling point, and let simmer fifty minutes. Pour over cooked spaghetti and let stand ten minutes. Serve very hot.

Liptaner Cheese

1 cream cheese	2 anchovies, finely chopped
¼ cup butter	1 shallot, finely chopped
1 teaspoon capers	½ teaspoon caraway seed
1 teaspoon paprika	½ teaspoon salt

Work cheese (large size) and add butter gradually. When thoroughly blended, add remaining ingredients. Press into a small mould and let stand in ice box to season. Remove from mould and serve with crackers.

Moulded Cheese with Bar-le-Duc Strawberries

Mash cream cheese and press into a cone-shaped mould. Remove from mould, cover with whipped cream sweetened with powdered sugar, and pour around strawberries. Serve with unsweetened wafer crackers.

Toasted Fromage Rolls

Cut fresh bread while still warm in as thin slices as possible, using a very sharp knife, and remove crusts. Work butter until creamy, add an equal measure of grated Young American cheese, and work until thoroughly blended; then season with salt and paprika. Spread bread with mixture and roll each piece separately. Toast over a clear fire and serve hot with the salad course.

Frozen Cheese Alexandra

½ cup butter	½ teaspoon paprika
¼ lb. Roquefort cheese	1 teaspoon finely cut chives
1 teaspoon salt	2 tablespoons Sherry

Cream butter, add cheese, and work until well blended; then add remaining ingredients. Pack in a small mould, surround with finely crushed ice and rock salt, using equal parts, and let stand one hour. Remove from mould and serve with hot toasted rye bread.

Pimiento Cheese Wafers

Mash a pimiento cream cheese, moisten with cream and force through a pastry bag and tube on unsweetened wafer crackers. If a pimiento cream cheese is not obtainable add one tablespoon finely chopped canned pimiento and a few grains salt to one ten-cent cream cheese.

Piquante Cheese Crackers

½ pound American Factory Cheese
3 tablespoons Sherry wine
2 tablespoons cream

2 tablespoons butter
1 teaspoon mustard
½ teaspoon salt
Few grains cayenne

Cut cheese in pieces and force through a meat chopper. Add Sherry wine, cream, butter worked until creamy, and seasonings. Force mixture through a pastry bag and tube on thin, unsweetened wafer crackers.

Walnut Deceits

Work a ten-cent cream cheese until smooth and add one-fourth cup olives, stoned and chopped, one-half teaspoon salt, and a few grains paprika. Shape in balls, roll in sifted cracker crumbs, flatten, and place halves of salted English walnuts opposite each other on each piece. The olives may be omitted and

PIMIENTO CHEESE WAFERS. — *Page* 46

WALNUT DECEITS. — *Page* 46.

PIQUANTE CHEESE CRACKERS. — *Page 46*

unsalted nuts may be used. Arrange on a plate covered with a lace paper doily.

Stuffed Figs

Mash cream cheese, moisten with heavy cream and season highly with salt and cayenne; then make into balls three-fourths inch in diameter. Wash and dry figs, make an incision in each, and stuff with cheese balls. Arrange in piles on a plate covered with a lace paper doily. Serve as an accompaniment to dressed lettuce or any light dinner salad.

Lenox Rarebit

1 tablespoon butter	Few grains cayenne
1 cup milk	6 eggs
1 teaspoon salt	1 small cream cheese
¼ teaspoon pepper	Unsweetened wafer crackers

Put butter in blazer and when melted add milk, seasonings, and eggs beaten slightly. Cook same as scrambled eggs, and when nearly done, add cheese worked until soft. Serve on crackers.

Chilaly

1 tablespoon butter	½ cup canned tomato pulp
2 tablespoons chopped green pepper	¾ pound soft mild cheese
	¾ teaspoon salt
1½ tablespoons chopped onion	Few grains cayenne
	2 tablespoons beer
1 egg	

Cook butter with pepper and onion three minutes, stirring constantly. Add tomatoes, from which liquor has been drained, and cook five minutes. Add cheese, cut in small pieces, salt, and cayenne. When cheese is melted, add beer and egg slightly beaten. Serve on squares of bread, toasted on one side, or zephyrettes.

Baked Rarebit

1 pound soft mild cheese	1½ cups milk
2 tablespoons butter	2½ cups stale bread
1¾ teaspoons salt	crumbs
⅛ teaspoon paprika	3 eggs

Cut cheese in thin slices. Sprinkle a layer of bread crumbs in buttered baking dish, cover with one-third cheese, sprinkle with one-third salt and paprika mixed, and repeat twice, making three layers. Beat eggs slightly, add milk, and pour over mixture. Bake in a moderate oven twenty-five minutes. Serve at once.

Shapleigh Luncheon Cheese

Cut stale bread in one-third inch slices. Spread with butter, remove crusts, and cut in finger-shaped pieces. Arrange near together around sides of a buttered baking dish, having bread extend about one inch above dish; also line bottom of dish.

Beat two eggs slightly, add one cup thin cream, one tablespoon butter, one teaspoon salt, one-half teaspoon mustard, one-fourth teaspoon paprika, a few grains cayenne, and one-half pound mild cheese, cut in small pieces. Pour mixture in dish and bake thirty minutes. Serve very hot.

CEREAL, CHEESE, AND VEGETARIAN DISHES 49

Cheese Soufflé

2 tablespoons butter	¾ teaspoon salt
3 tablespoons flour	Few grains cayenne
½ cup milk	Yolks 3 eggs
½ cup grated Young American Cheese	Whites 2 eggs

Melt butter in blazer, add flour, and stir until well blended; then pour on gradually, while stirring constantly, one-half cup milk. Bring to the boiling point and add cheese, salt, and cayenne. Put blazer over hot water pan and add yolks of eggs, beaten until thick and lemon-colored, and cut and fold in whites of eggs, beaten until stiff and dry. Put on cover of chafing dish and cook until firm.

Cheese Custard, Bread Sauce

4 eggs	3 tablespoons grated cheese
¾ cup cold water	½ teaspoon salt
⅓ cup heavy cream	⅛ teaspoon pepper
2½ tablespoons melted butter	Few grains cayenne
	Few drops onion juice

Beat eggs slightly and add remaining ingredients. Turn into buttered timbale moulds, set in pan of hot water and bake until brown. Remove to hot platter and pour around

Bread Sauce

1¼ cups milk	1½ tablespoons butter
⅛ cup fine stale bread crumbs	½ teaspoon salt
	Few grains pepper
1 onion	½ cup coarse stale bread crumbs
5 whole cloves	
1½ tablespoons butter	

Cook milk, bread, and onion stuck with cloves in double boiler, twenty-five minutes. Remove onion and add butter, salt, and cayenne. Pour over custard and sprinkle with coarse crumbs browned in frying pan in remaining butter.

Wellington Cheese Croquettes

3 tablespoons butter	⅛ teaspoon pepper
⅛ cup flour	Yolks 2 eggs
1 cup milk	2 tablespoons cream
½ teaspoon salt	2 cups soft mild cheese, cut in small cubes

Melt butter, add flour, and stir until well blended; then pour on gradually, while stirring constantly, milk. Bring to the boiling point and add egg yolks slightly beaten and diluted with cream, and cheese. Season with salt and pepper. Spread on a plate and cool. Shape, dip in crumbs, egg and crumbs, fry in deep fat, and drain on brown paper.

Cheese Cakes

2 tablespoons butter	Whites 3 eggs
3½ tablespoons flour	¼ teaspoon salt
4 tablespoons grated American cheese	Few grains cayenne

Melt butter, add flour, and stir until well blended. Remove from range and add cheese, salt, and cayenne. Fold in whites of eggs, beaten until stiff, and drop from tip of spoon on a buttered sheet one inch apart. Bake in a moderate oven twelve minutes.

Serve as an accompaniment to a dinner salad.

CEREAL, CHEESE, AND VEGETARIAN DISHES 51

Parmesan Cheese Sticks

Toss one cup bread dough on a floured board, pat and roll in rectangular shape as thin as possible. Spread with one tablespoon butter, dredge with flour, and fold from ends so as to make three layers. Repeat three times and cut in finger-shaped pieces. Arrange on sheet, cover, let stand fifteen minutes, and bake. Remove from oven, brush over with white of egg, and roll in grated Parmesan cheese, seasoned with salt and cayenne. Return to oven and bake four minutes.

Pea Roast

¾ cup bread crumbs	1 egg
½ cup canned pea pulp	¾ teaspoon salt
1 tablespoon sugar	⅛ teaspoon pepper
¼ cup English walnut meats, finely chopped	¼ cup butter
	¾ cup milk

Break stale bread in pieces, dry in oven, roll and put through a purée strainer; there should be three-fourths cup bread crumbs. Drain canned peas, rinse thoroughly with cold water, put in saucepan, cover with cold water, bring to the boiling point and let boil three minutes. Drain and force througt a purée strainer; there should be one-half cup pulp. Mix bread crumbs, pea pulp, sugar, nut meat egg slightly beaten, salt, pepper, butter and milk. Turn into a small bread pan lined with paraffine paper, and let stand fifteen minutes. Cover and bake in a slow oven forty minutes. Remove to hot serving dish, and garnish with Carrot Timbales (see p. 164).

Mock Sausages

Pick over one-half cup lima beans and soak over night in cold water to cover. Drain and cook in boiling, salted water until soft; again drain and force through a purée strainer; there should be three-fourths cup pulp. Add one-third cup rolled dried bread crumbs, three tablespoons heavy cream or butter, a few grains pepper, one-fourth teaspoon salt, one-half teaspoon sage, and one egg beaten slightly. Shape in the form of sausages, dip in crumbs, egg and crumbs, and fry in olive oil. Drain, arrange on serving dish and garnish with fried apple rings.

Pecan Nut Loaf

1 cup hot boiled rice	1 egg
1 cup pecan nut meats, finely chopped	1 cup milk
	1½ teaspoons salt
1 cup cracker crumbs	¼ teaspoon pepper
1 tablespoon melted butter	

Mix rice, nut meats, and cracker crumbs; then add egg well beaten, milk, salt, and pepper. Turn into a buttered small bread pan; pour over butter, cover and bake in a moderate oven one hour. Turn on a hot platter and pour around the following sauce:

Cook three tablespoons butter with two slices onion, three minutes, stirring constantly. Add three tablespoons flour and stir until well blended; then pour on gradually, while stirring constantly, one and one-half cups milk. Bring to the boiling point and add one-half teaspoon salt and a few grains pepper, and strain.

Mock Sausages with Fried Apple Rings.—*Page* 52

A Group of Dishes for Eggs, Vegetables and Entrées

CHAPTER VI

EGGS

Baked Eggs with Pimiento Potatoes

TO two cups hot riced potatoes, add two tablespoons butter, one-third cup rich milk, and one-half teaspoon salt. Beat vigorously three minutes, add one and one-half canned pimientos, forced through a strainer, and continue the beating until mixture is thoroughly blended. Pile evenly on a buttered baking dish, and make four cavities. In each cavity slip a raw egg, and bake until eggs are set.

French Poached Eggs

Put three pints boiling water in saucepan and add one tablespoon vinegar, and one-half tablespoon salt. Stir vigorously around and around edge of saucepan (using a wooden spoon held in a nearly upright position) while water is boiling vigorously.

As soon as well is formed in middle of water, slip in an egg. Remove to back of range and cook until white is set. Take out with a skimmer and trim. Repeat until the desired number of eggs is prepared.

Scrambled Eggs, New York Style

Cover a thin slice of ham with lukewarm water and let stand twenty-five minutes; then cut in thin Julienne-shaped pieces; there should be one cup. Put ham in omelet pan, add two tablespoons finely chopped onion and one and one-half tablespoons butter, and cook five minutes. Add five mushroom caps cut in slices, and cook five minutes. Arrange in a border around serving dish, fill centre with Scrambled Eggs (see The Boston Cooking School Cook Book, p. 98), and garnish with parsley.

Buttered Eggs à la Roberts

Cook six Buttered Eggs (see The Boston Cooking School Cook Book, p. 99), arrange on a hot platter, pour around Roberts Sauce, and garnish with parsley.

Roberts Sauce. — Melt three-fourths tablespoon butter, add three shallots finely chopped, and one-half tablespoon flour, and cook five minutes. Add one tablespoon vinegar, one-half cup white stock, two chopped pickles, one-half tablespoon chopped capers, one teaspoon chopped olives, one-half teaspoon French mustard, one-fourth teaspoon salt, and a few grains cayenne. Cook ten minutes, stirring constantly.

Eggs à la Benedict, 1912 Style

Split and toast English muffins. Place on each a circular piece of broiled ham, and over ham place a French poached egg. Pour over the following sauce:

Melt one and one-half tablespoons butter, add one and one-half tablespoons flour, and stir until well blended; then pour on gradually, while stirring constantly, one-half cup thin cream. Bring to the boiling point and add gradually the yolks of four eggs, and one-half cup butter. Season with one-half teaspoon salt, a few grains cayenne, and one and one-half tablespoons Tarragon vinegar. Add beef extract, by dipping two-tined fork in extract, then trailing through sauce, and repeating until trails of beef extract are through the sauce.

Florentine Eggs in Casseroles

Finely chop cooked spinach and season with butter and salt. Put one tablespoon spinach in each buttered individual casserole, sprinkle with one tablespoon grated Parmesan cheese, and slip into each an egg. Cover each egg with one tablespoon Béchamel Sauce and one-half tablespoon grated Parmesan cheese. Bake until eggs are set, and serve immediately.

Deerfoot Shirred Eggs

Cut six Deerfoot Farm Sausages in half-inch pieces and fry in one teaspoon melted butter six minutes. Add one cup tomato sauce, to which has been added one teaspoon finely chopped parsley. Put mixture in six buttered shirred egg dishes, crack two eggs in each dish and bake until eggs are set.

Eggs Molet Chasseur

2 shallots
1 tablespoon butter
6 mushroom caps
½ cup chicken stock
2 tablespoons Sherry wine
¼ teaspoon salt
Few grains pepper
Few grains cayenne
8 French poached eggs
4 tablespoons cream
2 tablespoons grated Parmesan cheese

Finely chop shallots and cook in butter, stirring constantly, three minutes. Add mushroom caps, peeled and chopped, and cook five minutes; then add stock, wine, salt, pepper, and cayenne. Bring to the boiling point and let simmer ten minutes. Turn into a shallow, buttered baking dish and place on sauce French poached eggs. Pour over cream, sprinkle with cheese and let stand in oven until cheese has melted.

Egg Cutlets

2 tablespoons butter
4 tablespoons bread flour
1 cup scalded milk
1 teaspoon salt
½ teaspoon paprika
¾ teaspoon finely grated onion
1 tablespoon finely chopped parsley
Few gratings nutmeg
8 hard-boiled eggs

Cream butter, add flour and stir until thoroughly blended. Pour on gradually the milk, and bring to the boiling point. Cook in double boiler five minutes and continue stirring. Cut eggs in coarse pieces, and add with remaining ingredients to sauce, cool and shape in the form of cutlets. Dip in flour, egg and crumbs, fry in deep fat and drain on paper. Make a cut at small end of each cutlet, and insert in each a two-inch piece of macaroni. Serve with White or Béchamel Sauce. The quantities given make eleven cutlets.

Omelet à la Columbia

Cut thinly sliced bacon in small squares; there should be one-half cup. Wash, pare, slice, and cut potatoes in fourth-inch cubes; there should be one cup. Fry bacon until crisp and brown, and drain. To bacon fat add potatoes and fry until delicately browned; then drain and mix with bacon dice.

Make a French omelet; fold one-half the bacon and potato with omelet, turn on a hot platter and surround with remaining bacon and potato. Garnish with parsley.

Omelet Soubise

Make a French omelet (see The Boston Cooking School Cook Book, p. 107), turn on a hot copper or fireproof platter, pour over Onion Sauce, sprinkle with two tablespoons Parmesan cheese, and place in a hot oven and bake until cheese is melted.

Onion Sauce. — Peel and finely chop one Bermuda onion and cook three minutes with two tablespoons butter, stirring constantly. Add two and one-half tablespoons flour and stir until well blended; then pour on gradually, while stirring constantly, one cup milk. Bring to the boiling point and let simmer three minutes; then add one egg yolk, slightly beaten and diluted with two tablespoons milk.

Japanese Lobster Omelet

Cook one teaspoon butter with one small onion, peeled and thinly sliced, five minutes. Add one stalk celery, washed, scraped, and thinly sliced crosswise, two tablespoons chicken stock, one-eighth teaspoon sugar, one teaspoon Soyou Sauce, and one-third cup lobster dice. Butter an individual omelet pan, turn in one-half the mixture add one egg, slightly beaten, spread evenly, and cook until egg is set. Turn and fold same as other omelets; repeat.

Savoyarde Omelet

1 cup potato cubes
¾ tablespoon butter
¾ teaspoon onion juice
¼ teaspoon salt
Few grains pepper
½ cup boiled leeks
1 tablespoon chopped parsley
3 tablespoons grated cheese
2 tablespoons butter
5 eggs
⅔ cup cream
½ teaspoon salt
⅛ teaspoon pepper

Wash potatoes and boil without paring until soft. Cool, pare, and cut in half-inch cubes. Put potato cubes with butter, onion juice, salt, and pepper, in small frying pan and cook until potatoes are slightly browned. Cut the white portion of leeks in thin slices crosswise, cook in boiling salted water until soft, and drain. Put two tablespoons butter in omelet pan and when melted pour in eggs, slightly beaten, to which have been added cream, salt, and pepper. As mixture cooks, prick and pick up with a fork; when about half done add prepared potatoes, leeks, and parsley, and continue the cooking until the whole is of a creamy consistency. Add cheese, place on hot part of range, that it may brown quickly underneath; fold and turn on a hot serving dish. Garnish with sprig of parsley.

Eggs à la Victoria

Cut bread in third-inch slices, shape with a round cutter and sauté in butter until delicately browned. On each round of bread place a sautéd chicken's liver, over liver a French poached egg, and pour over all tomato sauce. Sprinkle with finely cut chives and serve at once.

Egg and Pimiento Timbales

Line well-buttered timbale or Dario moulds with canned pimientos, fill with egg custard, place in pan of hot water, cover with buttered paper, and bake until firm. Turn on circular pieces of fried bread and serve with Bread Sauce.

Egg Custards, Bread Sauce

Beat three eggs slightly and add three-fourths cup milk. Season with one-half teaspoon salt, one-eighth teaspoon pepper, a few grains cayenne, and a few drops onion juice; then strain into buttered timbale moulds, set in pan of hot water (having water half surround moulds) and bake until firm. Remove to serving dish and pour around Bread Sauce. This recipe makes a sufficient quantity for six timbales.

Bread Sauce

1½ cups milk	Few grains cayenne
⅛ cup fine stale bread crumbs	⅛ teaspoon salt
	3 tablespoons butter
1 onion	½ cup coarse stale bread crumbs
5 cloves	

Cook milk twenty-five minutes in double boiler with fine bread crumbs and onion stuck with cloves. Remove onion, add salt, cayenne and one-half the butter. Pour sauce around the timbales and sprinkle with the coarse crumbs browned in remaining butter.

Creamed Eggs with Sardines

4 tablespoons butter	1 half-box sardines
¼ cup soft, stale bread crumbs	½ teaspoon salt
1 cup thin cream	¼ teaspoon paprika
2 hard-boiled eggs	⅛ teaspoon pepper

Melt butter, add bread crumbs and cream, and bring to the boiling point; then add eggs, finely chopped, sardines freed from skin and bones, and seasonings. Again bring to the boiling point and serve at once.

Windsor Eggs

Arrange four poached eggs on circular pieces of buttered toast, sprinkle with one and one-half tablespoons sautéd chopped mushroom caps, pour around Windsor Sauce and sprinkle sauce with one-half teaspoon finely chopped parsley, and one-half teaspoon finely cut chives.

Windsor Sauce. — Melt three tablespoons butter, add three tablespoons flour, and stir until well blended; then pour on gradually, while stirring constantly, three-fourths cup highly seasoned chicken stock, and one-fourth cup cream. Bring to the boiling point and add one-fourth teaspoon salt, one-eighth teaspoon pepper, and the yolk of one egg, slightly beaten.

Stuffed Eggs in Aspic

Cut six hard-boiled eggs in halves lengthwise, remove yolks and mash three. Add to mashed yolks three tablespoons melted butter, three anchovies, finely chopped, two teaspoons tarragon vinegar, one tablespoon French mustard, one-half tablespoon chopped capers, one-half teaspoon paprika, and one teaspoon salt. When well blended, fill halves of whites with mixture and coat with aspic. Arrange slices of chilled tomatoes on serving dish, marinate with French Dressing and place on each a prepared egg and surround with chopped aspic jelly colored light green.

Florentine Eggs

Remove shells from hard-boiled eggs. Dip one egg in water colored green, one in water colored violet, and leave one white. Cut in halves lengthwise and remove yolks and some of the white. Mash yolks and add one-fourth cup chopped lobster or crab meat, and two tablespoons sautéd chopped mushroom caps. Moisten with any salad dressing and refill whites with mixture. Arrange on a bed of watercress.

Jellied French Poached Egg

To two tablespoons, each, finely chopped carrot, onion, and celery, two sprigs parsley, one sprig thyme, two cloves, six peppercorns, and a bit of bay leaf, add one cup Madeira wine; bring to the boiling point and let simmer five minutes. Strain into a kettle and add one quart chicken stock, one tablespoon lemon juice, four tablespoons granulated gelatine, whites three eggs (unbeaten), one teaspoon salt, and a few grains cayenne. Heat gradually to the boiling point, while stirring constantly. Let boil two minutes, remove to back of range and let simmer thirty minutes; then strain through a double thickness of cheese cloth, placed over a fine strainer. Put a layer in a group of individual moulds, and when mixture becomes firm, decorate with truffle and red and green pepper, cut in fancy shapes. Place a cold French poached egg in centre of each, and gradually fill

Windsor Eggs. — *Page* 61.

Jellied French Poached Eggs. — *Page* 62

Bouillon Cups.

Toasted Triangles. — *Page* 77

moulds with jelly. Chill thoroughly, remove to serving dish, and garnish with watercress. Serve with

Remoulade Sauce.—To one cup Mayonnaise dressing add one-half tablespoon, each, finely chopped pickles and capers, and one teaspoon, each, finely chopped parsley, powdered tarragon, and anchovy essence.

CHAPTER VII

SOUPS AND SOUP ACCOMPANIMENTS

Mock Bouillon

2 quart cans tomatoes	3 cloves
2 cups water	½ teaspoon peppercorns
4 stalks celery	Blade of mace
8 slices carrot	⅛ cup Sherry
¾ onion sliced	½ teaspoon salt
1 small green pepper	⅛ teaspoon pepper

PUT tomatoes and water in saucepan, and add celery cut in pieces, carrot, onion, pepper (from which seeds have been removed), cloves, peppercorns and mace. Bring to the boiling point and let simmer fifteen minutes. Strain, and add Sherry, salt, and pepper. Cool and clear. Serve in bouillon cups.

Corn Mock Bisque Soup

1 can corn	½ can tomatoes
1 quart milk	¼ teaspoon soda
1 slice onion	⅛ cup butter
3 tablespoons flour	2 teaspoons salt
¼ cup cold water	⅛ teaspoon pepper

⅛ teaspoon paprika

Scald milk in double boiler with corn and onion. Mix flour with cold water to form a smooth paste and add to scalded milk; then cook twenty minutes, stirring constantly at first and afterward occasionally, and rub through a sieve. Cook tomatoes ten minutes, add soda, and rub through a sieve. Combine mixtures and strain into a tureen. Add butter bit by bit and seasonings.

Berkshire Soup

1 onion, finely chopped	2 tablespoons sugar
¼ cup butter	1 teaspoon salt
½ bay leaf	½ teaspoon pepper
12 peppercorns	2 cups water
2 tablespoons flour	1 can corn
1 can tomatoes	½ cup cream
2 egg yolks	

Cook onion and butter five minutes, stirring constantly. Add bay leaf, peppercorns, and flour, and cook two minutes; then add tomatoes, sugar, salt, pepper, and boiling water and simmer twenty minutes. Add corn, cook ten minutes, and force through a purée strainer. Just before serving add egg yolks, slightly beaten, and diluted with cream.

Celery and Tomato Purée

1 bunch celery	Bit of bay leaf
2 teaspoons salt	1 teaspoon peppercorns
3 pints cold water	2 sprigs parsley
2 tablespoons fat salt pork	1 clove garlic, crushed
1 onion, sliced	3½ tablespoons butter
1 small carrot, sliced	2 tablespoons flour
1 leek, sliced	1 pint tomatoes
½ teaspoon thyme	1 tablespoon sugar
2 cloves	Salt and pepper.

Break celery in one-inch pieces, and pound in a mortar. Add water and salt, bring slowly to the boiling point, and let simmer one hour. Try out pork fat, add vegetables and seasonings and cook ten minutes stirring constantly; then add tomatoes, sugar and salt and pepper to taste. Combine mixtures, thicken with two tablespoons flour mixed with one and one-half tablespoons butter. Cover and cook slowly one hour. Rub through a sieve, add remaining butter and serve at once.

French Tomato Soup

1 quart brown stock	1 teaspoon salt
1 can tomatoes	⅛ teaspoon pepper
1 onion, sliced	¼ teaspoon soda
2 cloves, garlic	½ tablespoon sugar
4 sprigs parsley	2 tablespoons butter
2 sprigs thyme	2 tablespoons cornstarch
Bit of bay leaf	1 cup cream
6 peppercorns	1 cup milk

Bring stock and tomatoes, mixed with vegetables, salt, and pepper, to the boiling point and let boil thirty minutes. Rub through a sieve, return to range, and add soda and sugar. Melt butter, add cornstarch, and when well blended, pour on hot soup. Bring to the boiling point, and just before serving add cream. Serve with croûtons.

Onion Soup

Wipe and make several gashes through the meat of a six-pound piece cut from a shin of beef. Put in kettle, add three quarts cold water, cover, heat slowly to the boiling point and let simmer six hours. Wipe, peel, and thinly slice five small onions; put in a frying pan and cook in enough butter to prevent burning (stirring constantly) until soft. Strain stock; there should be six cups. Add two and one-half teaspoons beef extract, onions, and salt to taste. Cut stale bread in one-third-inch slices and remove crusts. Toast on both sides. Place in tureen, sprinkle with three tablespoons grated Parmesan cheese and pour soup over bread just before sending to table.

Southdown Soup

Fore quarter lamb	½ tablespoon salt
3 quarts cold water	⅛ cup string beans
1 onion	⅛ cup boiled rice
½ teaspoon peppercorns	¼ teaspoon celery salt or curry powder

Wipe lamb, discarding skin and fat, and cut lean meat in small pieces. Put in kettle with bones and add cold water. Cover, bring gradually to the boiling point and let simmer four hours. During the last hour of the cooking add sliced onion, peppercorns, and salt. Strain, chill, and remove fat. Heat to the boiling point and to each quart of the stock add beans, cut on the diagonal, in small pieces, rice, and celery salt.

Veal Tomato Bisque

3 pints veal stock	½ teaspoon salt
⅛ cup tomato purée	Few grains pepper
¼ cup heavy cream	⅛ teaspoon soda

Mix veal stock, tomato purée, and cream. Bring to the boiling point and add seasonings.

To obtain tomato purée put one-half can tomatoes in saucepan, bring to the boiling point and let simmer until reduced two-thirds; then force through a purée strainer.

Chicken Gumbo

1 onion, finely chopped	2 teaspoons salt
4 tablespoons butter	¼ teaspoon pepper
1 quart chicken stock	½ green pepper, finely chopped
½ can okra	

Cook onion with butter five minutes, stirring constantly. Add to chicken stock to which have been added remaining ingredients. Bring to the boiling point and let simmer forty minutes.

Pimiento Bisque

½ cup rice	1½ teaspoons salt
3 pints chicken stock	½ teaspoon Tabasco Sauce
5 canned pimientoes	½ cup cream

Yolks 2 eggs

Cook rice and stock in double boiler until rice is tender; then rub through a sieve. Add pimientos, rubbed through a sieve, salt, and Tabasco Sauce. Bring to the boiling point and add egg yolks slightly beaten and diluted with cream.

Clear Mushroom Soup

Brush one-half pound mushrooms, finely chop stems and break caps in small pieces. Add to three pints consommé, bring gradually to the boiling point and let simmer thirty minutes. Cool and then clear, using the whites and shells of two eggs. Just before serving add Madeira wine to taste.

Cream Chestnut Soup

1 cup Italian chestnuts	1½ cups cream
1 quart chicken stock	½ teaspoon salt
⅛ teaspoon paprika	

Pick over, wash, and cook chestnuts in boiling water two minutes. Drain, gash, cool, and remove shells. Add stock, bring to the boiling point and let simmer until chestnuts are soft; then rub through a sieve and add remaining ingredients.

Potage Longchamps

1 can peas	1 tablespoon flour
2 slices onion	1 cup milk
1½ teaspoons sugar	Few sprigs fresh mint
3 cups chicken stock	¾ teaspoon salt
1 tablespoon butter	⅛ teaspoon pepper
⅓ cup cooked vermicelli	

Drain and rinse peas. Add onion, sugar, and chicken stock, bring to the boiling point and let simmer thirty minutes. Melt butter, add flour and stir until well blended; then pour on gradually, while stirring constantly, the hot stock. Again bring to the boiling point and put through a purée strainer. Add milk and, while soup is reheating, allow mint to remain in it until it has imparted a delicate flavor. Remove mint and add salt, pepper, and vermicelli.

Nymph Aurora

1 quart chicken stock	2 tablespoons cornstarch
2 slices onion	Leaf green
2 slices carrot	½ teaspoon salt
Bit of bay leaf	⅛ teaspoon pepper
Sprig of marjoram	2 tablespoons lemon juice
Blade mace	1 pint shrimps
½ teaspoon peppercorns	½ cup heavy cream

Cook chicken stock with onion, carrot, bay leaf, marjoram, mace, peppercorns, and cornstarch twelve minutes. Strain, color with leaf green and season with salt, pepper, and lemon juice; then add shrimps cut in pieces. Reheat, add cream beaten until stiff and serve at once.

Cream of Watercress Soup

1 bunch watercress	1 cup heavy cream
3 cups veal stock	¾ teaspoon salt
4½ tablespoons butter	⅛ teaspoon pepper
⅛ cup flour	Green coloring

Wash, pick over, and finely chop cress. Add to stock, bring to the boiling point and let simmer ten minutes; then strain through a double thickness of cheese-cloth. Melt butter, add flour and stir until well blended; then pour on gradually, while stirring constantly, hot stock. Bring to the boiling point. Add cream, salt, and pepper, and color delicately, using leaf green. Serve with Toasted Triangles (see p. 77).

Chicken and Oyster Consommé

1 pint oysters	1 teaspoon salt
½ cup cold water	Few grains cayenne
4 cups chicken stock	½ cup cream

Finely chop oysters (reserving the soft portion of twelve), add cold water and let simmer twenty-five minutes. Strain oyster liquor through a double thickness of cheese-cloth, placed over fine wire strainer, and add to chicken stock. Season with salt and pepper and add cream and the soft parts of oysters, cooked until plump. Reheat and serve at once.

Filippini Consommé

2 cups consommé	3 tablespoons Sherry wine
1 cup brown stock	½ teaspoon salt
4 tablespoons pimiento purée	Few grains cayenne

Mix ingredients and clear, using the white and shell of one egg. To obtain pimiento purée, drain canned pimientoes and force through a purée strainer.

Consommé Dubarry

5 pounds veal, cut from fore quarter	Bit of bay leaf
2 ox-tails	½ teaspoon peppercorns
3 quarts cold water	1 tablespoon salt
½ cup carrot, cut in small pieces	1½ tablespoons butter
½ cup celery, cut in small pieces	½ green pepper
	Flowerets cooked cauliflower
	¼ cup hot boiled rice
1 onion sliced	1 tablespoon shredded, blanched Jordan almonds
3 sprigs thyme	Royal custard

Wipe veal, remove meat, cut in small pieces and put with bones in soup kettle. Add ox-tails, wiped and cut in pieces, and pour over cold water. Heat gradually to the boiling point, skim, cover, and let simmer four hours. Cook carrot, celery, onion, thyme, bay leaf, and peppercorns with butter ten minutes, stirring constantly. Add to soup and let simmer two hours; then add green pepper cut in strips and cook fifteen minutes. Strain, cool, and remove fat. Reheat and add remaining ingredients.

A consommé that does not require clearing.

Consommé Montmorency

4-pound fowl	8 slices carrot
3 pounds knuckle of veal	2 sprigs parsley
3 quarts cold water	2 sprigs thyme
1 sliced onion	½ teaspoon peppercorns
2 stalks celery	2 tablespoons butter

Dress and clean fowl, put in a soup kettle and add veal cut in small pieces. Pour over water and add remaining ingredients, which have been cooked in butter eight minutes. Bring to the boiling point and let simmer until fowl is tender. Remove fowl and let stock boil one and one-half hours. Strain, cool, remove fat, and clear, allowing the white and shell of one egg and one cup uncooked beet to each quart. Garnish with one-fourth cup cooked green peas, one-fourth cup Julienne-shaped pieces of the white meat of cooked chicken, and one-fourth cup cooked pearl tapioca.

Iced Pimiento Consommé

Remove fat from one quart consommé, and clear, using the white of one egg and two pounded canned pimientos. Chill thoroughly and serve very cold in bouillon cups.

Consommé Tillyprone

8 lbs. shin of beef	2 sprigs parsley
4 lbs. knuckle of veal	2 sprigs marjoram
2 ozs. lean raw ham	3 sprigs thyme
4 quarts cold water	¾ teaspoon peppercorns
2 onions, sliced	4 cloves
1 small carrot	2 allspice berries
½ teaspoon celery seed	1 inch piece stick cinnamon
Small bay leaf	1 tablespoon salt
Blade of mace	1 egg
¾ cup Brussels sprouts	

Wipe beef and veal, remove lean meat from bones and cut in small pieces. Put in hot iron frying pan with ham and brown (turning frequently), using just enough butter to keep meat from burning. Remove to back of range, cover and cook one hour, turning occasionally. Put in soup kettle, add water, seasonings and bones sawed in pieces. Bring quickly to boiling point, skim, simmer six hours and strain through cheese-cloth placed over a fine wire strainer, when further clearing will not be necessary. Let stand twenty-four hours. Reheat and garnish with egg, slightly beaten, run through a strainer and cooked in soup.

Wash, pick over and slice Brussels sprouts crosswise and cook in boiling salted water, to which are added a few grains soda, until soft; drain and add to soup.

Consommé Japonais

3 pounds lean beef	10 peppercorns
3 pounds shin of beef	2 cloves
Carcass of roast chicken	5 allspice berries
1 sliced carrot	¼ teaspoon thyme
1 sliced onion	1 quart cold water
1 clove garlic	1½ quarts boiling water
1 stalk celery	Salt
1 sprig parsley	Pepper

Wipe meat, cut in small pieces, and put in a soup kettle. Add remaining ingredients except boiling water, salt, and pepper, cover and let stand on back of range one and one-half hours. Bring to the boiling point and let boil five minutes, stirring constantly. Add boiling water and let simmer one and one-half hours. Season with salt and pepper, and strain through a piece of cheese-cloth placed over a fine strainer.

Mock Turtle Soup

1 calf's head	½ teaspoon peppercorns
4 lbs. knuckle of veal	⅛ teaspoon celery seed
1 lb. marrow bone	4 allspice berries
4 quarts cold water	2 blades mace
1 small sliced carrot	½ tablespoon salt
2 sliced onions	1½ tablespoons butter
3 sprigs thyme	1½ tablespoons flour
2 sprigs marjoram	1½ tablespoons lemon juice
Bit of bay leaf	¼ cup Sherry wine
½ teaspoon clove	Salt and pepper

Clean and wash calf's head, put in kettle with veal and marrow bone; add cold water, cover, bring slowly to boiling point and let simmer until meat leaves bone. Cut face meat in one-half inch cubes — there should be one cup — and set aside with brains to use as garnish. Put tongue, remaining calf's head meat and veal through meat chopper. Return to kettle containing stock and add vegetables and seasonings and let simmer two hours. Strain, cool, remove fat, reheat and add butter and flour browned together. Add meat, lemon juice, Sherry and salt and pepper to taste. Then add egg balls.

Egg Balls. — Mash yolks of three hard-boiled eggs and add an equal measure of mashed calf's brains. Season highly with salt and pepper and add enough slightly beaten egg to hold mixture so that it may be shaped into small balls. Roll balls in flour and sauté in butter.

Bisque of Oysters, Capucine

1 quart oysters	½ cup rice
1½ quarts water	2 cups milk
2 stalks celery	2 teaspoons salt
2 leeks	⅛ teaspoon pepper
2 slices onion	⅛ teaspoon cayenne
2 sprigs parsley	⅛ teaspoon nutmeg
2 cloves	2 egg yolks
½ bay leaf	1 cup cream
1 cup canned peas	

Parboil oysters in their own liquor. Strain, reserve liquor, and finely chop the oysters. To liquor add water, celery, leeks, onion, parsley, cloves, bay leaf, chopped oysters, rice, and milk. Bring to the boiling point and let simmer one and one-quarter hours. Press through a sieve and add remaining seasonings; then egg yolks diluted with cream, and when boiling point is again reached, peas.

Manhattan Clam Bisque

2 quarts clams in shells	3½ tablespoons flour
½ cup cold water	½ teaspoon salt
Hot water	Few grains paprika
3 tablespoons butter	1 cup cream

Wash clams thoroughly, put in kettle, add cold water, cover, and cook until shells are partially opened. Strain liquor through double thickness of cheese-cloth, and add enough hot water to make one quart liquid. Brown butter, add flour and continue the browning; then pour on gradually the liquid. Bring to the boiling point and let simmer twenty minutes. Add seasonings and cream. Serve in bouillon cups with

Pimiento Cream. — Beat one-half cup heavy cream until stiff. Add the beaten white of one-half egg, two tablespoons pimiento purée and a few grains salt. To obtain pimiento purée drain canned pimientoes, dry on a towel and force through a sieve.

Corinthian Clam Bisque

2 dozen soft-shelled clams	2 cloves
¼ cup water	Blade mace
1 sliced onion	2 tablespoons cornstarch
Sprig parsley	2 tablespoons cold water
Salt and pepper	1 quart milk

Mock Cassava Bread in the Making. — *Page* 77

Mock Cassava Bread. — *Page* 77.

Pulled Bread. — *Page* 78.

Hominy Croûtons. — *Page* 78

Wash clams, put in kettle, add water, cover, bring to the boiling point, and cook until shells open. Remove clams from shells, chop finely and add to liquor; then add onion, parsley, clams, and mace and let simmer thirty minutes. Scald milk and thicken with cornstarch diluted with cold water. Cook ten minutes and add clam water, strained through a double thickening of cheese-cloth. Season with salt and pepper, and serve in bouillon cups with whipped cream.

SOUP ACCOMPANIMENTS

Toasted Triangles

Cut stale bread in one-eighth-inch slices and remove crusts; then cut in halves on the diagonal, making triangles. Toast under a gas flame or bake in a slow oven until crisp and delicately browned.

Mock Cassava Bread

Remove crusts from a small, stale baker's loaf in four pieces, using a sharp, long-bladed knife; then cut in very thin slices lengthwise and shape with an elliptical cutter. Dip each piece separately quickly in and out of cold water and shape over a form (using one-half-pound baking powder tins) and keep in place with soft twine. Place in dripping pan, brush over with melted butter and bake in a slow oven until crisp and delicately browned, turning frequently. Serve as an accompaniment to soup or five o'clock tea.

Pulled Bread

Cut off ends and remove crusts from a baker's French loaf; then cut in halves, crosswise. Pull apart into strips, using two three-tined forks. Put in dripping pan and bake in a slow oven until crisp and delicately browned.

Hominy Croûtons

Pack hominy mush in buttered one-fourth-pound baking powder box. When cold, remove from box, cut in one-fourth-inch slices and slices in one-fourth-inch cubes. Dip in fine crumbs, egg, and crumbs, and fry in deep fat.

Tapioca Garnish for Consommé

Soak one-fourth cup pearl tapioca over night in cold water to cover. Drain and cook in boiling salted water until transparent. Again drain and add to soup.

CHAPTER VIII

FISH

WAYS OF COOKING SHELLFISH

Sherry Oyster Cocktail

ALLOW six small oysters to each cocktail and pour over a dressing made of Sherry wine, salt, and cayenne, allowing two tablespoons wine and a few grains, each, salt and cayenne, to each cocktail. Let oysters stand in sauce in a cold place fifteen minutes before serving time.

Mayonnaise of Oysters

Clean selected oysters; put in omelet pan and parboil in their own liquor. Remove tough muscles and discard. Marinate soft portions with French Dressing and let stand in ice box until thoroughly chilled. Arrange for individual service on small, crisp lettuce leaves (placed on small plates), allowing three pieces of oyster for each portion. Garnish with Mayonnaise Dressing forced through pastry bag and tube and serve at once as a first course at dinner.

Norfolk Oysters

1½ cups hot boiled rice Butter
1 pint oysters Salt
1 cup white sauce Pepper
    1 cup buttered cracker crumbs

Cover bottom of buttered baking dish with one-half the rice, cover rice with one-half the oysters, pour over one-half the sauce, dot over with butter and sprinkle with salt and pepper; repeat, using remaining ingredients. Cover with crumbs, and bake in a hot oven thirty minutes.

Oysters Louisiane

Clean and parboil one quart oysters, reserve liquor, and add enough water to make one and one-half cups. Cook three tablespoons butter with two tablespoons chopped red pepper and one-half tablespoon finely chopped shallot, five minutes. Add four tablespoons flour and stir until well blended; then pour on gradually, while stirring constantly, oyster liquor. Bring to the boiling point and season with one-half teaspoon salt, one-eighth teaspoon paprika, few grains cayenne, and one tablespoon Sauterne wine. Arrange oysters in large buttered scalloped shells, pour over sauce, sprinkle with grated Parmesan cheese, and pipe around edge of shells a border of Duchess potatoes. Arrange in pan and bake until thoroughly reheated.

Devilled Oysters on Half Shells

1 pint oysters	Few grains cayenne
1 tablespoon butter	½ teaspoon made mustard
3 shallots, finely chopped	½ tablespoon Worcestershire Sauce
2 tablespoons flour	
½ cup milk	3 chopped mushroom caps
¼ cup cream	½ teaspoon chopped parsley
½ teaspoon salt	1 egg yolk
⅛ teaspoon nutmeg	Buttered cracker crumbs

Wash and chop oysters. Cook shallots in butter three minutes, add flour and stir until well blended; then add milk and cream. Bring to the boiling point and add oysters and remaining ingredients, except egg yolk and crumbs, and let simmer twelve minutes. Add egg yolk, put mixture in deep halves of oyster shells, cover with buttered crumbs, and bake fifteen minutes.

Scallop Cocktail I

Clean scallops, put in saucepan and cook until they begin to shrivel. Drain, chill and put in small fluted shells, allowing five for each shell. Arrange two shells on each plate of finely crushed ice, placing between shells a small glass containing cocktail dressing, same as used for Oyster Cocktail I (see The Boston Cooking School Cook Book, p. 180).

Scallop Cocktail II

1 teaspoon salt	½ teaspoon dry mustard
¼ teaspoon pepper	2 tablespoons vinegar
1 teaspoon chopped parsley	8 tablespoons Tomato
1 teaspoon chives, finely cut	Catsup
½ teaspoon chopped shallot	1 teaspoon grated horse-
½ teaspoon olive oil	radish root
10 drops Tabasco Sauce	1 pint scallops
1½ teaspoons Worcestershire Sauce	

Mix ingredients, except scallops. Cook scallops five minutes, drain, chill thoroughly, and cut in halves. Add to sauce and serve in cocktail glasses. This recipe makes six cocktails.

Savoy Scallops

1 quart scallops	3 tablespoons flour
Fish stock	½ cup Mayonnaise Dressing
3 tablespoons butter	½ teaspoon thyme

Parboil scallops, drain, and cut in quarters. To scallop liquor add enough fish stock to make one and one-third cups. Melt butter, add flour and stir until well blended; then pour on gradually, while stirring constantly, fish liquor. When boiling point is reached remove to back of range and add gradually Mayonnaise Dressing; then scallops and thyme. Keep hot in chafing dish, but do not allow mixture to boil. For the thyme remove the tiny leaves from sprigs of dried thyme.

Samoset Scallops

1 pint scallops	Few grains soda
1 tablespoon butter	1 cup finely cut, soft mild cheese
1 tablespoon flour	
½ cup thin cream	1 egg
⅛ cup stewed and strained tomatoes	Salt
	Mustard
Cayenne	

Parboil scallops, drain and cut in quarters. Melt butter, add flour and stir until well blended; then pour on gradually, while stirring constantly, cream. Bring to the boiling point and add tomatoes mixed with soda. Again bring to the boiling point, add cheese and, as soon as cheese has melted, egg slightly beaten, scallops, and seasoning. Serve on squares of toasted bread.

Scalloped Scallops

1 pint scallops	½ cup soft bread crumbs
½ cup butter	½ cup cream
1 cup cracker crumbs	Salt
Pepper	

Wash and pick over scallops. Melt butter and add cracker and bread crumbs. Put a layer of crumbs in buttered dish, cover with scallops, add one-half the cream and season with salt and pepper; repeat, cover with buttered crumbs and bake until crumbs are brown, the time required being about twenty-five minutes.

Scallops Bresloise

1 pint scallops	3 tablespoons fresh bread crumbs
½ cup water	
½ cup white wine	½ clove garlic, finely chopped
½ teaspoon salt	
⅛ teaspoon pepper	1 teaspoon chopped parsley
1 small white onion	1 egg yolk
2 tablespoons butter	¾ cup buttered bread crumbs
1 tablespoon flour	

Cook scallops in water and wine, to which salt and pepper have been added, five minutes; drain and chop. Chop onion and cook with butter five minutes, stirring constantly; add flour and stir until well blended; then pour on gradually, while stirring constantly, liquor drained from scallops. Bring to the boiling point and add scallops and remaining ingredients, except buttered bread crumbs. Fill buttered shells with mixture, sprinkle with buttered crumbs, arrange in pan, and bake until crumbs are brown.

Fried Scallops à la Huntington

Clean one quart scallops and pour over the juice of one lemon, one tablespoon olive oil, one-half teaspoon finely chopped parsley, one teaspoon salt, and one-half teaspoon pepper. Cover, let stand thirty minutes, and drain. Mix three tablespoons chopped cooked ham, four tablespoons soft, stale bread crumbs, two tablespoons grated Parmesan cheese, and one teaspoon chives, finely cut. Dip scallops in egg, roll in mixture, fry in deep fat and drain on brown paper. Sprinkle with salt, remove to hot platter, and garnish with parsley.

How to Boil Lobsters

Have ready a large kettle containing vigorously boiling water, adding one tablespoon salt to each quart of water. Put in live lobsters, tail end down, one at a time, having the water come to the boiling point between each addition. Lobsters should be entirely covered by water. Cover and let boil twenty minutes.

Spanish Lobster in Casseroles

Remove meat from a two-pound lobster and cut in small pieces. Put body bones and claw meat in a stewpan, cover with two and one-half cups cold water and add one slice, each, carrot and onion, sprig of parsley, and stalk of celery. Bring to the boiling point and let boil until reduced to one and one-half

SCALLOP COCKTAIL. — *Page* 81.

SARDINE COCKTAIL. — *Page* 372

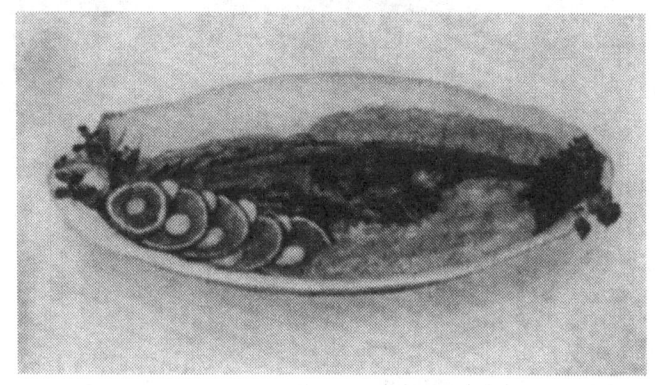

BROILED POMPANO, CUCUMBER HOLLANDAISE. — *Page* 88

SHATTUCK HALIBUT. — *Page* 89.

cups; then strain. Melt four tablespoons butter, add four tablespoons flour and stir until well blended; then pour on gradually lobster stock. Bring to the boiling point and add one-half cup heavy cream, yolks two eggs, slightly beaten, and lobster dice. Season with one tablespoon lemon juice, one-half teaspoon salt, one-fourth teaspoon paprika, and one-eighth teaspoon pepper. Put one tablespoon boiled rice in each buttered individual casserole, fill with lobster mixture, and on top place a small slice broiled tomato, brushed over with melted butter and seasoned with salt and pepper.

Planked Live Lobster

Split a one and one-half pound live lobster (see The Boston Cooking-School Cook Book, p. 189), put in dripping pan, brush shell over with olive oil or melted butter and bake in a hot oven fifteen minutes. Remove to plank and garnish with Julienne potatoes, slices of peeled and chilled tomatoes, overlapping one another, slices of cucumber and parsley. Pour over lobster melted butter, seasoned with salt, pepper and lemon juice.

Planked Live Lobster with Oysters

Split and bake a lobster, same as for Planked Live Lobster, cooking only twelve minutes. Clean and pick over one cup oysters, put over tail and body meat of lobster, sprinkle with salt and pepper and dot over generously with butter. Put in oven and bake until oysters are plump and edges curl. Garnish with Saratoga Chips (see The Boston Cooking School Cook Book, p. 314) and sprigs of parsley.

Crab Meat Urzini

3 tablespoons butter	¾ teaspoon salt
3 tablespoons flour	½ pound crab meat
¾ cup milk	¼ pound mushroom caps
¾ cup cream	1 canned pimiento

Melt butter, add flour and stir until well blended; then pour on gradually, while stirring constantly, milk and cream. Bring to the boiling point, season with salt and add crab meat, mushroom caps (sliced and sautéd in butter), and pimiento (cut in long, thin strips). Use as a filling for patties, vol-au-vent, or Swedish timbales.

Crab Meat Mornay

4½ tablespoons butter	¾ cup chicken stock
3 tablespoons flour	¾ cup milk
2½ tablespoons cornstarch	Yolks 2 eggs
¾ teaspoon salt	1¼ cups crab meat
½ cup grated Young America cheese	

Melt butter, add flour, cornstarch, and salt, and stir until well blended; then pour on gradually, while stirring constantly, chicken stock; bring to the boiling point and let boil three minutes. Add milk gradually, again bring to the boiling point and add egg yolks, slightly beaten. Butter eight individual casseroles, cover bottoms with crab meat, cover

FISH 87

meat with sauce, and sprinkle with cheese. Run under gas flame to melt cheese, and brown.

Crabs Ravigôte

1 pound fresh crab meat	½ teaspoon finely chopped
1 teaspoon salt	parsley
⅛ teaspoon cayenne	1 hard boiled egg, finely
1 teaspoon made mustard	chopped
1 tablespoon olive oil	3 tablespoons vinegar

Season crab meat with remaining ingredients, mix thoroughly and arrange in six scallop shells, spread evenly with Ravigôte Mayonnaise (see The Boston Cooking-School Cook Book, p. 344) and garnish with fillets of anchovies, arranged lattice fashion.

WAYS OF COOKING OTHER FISH

Fisherman's Haddock

Remove head and tail from a four-pound haddock, split and wipe with a piece of cheese-cloth wrung out of cold water. Sprinkle inside with one cup salt, cover and let stand over night. In the morning remove salt, rinse thoroughly, tie in cheese-cloth, and cook in boiling water until tender. Drain thoroughly, and remove from cheese-cloth to hot platter. Garnish with steamed potatoes of uniform size and boiled beets (cut in slices and slices cut in fancy shapes; then seasoned with butter and salt), alternating vegetables. Cut four one-fourth-inch slices fat salt pork in small cubes and try out. Serve fish with pork scraps, pork fat, and two cups white sauce.

Broiled Pompano, Cucumber Hollandaise

Order fish dressed for broiling; wipe, sprinkle with salt and pepper, and place in a greased broiler. Broil flesh side until well seared, brush flesh side sparingly with olive oil or melted butter and continue broiling on flesh side until fish begins to brown, again brush over with butter or oil and continue broiling on flesh side until well browned. Turn and broil skin side until fish is done. Remove to heated platter, pour over Cucumber Hollandaise (see p. 157) and garnish at one end of platter with ten thin slices of lemon (from which seeds have been removed) and ten thin slices of round radishes, alternating and overlapping them. In middle of garnish thus arranged, place a sprig of parsley.

Baked Halibut, Swedish Style

1 pound slice halibut	¾ cup canned tomatoes
Salt	½ teaspoon powdered sugar
Pepper	½ onion
Melted butter	⅛ cup heavy cream

Wipe halibut and remove skin. Place in an earthen baking dish, sprinkle with salt and pepper and brush over with melted butter. Drain tomatoes and add sugar. Spread over fish, then cover with onion, thinly sliced. Bake twenty minutes, pour over cream and bake ten minutes. Remove onion and serve at once, from dish in which it was cooked.

FISH 89

Shattuck Halibut

Wipe a one and one-half pound slice chicken halibut with a piece of cheese-cloth, wrung out of cold water. Put in a buttered copper platter or dripping pan, and sprinkle with salt and pepper. Arrange on top five three-fourth-inch slices cut from medium-sized tomatoes, which have been peeled; then sprinkle with Julienne-shaped pieces cut from a green pepper. Bake in a hot oven twenty-five minutes, basting four times, using one-third cup melted butter and after that is gone, liquor in platter.

Halibut à la Suisse

Wipe a two-pound piece of halibut with cheese-cloth, wrung out of cold water. Put in baking pan of correct size, sprinkle with salt and pepper and put on top one-half cup butter. Bake fifteen minutes, basting twice; then cover with one-fourth pound mushrooms, broken in pieces, and pour over one cup cream. Again bake fifteen minutes, add one teaspoon beef extract and bake ten minutes, basting twice. Remove to hot serving dish, pour around sauce remaining in pan, and garnish with parsley.

Halibut Veronique

Wipe two three-fourth-pound slices chicken halibut and cut into eight fillets. Sprinkle with salt and pepper, brush over with lemon juice, and put a thin slice of onion on each. Cover, and let stand two hours. Remove onion, place fillets in buttered pan of correct size and pour over the following sauce:

Melt three tablespoons butter, add three tablespoons flour and stir until well blended; then pour on gradually, while stirring constantly, two-thirds cup fish stock, and one-half cup cream. The fish stock used is made from bones, skin, and trimmings of fish.

Cover and bake in a hot oven five minutes. Transfer fish to a copper platter.

Remove skin and seeds from three-fourths cup Malaga grapes, pour over three tablespoons Tokay wine, cover, and let stand thirty minutes. Drain, add to sauce which has been strained, seasoned with salt, and cooked five minutes; then add two teaspoons wine in which grapes have soaked and pour over fish.

Serve in copper platter.

Halibut Loomis

2 1-pound slices chicken halibut	Bit of bay leaf
1 onion	½ cup white wine
2 sprigs parsley	1 tablespoon vinegar
1 sprig thyme	¾ teaspoon salt
2 cloves	⅛ teaspoon pepper
	Cold water

Slice onion and add parsley, thyme, cloves, and bay leaf. Put in pan, lay fish over vegetables, sprinkle with salt and pepper, and add wine, vinegar, and cold water to cover. Cover and let stand two hours. Place on range, bring to boiling point and let boil fifteen minutes. Remove to hot platter and pour over the following sauce: Melt two tablespoons butter, add three tablespoons flour and stir until well blended; then pour on gradually, while stirring constantly, one-half cup milk, and one-third cup liquor, in which fish was cooked. Bring to the boiling point and add two tablespoons grated cheese, one-fourth teaspoon salt, few grains pepper, and the yolk of one egg, slightly beaten. Dot over with one tablespoon butter, place in a hot oven and bake until well browned. Sprinkle with one-half tablespoon finely chopped parsley and serve at once.

Fillets of Halibut à la Hollanden

2 ¾-pound slices halibut	3 tablespoons butter
6 thin slices fat salt pork	3 tablespoons flour
1 sliced onion	¾ cup buttered cracker crumbs
½ bay leaf	

Wipe fish and cut into eight fillets. Take up each fillet separately, roll, and fasten with a wooden skewer. Arrange pork in pan, cover with onion and bay leaf, broken in pieces, and place fillets over all. Work butter until creamy, add flour and stir until well blended. Then mask fillets with mixture, sprinkle with buttered crumbs, and bake in a hot oven. Remove to serving dish, take out skewers, and pour around the following sauce:

To two and one-half tablespoons fat, remaining in pan, add two tablespoons flour and stir until well blended; then pour on gradually, while stirring constantly, one cup rich milk or cream. Bring to the boiling point and season with one-fourth teaspoon salt, one-eighth teaspoon pepper, and one tablespoon butter, bit by bit.

Huntington Halibut, Sauce Verte

Wipe a slice of halibut, weighing about one pound, with a piece of cheese-cloth wrung out of cold water. Free from skin and bones and force through a meat chopper; there should be one and three-fourths cups. Put in mortar and add whites two eggs gradually, while working constantly until mixture is smooth, then add one and one-fourth cups heavy cream and salt, pepper and cayenne to taste. Rub through a sieve, line buttered individual moulds with mixture and nearly fill spaces with creamed shrimps or crab meat and cover with forcemeat. Set in pan of hot water, cover with buttered paper and bake until firm. Remove to hot serving dish and pour around Sauce Verte (see p. 160).

Haddock à la Metropole

5-pound haddock
2 cups cold water
3 slices carrot
1 slice onion
2 sprigs parsley
6 peppercorns
2½ tablespoons butter
3½ tablespoons flour

½ teaspoon salt
⅛ teaspoon pepper
½ cup heavy cream
1¼ tablespoons pimiento purée
½ tablespoon finely chopped chives
¼ teaspoon salt

¾ cup buttered coarse bread crumbs

Skin, bone, and cut haddock into fillets for individual service. Cover bones, skin, and trimmings with water, add carrot, onion, parsley, and pepper; bring to the boiling point and let simmer until reduced one-half. Melt butter, add flour and stir until well blended; then add fish stock, which has been strained, and bring to the boiling point. Arrange fish in buttered pan, brush over with lemon juice (using one and one-half tablespoons), sprinkle with salt and pepper, and pour over sauce. Cover with buttered paper and bake fifteen minutes. Beat cream until stiff, add pimiento purée, chives, and salt. Spread fillets with cream. Sprinkle with buttered crumbs, and bake until crumbs are brown. To obtain pimiento purée drain canned pimientos and force through a purée strainer.

Stuffed Baked Haddock à la Preston

Wipe, skin, and fillet a four-pound haddock. Brush over with lemon juice and sprinkle with salt and pepper. Put one fillet in buttered pan, spread with mushroom filling, cover with remaining fillet, pour over two-thirds cup cream, and bake twenty-five minutes. Sprinkle with two-thirds cup buttered bread crumbs and bake until crumbs are brown. Remove to hot serving dish and strain around liquor remaining in pan.

Mushroom Stuffing. — Mix one-half cup bread crumbs with three tablespoons melted butter and one-third cup mushroom caps, cut in pieces; then add one-half teaspoon salt and a few grains pepper.

Baked Bluefish à la Muisset

Wipe, scale, cut off fins, and remove large bones from a three-pound fish. Place on a buttered fish sheet in dripping pan and sprinkle with one teaspoon salt mixed with one-half teaspoon curry powder. Work one tablespoon butter until creamy, add one teaspoon anchovy essence, and spread over fish. Bake twenty-five minutes, basting four times with melted butter, using one-third cup. Mix two ounces blanched and chopped almonds and one tablespoon capers. Add one-half cup chicken or brown stock, bring to the boiling point and let simmer five minutes. Pour over fish, sprinkle with coarse bread crumbs, and bake until crumbs are brown. Remove to hot serving dish and garnish with parsley.

Stuffed Turbans of Flounder

2 large flounders
¾ cup chopped mushroom caps
Few drops onion juice
3 tablespoons butter
4½ tablespoons flour
½ cup cream
12 chopped bearded oysters
½ teaspoon salt
⅛ teaspoon pepper
Few grains cayenne
Few grains mace

Wipe, skin, and cut flounders into eight fillets. Trim and coil around inside of buttered muffin rings, placed in a buttered pan. Cook mushroom caps and onion juice with butter one minute. Add

THE PREPARING OF STUFFED TURBANS OF FLOUNDER. — *Page 94*

STUFFED TURBANS OF FLOUNDER. — *Page 94.*

FILLET OF FLOUNDER IN PAPER COVER READY FOR OVEN. — *Page 95*

FILLET OF FLOUNDER IN PAPER COVER. — *Page 95.*

flour and stir until well blended; then pour on gradually, while stirring constantly, cream. Bring to the boiling point and add oysters and seasonings. Fill muffin rings with mixture, cover with buttered paper, and bake fifteen minutes. Sprinkle with buttered bread crumbs and continue baking until crumbs are brown.

Fillets of Flounder in Paper Cases

Cut cold boiled ham in one-fourth-inch slices, then in oblong-shaped pieces with rounding corners. Fillet large flounders and cut in pieces. Arrange a thick piece on each piece of ham, sprinkle with salt and pepper, put in paper cases and turn edges, thus preventing escape of juices. Put in pan, brush cases with melted butter and bake in a hot oven fifteen minutes. Arrange on hot serving plates without removing cases. Serve with melted butter.

Fillets of Sole, St. Malo

Clean, wipe, and fillet three flounders. Put in buttered pan, sprinkle with salt and pepper, and pour over three-fourths cup fish stock (made from trimmings and bones), one-half cup white wine, liquor drained from one-half pint parboiled oysters, two slices, each, carrot and onion, bit of bay leaf, sprig of parsley, and stalk of celery, broken in pieces. Cover with buttered paper and bake twenty minutes. Remove fillets to copper platter. Melt three tablespoons butter, add three tablespoons flour and stir until well blended; then pour on gradually, while stirring constantly, one cup liquor remaining in pan. Bring to the boiling point, add one-half cup heavy cream, and season with one-half teaspoon salt and a few grains paprika.

Strain sauce over fillets, place a parboiled oyster on each, sprinkle with six tablespoons Parmesan cheese, and bake until cheese is melted.

Fillets of Sole Marguery

Wipe, skin and fillet two sole. Put in buttered dripping pan, sprinkle with salt and paprika and pour over one-third cup white wine. Cover with buttered paper and bake in a moderate oven fifteen minutes. Put bones and trimmings of fish in saucepan, add body bones from a small lobster and six little neck clams. Cover with two and one-half cups cold water, bring to the boiling point and let simmer until stock is reduced to one cup. Melt three tablespoons butter, add three tablespoons flour and stir until well blended, then pour on gradually the fish stock. Bring to the boiling point and add one-fourth cup wine in which fish has cooked and season with salt and pepper. Arrange fillets on copper platter, strain over sauce and garnish with slices of lobster meat, chopped truffle and one dozen little neck clams. Sprinkle with grated Parmesan cheese and bake until thoroughly heated.

FISH 97

Baked Shad, Roe Sauce

Clean and split a three-pound shad. Place in an oiled dripping pan, sprinkle with salt and pepper, brush over with melted butter and bake in a hot oven thirty minutes. Remove to serving dish and pour around Roe Sauce (see p. 159).

Petite Halibut, Lobster Sauce

Free raw halibut from skin and bones and force through a sieve; there should be one cup. Pound in a mortar, and add gradually the white of one egg; then add gradually one cup heavy cream, and season with three-fourths teaspoon salt, one-eighth teaspoon pepper, and a few grains cayenne. Turn into slightly buttered individual fish moulds, set in pan of hot water, cover with buttered paper, and bake until firm; the time required being about fifteen minutes. Remove from moulds to hot serving dish and insert peppercorns to represent eyes. Pour around Lobster Sauce and garnish with fan-shaped pieces of lemon, or diamond-shaped pieces of red pepper, and slices of cucumber cut in the shape of fishes.

Lobster Sauce

Melt two tablespoons butter, add two tablespoons flour and stir until well blended; then pour on gradually, while stirring constantly, one-third cup lobster stock and one-fourth cup cream. Bring to the boiling point and add one-fourth cup butter, bit by bit, yolks two eggs, one tablespoon lemon juice, one-half teaspoon salt, one-eighth teaspoon pepper, a few grains cayenne, and two tablespoons lobster meat cut in cubes.

Moulded Rolled Fillets of Halibut

Wipe, skin, and fillet a three-pound chicken halibut or turbot. Cut each of the four fillets in halves, lengthwise. Trim into shape, sprinkle with salt and lemon juice, and spread with salmon forcemeat. Roll like a jelly roll and roll in buttered cheesecloth, fastening ends with soft twine. Cook over boiling water twenty minutes. Cool, remove from cheese-cloth, and cut in one-third-inch slices, crosswise. Line buttered charlotte russe moulds with prepared fish, spread with halibut forcemeat to keep pieces in shape and fill cavity with a mixture of three-fourths cup cold, cooked, flaked salmon and halibut (using equal parts), and one-fourth cup chopped mushrooms, moistened with sauce made from one and one-half tablespoons, each, butter and flour and one-third cup fish stock. Cover with salmon forcemeat, set in a pan of hot water, cover with buttered paper and bake until firm, the time required being about forty-five minutes. Remove from moulds to hot platter, as shown in illustration and garnish with thin slices of lemon, shrimps, and parsley. Pour around English Fish Sauce.

Petite Halibut, Lobster Sauce. — *Page* 97.

Moulded Rolled Fillet of Halibut. — *Page* 98

IROQUOIS STEAK.—*Page* 107.

TOURNADOES OF BEEF.—*Page* 109

Salmon Forcemeat. — Cut stale, baker's bread in slices, remove crusts, break, crumb in small pieces and pack solidly in cup; there should be three-fourths cup. Cover crumbs with cold water and let stand one minute. Drain in cheese-cloth and squeeze as dry as possible. Put in saucepan, add three-fourths tablespoon butter and cook, stirring constantly, until a paste is formed; then spread on a plate to cool. Force two-thirds cup of cold, cooked salmon through meat chopper, pound in a mortar with bread mixture and add one-third cup heavy cream, two eggs, three-fourths teaspoon salt, one-eighth teaspoon pepper, and a slight grating nutmeg.

Halibut Forcemeat. — Melt three tablespoons butter, add six tablespoons flour and stir until well blended; then pour on gradually, while stirring constantly, one-third cup fish stock. Remove from range, cool, put in mortar and pound with one and one-half cups uncooked halibut, forced through a meat chopper. When well blended, add two eggs and three egg yolks, two teaspoons salt, one-fourth teaspoon pepper, and one-half cup heavy cream. Force through a purée strainer.

English Fish Sauce. — Make a stock from trimmings from salmon and halibut, a nape of halibut, one sprig, each, parsley, and thyme, one onion, cut in halves, bit of bay leaf, one-fourth cup white wine, two tablespoons Sherry wine, one tablespoon lemon juice, and five cups water. Cook until reduced to two cups.

Melt three and one-half tablespoons butter, add three and one-half tablespoons flour and stir until well blended; then pour on gradually, while stirring constantly, one and one-third cups stock, the remaining two-thirds being used for forcemeat, and fish and mushroom mixture. Bring to the boiling point and season with salt and pepper.

Finnan Haddie, Caledonian Style

Cut a four-pound finnan haddie in halves, lengthwise, put one-half in dripping pan, surround with milk and water, using equal proportions, place on back of range, where it will heat slowly, and let stand twenty-five minutes. Trim fish to fit a copper platter or granite ware pan, by cutting off flank and a piece from tail end. Pour over a cream sauce and surround with six halves of potatoes of uniform size, washed and smoothly pared. Bake until potatoes are soft (the time required being about forty minutes), basting with the cream sauce four times during the cooking.

If cooked in copper platter, serve from it; if cooked in pan, remove to hot serving dish and pour around sauce. For the *Cream Sauce* melt two tablespoons butter, add two tablespoons flour, and stir until well blended; then pour on gradually, while stirring constantly, one cup milk and one-half cup cream. Bring to the boiling point and season with a few grains pepper.

Epicurean Finnan Haddie

3-pound finnan haddie	¼ cup butter
½ tablespoon finely chopped shallot	1 teaspoon salt
	½ teaspoon paprika
1 tablespoon finely chopped green pepper	Few grains cayenne
	4 tablespoons flour
½ tablespoon finely chopped red pepper	1 cup cream
	1 cup milk

Soak finnan haddie in milk to cover, one hour. Bake in a moderate oven thirty minutes and separate in flakes; there should be two cups. Cook shallot and pepper in butter five minutes, stirring constantly. Add salt, paprika, and cayenne mixed with flour and stir until well blended; then pour on gradually, while stirring constantly, milk and cream. Bring to the boiling point and add finnan haddie. Serve on squares of toasted bread, or turn into a buttered baking dish, cover with buttered crumbs and bake until crumbs are brown.

Savory Finnan Haddie

Soak a finnan haddie in milk to cover one hour; then cook until tender and separate into flakes; there should be one cup. Cut a two-inch cube of fat salt pork in tiny dice and try out. To two tablespoons of the pork fat add two tablespoons flour and stir until well blended; then pour on gradually, while stirring constantly, one cup rich milk. Bring to the boiling point and add finnan haddie, pork scraps, yolks of two eggs, slightly beaten, and one and one-half cups small potato balls or cubes, which have been cooked in boiling, salted water until soft. Season with salt and pepper and serve as soon as thoroughly heated.

Epicurean Fish Cutlets

1¾ cups flaked cooked haddock	3 tablespoons butter
½ tablespoon shallot, finely chopped	⅛ cup flour
	¾ teaspoon salt
2 tablespoons red pepper, finely chopped	¼ teaspoon paprika
	½ cup milk
½ cup cream	

Cook shallot and red pepper with butter five minutes, stirring constantly. Add flour mixed with salt and paprika and stir until well blended; then pour on gradually, while stirring constantly, milk and cream. Bring to the boiling point, add fish, and spread on a plate to cool.

Shape, dip in crumbs, egg, and crumbs, fry in deep fat and drain on brown paper. Arrange on a serving dish, garnish with sprigs of parsley, and serve with or without

Epicurean Sauce. — Mix one tablespoon tarragon vinegar, two tablespoons grated horseradish root, one teaspoon English mustard, one-half teaspoon salt, and a few grains cayenne; then add one-half cup whipped cream and three tablespoons Mayonnaise Dressing.

Smelts au Beurre Noir

Split and bone eight selected smelts, sprinkle with salt and pepper, roll in flour and sauté in butter. Remove serving dish, pour over *Beurre Noir* and sprinkle to with one-half tablespoon finely chopped parsley.

Beurre Noir. — To fat in pan add two and one-half tablespoons butter and stir until well browned; then add one teaspoon lemon juice and a few grains, each, salt and pepper. Strain over fish.

Smelts à la Guaymas

Wipe, split, and bone six selected smelts. Sprinkle with salt, pepper, onion juice, and lemon juice; cover and let stand fifteen minutes. Parboil a red pepper, remove seeds and outside skin and rub pulp through a sieve; then add one tablespoon grated Parmesan cheese. Spread smelts with mixture, roll, fasten with wooden skewers, dip in crumbs, egg, and crumbs, fry in deep fat and drain. Serve with Guaymas Sauce (see p. 159).

Smelts Veronique

Clean eight selected smelts, sprinkle with salt and pepper, roll in flour and sauté in olive oil until delicately browned, turning frequently. Remove to hot serving dish and sprinkle with one-fourth cup Jordan almonds, blanched, cut in thin slices crosswise and sautéd in olive oil. Garnish with Fried Potato Curls.

Fried Smelts, Britannia

Clean smelts, remove heads and tails, and cut in one-half-inch slices crosswise. Cut thin slices of bacon in pieces. Arrange fish and bacon alternately on skewers having four of each for a service. Brush over with olive oil, seasoned with salt and pepper, roll in crumbs, fry in deep fat and drain on brown paper. Garnish with parsley and serve with sections of lemon.

Planked Smelts

Clean and bone eight selected smelts and arrange on a buttered plank in the shape of a large fish. Sprinkle with salt and pepper, spread with Maître d'Hôtel Butter and bake twelve minutes. Garnish around edge with potato roses, made by forcing Duchess potatoes through a pastry bag and rose tube, and bake until fish is done and potatoes are brown. Remove from oven, sprinkle with finely chopped parsley and between roses place slices of cucumber and sections of small tomatoes, each, dressed with French dressing. Serve at once from plank.

Gloucester Salt Codfish

Cut boneless salt codfish in two-inch pieces, cover with lukewarm water and let stand fifteen minutes. Drain, dry on a towel and sauté in butter in a hot frying pan until delicately browned. Add rich milk or thin cream to about half cover fish and bring gradually to the boiling point. Pour into hot serving dish.

Spanish Codfish

Pick over salt codfish and separate in small pieces; there should be two-thirds cup. Cover with lukewarm water, soak until soft, and drain. Cut four medium-sized cold boiled potatoes in slices. Arrange alternate layers of potatoes and fish in buttered baking dish, sprinkle with salt and pepper and cover with one and one-half canned pimientos cut in strips; repeat. Pour over one cup tomato sauce, cover with buttered cracker crumbs and bake until crumbs are brown.

Salmon Soufflé, Spanish Sauce

1 can salmon	½ cup soft bread crumbs
¼ teaspoon salt	½ cup milk
⅛ teaspoon paprika	Yolks 3 eggs
2 teaspoons lemon juice	Whites 3 eggs

Thoroughly rinse salmon, remove bones and skin, separate into flakes and add seasonings. Cook bread crumbs in milk five minutes, add salmon and the egg yolks beaten until thick and lemon-colored; then cut and fold in whites of eggs, beaten until stiff and dry. Turn into a buttered dish, set in a pan of hot water, and bake in a moderate oven until firm. Serve with Spanish Sauce (see p. 154).

Spiced Salmon

Remove fish from one can choice selected salmon. Rinse thoroughly with hot water and remove skin and bones. Put one cup vinegar in saucepan and add one teaspoon whole cloves, one-half teaspoon allspice berries, eight peppercorns, and one-fourth teaspoon salt. Bring to the boiling point, pour over fish, cover and let stand two hours. Drain and separate into flakes.

Court Bouillon

1/8 cup, each, carrot, onion and celery, cut in small pieces	2 cloves
2 sprigs parsley	1/2 bay leaf
2 tablespoons butter	1 tablespoon salt
6 peppercorns	2 tablespoons vinegar
	2 quarts water

Cook carrot, onion, celery, and parsley with butter three minutes, add remaining ingredients and bring to boiling point. To be used for stock in which to boil fish.

CHAPTER IX

BEEF

Iroquois Steak

Season one and one-fourth pounds Hamburg steak with salt and pepper and form into one large elliptical-shaped cake. Put in a slightly greased hot iron frying pan, sear on one side, turn and sear on other side. Remove to copper platter and bake in a hot oven. Spread with softened butter, sprinkle with salt and pepper and garnish with fried strips of green pepper. Arrange glazed silver-skinned onions at each end of platter. Fry the strips of pepper in deep fat; then strip off the outside skin that blisters during the process.

Steven Steak

Cut flank end from a sirloin or Porterhouse steak, wipe and remove superfluous fat. Force through a meat chopper or finely chop and add two tablespoons cracker crumbs, one-half teaspoon salt, one-eighth teaspoon paprika and one-half egg, slightly beaten. Shape into a cake, using as little preserve as possible and sauté in a hot iron frying pan. Remove to platter, pour around one cup White Sauce I (see The

Boston Cooking-School Cook Book, p. 266), to which is added one-fourth teaspoon beef extract. Garnish with parsley.

Smothered Round Steak

Try out, in a hot iron frying pan, three slices fat salt pork three by four inches and add one onion, peeled and cut in thin slices. Cook, stirring constantly, until onion is brown. Wipe a two pound slice of round steak, put in frying pan and pour over one and one-half cups cold water and add one-fourth teaspoon salt. Bring quickly to the boiling point, cover closely, remove to back of range and let simmer until meat is tender. Remove steak to hot platter and strain stock of which there should be one cup. Melt one tablespoon butter, add two tablespoons flour and stir until well blended; then pour on gradually, while stirring constantly hot stock. Bring to the boiling point, season with salt and pepper and pour over steak.

Planked Rump Steak

Wipe a rump steak, cut two inches thick, and panbroil for ten minutes. Pipe a border of mashed potatoes (using a pastry bag and rose tube) around edge of slightly buttered plank; put steak in centre and place in oven to brown potatoes and finish cooking meat. Garnish with Glacéd Onions (The Boston Cooking-School Cook Book, see p. 296), Julienne Potatoes, buttered carrot slices, Littleton Stuffed

Planked Sirloin Steak.— *Page* 109

THE LARDING OF A FILLET OF BEEF.—*Page* 110

COLD ROAST BEEF À LA SHAPLEIGH.—*Page* 116.

BEEF 109

Peppers (see p. 174) and sautéd mushroom caps. Place plank on platter and surround with parsley.

Planked Sirloin Steak

Wipe a sirloin steak, cut two inches thick, remove flank end, and pan-broil ten minutes. Pipe a border of mashed potatoes around edge of slightly buttered plank and make eight nests of mashed potatoes. Place steak on plank and put in oven to brown potatoes and finish cooking steak. Fill potato nests with canned peas, reheated and seasoned, and arrange around at equal distances piles of buttered carrot cubes and stuffed tomatoes. Fit plank into nickel frame and send to table.

Tournadoes of Beef

Wipe a fillet of beef, cut in three-fourth-inch slices and trim in circular shapes. Sauté in butter in a hot iron frying pan six minutes. Arrange on serving dish, place a Hominy and Horseradish Croquette on each and on each croquette place a section of banana, sautéd in butter. To fat remaining in frying pan add two tablespoons boiling water, one-half teaspoon beef extract and one tablespoon butter. Pour around beef.

Beef Tenderloins à la Wright

Cut six three-quarter-inch slices from a tenderloin of beef, trim and shape into rounds and broil four minutes. Wipe and chop ten mushrooms, add three tablespoons butter and cook five minutes; then add two tablespoons flour, one-half cup cream, two tablespoons Sherry wine, one and one-half teaspoons salt, one-eighth teaspoon, each, nutmeg and cayenne and cook five minutes. Put mixture in eight puff paste cases, cover with broiled tenderloin and garnish top of each with a sautéd mushroom cap. Serve with Sauce Béarnaise (The Boston Cooking-School Cook Book, see p. 275).

Larded Fillet of Beef, Madeira Sauce

Wipe a fillet of beef, remove fat, veins and tendonous portions, skewer in shape and lard upper side with grain of meat. Place on rack in pan, sprinkle with salt and pepper, dredge with flour and put in bottom of pan small pieces of pork. Bake in a hot oven twenty-five minutes, basting three times. Take out skewer, remove meat to hot platter, pour around Madeira sauce and garnish with parsley. For the sauce brown four tablespoons butter, add five tablespoons flour and stir until well browned. Then pour on gradually, while stirring constantly, one and one-fourth cups brown stock. Bring to the boiling point and add two canned pimientos (drained and cut in thin strips), one-half teaspoon salt and a few grains pepper. Again bring to the boiling point and add one and one-half tablespoons Madeira wine.

BEEF 111

Fillet of Beef à la Newport

Wipe, remove fat, veins and tendinous portions from a fillet of beef. Put one-fourth cup butter in hot frying pan and add two tablespoons finely chopped parsley and two slices lemon. When butter is melted, add fillet and turn frequently until entire surface is seared and well browned. Cook, turning occasionally, twenty minutes; then pour over one-fourth cup Sherry wine, cover and let stand eight minutes. Place on hot platter, remove lemon and pour liquid in pan over meat. Garnish with parsley.

Hungarian Goulasch

Wipe two pounds beef cut from lower part of round with a piece of cheese-cloth, wrung out of cold water, and cut in one and one-half inch cubes. Put in saucepan, add one quart boiling water, to which has been added two cloves of garlic and let boil five minutes. Cover and let simmer until meat is tender.

Pare potatoes and cut in three-quarter-inch slices, then cut slices in cubes; there should be one and one-half cups. Cover with boiling salted water and let boil five minutes; drain and add to meat fifteen minutes before serving-time to finish the cooking. Peel twenty-four tiny onions and cook in boiling salted water to cover; drain and add to goulasch. Cream three tablespoons butter, add three tablespoons flour and work until smooth; then add by small pieces to stock in stewpan (of which there should be two cups), stirring constantly. Season with salt and pepper and turn on a hot platter.

Pot Roast

Wipe one and one-half pounds lean beef, cut from forequarter, with a piece of cheese-cloth, wrung out of cold water, and cut in one and one-half inch pieces. Put in an earthen dish (a bean-pot will answer the purpose) or casserole dish, and add one onion, peeled and sliced, eight slices of carrot cut one-fourth inch thick, two sprigs parsley, one and one-half teaspoons salt, and a half teaspoon peppercorns. Add meat and two cups, each, hot water and canned tomatoes. Cover and bake in a slow oven three and one-half hours. Half an hour before serving time thicken with three tablespoons butter, worked until creamy and mixed with three tablespoons flour, and add one cup canned peas, which have been thoroughly rinsed with cold water and allowed to become reoxygenated. Remove onion, carrot, parsley and peppercorns and turn on a hot serving dish.

Pot Roast, American Style

Buy four pounds beef, cut from top of shin or from a rib roll. Wipe with a piece of cheese-cloth, wrung out of cold water, rub over with salt and sprinkle with pepper. Roll in flour and sear the entire surface in hot fat salt pork. Place in a casserole dish or porcelain-lined kettle. Add one-half cup hot water, cover and cook four hours, adding more water as needed, and turning three times during the cooking. If done in a casserole dish, bake in the oven; if in either of the other vessels mentioned, cook on top of range.

Wash and scrape two carrots, cut in one-eighth-inch slices, cook in boiling salted water until soft; drain and season with butter, salt and pepper. Wash, pare and soak eight small potatoes of uniform size and cut in eighths, lengthwise. Cook in boiling salted water to cover; drain, sprinkle with salt and pour over one-fourth cup clarified butter. Remove meat to a hot serving dish, surround with carrot and potatoes and garnish with parsley. If cauliflower is at hand, it makes a most agreeable addition to this dish.

Cannelon of Beef

Wipe one and one-half pounds lean beef, cut from round, and finely chop. Add one-third cup finely chopped fat salt pork and season with salt and pepper. Shape in a roll, wrap in buttered paper, place on rack in dripping pan and bake in a hot oven thirty-five minutes, basting every five minutes with butter, melted in boiling water, using three tablespoons butter and three-fourths cup water. Remove from paper to serving dish. Pour around tomato sauce and garnish with parsley.

Swedish Meat Balls

Wipe one pound beef, cut from lower part of round, with a piece of cheese-cloth wrung out of cold water. Force through a meat-chopper or chop finely; there should be two cups. Add one-half cup stale bread crumbs and one egg, slightly beaten; then season with two-thirds teaspoon salt, one-eighth teaspoon pepper and a few grains nutmeg. Make into balls, using as little pressure as possible, one and one-half inches in diameter; cover and let stand one hour. Try out three slices fat salt pork three inches square and brown meat-balls in pork fat. Melt two tablespoons butter, add two tablespoons flour and stir until well blended; then pour on gradually, while stirring constantly, one and three-fourths cups brown stock. Bring to the boiling point and season with salt and pepper. Add balls to sauce, cover and let simmer one and one-half hours. Swedish meat balls are frequently served with dumplings.

Canadian Meat Pie

1½ lbs. top of round steak
3 lambs' kidneys
1½ sliced onions
2½ tablespoons butter
1½ cups boiling water
1¼ tablespoons Worcestershire Sauce
2 tablespoons flour
½ teaspoon salt
⅛ teaspoon pepper

Wipe steak, remove fat and cut lean meat in three-fourths-inch cubes. Soak, pare, trim and cut kidneys in one-fourth-inch cubes. Try out fat, removed from steak; add onion and stir constantly until well browned. Add one tablespoon butter, beef and kidneys and stir constantly until entire surface of meat is well seared and browned; then remove to stewpan. To fat remaining in pan, add boiling water and strain; then add Worcestershire Sauce, salt and pepper. Pour over meat, cover tightly and let cook on back of range, or over gas flame (over which is placed an asbestos cover), until meat is tender. Strain off liquid remaining in pan and thicken with remaining butter and flour mixed together. When meat is cold, turn into an elliptical-shaped granite-ware baking dish (having a half-inch rim) in the centre of which is placed an earthen cup, and pour over one-half the sauce, reserving the remainder to pass separately, when the pie is served. Place on rim of pan a three-fourths-inch strip of paste, brush over with cold water and put on a cover from the centre of which a circular piece has been cut. Garnish, as shown in illustration, with a braid of paste and four diamond-shaped pieces. Around edge make a row of parallel creases, one-half inch apart, using the back of a knife. Between each two creases snip paste three times, using scissors. Bake in a hot oven.

Casserole of Beef

Cut cold roast beef and cold broiled steak, alone or in combination, in one-inch cubes; there should be one quart. Put in a casserole dish and add two cups brown sauce or beef gravy, one-half cup celery cut in small pieces, one-half cup carrot cut in small cubes, one onion thinly sliced, one cup canned tomatoes, one teaspoon Worcestershire Sauce, one-half teaspoon salt and one-eighth teaspoon pepper. Cover and bake one hour; then add one cup peas, beans or mushrooms, canned or fresh, one cup potato balls or cubes, which have been cooked in boiling salted water ten minutes, and two tablespoons Sherry wine. Again cover and cook thirty minutes, or until potatoes are soft. Serve from casserole.

Cold Roast Beef à la Shapleigh

Cut cold roast beef in thin slices and arrange slices overlapping one another, lengthwise of platter. Mix six tablespoons olive oil, two tablespoons Tarragon vinegar, one teaspoon salt, one-fourth teaspoon pepper, one-half teaspoon, each, paprika and dry mustard, and one tablespoon, each, finely chopped shallot, parsley and red pepper. Pour dressing over meat and garnish with crisp lettuce leaves, stoned olives and curled celery.

Baked Larded Liver, Claret Sauce

Skewer, tie in shape and lard upper surface of calf's liver. Place in pan and spread with the following mixture: Cream three tablespoons butter and add one and one-fourth teaspoons salt and one-half teaspoon, each, ground clove and pepper. Pour around liver one-half cup boiling water and cook in a moderate oven one hour, basting every ten minutes. Remove to hot serving dish, skim off fat from liquor remaining in pan, add one cup claret wine and strain sauce around liver.

Fricandeau of Liver

¾ cup chopped, cold, cooked liver	2 tablespoons flour
	¾ cup cream
3 tablespoons butter	½ teaspoon salt
1 tablespoon onion, finely chopped	⅛ teaspoon paprika
	2 tablespoons Sherry wine

Six slices buttered toast

Cook butter with onion three minutes, stirring constantly. Add flour and stir until well blended; then pour on cream, gradually, while stirring constantly. Bring to the boiling point and add salt, paprika and liver. When thoroughly heated add Sherry wine, and pour over toast (from which crusts have been removed). Garnish with toast points and parsley.

Calf's Liver à la Madame Beque

Wipe liver and cut in one-inch cubes. Sprinkle with salt and pepper and cover with thin slices onion and three sprigs parsley. Let stand two hours, fry in deep fat one minute and drain on brown paper. Remove to hot serving dish and garnish with slices of lemon and sprigs of parsley.

Calf's Brains à la York

Wash brains and cook thirty minutes in boiling, salted, acidulated water, to which has been added one slice, each, onion and carrot, sprig of parsley, bit of bay leaf and stalk of celery, broken in pieces. Remove from stock, drain and place under a weight; when cold cut in small cubes, pour over one-half cup Sherry wine, cover and let stand one hour. Brush and peel one-fourth pound mushroom caps, cut in slices, and sauté in butter. Melt three tablespoons butter, add three tablespoons flour and stir until well blended. Then pour on gradually, while stirring constantly, one cup thin cream and one-half cup heavy cream. Bring to the boiling point, add brains and mushroom caps and season with one teaspoon salt, one-fourth teaspoon paprika and a few grains cayenne.

Corned Beef Tomato Toast à la Bradley

3½ tablespoons butter
3 tablespoons flour
1½ cups stewed and strained tomatoes
¼ teaspoon soda
½ cup milk
½ teaspoon salt
8 slices dry toast
⅛ cup chopped remnants cooked corned beef
2 tablespoons grated cheese

Melt butter, add flour and stir until well blended; then pour on gradually, while stirring constantly, tomatoes, to which soda has been added. Bring to the boiling point and add milk and salt and again bring to the boiling point. Dip toast (from which crusts have been removed) separately in sauce, and when soft remove to serving dish. To remaining sauce add chopped corned beef and pour over all. Sprinkle with cheese and garnish with toast points and parsley.

CHAPTER X

LAMB AND MUTTON

Lamb Chops, Reforme

Wipe six French chops and sprinkle with one-half teaspoon salt and one-fourth teaspoon pepper. Roll in flour, egg (slightly beaten and diluted with one and one-half tablespoons water) and five tablespoons finely chopped raw ham. Sauté in a hot iron frying pan, arrange on a hot platter and pour around the following sauce: Cut in thin strips two gherkins, one small truffle, six mushroom caps, and white one hard-boiled egg. Add one tablespoon Sherry and three-fourths cup brown stock. Bring to the boiling point and let simmer five minutes. Season to taste with salt.

Spanish Lamb Chops, Truffle Sauce

Wipe six French chops, cut one and one-half inches thick, split meat in halves, cutting to bone, and stuff with the following mixture: Mix six tablespoons soft bread crumbs, three tablespoons chopped mushroom caps, two tablespoons melted butter and salt and cayenne to taste. Dip chops in crumbs, egg and crumbs, and fry in deep fat. Serve with Truffle Sauce (see p. 154).

LAMB AND MUTTON

Kernels of Lamb, Currant Mint Sauce

Wipe eight lamb chops, remove eye of meat and sauté in a hot iron frying pan or blazer from six to eight minutes, sprinkling with salt the last two minutes of the cooking. Remove to hot dish and serve with Currant Mint Sauce (The Boston Cooking-School Cook Book, see p. 219).

Tournadoes of Lamb

Order six kidney lamb chops cut two inches thick. Remove fat and bone and skewer lean meat into six circular pieces. Coil around each a thinly cut strip of bacon, having bacon overlap one inch, and fasten with wooden skewers. Sprinkle with salt and pepper; place in a greased broiler, and broil over a clear fire or bake in a hot oven; the time required being about fifteen minutes. Remove to hot platter and garnish with Savory Potatoes (see p. 182) and parsley. Mint jelly should accompany this dish.

Sautéd Fillets of Lamb

Order two pounds lamb cut from fore quarter. Remove bones and cut meat in strips one inch in thickness; then flatten with a cleaver to three-fourths inch in thickness. Arrange on a platter and pour over a marinade, made by mixing three tablespoons olive oil, three tablespoons vinegar, two-thirds teaspoon salt, one-half onion finely chopped, and one tablespoon parsley finely chopped. Cover and let stand over night or for several hours. Remove pieces of vegetables from fillets and sauté in a hot frying pan, using as little butter as possible.

Lamb Chops à la Rector

Force a border of Duchess Potato mixture around edge of plank, using a pastry bag and tube. In centre place two thin pieces of broiled ham and on ham place two thick broiled chops, the bone ends of which are garnished with paper frills. At ends of plank place canned artichoke bottoms, drained, heated and seasoned with melted butter, salt and pepper. Fill artichoke bottoms with Rector Potatoes (see p. 187). Place sautéd mushroom caps between chops. Garnish with sprigs of parsley.

Mutton Duck

Remove the bones from a fore quarter of lamb, excepting the leg bone, from the inside end of which a piece should be sawed, so as to make a shape more like a duck. From outside end saw off pieces, that bone may be left to better represent bill. Scrape removed blade bone, trim, point end and insert to represent tail. Stuff, sew, skewer, cover parts representing head and tail with buttered paper and tie into shape. Place on rack in dripping pan, sprinkle with salt and pepper, dredge meat and bottom of pan with flour, and arrange three gashed thin slices of fat salt pork on meat and one slice cut

Lamb Chops à la Rector. — *Page* 122.

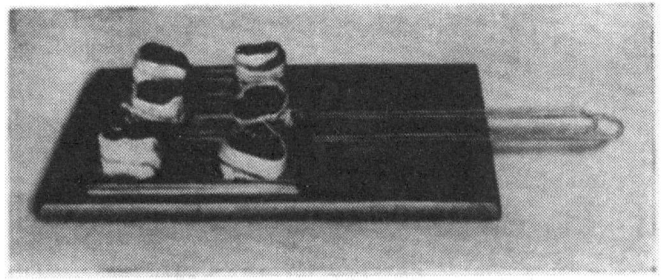

Tournadoes of Lamb Ready for Cooking. — *Page* 121

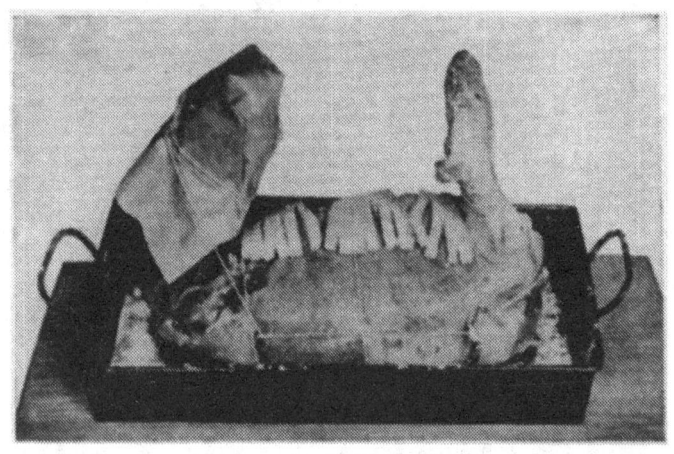

MUTTON DUCK READY FOR OVEN. — *Page* 122.

MUTTON DUCK GARNISHED FOR SERVING. — *Page* 122

in pieces in bottom of pan. Roast in a hot oven two hours, basting every fifteen minutes, with one-third cup butter melted in two-thirds cup boiling water, and after that is gone, with fat in pan. Remove string, paper and skewers, place on serving dish and garnish with fried potatoes and Baked Egg Plant in Pimiento Cases.

Serve with a brown gravy made from fat in pan.

A fore quarter of lamb may be ordered dressed for a mutton duck at any first-class city market, when it will be necessary to remove stitches if one cares to use stuffing. It may be roasted without stuffing.

Devonshire Saddle of Mutton

Wipe a saddle of mutton, sprinkle with salt and pepper, place on rack in dripping pan, and dredge meat and bottom of pan with flour. Bake in a hot oven one and one-quarter hours, basting every ten minutes with fat in pan. Serve with Devonshire Sauce (see p. 159).

Lamb Réchauffé

½ tumbler currant jelly
1 cup heavy cream
2 tablespoons Sherry wine
Salt

Cayenne
¼ teaspoon arrowroot
1 tablespoon milk
Cold roast lamb, thinly sliced

Melt jelly in chafing dish and add cream and wine. Season with salt and cayenne. Dilute arrowroot with milk and add to mixture and when thickened add lamb. Serve as soon as meat has thoroughly heated.

Lamb à la Breck

Finely chop cold roast lamb; there should be one cup. Season with one-half teaspoon salt, one-eighth teaspoon pepper, one-eighth teaspoon celery salt and a few drops onion juice. Put one cup boiled macaroni in a buttered baking dish, cover with lamb and pour over one and one-half cups milk, to which have been added four eggs, slightly beaten. Bake in a moderate oven until firm.

Cold Roast Lamb, Family Style

Cut cold roast lamb in slices and arrange, overlapping one another, around chop plate. In centre place individual moulds of seasoned, hot, chopped boiled spinach, seasoned with butter, salt and pepper. Make a depression in each mould and in cavity thus made drop a poached egg. Garnish with watercress.

CHAPTER XI

VEAL AND SWEETBREADS

Bavarian Veal Chops

WIPE six loin chops and put in a stewpan with one-half sliced onion, eight slices carrot two stalks celery, one-half teaspoon peppercorns four cloves and two tablespoons butter. Cover with boiling water and let simmer until chops are tender. Drain, season with salt and pepper, dip in flour, egg and crumbs, fry in deep fat and drain on brown paper. Arrange on hot serving dish and surround with two cups boiled macaroni, broken into two-inch pieces and mixed with the following sauce: Peel and slice onions; there should be two cups. Cover with boiling water, cook five minutes, drain, again cover with boiling water and cook until soft; again drain and rub through a sieve. Melt two tablespoons butter, add two tablespoons flour and stir until well blended; then pour on gradually, while stirring constantly, one cup chicken stock. Bring to the boiling point and add onion purée and one-half cup cream or milk. Season with one-half teaspoon salt and a few grains pepper.

Veal Holstein

Wipe and trim two slices of veal, cut from the leg; then pound by using edge of saucer or plate and cut in pieces for serving. Sprinkle with salt and pepper, dip in stale bread crumbs, egg and crumbs, and sauté in a hot iron frying pan, until well browned, using two-thirds pork fat to one-third butter. Place on back of range, pour over one and one-half cups brown sauce, cover and let simmer until meat is tender, the time being from one to one and one-half hours. Remove to serving dish and strain sauce around cutlets. Garnish each with a poached egg and around dish arrange thin slices of cucumber pickles, thin slices of cooked beets (cut in fancy shapes), slices of lemon (sprinkled with finely chopped parsley) and stoned olives stuffed with capers and anchovies.

Stuffed Cushion of Veal, Brown Mushroom Sauce

Order a five-pound cushion of veal (a piece cut from the upper part of the leg). Wipe, stuff and truss. Put one-fourth pound butter in a hot iron frying pan and when melted add veal and cook until the entire surface is seared and well browned, turning frequently, using a two-tined fork to prevent piercing. Cover and bake in a hot oven from one and one-half to two hours. Remove to hot platter, garnish with parsley and serve with Brown Mushroom Sauce.

Stuffing. — Toast six slices of stale baker's bread,

cut one-half inch in thickness, with crusts removed. Pour over brown or chicken stock to moisten. Add one two-inch cube fat salt pork, finely chopped, one hard-boiled egg, finely chopped, and one-fourth pound mushroom caps, cleaned, peeled, sautéd in butter three minutes and cut in strips. Season with salt and pepper.

Brown Mushroom Sauce. — Pour off one-fourth cup fat remaining in pan, add five tablespoons flour and stir until well blended; then pour on gradually, while stirring constantly, one and one-fourth cups brown stock, bring to the boiling point and add one-third cup mushroom liquor (obtained by cooking stems and peeling of mushroom caps). Season with salt and pepper, add fat remaining in pan, stirring vigorously, and strain through a double thickness of cheese-cloth, placed over a strainer. Add one-half pound mushroom caps, cleaned, peeled, cut in slices and sautéd in butter three minutes. Bring to the boiling point and serve at once.

Loin of Veal, Allemande

Order a piece cut from loin of veal with ribs and flank attached. Remove meat which lies nearest the backbone in one piece. Remove meat from flank, discarding skin; then force through a meat chopper; there should be seven-eighths cup. Add one-third cup beef suet, finely chopped, and mix thoroughly. Cook three-fourths cup stale bread crumbs with three-fourths cup milk, until reduced to a thick paste. Add three tablespoons butter, one egg and one egg yolk, slightly beaten, one tablespoon tomato catsup, one-eighth teaspoon grated nutmeg, and salt, pepper and cayenne to taste. Combine mixtures, shape in a loaf, roll in crumbs, egg and crumbs. Arrange four slices of fat salt pork lengthwise of centre of dripping pan. Place on pork the long rib bones (which have been removed), on bones, the meat roll, and over roll the piece of lean meat. Sprinkle with salt and pepper, dredge meat and bottom of pan with flour and over meat arrange pieces of fat salt pork. Bake in a slow oven two hours. As soon as flour in pan is brown, baste with fat in pan and continue the basting every ten minutes, using two cups stock, which has been made from bones and trimmings. During the last half-hour of the cooking pour over one-half cup sour cream. Remove to platter and garnish with Deerfoot Potatoes (see p. 187) and parsley.

Serve with a brown gravy made from fat in pan.

Sweetbreads à la Root

Parboil three pair sweetbreads, drain, then cool and insert strips of truffles, using a larding needle. Put in a pan six slices carrot, one-half small onion, sliced, one stalk celery, cut in pieces, one sprig parsley, a bit of bay leaf and a two-inch cube fat salt pork, cut in pieces. Place sweetbreads over vegetables, add one-half teaspoon salt and one-fourth teaspoon pepper; cook on range ten minutes. Pour

Loin of Veal Allemande Ready for Oven. — *Page* 127

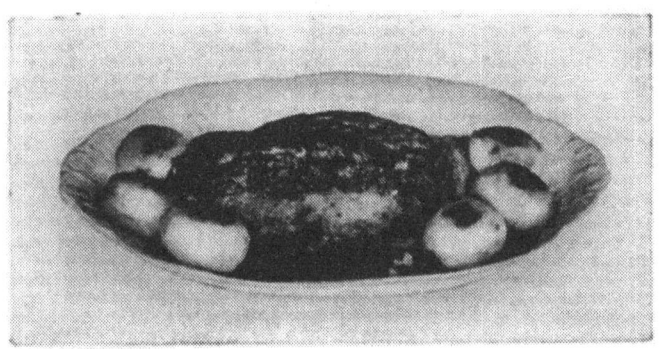

Loin of Veal Allemande. — *Page* 127.

KERNELS OF PORK. — *Page* 132.

ROAST CROWN OF PORK. — *Page* 132

over one cup white stock, one-fourth cup white wine and two tablespoons port wine. Cover and bake thirty minutes.

Arrange around platter a purée of French chestnuts, forced through a pastry bag and tube. Place sweetbreads in centre. Strain sauce, remove fat and add one-third cup finely chopped mushroom caps, cooked in one-half tablespoon butter, two minutes. Pour sauce over sweetbreads and garnish with sprigs of watercress.

South Park Sweetbreads

Parboil two sweetbreads in milk, cool and cut in one-half-inch cubes. Work one-fourth cup butter until creamy and add the yolks of four hard-boiled eggs, forced through a potato ricer, and one tablespoon brandy. Melt two tablespoons butter, add two tablespoons flour and stir until well blended; then pour on gradually, while stirring constantly, one-half cup cream. Bring to the boiling point and add egg paste, one-fourth cup Sherry wine, three-fourths teaspoon salt, one-eighth teaspoon pepper, a few gratings nutmeg, whites of four hard-boiled eggs, finely chopped, and sweetbreads. Serve in timbale cases, patty shells or puff paste vol-au-vents.

Sweetbreads Monroe

Parboil a sweetbread and cut in six pieces. Put in a saucepan and add one small sliced onion, one stalk celery, cut in slices crosswise, four slices fat salt pork, cut in cubes, one tablespoon butter, one teaspoon salt and one-eighth teaspoon pepper. Cook six minutes, stirring almost constantly; then add three-fourths cup chicken stock and one-fourth cup white wine. Cover and let simmer thirty-five minutes. Remove sweetbreads and strain stock. Melt one tablespoon butter, add one tablespoon flour and stir until well blended; then pour on gradually, while stirring constantly, stock. Add one can French peas (drained and rinsed) and let simmer ten minutes. Divide peas in six small casseroles, place a piece of sweetbread on each, cover with Béarnaise Sauce (The Boston Cooking-School Cook Book, see p. 275) and garnish with a piece of truffle.

Waldorf Sweetbreads

Soak two pair sweetbreads in cold water to cover one hour and cook in equal parts of white wine and boiling water (to which has been added one-half tablespoon salt) ten minutes. Drain, trim, place under a weight and let stand one-half hour. Put in a saucepan, cover with thin strips of fat salt pork, two slices each of onion and carrot, sprig of parsley and one and one-half cups chicken stock. Bring to the boiling point and let simmer one-half hour. Drain, cut in pieces and arrange on canned artichoke bottoms (re-heated and seasoned with butter, salt and pepper) around a mound of cooked hominy sprinkled with finely chopped parsley.

Pour around Waldorf Sauce (see p. 155) and garnish with cutlet-shaped pieces of sautéd bread (the top being sprinkled over with white of eggs, then dipped in finely chopped parsley), watercress and parsley.

Mock Sweetbreads

Finely chop one pound lean veal, add two ounces finely chopped fat salt pork, and work, using the hands, until well blended; then add two-thirds cup soft bread crumbs, two eggs, slightly beaten, one-third cup flour, one-half cup rich milk, one-half teaspoon salt and one-eighth teaspoon pepper. Form into eight elliptical-shaped pieces, put in dish, dot over with butter, using one and one-half tablespoons, and pour around three-fourths cup chicken stock. Cover and bake one hour, basting every ten minutes of the cooking. Remove to hot serving dish and pour around white, brown or tomato sauce.

CHAPTER XII

PORK

Kernels of Pork

WIPE a spare rib of pork and remove lean meat in one piece. Cut in three-fourth-inch slices crosswise, sprinkle with salt and sauté in a hot iron frying pan, rubbed over with pork fat. Arrange down the centre of a hot platter and surround with nests made of Savory Potatoes filled with Creamed Silver Skins. Garnish with sprig of parsley.

Roast Crown of Pork

Select parts from two loins containing ribs, scrape flesh from bone between ribs, as far as lean meat, and trim off backbone. Shape each piece in a semicircle, having ribs outside, and sew pieces together to form a crown. Trim ends of bones evenly, care being taken that they are not left too long. Sprinkle with salt, dredge with flour and place on rack in dripping pan (bones down) and bake in a hot oven two hours, basting every fifteen minutes with fat in pan, which comes from trimmings of pork fat placed in pan, as that which comes from crown is insufficient.

Remove to chop plate, surround with groups of

PORK 133

Baked Potato Apples (see p. 185) at regular intervals, and between potato apples, halves of baked apples. Garnish ends of bones with paper frills and put a large bunch of parsley in centre of crown.

Fort Lincoln

Cut three slices fat salt pork (three inches by four inches) in small cubes and try out. To two tablespoons pork fat add three tablespoons flour and stir until well blended; then pour on gradually, while stirring constantly, one cup milk, bring to the boiling point and season with one-half teaspoon salt and a few grains pepper. Add one and one-half cups cold roast pork, cut in cubes, and when thoroughly heated add pork scraps. Make a border in fort shape of mashed potatoes, fill with mixture and garnish with fried potato balls and parsley.

Little Roast Pig

Clean, stuff, truss and skewer a suckling pig. Make four parallel gashes, three inches long, through skin on each side of backbone. Put on rack in dripping pan, brush entire surface with melted butter, sprinkle with salt, pour around two cups boiling water and cover with buttered paper. Roast in a hot oven three hours, basting every fifteen minutes with liquor in pan. Remove paper after cooking two and one-half hours and brush over with heavy cream. Remove to serving dish, put small red apple in mouth, cranberries in eye sockets and laurel wreath around neck. Garnish with nest-shaped hominy croquettes filled with Apple Ball Sauce (see p. 391), sections of red apples and watercress.

Stuffing

6 onions
20 sage leaves
3 cups soft stale bread crumbs
½ cup soft butter
1 egg
Salt and pepper

Peel onions, add boiling water to cover and parboil ten minutes. Add sage leaves and cook two minutes longer; then drain off water. Finely chop onions and sage and add to bread crumbs, with butter and egg slightly beaten. Season with salt and pepper.

Fried Salt Pork, Country Style

Cut fat salt pork in thin slices, and slices in halves crosswise (making pieces about three by two inches), and gash each rind edge four times. Dip in a mixture of corn meal and flour, using two parts corn meal to one part flour; put in a hot iron frying pan and cook until crisp and well browned, turning frequently. Remove from pan and strain fat through a double thickness of cheese-cloth placed over a fine strainer. Put one and one-half tablespoons fat in saucepan, add two and one-half tablespoons flour and stir until well blended; then pour on gradually, while stirring constantly, one cup milk. Bring to the boiling point and add one-fourth teaspoon salt, a few grains pepper and one tablespoon butter, bit by bit; then add one and one-half cups boiled potato cubes. Pile in centre of hot serving dish and surround with prepared pork. Garnish with sprigs of parsley.

Bacon Curls

Cut bacon in as thin slices as possible and remove rind. Put in a hot iron frying pan and during the cooking shape in the form of curls, using a knife and fork. Drain on brown paper and arrange on serving dish around a mound of Corn Oysters (see p. 167).

Ham à la Van Voast

Wash and soak ham over night in cold water to cover. Put in kettle, cover with cold water and add six slices carrot, six slices onion, two stalks celery, three sprigs parsley, one teaspoon whole cloves, one teaspoon allspice berries and one-half teaspoon peppercorns.

Bring to the boiling point and let simmer until meat is tender. Cool in water in which it has been cooked, take from water, remove skin and cover with the following paste: Mix one cup soft stale bread crumbs, one cup brown sugar, and enough mustard mixed with vinegar to hold the mixture together. Pour over two cups cider and bake in a slow oven one hour, basting every ten minutes.

Roast Ham, Cider Sauce

Soak a twelve-pound ham several hours, or over night, in cold water to cover. Wash thoroughly, scrape and trim off hard skin near end of bone. Put in a kettle with one-half cup, each, sliced onion and carrot, two sprigs parsley, one-half bay leaf, four cloves and five peppercorns. Cover with cold water, bring slowly to boiling point and let simmer until tender, the time required being about four hours. After two hours of the cooking, add one quart cider. Allow ham to cool in liquor. Remove from liquor, take off skin, sprinkle with sugar and fine bread crumbs. Put dashes of paprika over ham, about every two inches, and insert a clove in centre of each dash. Bake one hour in a slow oven. Serve hot with Cider Sauce (see p. 160).

Frosted Ham

Remove outside skin from a cold boiled ham and trim off most of the fat, leaving as smooth a surface as possible. Rub over with cracker dust (made from hard crackers, rolled and put through a fine sieve) and spread with Ornamental Frosting. Decorate with Ornamental Frosting (colored pink and green) forced through a pastry bag and tube. Remove to platter, garnish bone with paper frill and bone end with silver skewer stuck with a large truffle between two pimolas. Arrange around ham a border of small lettuce leaves and watercress.

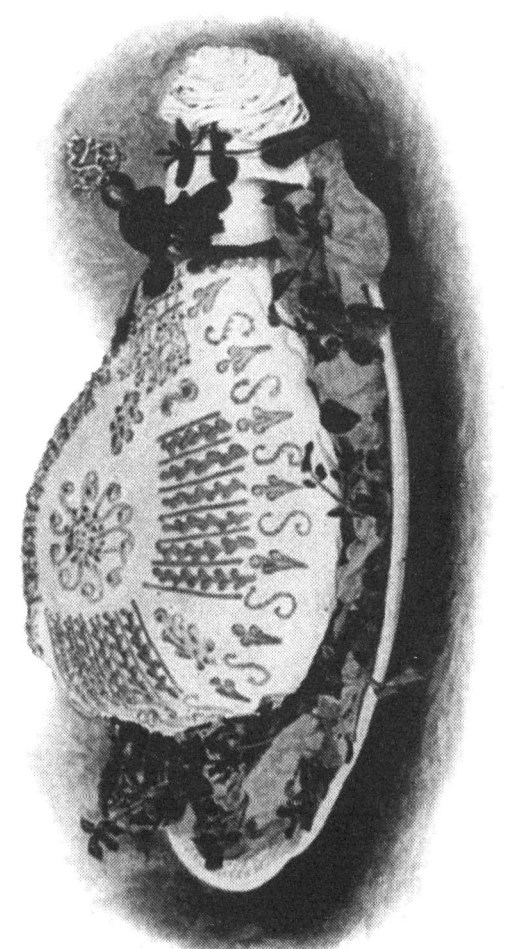

FROSTED HAM.—*Page* 136

Sausages à la Maître d'Hôtel

Cut apart a string of small sausages and pierce each several times with a fork. Put in a frying pan, cover with boiling water and cook ten minutes. Drain, return to pan and fry until well browned, turning frequently. Remove to hot platter, pour over Maître d'Hôtel Butter (see The Boston Cooking-School Cook Book, p. 273) and garnish with watercress.

Miss Daniel's Meat Loaf

1 pound fresh pork	1 cup milk
1 pound veal	1 tablespoon salt
2 pounds beef	⅛ teaspoon pepper
1 cup bread crumbs	3 eggs, slightly beaten

Chop meat finely, mix and add remaining ingredients in order given. Shape into a loaf, put in pan and lay across top six thin slices fat salt pork. Roast in a hot oven one and one-half hours, basting every ten minutes, at first with one-half cup hot water and after that has gone, with fat in pan. Remove to platter, pour around tomato or brown sauce and garnish with parsley. Many think one small onion, peeled and finely chopped, an agreeable addition to this dish.

German Loaf

1 pound ham	1 teaspoon pepper
1 pound fresh pork	2 teaspoons curry powder
1 clove garlic	1½ tablespoons sage
1 small onion	White 1 egg
1 tablespoon salt	⅓ cup cream

Force ham, pork, garlic and onion through meat chopper. Add seasonings and again force through meat chopper; then add egg white and cream and mix thoroughly. Put four strips of uncooked ham fat on centre of square of cheese-cloth, press mixture into shape and place over fat. Roll in cheese-cloth and tie. Place on trivet in kettle and add three quarts boiling water, one-fourth cup vinegar and one teaspoon salt. Cover and let simmer two and one-half hours. Drain, cool and put under a weight. Cut in thin slices for serving.

CHAPTER XIII

POULTRY

Smothered Chicken, Swedish Style

DRESS, clean and split two young, small broilers. Sprinkle inside and outside with salt and pepper, dredge outside sparingly with flour and fold over. Heat a Scotch kettle, pour in one cup heavy cream and add chickens. Cook until chickens are well browned, turning frequently and adding more cream as necessary. Cover and cook until chickens are tender and remove to hot platter. To three tablespoons fat remaining in kettle add three tablespoons flour and stir until well blended; then pour on gradually, while stirring constantly, one and one-half cups chicken stock and one-half cup cream. Bring to the boiling point, season with salt and pepper and strain. Pour around broilers and garnish with parsley.

Chicken en Casserole

Dress and clean a young, tender fowl and cut in pieces for serving. Spread with one-third cup butter, put in a casserole and sprinkle with salt and pepper. Pour over one cup boiling water, cover, and cook until chicken is tender, the time required being about one hour. Add one cup cream and two cups fresh mushroom caps, broken in pieces. Cook ten minutes and thicken with one tablespoon flour, diluted with two tablespoons water.

Chicken Paprika

Dress, clean and cut two chickens in pieces for serving; then sprinkle with salt and pepper. Cook four and one-half tablespoons butter with one-half onion finely chopped, fifteen minutes, stirring almost constantly to prevent burning. Add chicken, sprinkle with four and one-half tablespoons flour, mixed and sifted with one teaspoon paprika, and pour over one and one-half cups chicken stock. Bring to the boiling point and let simmer twenty minutes, adding more chicken stock if necessary. Remove to casserole dish, cover and cook until chicken is tender.

Delmonico's Devilled Chicken

Wipe a chicken, dressed same as for broiling, sprinkle with salt and pepper, place in a well-greased broiler and broil over a clear fire eight minutes. Remove to pan and rub over with the following mixture: Cream four tablespoons butter and add one teaspoon made mustard, one-half teaspoon salt, one teaspoon vinegar and one-half teaspoon paprika. Sprinkle with three-fourths cup buttered, soft bread crumbs and bake until chicken is tender and crumbs are browned.

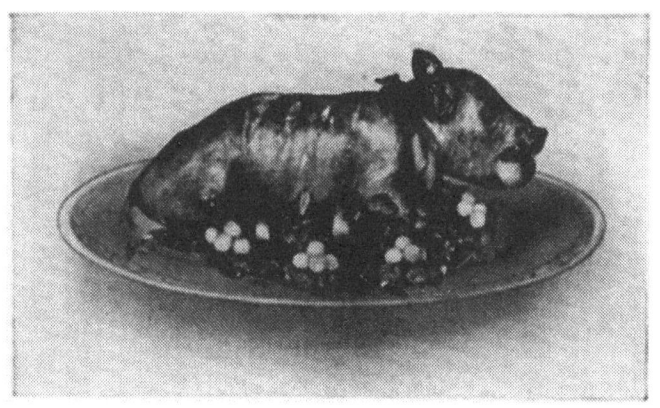

LITTLE ROAST PIG. — *Page* 133.

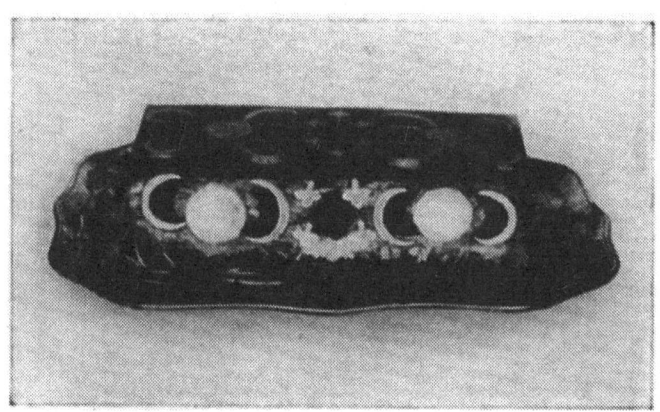

MOULDED JELLIED CHICKEN. — *Page* 143

CANADIAN MEAT PIE. — *Page* 114.

CHICKEN PIE, COUNTRY STYLE. — *Page* 141

Chicken Pie, Country Style

Dress, clean and cut up two fowls. Put in a stewpan with one onion, cover with boiling water, bring to the boiling point and let simmer until meat is tender. When half cooked, add one-half tablespoon salt and one-eighth teaspoon pepper. Remove chicken, strain stock, skim off fat, return to stewpan and let simmer until reduced to four cups. Thicken stock with one-third cup flour, diluted with enough cold water to pour easily. When boiling point is reached, add three tablespoons butter, bit by bit, and more salt if necessary. Place a small cup in the centre of baking dish, arrange pieces of chicken around it (removing some of the larger bones) and pour over gravy.

Cover with a baking powder crust one-half inch in thickness from the centre of which a circular piece two inches in diameter has been removed. Roll remaining dough, one-fourth inch in thickness, in rectangular shape, cut in thirds lengthwise and braid strips. Put around opening in crust, and bake in a hot oven. Remove to plate and arrange a paper collar around dish.

Baking Powder Crust. — Mix and sift three cups bread flour, two tablespoons baking powder and one and one-half teaspoons salt. Work in three tablespoons each butter and lard, using the tips of the fingers; then add one and one-fourth cups milk.

Planked Boned Chicken

Bone a chicken, sprinkle with salt and pepper, dredge with flour and dot over with two tablespoons butter. Put in a buttered pan and bake in a moderate oven thirty-five minutes. Pipe around plank brushed over with melted butter, a border of mashed sweet potatoes. Put chicken on plank and bake until potato is re-heated and well browned. Garnish with Saratoga Potatoes (see The Boston Cooking-School Cook Book, p. 314), Hominy and Horseradish Croquettes (see p. 41), sautéd sliced mushroom caps and sprig of parsley.

Ambassadrice Capon

Dress, clean, stuff, truss and roast a capon. Cut a slice in such fashion as to remove wishbone, not quite cutting off; then cut around second joints at body, not quite cutting off, and then force wings back. Cut breast meat in slices. Cut as many one-third-inch slices of bread as there are slices of breast meat and shape in cutlet forms; spread one side with paté-de-fois-gras and sauté in butter. Place bird on platter and arrange around bird, croûtons on which is placed breast meat; then garnish each with a circular piece of truffle. With a sharp knife or scissors cut out breast bone and fill cavity with cooked asparagus tips or stalks seasoned with butter and salt.

Garnish with parsley. Serve with a gravy made

POULTRY 143

from four tablespoons fat remaining in pan, four tablespoons flour, one cup, each, chicken stock and cream, and salt and pepper to taste.

Knickerbocker Suprême of Chicken

Remove breast meat from three young chickens and trim into cutlet shape. Sprinkle with salt and pepper, dip in heavy cream, roll in flour and sauté in butter until delicately browned. Arrange in pan, dot over with two tablespoons butter, cover with buttered paper and bake ten minutes, or until tender. Remove to cutlet-shaped pieces thinly sliced hot broiled ham, garnish top of each with three asparagus tips and pour around the following sauce: Melt three and one-half tablespoons butter, add three and one-half tablespoons flour and stir until well blended; then pour on gradually, while stirring constantly, one cup chicken stock and one-half cup cream; bring to the boiling point, and add one-half teaspoon salt, one-eighth teaspoon paprika and the yolk one egg slightly beaten. Sautéd mushroom caps, arranged overlapping one another, lengthwise of centre of dish, adds to the attractive appearance of this dish.

Moulded Jellied Chicken

Wipe a knuckle of veal, put in soup kettle, cover with cold water and bring to boiling point; then add a six-pound fowl, and cook until meat is tender, adding, the last hour of cooking, one teaspoon salt. Remove fowl and put aside to cool, when it should be cut in slices. Force lean meat from veal through meat chopper; there should be one and one half cups. Let stock simmer until reduced to two cups; then add one-fourth teaspoon salt, one-eighth teaspoon pepper and a few drops onion juice; cool and clear.

Add to veal one cup stock and season to taste, with salt, paprika, onion and lemon juice. When well mixed add one cup celery, cut in small pieces.

Place a bread pan in pan of ice-water, pour in stock one-eighth inch deep; when firm decorate with whites and yolks of hard-boiled eggs, canned pimientoes, cut in fancy shapes, and fresh mint leaves. Add remaining stock by spoonfuls, lest the decoration be disarranged. When firm add alternate layers of veal and sliced chicken until all is used. Cover top layer with buttered paper; on this place pan and weight. Let stand for several hours or over night in ice box. Remove from pan to serving dish and garnish with cress.

Chicken à la Cadillac

¾ cup cold, cooked chicken, cut in cubes

¼ cup cold, cooked ham, cut in cubes

1 cup white sauce

Cooked asparagus stalks

Heat chicken and ham cubes in sauce and put in individual casserole dishes. Arrange short stalks of hot, buttered asparagus on each dish.

PLANKED BONED CHICKEN. — *Page* 142

AMBASSADRICE CAPON. — *Page* 142.

KNICKERBOCKER SUPRÊME OF CHICKEN.—*Page* 143

CHICKEN À LA CADILLAC.—*Page* 144.

Meat Cakes

1 cup chopped, cold, cooked meat (chicken, turkey or lamb)	1 egg, slightly beaten
1 tablespoon heavy cream	¼ teaspoon salt
	Few grains pepper

Mix ingredients in order given, shape in small, flat cakes, dip in egg and crumbs, and sauté in butter until well browned on both sides. Remove to hot platter and pour around one cup White Sauce, to which has been added (just before serving time) one-third cup celery cut in small pieces.

Turkey Tetrazzini

2 tablespoons butter	½ cup cooked spaghetti, cut in ½ inch pieces
3 tablespoons flour	
1 cup cream	½ cup sautéd sliced mushroom caps
1 teaspoon salt	
¼ teaspoon celery salt	⅛ cup grated Parmesan cheese
⅛ teaspoon pepper	¾ cup buttered cracker crumbs
1 cup cold turkey cut in thin strips	

Make a sauce of butter, flour, cream, salt, celery salt and pepper. When boiling point is reached, add turkey, spaghetti and mushrooms. Fill buttered ramekin dishes with mixture, sprinkle with cheese and crumbs and bake until crumbs are brown.

CHAPTER XIV

GAME

Venison Steak, Port Wine Sauce

WIPE venison steak, place on a well-greased broiler and broil over a clear fire. Remove to hot platter, pour around Port Wine Sauce and garnish with parsley.

Port Wine Sauce

2 tablespoons butter	2 tablespoons butter
3 tablespoons currant jelly	1½ tablespoons cornstarch
½ teaspoon peppercorns	2 teaspoons lemon juice
2 cloves	½ teaspoon salt
Bit of stick cinnamon	Few grains cayenne
2 teaspoons finely chopped onion	¼ cup port wine
	1½ tablespoons Maraschino cherries
1 cup brown stock	

12 slices poached beef marrow

Cook butter and currant jelly three minutes, stirring constantly. Add peppercorns, cloves, cinnamon, onion, port wine and brown stock and cook two minutes. Melt butter, add cornstarch and stir until well blended; then pour on gradually, while stirring constantly, the hot liquid. Bring to the boiling point and add lemon juice, salt, cayenne and remaining port wine. Strain, reheat, and add glacéd cherries, cut in halves, and marrow.

To poach Marrow. — Remove marrow from marrow bone and cut in one-half-inch slices crosswise. Put in boiling salted water, cover and let simmer eight minutes.

Rabbit à la Southern

Dress and clean two rabbits and disjoint in pieces for serving. Cover with three pints cold water to which have been added one and one-half tablespoons salt and let stand three hours. Drain, wipe, sprinkle with salt and pepper and roll in flour. Try out one-half pound of bacon cut in pieces; there should be two-thirds cup fat. Put in iron frying pan, add rabbit, cover and cook slowly one and one-half hours, turning frequently. Pour over one cup milk and cook thirty minutes. Remove to serving dish and garnish with parsley.

Pigeon Pie

Dress, clean and truss six pigeons and sauté in salt pork fat until entire surface is seared, turning frequently. Put in a kettle, nearly cover with boiling water and add one-half teaspoon peppercorns, one onion, stuck with eight cloves, eight slices carrot, two sprigs parsley and two stalks celery and let simmer five hours. Remove pigeons, strain liquor and thicken with four tablespoons butter melted and cooked with three tablespoons flour. Reheat pigeons in sauce, arrange in a pastry case and cover with a pastry top.

Squabs en Casserole

Dress, clean and truss three jumbo squabs. Put in casserole, brush over with melted butter, cover and bake ten minutes. Add one-half cup chicken stock, again cover and cook until squabs are tender. Add one cup boiled potato balls, one bunch cooked asparagus and five Bermuda onions, peeled, cut in one-fourth-inch slices, broiled over a clear fire and then brushed over with melted butter and sprinkled with salt.

Sautéd Quail à la Moquin

Dress, clean and truss six quail. Put in a copper saucepan one-half cup butter, two finely chopped shallots, two cloves garlic, finely chopped, one-half bay leaf, one teaspoon peppercorns and two cloves, and cook, stirring constantly, eight minutes. Sauté quail in mixture until well browned. Pour over one pint white wine and let simmer thirty minutes. Remove quail, strain sauce into casserole and add slowly one pint heavy cream. Season with one-half teaspoon salt, one-eighth teaspoon pepper, a few grains cayenne and one teaspoon finely cut chives. Put quail in casserole, cover and heat to the boiling point. Serve in casserole.

Larded Stuffed English Partridge
Cold Orange Sauce

Clean, stuff, lard and truss three birds. Put in casserole and add one-third cup trimmings from

LARDED BREASTS OF GUINEA CHICKEN. — *Page* 149

SQUABS EN CASSEROLE. — *Page* 148.

pork cut in small pieces. Put in hot oven and cook uncovered fifteen minutes, basting three times, using three tablespoons melted butter. Pour over one-half cup Sherry wine, cover and cook twenty-five minutes. Remove to serving dish on slices of toasted bread, garnish with watercress and serve with Cold Orange Sauce (see p. 160).

Larded Breasts of Guinea Chicken

Remove breasts from bird, leaving wing joints attached, and scrape and trim bones. Lard upper side of breasts, using four lardoons to each. Put in dripping pan, sprinkle with salt and pepper, dredge with flour and brush over with cream. Bake in a hot oven thirty minutes, basting three times with fat in pan. Remove to thin slices of hot, fried or broiled ham and serve with Brown Nut Sauce (see p. 155). Put frills on bones and garnish with potato balls and pastry boats filled with Asparagus Mousselaine.

Game Mousse, Sauce Bigarrade

Force one pound uncooked duck meat through a meat chopper; repeat, and add gradually the whites of two eggs. When thoroughly blended rub through a sieve. Add heavy cream to make of right consistency, the amount required being about two cups. Season with salt, cayenne and nutmeg. Sprinkle a buttered mould with chopped truffle, pour in mixture, cover with buttered paper, set in pan of hot water and bake until firm. Remove from mould to serving dish, pour around Sauce Bigarrade and garnish with parsley.

Sauce Bigarrade. — After breast meat has been removed from one pair ducks, put remainder of birds, broken in pieces, in kettle; cover with cold water and add one-half onion. six slices carrot, two sprigs celery, one sprig parsley, bit of bay leaf and one-half teaspoon peppercorns. Bring to the boiling point and let simmer until stock is reduced to two cups; then strain. Melt three tablespoons butter, add three tablespoons flour and stir until well blended, then pour on gradually, while stirring constantly, stock. Again bring to the boiling point and season with one-half teaspoon salt, one-eighth teaspoon pepper and a few grains paprika; then add one-third cup orange juice, one tablespoon lemon juice and the rind of one-fourth orange (parboiled two minutes in boiling water, freed from white portion and cut in Julienne-shaped pieces).

CHAPTER XV

STUFFINGS FOR GAME AND POULTRY

Cracker Stuffing

3 cups cracker crumbs
⅛ cup melted butter
1¼ cups boiling water
Salt and pepper
Poultry seasoning or sage

Add water to butter and pour over crackers to which seasonings have been added.

New England Stuffing

1 small stale baker's loaf
Hot water
⅛ cup fat salt pork
1 egg
Salt and pepper
Sage

Remove outside crusts from bread. Cut bread in slices and toast until delicately browned; then put in chopping bowl and chop while adding hot water to moisten. Add pork finely chopped, egg well beaten and seasonings to taste.

Fall River Stuffing

Put turkey giblets in saucepan and cover with one quart cold water. Place on range and heat gradually until boiling point is reached; then let simmer until giblets are tender. The liver will cook in less time than the heart and gizzard, and should be removed as soon as done. Split and spread sixteen common crackers with butter, allowing one-half tablespoonful to each half-cracker. Pour over crackers two and three-fourths cupfuls of stock in which giblets were cooked. As soon as crackers have absorbed stock, add giblets chopped and seasoned with salt and pepper. Summer savory, sage or marjoram may be added as desired.

Swedish Stuffing

2 cups stale bread crumbs	1 teaspoon salt
⅜ cup melted butter	⅛ teaspoon pepper
½ cup raisins seeded	½ teaspoon sage
½ cup English walnut meats	

Mix ingredients in the order given; raisins should be cut in pieces and nut meats broken in pieces.

Bread and Celery Stuffing

3½ cups baker's stale bread crumbs	1½ teaspoons salt
	¼ teaspoon pepper
1 cup boiling water	¾ cup finely cut celery
1 tablespoon poultry seasoning	½ cup melted butter

Pour water over bread and let stand twenty minutes; then squeeze out all the water that is possible. Add remaining ingredients and mix thoroughly.

Oyster Stuffing

1½ cups stale bread crumbs	¼ cup oyster liquor
1½ cups cracker crumbs	2½ teaspoons salt
½ cup melted butter	½ teaspoon pepper
1 pint oysters	¼ teaspoon mace

Mix bread and cracker crumbs and add melted butter, oysters washed and bearded, oyster liquor and seasonings. To beard oysters remove and discard tough muscles.

Sausage Stuffing (for Turkey)

1 small onion	¼ teaspoon pepper
2 tablespoons butter	⅛ teaspoon powdered thyme
½ pound sausage meat	2 teaspoons parsley, finely
4 dozen French chestnuts	chopped
2 teaspoons salt	2 ounces fresh bread crumbs

Finely chop onion and cook in butter three minutes; then add sausage meat and cook five minutes. Boil chestnuts and mash one-half. Add to first mixture with remaining ingredients, and when thoroughly blended add whole chestnuts.

Potato Stuffing

2 cups hot mashed potato	Giblets
2 cups cracker crumbs	Hot water
⅛ cup melted butter	Salt and pepper
⅛ cup sausage fat	Sage

Mix first four ingredients in the order given. Add one-half cup giblets, cooked and finely chopped. Moisten with hot water and add seasonings to taste.

CHAPTER XVI

MEAT AND FISH SAUCES

Allemande Sauce

Melt three tablespoons butter, add three tablespoons flour and stir until well blended; then pour on gradually, while stirring constantly, one-half cup chicken stock and one-half cup cream. Bring to the boiling point and add three tablespoons grated Parmesan cheese, the yolk of one egg, one-half teaspoon salt and a few grains pepper.

Spanish Sauce

3 tablespoons butter	½ cup cream
3 tablespoons flour	1 teaspoon salt
1 cup milk	⅛ teaspoon pepper
½ cup pimiento purée	

Melt butter, add flour and stir until well blended; then pour on gradually, while stirring constantly, milk and cream. Bring to the boiling point and add seasonings and pimiento purée.

To obtain pimiento purée, drain canned pimientoes and force through a purée strainer.

Truffle Sauce

Melt three tablespoons butter, add three tablespoons flour and stir until well blended; then pour on gradually, while stirring constantly, one cup milk and one-half cup cream. Bring to the boiling point and add one and one-half tablespoons chopped truffles, two tablespoons Madeira wine and salt and pepper to taste.

Waldorf Sauce

Melt three tablespoons butter, add three tablespoons flour and stir until well blended; then pour on gradually, while stirring constantly, one and one-half cups chicken stock. Bring to the boiling point, add one-half tablespoon beef extract and two tablespoons chopped truffles. Season with one-fourth teaspoon salt and a few grains pepper.

Bread Sauce

Cook one and one-fourth cups milk in double boiler with one-third cup fine, stale bread crumbs and one onion, stuck with five cloves, twenty-five minutes. Remove onion, add one and one-half tablespoons butter, one-half teaspoon salt and a few grains cayenne. Sprinkle with one-half cup coarse, stale bread crumbs, browned in one and one-half tablespoons butter.

Brown Nut Sauce

2 tablespoons butter	½ teaspoon salt
2 tablespoons peanut butter	Few grains pepper
3½ tablespoons flour	⅛ cup coarse bread crumbs
1½ cups chicken stock	1 tablespoon butter

Brown butter, add peanut butter and when well mixed add flour and continue the browning; then pour on gradually, while stirring constantly, chicken stock. Bring to the boiling point and add salt and pepper. Pour around meat with which it is to be served and sprinkle with bread crumbs browned in one tablespoon butter.

Epicurean Sauce

½ cup heavy cream	1 tablespoon tarragon vinegar
3 tablespoons Mayonnaise Dressing	1 teaspoon English mustard
	½ teaspoon salt
2 tablespoons grated horseradish root	Few grains cayenne

Beat cream until stiff, using a Dover Egg Beater. Remove beater and stir in remaining ingredients.

Mock Hollandaise Sauce

2 tablespoons butter	⅛ teaspoon pepper
2 tablespoons flour	Few grains cayenne
½ cup milk	Yolks 2 eggs
½ teaspoon salt	½ cup butter
1 tablespoon lemon juice	

Melt butter, add flour and stir until well blended; then add milk, salt, pepper and cayenne, and bring to the boiling point. Stir in the egg yolks, butter bit by bit, and lemon juice.

Horseradish Hollandaise

½ cup butter	½ teaspoon salt
Yolks 3 eggs	4 tablespoons grated horseradish root
½ tablespoon vinegar	
2 tablespoons heavy cream	

Wash butter and divide in thirds. Put one-third in small saucepan with egg yolks, vinegar and salt. Place saucepan in larger saucepan containing boiling water, and stir constantly until butter is melted; then add second piece of butter and, as mixture thickens, third piece. Remove from fire and add grated horseradish root, and heavy cream, beaten until stiff.

Cucumber Hollandaise

4 tablespoons white tarragon vinegar	¾ cup washed butter
	½ teaspoon salt
1 red pepper	Few grains cayenne
Yolks 5 eggs	2 cucumbers

Cook vinegar with pepper (one of the small ones found in pepper sauce) until reduced to two tablespoons. Strain into saucepan, add egg yolks and one-third of the butter and stir constantly until mixture becomes heated, holding saucepan over boiling water in larger saucepan, placed on range. When butter is melted and mixture begins to thicken, add remaining butter in pieces, continuing the stirring. Add seasonings and cucumbers pared, chopped and drained from their liquor, then squeezed in cheese-cloth.

Sauce Béarnaise I

To three finely chopped shallots add two tablespoons tarragon vinegar; bring to the boiling point and let simmer until reduced one-half. Strain, add gradually to two egg yolks, slightly beaten, and cook slowly, while stirring constantly, four minutes; then add five tablespoons melted butter, one-fourth teaspoon salt, one-eighth teaspoon cayenne and one-half teaspoon finely chopped parsley.

Sauce Béarnaise II

3 tablespoons water	Yolks 4 eggs
3 tablespoons tarragon vinegar	½ teaspoon salt
½ onion	⅛ teaspoon paprika
4 tablespoons butter	

Put water, vinegar and onion in small saucepan and heat to boiling-point. Beat yolks of eggs slightly and pour on gradually hot liquid, from which onion has been removed; then add seasonings. Place saucepan in larger saucepan, containing boiling water, and cook, stirring constantly, until mixture thickens slightly; then add butter which has been worked until creamy, one tablespoon at a time, stirring constantly during the entire cooking.

Mousselaine Sauce

3 tablespoons butter	¼ teaspoon salt
3 tablespoons flour	Few grains pepper
1 cup chicken stock	Yolks 2 eggs
½ cup cream	½ tablespoon lemon juice

Melt butter, add flour and stir until well blended; then pour on gradually, while stirring constantly, stock and cream. Bring to the boiling point and add salt and pepper. Just before serving add egg yolks, slightly beaten, and lemon juice.

MEAT AND FISH SAUCES

Vinaigrette Sauce

Mix one teaspoon salt, one-fourth teaspoon paprika, a few grains pepper, one tablespoon tarragon vinegar, two tablespoons cider vinegar, six tablespoons olive oil, one tablespoon, each, chopped green pepper and cucumber pickle and one teaspoon each finely chopped parsley and chives.

Guaymas Sauce

To one-half cup tomato sauce add, just before serving, one-third cup Mayonnaise Dressing and three tablespoons shredded olives.

Devonshire Sauce

To one and one-half cups brown sauce add one-third cup currant jelly, beaten with a fork, one-half cup claret wine, one teaspoon lemon juice and three drops essence of anchovy.

Roe Sauce

Put two tablespoons, each, Sherry wine, white wine and butter in small shallow pan and add one-half shad roe sprinkled with salt, pepper, cayenne and a few gratings nutmeg. Cover with buttered paper and bake thirty minutes. Take from oven and remove membranes. Brown three tablespoons butter, add four tablespoons flour and continue the browning; then pour on gradually, while stirring constantly, one cup chicken stock. Bring to the boiling point and add one-fourth teaspoon beef extract, roe and one-fourth teaspoon salt.

Cold Orange Sauce

6 tablespoons currant jelly	2 tablespoons lemon juice
3 tablespoons sugar	2 tablespoons Port wine
Grated rind 2 oranges	¼ teaspoon salt
2 tablespoons orange juice	⅛ teaspoon cayenne

Put first three ingredients in a bowl and beat for five minutes; then add remaining ingredients and stir until well blended.

Currant Mint Sauce

Separate one-half tumbler currant jelly in small pieces, but do not beat it. Add one and one-fourth tablespoons finely chopped fresh mint leaves and thin, short shavings from one-fourth the rind of an orange.

Cider Sauce

3 tablespoons butter	2 cups ham liquor
4 tablespoons flour	4 tablespoons cider
Salt	Pepper

Melt butter, add flour, and pour on gradually, while stirring constantly, hot ham liquor. Bring to the boiling point and add cider, and salt to taste.

Sauce Verte

2 tablespoons butter	½ teaspoon salt
3 tablespoons flour	Few grains pepper
1 cup fish stock	Few grains cayenne
⅛ cup heavy cream	2 tablespoons sauterne
Green coloring	

Melt butter, add flour and stir until well blended; then pour on stock gradually while stirring constantly. Bring to the boiling point and add cream and seasonings. Again bring to the boiling point and color green.

CHAPTER XVII

VEGETABLES

French Artichokes, Vinaigrette Sauce

TRIM tops and wash French artichokes. Cook in boiling, salted water to cover until soft. Remove from water, drain, and separate the scales of each, so as to represent a flower. Serve with Vinaigrette Sauce (see p. 159).

Jerusalem Artichokes

Wash and pare one quart Jerusalem artichokes and cook in boiling, salted water until soft. Drain, add one-fourth cup butter, two tablespoons lemon juice, two tablespoons finely chopped parsley, one-half teaspoon salt, and a few grains cayenne. Cook three minutes and serve very hot.

Arlington Asparagus

Arrange boiled asparagus stalks through rings (one-third inch wide) cut from peel of a lemon. Place on oblong pieces of buttered toast (from which crusts have been removed), moistened with water in which asparagus was cooked. Brush lemon rings with melted butter; place in oven to re-heat asparagus and arrange on serving dish.

Asparagus Mousselaine

Arrange short stalks of cooked asparagus in individual baking dishes, allowing eight to each portion, and pour over Mousselaine Sauce (see p. 158).

Lima Beans Fermière

Soak two cups dried lima beans over night in cold water to cover. Drain, put in a casserole dish, and sprinkle with one-half teaspoon salt and one-eighth teaspoon pepper. Cut a two-inch cube of fat salt pork in small pieces, try out, and strain. To fat add one small onion, thinly sliced, and one-half cup one-third-inch carrot cubes and stir constantly until vegetables are browned. Add to beans, dot over with two tablespoons butter and add water to half the height of the beans. Cover and cook in a slow oven until beans are soft.

Brussels Sprouts with Celery

Remove wilted leaves from one quart Brussels sprouts and soak in cold water fifteen minutes. Drain and cook in boiling, salted water twenty minutes, or until easily pierced with a skewer; again drain. Wash celery and cut in small pieces; there should be one and one-half cups. Melt three tablespoons butter, add celery, and cook two minutes,

French Artichoke, Vinaigrette Sauce. — *Page* 161.

Peppers Stuffed with Fresh Green Corn. — *Page* 173

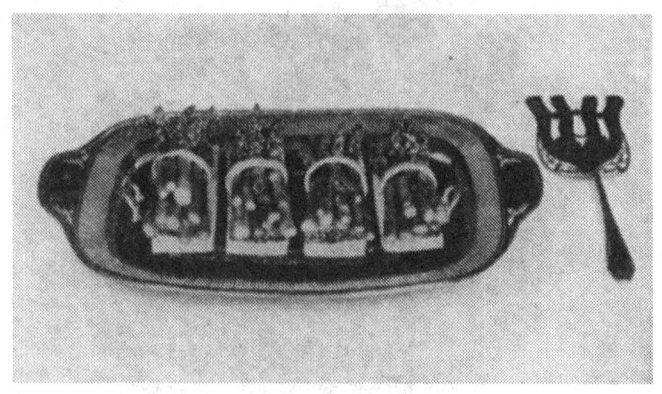

ARLINGTON ASPARAGUS. — *Page* 161.

ASPARAGUS, MOUSSELAINE SAUCE. — *Page* 162

VEGETABLES 165

then add three tablespoons flour and pour on gradually one and one-half cups scalded milk. Bring to the boiling point, add sprouts, season with salt and pepper and serve as soon as sprouts are re-heated.

Brussels Sprouts with Chestnuts

Pick over one quart Brussels sprouts, remove wilted leaves and soak in cold water to cover, to which has been added one-eighth teaspoon soda. Drain and cook in boiling, salted water to cover, until soft. Drain and sauté in three tablespoons butter.

Remove shells from French chestnuts and cook in boiling, salted water to cover until soft; there should be one cup. Cook one-fourth cup butter with two teaspoons sugar until well browned, stirring constantly. Add chestnuts and cook until chestnuts are browned; then add sautéd sprouts, one-third cup brown stock, one-half teaspoon beef extract, one-half teaspoon salt, a few grains cayenne, and two tablespoons brandy.

Smothered Cabbage

Take off outside wilted leaves from a firm, medium-sized cabbage, cut in quarters and remove tough centre portion; then finely chop or force through a meat chopper; there should be five cups. Melt five tablespoons butter in hot iron frying pan, add two tablespoons flour and stir until well blended; then pour on gradually, while stirring constantly, one cup milk. Bring to the boiling point and add two teaspoons salt, one-fourth teaspoon pepper, and cabbage. Mix thoroughly, cover, put on back of range and cook slowly from fifty to sixty minutes.

Mint Glazed Carrots with Peas

Scrape three medium-sized carrots, cut in one-fourth-inch slices, then in strips or fancy shapes, using French vegetable cutters. Cook in boiling, salted water fifteen minutes and drain. Put in saucepan with one-half cup butter, one-half cup sugar and one tablespoon chopped fresh mint leaves. Cook slowly until soft and glazed. Drain and rinse thoroughly one can French peas. Cook ten minutes in boiling water to cover, drain, and season with butter, salt, and pepper. Turn peas on hot serving dish and surround with carrots.

Carrot Timbales

Wash and scrape carrots. Cut off the deepest-colored portion in thin slices, lengthwise of vegetables, and fill a quart measure packed solidly. Cook in two tablespoons butter ten minutes, stirring constantly; then cover with boiling water or stock and cook until soft. Drain and force through a purée strainer. Add two whole eggs and one egg yolk slightly beaten, and season with salt and pepper. Fill buttered timbale moulds (garnished with hard-boiled egg, cut in fancy shapes) two-thirds full, set in pan of hot water, cover with buttered paper and bake fifteen minutes.

Cucumber Jelly

2 cups chicken stock	2 cucumbers
1 slice onion	1½ tablespoons granulated
1 sprig parsley	gelatine
	Green coloring

To chicken stock add onion, parsley and cucumbers, pared and grated. Cover and let stand two hours. Heat gradually to the boiling point, add gelatine, and color green. Let stand until nearly cold; then strain into individual paper cases, in the bottom of each of which is a slice of cucumber. Garnish tops with Mayonnaise Dressing and halves of blanched Jordan almonds.

Baked Egg Plant

Pare an egg plant, cut in one-fourth-inch slices, crosswise, and soak, in cold water to cover, two hours. Drain and cook in boiling, salted water to cover until soft. Again drain and mash; then add one-fourth cup butter, one-half cup stale bread crumbs, two eggs, well beaten, a few drops onion juice, one-half teaspoon salt, and one-eighth teaspoon pepper. Line buttered Dario or individual moulds with canned pimientes (drained and dried). Fill with egg plant mixture, sprinkle with buttered crumbs, and bake in a hot oven fifteen minutes. Remove from moulds and garnish with sprigs of parsley.

Baked Stuffed Egg Plant

Wipe egg plant and cut in quarters, lengthwise. Remove pulp close to skin, leaving thin shells.

Force pulp through a meat chopper and drain; there should be two and two-thirds cups. Put in a saucepan, add one and one-half cups ham stock, bring to the boiling point and let boil twenty minutes. Add three-fourths cup coarse, dried bread crumbs, one-fourth cup melted butter, one teaspoon lemon juice, one-half teaspoon salt, and one egg, slightly beaten. Fill shells with mixture, sprinkle with buttered crumbs, and bake in a hot oven fifteen minutes.

Egg Plant Turque

Wipe three small egg plants, cut in halves, lengthwise, fry in deep fat twelve minutes and drain. Scoop out inside and finely chop. Put two tablespoons olive oil in saucepan, and when heated add one tablespoon finely chopped onion, and cook five minutes. Add three tablespoons uncooked rice, and one-half clove of garlic, finely chopped, and cook five minutes; then add chopped egg plant, one cup tomato sauce, one-half teaspoon salt, and one-fourth teaspoon grated nutmeg. Turn into a buttered dish and bake forty-five minutes. Add yolks two eggs, slightly beaten, and stuff egg plant shells with mixture. Cover with buttered crumbs and bake until crumbs are brown.

Creamed Mushrooms

1 pound mushrooms	Few grains pepper
5 tablespoons butter	1½ tablespoons flour
½ teaspoon salt	½ cup thin cream

Clean mushrooms, remove caps, and cut both stems and caps in thin slices. Melt butter, add sliced mushrooms and cook three minutes. Sprinkle with salt and pepper, dredge with flour and pour over cream. Cook five minutes, stirring constantly.

Mushroom and Tomato Toast

Cut stale bread in one-third-inch slices, shape with a large round cutter and sauté in butter until delicately browned. Wipe mushrooms and cut in pieces; there should be two cups; then cook in two tablespoons butter five minutes. Cook one tablespoon butter and one-half teaspoon finely chopped shallot three minutes. Add one cup tomato purée, bring to the boiling point and let simmer three minutes; then add one-half teaspoon salt, one-eighth teaspoon pepper, and a few grains paprika. Arrange mushrooms on six rounds of bread, pour over tomato, and sprinkle with one tablespoon finely chopped parsley.

Creamed Silver Skins

Peel three cups small silver skinned onions and cook in boiling, salted water to cover, fifteen minutes. Drain, add one cup thin cream, and cook in double boiler until soft, adding three-fourths teaspoon salt the last ten minutes of the cooking.

Onion Soufflé

Cook onions in boiling salted, water until soft, drain and force through a sieve; there should be one and one-fourth cups onion pulp. Melt four tablespoons butter, add four tablespoons flour, and pour on gradually one-third cup water in which onions have been cooked and one-third cup cream; then add onion pulp and bring to the boiling point. Season with salt and pepper. Beat yolks of three eggs until thick and lemon-colored and add to first mixture. Cut and fold in whites of eggs beaten until stiff and dry. Turn into a buttered baking dish and bake twenty-five minutes in a moderate oven. Serve at once.

Onion Farci

Peel six large Bermuda onions and remove a part of the inside. Put in saucepan, cover with boiling water and let boil six minutes. Drain, and stuff with veal forcemeat. Place onions in pan on six thin slices fat salt pork, pour around one cup brown or chicken stock and bake until onions are soft; the time required being about thirty-five minutes. Remove onions to serving dish, strain stock, skim off all fat that is possible, add one teaspoon beef extract, one-fourth tablespoon butter, and salt and pepper to taste. Pour over onions.

Veal Forcemeat. — Finely chop raw veal; there should be one-half cup. Add two tablespoons finely chopped fat salt pork and one-half cup soft bread crumbs, cooked with one tablespoon butter and one tablespoon finely chopped onion, three minutes. When mixture is well blended add one-half teaspoon salt, one-eighth teaspoon pepper, and one egg, slightly beaten.

Oyster Plant with Fine Herbs

Wash and scrape one bunch oyster plant. Put at once into cold acidulated water and let stand ten minutes. Cut in one-inch slices crosswise and cook in boiling salted water to cover until soft. Drain, put in pan with three tablespoons butter, reheat. Add one teaspoon finely chopped parsley and one-half teaspoon finely chopped chives. Sprinkle with salt and pepper.

Sautéd Parsnips

Cut cold, boiled young parsnips in sixths, lengthwise. Sauté in butter until delicately browned and sprinkle with salt and pepper.

Peppers Stuffed with Fresh Green Corn

Cut a thick slice from the stem end of each pepper, remove seeds and parboil peppers fifteen minutes in boiling salted water to which is added one-eighth teaspoon soda. Drain, fill with corn mixture, arrange on serving dish, sprinkle tops with paprika, and garnish with parsley.

Corn Mixture. — Remove husks and silky threads from one dozen ears of green corn. Cut lengthwise of cob through each row of kernels and scrape with a knife to remove pulp; there should be two and one-half cups. Put pulp in omelet pan, add one-half cup milk and cook slowly, on back of range, twenty-five minutes, stirring frequently. If cooked on a gas range, gas flame should be turned low and covered with an asbestos mat. Season with butter, salt and pepper.

Jarvis Stuffed Peppers

Cut slices from stem ends of six green peppers, remove seeds and parboil three minutes in one quart boiling water to which has been added one-eighth teaspoon soda. Bring one-half can tomatoes to boiling point and let simmer twenty-minutes; then rub through a sieve and continue the simmering until there is one-half cup tomato purée. Season with salt and pepper and add one-half cup hot boiled rice. Let stand until rice has absorbed tomato; then add one sweetbread, parboiled and cut in small cubes. Season with one-half teaspoon salt and one-eighth teaspoon paprika. Fill peppers with mixture, arrange in a pan, sprinkle tops with buttered bread crumbs, and bake until crumbs are brown. Remove to circular pieces of sautéd bread and pour around

Littleton Sauce. — Mix one teaspoon flour and one teaspoon mustard, and when thoroughly blended add one tablespoon melted butter, one tablespoon vinegar, one-half cup boiling water and the beaten yolks of three eggs. Cook in double boiler, stirring constantly, until mixture thickens. Add one-fourth teaspoon salt, and a few grains, each, pepper and cay-

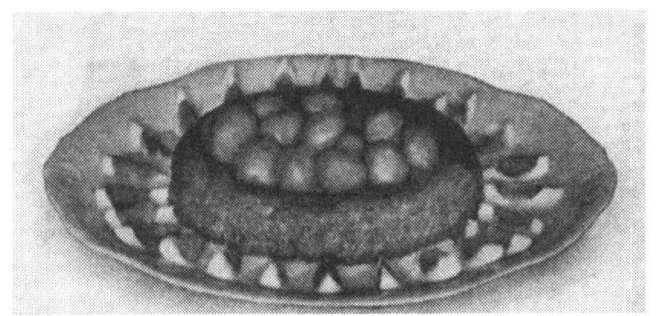

MOULDED SPINACH. — *Page* 175.

MOULDED SPINACH ON ARTICHOKE BOTTOMS. — *Page* 176

Radishes Cut for Garnishing.

Delmonico Tomatoes. — *Page* 178

enne. Just before serving add one tablespoon currant jelly separated in small pieces.

Templeton Stuffed Peppers

Wipe four long, green peppers and parboil ten minutes in one quart boiling water, to which has been added one-fourth teaspoon soda. Drain, cut in halves, lengthwise, remove seeds, stuff, arrange in pan, cover with buttered crumbs, and bake until crumbs are brown.

For the stuffing cook one-half tablespoon chopped onion, and one-half tablespoon green pepper, cut in small pieces, in two tablespoons butter five minutes, stirring constantly. Add two tablespoons flour mixed with one teaspoon salt, one-fourth teaspoon paprika, one-fourth teaspoon mustard, and a few grains cayenne. Pour on gradually, while stirring constantly, one-half cup milk; bring to the boiling point, add one cup canned corn and cook five minutes; then add one egg, slightly beaten, and two-thirds cup dry bread, broken in very small pieces and sautéd in butter until well browned.

Moulded Spinach

Pick over and wash one peck spinach. Cook in an uncovered vessel with a large quantity of boiling, salted water, to which have been added two-thirds teaspoon soda and one teaspoon sugar. Drain very thoroughly and finely chop. Season with one-third cup butter and three-fourths teaspoon salt, and reheat. Press into a buttered border mould, and keep in a warm place until serving time. Remove to hot platter and fill centre with seasoned, small boiled beats. Pour around one and one-half cups White Sauce, and surround with four hard-boiled eggs, cut in sixths, lengthwise.

Mounded Spinach on Artichoke Bottoms

Wash and pick over one-half peck spinach. Cook twenty-five minutes in an uncovered vessel in a large quantity of boiling, salted water, to which have been added one-third teaspoon soda and one-half teaspoon powdered sugar. Drain, finely chop and season with butter, salt, and pepper.

Drain canned artichoke bottoms, put in a shallow or omelet pan, cover bottom of pan with boiling water and add three tablespoons vinegar and one teaspoon salt. Cover and cook until artichokes are thoroughly heated. Drain, mound with cooked spinach, put in oven to re-heat and garnish with yolks of hard-boiled eggs rubbed through a coarse strainer, and whites of hard-boiled eggs cut in fancy shapes.

Soubrics of Spinach

Wash, boil, and drain two quarts spinach; then chop. Add two tablespoons grated Parmesan cheese and two egg yolks, slightly beaten, and season with one-half teaspoon salt and a few grains, each, cayenne and nutmeg. Cook five minutes, stirring constantly. Remove from range and stir in the unbeaten white of one egg. Measure by rounding tablespoonfuls, sauté in butter, arrange on hot serving dish and pour around one cup white sauce.

Squash Soufflé

Cut winter squash in pieces, remove seeds and stringy portion, and pare. Place in a steamer or strainer and cook over boiling water thirty-five minutes, or until soft. Mash and season with butter, salt, and pepper. To two cups mashed and seasoned squash add gradually one cup cream, and when thoroughly blended, add the yolks of two eggs, beaten until thick and lemon-colored; then the whites of two eggs, beaten until stiff and dry. Turn into a buttered dish and bake in a slow oven until firm.

Broiled Tomatoes
Horseradish Hollandaise

Wipe and remove skins from medium-sized tomatoes. Cut in halves, crosswise, sprinkle with salt and pepper, brush over with melted butter and broil from six to eight minutes. Remove to circular pieces of sautéd bread or buttered toast and on each put a tablespoon Horseradish Hollandaise (see p. 156).

Creole Tomatoes

Wipe six medium-sized tomatoes, remove a slice from the top of each, scoop out some of the pulp, sprinkle insides with salt, invert and let stand one hour. Melt one tablespoon butter, add one tablespoon flour mixed with one-half teaspoon salt, one-fourth teaspoon paprika, and a few grains pepper, and when well blended, pour on gradually, while stirring constantly, one-half cup cream. Bring to the boiling point and add one cup crab meat, one tablespoon Sherry wine, and one-half tablespoon, each, red and green pepper, finely chopped. Fill tomatoes with mixture, sprinkle tops with coarse, buttered bread crumbs, and bake in a moderate oven until tomatoes are soft.

Stuffed Tomatoes

Wipe and remove stem end from six small tomatoes. Take out seeds and most of pulp, sprinkle inside of tomatoes with salt, invert and let stand twenty minutes. Cook three tablespoons butter with six tablespoons chopped green pepper, five minutes. Add three-fourths cup soft, stale bread crumbs, one-half cup removed tomato pulp, one-fourth teaspoon salt, one-eighth teaspoon pepper, and a few drops onion juice. Fill tomatoes with mixture, put in buttered pan and bake fifteen minutes in a hot oven.

Delmonico Tomatoes

Wipe and remove a thick slice from stem ends of eight small tomatoes, scoop out inside, sprinkle with salt, invert and let stand two hours.

Wipe, remove seeds, and chop three green peppers.

Add one-half onion finely chopped and one-fourth teaspoon soda and cook with one tablespoon butter five minutes, stirring constantly. Add one tablespoon thick brown sauce to bind mixture together. Line tomatoes with pepper mixture, having mixture extend over top of tomatoes. Put three cubes parboiled sweetbreads in each, cover with buttered bread crumbs and bake twelve minutes in a hot oven. Place on circular pieces of sautéd bread and cover with brown sauce diluted with brown stock or water.

Soufflé of Tomatoes, Neapolitan Style

Melt two tablespoons butter, add two tablespoons flour, and stir until well blended; then pour on gradually, while stirring constantly, one-half cup rich milk and one cup tomato purée. Bring to the boiling point and let simmer two minutes; then add two-thirds cup grated Parmesan cheese, one-half teaspoon salt, and a few grains pepper. Break macaroni in one-half-inch pieces (there should be one-half cup) and cook in boiling, salted water until soft; drain and add one and one-half tablespoons melted butter. Add to tomato mixture; then add the yolks of three eggs, beaten until thick and lemon-colored, and cut and fold in the whites of three eggs, beaten until stiff. Turn into a buttered baking dish and bake until firm. Serve immediately.

To obtain tomato purée, simmer one can tomatoes until reduced one-half, then force through a purée strainer and again let simmer until reduced to one cup.

Tomatoes, Virginia Style

Select six sound, ripe, medium sized-tomatoes. Wipe, prick each several times with a fork, arrange in baking dish and bake in a moderate oven until soft. Remove skins, arrange on serving dish and pour over a sauce made of two tablespoons butter, three tablespoons flour, one-half teaspoon salt, one-eighth teaspoon pepper, and one cup thin cream.

Turnip Cones

Wash turnips, pare, and cut in cone shapes, using a French vegetable cutter; there should be three cups. Put in a casserole with one and one-half teaspoons salt, one and one-half teaspoons sugar, one-fourth cup butter, and one-third cup water or stock. Cover and cook in a moderate oven until turnips are soft.

Vegetables en Casserole

6 medium-sized potatoes	¼ cup rice
1 small turnip	1 teaspoon salt
1 cup canned peas	⅛ teaspoon pepper
1 cup canned tomatoes	⅛ teaspoon allspice
1 onion	4 cups brown stock

Wash, pare and thinly slice potatoes. Wash and pare turnip, cut in one-half-inch slices and slices in cubes. Peel and slice onion. Pick over and wash rice. Put ingredients in alternate layers except stock in casserole, pour over stock, cover and cook in a slow oven three hours.

Jellied Vegetable Ring

Soak one tablespoon granulated gelatine in one-fourth cup cold water and dissolve in one cup boiling water; then add one fourth cup, each, sugar and vinegar, two tablespoons lemon juice and one teaspoon salt. Strain, cool, and when beginning to stiffen, add one cup celery cut in small strips, one-half cup shredded cabbage, one-third cup small cucumber cubes, one-fourth cup cold, cooked green peas, and one-fourth cup cold, cooked beets (cut in thin slices; then in fancy shapes). Turn into ring mould and chill. Remove to serving dish and arrange around jelly thin slices of cold cooked meat. Fill centre with Horseradish Cream Dressing (see p. 215) and garnish with watercress.

Vegetable Panachée

Cut cold boiled turnip and carrots in one-fourth-inch slices and slice in strips of uniform size. Line sides of a generously buttered oval mould with alternate strips of prepared vegetables and garnish bottom of mould with vegetables shaped with French cutters. Fill with finely chopped boiled spinach, seasoned with butter, salt, and pepper. Set mould in pan of hot water and bake until thoroughly heated. Remove to hot serving dish and serve with or without White Sauce.

CHAPTER XVIII

POTATOES

Potatoes en Casserole

WASH and pare eight smooth round potatoes of uniform size. Cover with cold water and let stand two hours. Drain, put in a casserole dish, sprinkle with salt and add butter, allowing one teaspoon to each potato. Cover and bake until soft (the time required being about forty-five minutes), turning every fifteen minutes.

Spanish Potatoes

Season three cups hot riced potatoes with three tablespoons butter, one-half cup cream, and salt to taste. Beat vigorously five minutes, add one and one-half canned pimientos (cut in small pieces or forced through a purée strainer) and beat until well blended. Re-heat and pile on a hot serving plate.

Savory Potatoes

Force hot boiled potatoes through a potato ricer; there should be two cups. Season with three tablespoons butter, one and one-half teaspoons salt, and moisten with one-third cup milk or cream. Beat vigorously and add one tablespoon chopped watercress and one teaspoon chopped fresh mint leaves.

Chantilly Potatoes

Pile on a serving dish three cups well-seasoned mashed potatoes. Beat one-half cup heavy cream until stiff, add one-half cup grated cheese, and season with salt and pepper. Spread over potatoes, place in a hot oven and bake until cheese is melted and cream is delicately browned.

Pomme Fondante

Force hot boiled potatoes through a potato ricer; there should be three and one-half cups. Season with three tablespoons butter, one and one-half teaspoons salt, and one-fourth teaspoon pepper. Add gradually, while beating constantly, two-thirds cup hot milk and beat vigorously three minutes. Turn into a buttered baking dish, pour over one-half cup heavy cream and sprinkle with three-fourths cup coarse stale bread crumbs. Bake in a hot oven until crumbs are brown.

Pittsburg Potatoes

1 quart ⅛-inch potato cubes	2 cups white sauce
1 onion	½ pound mild cheese
½ can pimientos	½ teaspoon salt

Cook potato cubes and onion, finely chopped, in boiling, salted water to cover, five minutes. Add pimientos, cut in small pieces, and cook seven minutes; then drain. Turn into a buttered baking dish and pour over white sauce, mixed with cheese and salt. Bake in a moderate oven until potatoes are soft.

Alphonso Potatoes

Wash and pare five medium-sized potatoes and cook in boiling, salted water until soft; then cut in one-fourth-inch cubes. Parboil one green pepper, from which seeds have been removed, six minutes and cut in one-eighth-inch squares. Add to potato cubes with three-fourths cup milk, and one-half teaspoon salt. Let simmer fifteen minutes. Put in a buttered baking dish, sprinkle with one and one-half tablespoons grated Parmesan cheese, and bake ten minutes.

Potatoes à la Goldenrod

Cut boiled potatoes in cubes; there should be two cups. Separate yolks from whites of four hard-boiled eggs. Chop the whites and force the yolks through a potato ricer or strainer. Add potato cubes and chopped whites to one and one-half cups white sauce, turn into a hot serving dish. Sprinkle with yolks and garnish with parsley.

White Sauce

3 tablespoons butter
3 tablespoons flour
1½ cups milk
2 slices onion
½ teaspoon salt
Few grains paprika

JELLIED VEGETABLE RING. — *Page* 181

VEGETABLE PANACHÉE. — *Page* 181.

Potatoes à la Suisse. — *Page* 186

Lorrette Potatoes. — *Page* 188.

Melt butter, add flour and pour on gradually, while stirring constantly, the milk which has been scalded with the onion, then the onion removed. When boiling point is reached, add seasonings and beat until smooth and glossy.

Potato Moulds

Remove the inside from three baked potatoes and force through a potato ricer. Season with two tablespoons butter, one-half teaspoon salt and a few grains pepper and add the white of one egg, beaten until stiff. Mould with a tablespoon; place on a buttered sheet, brush over with melted butter and bake in a hot oven until well browned.

Martinique Potatoes

Scoop out inside of four large hot baked potatoes and force through a potato ricer. Add one and one-half tablespoons butter, three tablespoons cream, one egg yolk slightly beaten, one-half teaspoon salt, one-eighth teaspoon pepper and a few gratings nutmeg. Set on range and cook three minutes, stirring constantly; then add, gradually, the white of one egg, beaten to a stiff froth. Shape between two buttered tablespoons, place on a buttered sheet and bake until delicately browned.

Baked Potato Apples

1½ cups hot riced potatoes   2 tablespoons butter
Yolk ½ egg   ½ teaspoon salt
          Few grains pepper

Mix ingredients and stir until well blended. Shape into forms representing small apples, using one tablespoon mixture to each apple. Arrange on buttered sheet, brush over with yolk of egg, diluted with one-half tablespoon cold water, and insert cloves in both stem and blossom ends. Bake in a hot oven until thoroughly heated and glazed.

Potatoes à la Suisse

Wash smooth, round, medium-sized potatoes; put in dripping pan and bake in a hot oven until soft. Remove a slice from each and scoop out most of the inside. Force through a potato ricer, season with butter, salt and pepper and add a small quantity of milk. Slip an egg into each potato case and force potato mixture through a pastry bag and tube around edge. Return to oven and bake until eggs are set. Arrange on serving dish and garnish with watercress.

Anchovied Stuffed Potatoes

Wash and peel six medium-sized potatoes, arrange in a pan and bake in a hot oven, turning frequently; the time required being about fifty minutes. Cut slice from each lengthwise, scoop out inside and force through a potato ricer. Add one-half cup hot milk, two tablespoons butter, twelve anchovies, cut in small pieces, one-eighth teaspoon grated nutmeg and salt and pepper to taste. Refill shells with mixture, sprinkle with grated cheese and bake until delicately browned.

Deerfoot Potatoes

Wash and pare potatoes of uniform size. Remove from each two portions, using an apple corer. Fill cavities thus made with sausages and insert rounds of potatoes to conceal sausages. Put in a pan and bake in a hot oven until potatoes are soft.

French Fried Potatoes

Wash and pare small potatoes, cut in eighths lengthwise, and soak one hour in cold water to cover. Drain and parboil in boiling salted water to cover two minutes; again drain, plunge into cold water, dry between towels, fry in deep fat until delicately browned, a few at a time, and drain on brown paper. Heat fat to a higher temperature, return all the potatoes to fat, using a frying basket, and fry until crisp and brown, keeping the basket in motion. Again drain on brown paper and sprinkle with salt.

Rector Potatoes

Wash, pare and shape potatoes, using an elliptical shaped French cutter. Fry in deep fat and drain.

Fried Potato Curls

Wash and pare potatoes and cut in one-half-inch slices. Cut round and round so as to make curls. Put in cold water and let stand thirty minutes. Drain, dry on a towel and fry in deep fat. Drain on brown paper and sprinkle with salt.

Fried Potato Dots

Wash and pare large potatoes and shape with an apple corer; then cut pieces thus formed in one-fourth-inch slices, crosswise. Soak in cold water eight minutes, drain, cook in salted boiling water two minutes; again drain, put in ice water and let stand ten minutes. Drain, dry between towels, fry in deep fat, drain on brown paper and sprinkle with salt.

Lorrette Potatoes

Wash and pare large potatoes, and shape with a cutter, especially made for the purpose of cutting vegetables. Cover with boiling salted water and let boil five minutes. Drain and plunge into ice-water and let stand one minute. Again drain, dry between towels, fry in deep fat and drain on brown paper. Sprinkle with salt.

Princess Potatoes

3 cups ½-inch potato cubes
1 cup white sauce
1 teaspoon beef extract
½ tablespoon lemon juice
1 teaspoon finely chopped parsley
1 tablespoon butter

Fry potato cubes in deep fat until delicately browned and drain on brown paper. Make sauce of two tablespoons butter, two tablespoons flour, one-third teaspoon salt, a few grains pepper and one cup milk. Add beef extract, lemon juice, parsley and butter, bit by bit; then add potatoes and serve at once.

Potatoes Rissolée

Wash, pare and trim eight new potatoes of uniform size. Let stand in cold water fifteen minutes, drain and dry between towels. Fry in deep fat until delicately browned and drain on brown paper. Put in baking pan and bake in a hot oven until soft, the time required being about twenty-five minutes. Remove to serving dish and pour over one cup rich white or cream sauce.

Sultan Potatoes

Wash and pare large potatoes and shape in circular pieces, two and one-half inches long and one-third inch in diameter, using a French vegetable cutter. Fry in deep fat and drain on brown paper; there should be three cups. Arrange on hot serving dish to represent a wood pile and pour over sauce, same as for Princess Potatoes, omitting the parsley (see p. 188).

Fried Potatoes, Bourgoyne

Wash, pare and cut potatoes in one-fourth-inch slices; then slice in strips; there should be three cups. Parboil one minute in boiling salted water, drain, dry on towel, fry in deep fat and drain on brown paper. Melt three-fourths teaspoon butter in hot iron fry pan, and add three-fourths teaspoon finely cut chives; add potatoes and stir until potatoes have absorbed fat.

Potato and Spinach Croquettes

Force hot boiled potatoes through a potato ricer; there should be two cups. Add two tablespoons butter, yolks two eggs, slightly beaten, and one-fourth cup finely chopped cooked spinach. Season with salt and pepper. Shape, dip in crumbs, egg and crumbs, fry in deep fat and drain on brown paper.

Nut and Potato Croquettes

2 cups hot riced potatoes	¼ cup bread crumbs
3 tablespoons cream	¼ cup cream
½ teaspoon salt	½ egg yolk
⅛ teaspoon pepper	¼ teaspoon salt
Few grains cayenne	⅛ cup chopped pecan nut meats
Few drops onion juice	
Yolk 1 egg	

Mix first seven ingredients and beat thoroughly. Cook bread crumbs with cream to make a thick paste and cool; then add remaining ingredients. Shape potato mixture in nests, fill with nut mixture, cover with potato mixture, roll until of the desired length and flatten ends. Dip in crumbs, egg and crumbs, fry in deep fat and drain on brown paper. Stand in circular form on serving dish and fill centre with a bunch of parsley.

Piedmont Potato Croquettes

To two cups hot riced potatoes add three tablespoons butter, three-fourths teaspoon salt, one and one-half tablespoons finely chopped truffles and the

POTATOES 191

yolks of three eggs slightly beaten. Shape in balls (allowing one rounding tablespoon of mixture to each croquette), roll in flour, dip in egg and roll in Jordan almonds, blanched and shredded. Fry in deep fat and drain on brown paper.

Creamed Sweet Potatoes, Club House Style

Cut cold boiled sweet potatoes in one-half-inch cubes; there should be two cups. Put in a saucepan with two tablespoons butter and cook three minutes. Season with one-half teaspoon salt, one-eighth teaspoon black pepper and few grains paprika; then sprinkle with two tablespoons flour and pour over one cup rich milk. Cook very slowly twenty minutes.

Candied Sweet Potatoes

Wash and cook six medium-sized sweet potatoes in boiling salted water to cover. Drain, peel, cut in halves, lengthwise, arrange in buttered baking dish, sprinkling each layer with brown sugar, using one cup in all. Pour over one-half cup melted butter. Cook in a slow oven two hours.

Sweet Potatoes, Brulé

Cut three medium-sized cold boiled sweet potatoes in one-third-inch slices and sauté in butter until delicately browned. Put one-fourth cup sugar and one tablespoon boiling water in small saucepan, place on range, bring to the boiling point and let boil until of the consistency of a thick syrup. Put one-half tablespoon syrup in chafing dish, add potatoes, sprinkle with salt, paprika and a few grains cayenne. Add one-fourth cup brandy, put lighted match to brandy, and as soon as brandy begins to burn, toss potatoes (using a fork and spoon) until brandy stops burning.

Sautéd Sweet Potatoes with Rum

Wash and pare medium-sized sweet potatoes, and cut in one-third-inch slices, lengthwise. Parboil in boiling salted water eight minutes, drain and sauté in butter until well browned on both sides. Remove to a hot serving dish, pour over Jamaica rum and light when sending to table.

Sweet Potatoes, Flambant

Wash and pare large sweet potatoes. Cook in boiling salted water until soft, drain, cut in one-fourth-inch slices lengthwise and trim in oblong shapes of uniform size. Sprinkle with salt and sauté until browned. Arrange pieces overlapping one another on a silver platter and pour over and around brandy. Light liquor and baste, using brandy in dish until it stops burning.

Scalloped Sweet Potatoes and Apples

2 cups cold boiled sweet potatoes cut in ¼ inch slices
½ cup brown sugar
1½ cups thinly sliced sour apples
4 tablespoons butter
1 teaspoon salt

Nut and Potato Croquettes. — *Page* 190.

Piedmont Potato Croquettes. — *Page* 190

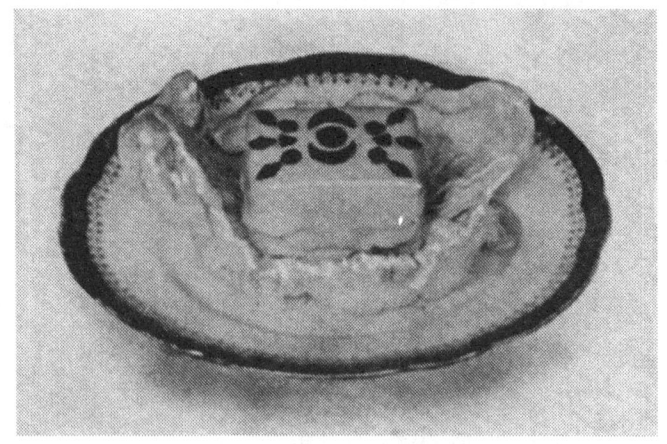

RECTOR SALAD. — *Page* 196

CARLTON SALAD. — *Page* 196.

Put one-half the potatoes in buttered baking dish, cover with one-half the apples, sprinkle with one-half the sugar, dot over with one-half the butter and sprinkle with one-half the salt; repeat and bake in a moderate oven one hour.

CHAPTER XIX

SALADS

Lettuce and Pimiento Salad

REMOVE leaves from one head lettuce, wash, drain and dry. Arrange in bowl as near the original shape as possible and sprinkle with one-half cup canned pimientos cut in strips. Just before sending to table pour over Columbia French Dressing (see p. 213).

Chiccory and Celery Salad

Wash and scrape celery and cut in one and three-fourths inch pieces crosswise; then cut in thin strips lengthwise. Chill in cold water to which have been added a few drops lemon juice. Drain and dry in cheese-cloth. Pick over and wash one head chiccory, drain and dry on cheese-cloth. Arrange in salad bowl, sprinkle with celery and serve with French Dressing.

Good Luck Salad

Wipe a long selected cucumber, pare, cut in thin slices crosswise and trim. Arrange horse-shoe fashion on a bed of romaine, also trimmed and arranged horse-shoe fashion. Garnish with pieces of truffle cut to represent nail heads. Serve with Cream French Dressing (see p. 213).

Cucumber Cups

Pare cucumbers and remove a thick slice from each end and with a sharp-pointed knife make eight grooves at equal distances lengthwise of cucumber. Cut in pieces crosswise and remove some of the inside, leaving cups; then cut in thin slices crosswise, keeping the original shapes. Arrange on nest of lettuce leaves and fill with Cream French Dressing (see p. 213).

Dressed Cucumber

(An accompaniment to a fish course)

Wipe a long selected cucumber. Beginning at blossom end, make nine incisions, at equal distances, through skin lengthwise of cucumber to one inch of stem end. Pass knife under sections of skin and cut down almost as far as incisions extend. Remove cucumber at that point and pare with a fluted knife, then cut in thin slices crosswise. Replace prepared cucumber in skin, place on a glass dish and garnish with watercress and radishes cut to represent flowers (see illustration). Pour over French Dressing.

Rector Salad

Pare long selected cucumbers and cut in box-shaped pieces two inches long, one and one-half inches wide and one and one-fourth inches high; then cut in thin slices, crosswise, keeping in original shape. Soak one-half teaspoon granulated gelatine in two teaspoons cold water five minutes. Set cup containing gelatine in small saucepan of boiling water and stir until gelatine has dissolved. Strain, cool and add gradually to one cup Mayonnaise Dressing. Spread cucumber boxes evenly with prepared Mayonnaise Dressing, and garnish with small rounds of red pepper and diamond-shaped pieces of truffle, arranged in regular fashion. Arrange in nests of crisp lettuce leaves.

Carlton Salad

Separate French Endive into pieces and clean; drain and chill. Cut cold cooked beets in one-quarter-inch slices and slices into rings and fancy shapes, using a French vegetable cutter. Arrange pieces of endive through beet rings. Arrange for individual service on crisp lettuce leaves, allowing two leaves, two bunches of endive in rings and five shapes for each portion.

Serve with Carlton Salad Dressing (see p. 217).

Nugget Salad

Wipe, peel and cut in halves small yellow tomatoes. Chill thoroughly, arrange on a bed of lettuce leaves,

Indian Salad.—*Page* 198

Spring Salad —*Page* 198.

pour over French Dressing and sprinkle with finely chopped parsley.

German Tomato Salad

Chill six small tomatoes of uniform size. Peel (which is best accomplished by scraping entire surface with the back of a vegetable knife, when skin may be easily removed) and cut in eighths, without severing sections. Open in such fashion as to represent the petals of a flower. In centre of each place a teaspoon of pearl onions. Serve with French Dressing.

Poinsettia Salad

Chill, cut and arrange tomatoes same as for German Tomato Salad. In centre of each put one tablespoon cream cheese, mashed, moistened with French Dressing, seasoned with salt and paprika and forced through a purée strainer. Serve with Martinique French Dressing.

Huntington Salad

Wipe, peel and chill medium-sized tomatoes, then cut in five vertical slices, crosswise, not severing sections. Mash a cream cheese, moisten with French Dressing, pack into a timbale mould and chill thoroughly. Remove from mould, cut in one-fourth-inch slices, crosswise, and fit slices between incisions in tomatoes. Serve in nests of crisp lettuce leaves with French Dressing.

Joplin Stuffed Tomato Salad

Wipe and skin six small tomatoes. Cut a piece from stem end of each, scrape out soft inside, sprinkle inside surface with salt, invert and let stand one-half hour. Mash one-half a cream cheese, and add six chopped pimolas, one tablespoon finely chopped parsley, one tablespoon tomato pulp, and one-fourth teaspoon dry mustard and moisten with French Dressing. Fill tomatoes with mixture, arrange in nests of crisp lettuce leaves and serve with Mayonnaise Dressing.

Indian Salad

Wipe and peel six medium-sized tomatoes. Scoop out centres, sprinkle inside with salt, invert and let stand until thoroughly chilled. Insert in each from six to eight short stalks of cold boiled asparagus. Put over asparagus, resting on rims of tomato, one-fourth-inch rings cut from a cold boiled beet. Over beet rings arrange one-fourth-inch rings cut from green pepper, and over green pepper rings, red pepper rings. Arrange for individual service on crisp lettuce leaves and serve with Indian Dressing.

Spring Salad

Cut four hard-boiled eggs in halves crosswise, remove yolks, and cut a thin slice from each end of whites, thus making cups that will stand upright. Mash yolks and moisten with cream salad

German Tomato Salad. — *Page* 197

Huntington Salad. — *Page* 197.

Celery Salad Bonne Femme. — *Page* 200

Flemish Beauty Salad. — *Page* 202.

dressing. Fill cups with one-half cup tiny cucumber cubes mixed with three tablespoons chopped sweet cucumber pickles, and moistened with cream salad dressing. Garnish top of each with yolk mixture, forced through a pastry bag and rose tube and garnish with diamond-shaped pieces of pickle. Arrange thick slices of tomato on lettuce leaves and on each slice of tomato place an egg cup. Garnish with watercress.

Porcupine Salad

Wipe and peel eight small tomatoes and stick with two-inch narrow strips of celery and green pepper at regular intervals, allowing seven of each to each tomato. Put a tablespoon Waltham Salad Dressing (see p. 216) on each serving plate, place tomato on dressing and sprinkle with finely chopped parsley, allowing one tablespoon to the eight tomatoes.

To be accompanied with dressed lettuce or may be served on lettuce leaves.

Heliofolis Salad

Wash, scrape and cut celery in thin slices crosswise; there should be one-half cup. Wipe, pare and cut an apple in eighths, lengthwise, then sections in thin slices, crosswise. Parboil a small green pepper in boiled salted water to cover eight minutes. Cut in halves, remove seeds and cut in Julienne-shaped pieces. Wipe and peel four tomatoes of uniform size and cut in sections. Marinate each separately and chill thoroughly. Arrange on a nest of crisp lettuce leaves and serve with Cream Mayonnaise.

Dixie Salad

Wash, drain, chill and arrange French endive in salad bowl and on endive arrange thin lengthwise slices cut from sections of pared apples, small tomatoes peeled and cut in quarters, whites of hard-boiled eggs, finely chopped, and yolks of hard-boiled eggs forced through a potato ricer or purée strainer. Serve with Cream Salad Dressing.

Celery Salad, Bonne Femme

Wash, scrape and cut celery in small pieces. Chill in cold or ice water, drain and dry on a towel. To celery add an equal measure of apples, pared, cored and cut in small pieces. Moisten with Denver Cream Dressing and arrange in a salad bowl made of a small solid white cabbage, placed on a bed of crisp lettuce leaves. Cut rim of bowl in points and insert sections of bright red apples and whole cloves as shown in the illustration.

Asparagus Salad I

Arrange one-half bunch of cooked asparagus, which has been thoroughly chilled, on a bed of crisp lettuce leaves, and arrange the following mixture to represent a band across the middle of bunch: To the white of one hard-boiled egg, finely chopped, add one

Asparagus Salad I.—*Page* 200

Easter Salad.—*Page* 201.

SALADS 201

tablespoon, each, pickle and pimiento, finely chopped, and one-half tablespoon finely chopped parsley. Pour over a dressing made of four tablespoons olive oil, two tablespoons lemon juice, one-half teaspoon salt and one-eighth teaspoon pepper.

Asparagus Salad II

Arrange cold cooked asparagus on a bed of crisp lettuce leaves and pour over Vinaigrette Sauce (see p. 159).

Allerton Salad

Wipe and pare a cucumber; cut in one-third-inch slices and slices in one-third-inch cubes. Add an equal measure of celery (cut in thin slices, crosswise), one-half the measure of English Walnut meats, broken in pieces, and one-third the measure of a red or green pepper, finely chopped. Moisten with Ruthven Salad Cream, mound on three-fourth-inch slices of peeled, chilled tomatoes, arrange in nests of lettuce leaves and sprinkle with finely cut chives.

Easter Salad

Put eggs in saucepan, cover with boiling water and let boil fifteen minutes. Remove shells and while hot hold between thumb and finger, while pressing into apple shapes keeping under a stream of cold water. Mix a bit of Fruit Red with cold water and apply to eggs, using a brush. Insert a clove to represent blossom end, and a stem and leaves to represent stem end (hot-house lilac leaves answer the purpose) and arrange on lettuce leaves.

Serve with Mayonnaise Piquante (see p. 214).

Flemish Beauty Salad

Cook eggs same as for Easter Salad and when still hot, press into pear shapes. Mix a bit of Fruit Green with cold water and put on pears, using a camel's hair brush. Insert cloves and stem and leaves same as in Easter Salad. Arrange on lettuce leaves and serve with Mayonnaise Piquante (see p. 214).

Romaine Salad

Separate one head romaine in quarters. Put sections on salad plates for individual service and arrange on each sections of grape fruit, oranges and pears, using two of each. Place at ends pickled walnuts. Serve with French Dressing.

Dinner Salad

Arrange for individual service alternate sections of orange and grape fruit on romaine, allowing six sections of fruit and two romaine leaves to each portion. Garnish between sections with thin strips of canned pimiento. Serve with French Dressing.

PARISIAN GRAPE FRUIT SALAD. — *Page* 203

TOURAINE GRAPE FRUIT SALAD. — *Page* 203

Cherry Nut Salad.—*Page* 205

Campestris Salad.—*Page* 206.

Peanut Salad

Shell, skin and chop one pint peanuts; there should be one-half cup. Add one cup celery, washed, scraped, cut in small pieces, chilled in ice water, drained and dried in a towel. Marinate with French Dressing. Wipe peppers, cut in halves lengthwise, and remove seeds. Arrange on a bed of lettuce leaves, fill with prepared mixture and garnish top of each with three thin slices of radish overlapping one another.

Parisian Grape Fruit Salad

Drain canned artichoke bottoms, marinate with French Dressing and let stand in ice box one hour. Peel grape fruit, remove pulp by sections and cut in halves, crosswise. Mould halves of sections dome-shaped on artichoke bottoms and arrange between each section a narrow strip of canned pimiento and garnish top with pimiento shaped with a French vegetable cutter. Arrange each on crisp lettuce leaves for individual service. Pour over Red Wine French Dressing.

Touraine Fruit Salad

Remove pulp from one grape fruit and one large orange. Wipe and remove skins from pears and scoop out balls, using a French vegetable cutter, having the same measure as of orange pulp. Drain juice from fruits and moisten with a Cream French Dressing (see p. 213).

Take a quart bowl and line with alternate sections of grape fruit and orange. Fill centre with prepared fruit and chill. Remove from bowl to salad dish, place a canned artichoke bottom (marinated with French Dressing) on top and garnish with small triangular pieces cut from thin slices of truffle and three or four small heart lettuce leaves.

Lakewood Salad

Cut one grape fruit and two oranges in sections and free from seed and membrane. Skin and seed white grapes; there should be three-fourths cup. Cut pecan nut meats in pieces; there should be one-third cup. Mix prepared ingredients, arrange on a bed of romaine, pour over dressing and garnish with thin strips of red pepper.

For the dressing mix four tablespoons olive oil, one tablespoon grape fruit juice, one-half tablespoon vinegar, one teaspoon salt, one-fourth teaspoon paprika, one-eighth teaspoon pepper and one tablespoon finely chopped Roquefort cheese.

Moquin Salad I

Seed and peel white grapes and stuff with strips of canned pimiento; there should be one cup. Separate tangerines into sections and free from skin and seeds; there should be one and one-fourth cups. Mash a ten cent cream cheese, add one-fourth cup chopped pecan nut meats and moisten with French Dressing;

SALADS 205

then make into balls about size of grapes. Arrange grapes, tangerines and cheese balls on lettuce leaves, and serve with French Dressing.

Strawberry Salad

Wash, hull and cut one pint selected strawberries in halves, lengthwise. Sprinkle with powdered sugar and add one teaspoon kirsch. Cover and let stand in ice box until thoroughly chilled. Arrange in eight nests of white lettuce leaves and cover fruit with one-half pint whipped cream (seasoned with salt and paprika) to which has been added one-half cup Mayonnaise Dressing. Garnish with halves of strawberries and chopped pistachio nut meats.

Rosalie Salad

Cook celery roots in boiling salted water to cover. Drain, chill and cut in thin slices. Drain halves of canned peaches and fill cavities with chopped Pistachio nut meats. Cut cold boiled beets in thin slices. Arrange prepared vegetables and fruit on a bed of escarole, and when thoroughly chilled, pour over French Dressing.

Cherry Nut Salad

Wipe fresh or drain canned cherries. Remove stones and fill cavities thus made with pecan nut meats. Arrange on a bed of crisp lettuce leaves and garnish with cherries, from which the stems have not been removed, if any are at hand. Serve with Cream Mayonnaise.

Rochester Salad

Remove pimientos from can, drain thoroughly and dry on a towel. Line timbale moulds with pimientos and pack solidly with the following mixture: Work a small cream cheese until smooth, add two tablespoons pecan nut meats, broken in pieces, and moisten with French Dressing. Chill thoroughly, remove from moulds and cut in one-third-inch slices crosswise. Arrange for individual service on crisp lettuce leaves, allowing three slices for each portion. Serve with California French Dressing.

Cheese and Apple Salad

Wipe and pare apples and shape with a French vegetable cutter, having twenty-four small balls; then marinate with French Dressing and let stand until chilled.

Mash a cream cheese and add one teaspoon, each, Worcestershire Sauce and salt, and one tablespoon chopped canned pimiento. Shape into twelve balls, same size as apple balls. Arrange on bed of lettuce leaves and garnish with strips of canned pimiento. Serve with French Dressing.

Campestris Salad

Mash a five cent Neufchâtel cheese, season with one-fourth teaspoon salt and one-eighth teaspoon

GRAPE FRUIT JELLY SALAD. — *Page* 207

BANANA SALAD. — *Page* 208.

Ginger Ale Salad. — *Page 209.*

Los Angeles Fruit Salad. — *Page 208*

paprika and moisten with one-half tablespoon French Dressing. Shape to represent mushroom caps and stems, roll in finely chopped salted almonds put through a purée strainer and put caps on stems. Place on thin unsweetened wafer crackers around a basket (made from the skin of an orange), filled with Red Bar-le-duc Currants, and garnish with sprigs of green. Pass with dressed lettuce.

Grape Fruit Jelly Salad

Mash a large cream cheese, moisten with heavy cream, and season highly with salt, pepper and onion juice. Pipe around a mould of Grape Fruit Jelly, sprinkle with chopped English walnut meats, and garnish with watercress. Serve with Huntington French Dressing, made by mixing one-half teaspoon salt, one-fourth teaspoon paprika, one tablespoon, each, vinegar and lemon juice, and four tablespoons olive oil. Stir until well blended.

Grape Fruit Jelly. — Put one-third cup sugar in small saucepan, pour over one-third cup water, bring to the boiling point and let boil three minutes. Remove from range, add one and one-half tablespoons granulated gelatine, soaked in two tablespoons cold water, one-half cup grape fruit juice, one tablespoon lemon juice and a few grains salt. Strain into a bowl.

Moquin Salad II

Drain slices of canned pineapple, cut in halves, crosswise, and arrange for individual service on lettuce leaves.

Work a cream cheese and moisten with French Dressing. Force through a potato ricer over pineapple. Serve with French Dressing.

The New Vanderbilt Salad

Arrange thin slices of fresh pineapple (cut crosswise of fruit with centre removed) on nests of lettuce leaves. Pile in centre celery cut in thin one and one-half inch Julienne-shaped pieces mixed with an equal measure of chopped English walnut meats. Garnish pineapple circle at equal distances with two sections, each, of grape fruit and orange. Serve with Cream Mayonnaise (see The Boston Cooking-School Cook Book, p. 327).

Banana Salad

Remove skins from bananas, scrape, using a silver knife, and cut in thirds crosswise; then cut each third in pieces lengthwise, and roll in finely chopped peanuts. Arrange with slices of tangerine on a bed of lettuce leaves and pour over French Dressing.

Los Angeles Fruit Salad

Cut marshmallows in thin strips; there should be one and three-fourths cups. Add one-half can

SALADS 209

sliced pineapple, drained and cut in small cubes, two and three-fourths cups Malaga grapes, skinned, seeded and cut in halves, one and one-half cups sections of oranges, one-half cup English walnut meats, cut in pieces, and a few grains salt.

Make cups of halves of orange peel, arrange on nests of lettuce leaves and fill with mixture. Cover with Cream Salad Dressing and garnish top of each with thin strips of canned pimiento, one-half grape, skinned and seeded, and finely chopped parsley.

Fruit and Ginger Ale Salad

Soak two tablespoons granulated gelatine in two tablespoons cold water and dissolve in one-third cup boiling water; then add one-fourth cup lemon juice, two tablespoons sugar, a few grains salt and one cup ginger ale. Let stand until mixture begins to set and fold in one-third cup Malaga grapes, skinned, seeded and cut in halves, one-third cup celery, cut in slices crosswise, one-third cup apple, cored, pared and cut in Julienne-shaped pieces, two tablespoons Canton ginger, cut in small pieces, and four tablespoons canned pineapple cut in small cubes.

Turn into a border mould, chill and remove to serving dish. Garnish with watercress and celery tips. In centre place small dish, fill with Cream Mayonnaise Dressing and garnish with curled celery.

Runnymede Salad

Wipe two long cucumbers, remove a thick slice from each end and cut crosswise in two-inch pieces.

Remove centres, leaving cups. Cut white meat of cold cooked chicken in thin slices, then in one-half-inch squares; there should be one-half cup. Mix with an equal measure, each, of cold boiled potatoes and artichoke bottoms, cut in the same fashion, and two tablespoons truffle, cut in small pieces. Moisten with Chutney Mayonnaise (see p. 214) and fill cups. Arrange on nests of lettuce leaves.

After Theatre Salad

Cook salt herring in boiling water to cover, fifteen minutes. Drain, cool and separate into flakes; there should be one cup. Add an equal measure of one-third-inch cubes of cold boiled potatoes and one-fourth the measure of finely chopped whites of hard-boiled eggs. Mix thoroughly, moisten with French Dressing, cover and let stand in a cold place one hour. Beat one-fourth cup heavy cream until stiff and add two tablespoons canned pimiento purée. Mix with an equal measure of Mayonnaise Dressing, moisten mixture with dressing and mound on a nest of lettuce leaves.

Potato and Egg Salad

Cut cold boiled potatoes in one-half-inch cubes; there should be one and one-half cups. Add one canned pimiento, drained and cut in thin strips, and two slices onion, finely chopped. Moisten with Waltham Salad Dressing (see p. 216), arrange in a mound and garnish with three hard-boiled eggs.

Chop whites and arrange on two-fourths of the mound opposite each other; force yolks through a potato ricer and arrange on other two-fourths. Put single sprigs of parsley in lines dividing whites from yolks. Garnish top with a slice of hard-boiled egg and parsley.

Shad Roe Salad

In each of six well-buttered cups or other individual moulds drop the white of an egg. Sprinkle with salt and pepper and in centre of each place a one-inch piece of cooked shad roe. Set moulds in pan of hot water and bake until white is set. Remove from moulds and marinate with French Dressing.

When thoroughly chilled, arrange in nests of lettuce leaves and garnish with Mayonnaise Dressing, forced through a pastry bag and tube, and thin strips of red pepper.

Mock Chicken Salad

> 2 cups ½-inch cubes roast pork
> 1 cup celery, cut in small pieces
> 4 stoned and chopped olives
> ½ red pepper

Mix pork cubes, celery and olives and add one-half of the pepper, which has been washed, parboiled and seeds removed, then cut in thin strips. Moisten with Mayonnaise or Waltham Salad Dressing. Mound in salad bowl and garnish with celery tips and remaining strips of red pepper.

CHAPTER XX

SALAD DRESSINGS

Martinique French Dressing

TO French Dressing (see The Boston Cooking-School Cook Book, p. 323) add one-half teaspoon finely chopped parsley and one-half tablespoon finely chopped green pepper.

Breslin French Dressing

To French Dressing add one-half tablespoon chopped pistachio nuts and one-fourth teaspoon finely chopped truffle.

Red Wine French Dressing

½ teaspoon salt
⅛ teaspoon paprika
2 tablespoons red wine vinegar
4 tablespoons olive oil

Mix ingredients in order given, and stir until well blended.

California French Dressing

4 tablespoons olive oil
2 tablespoons grape fruit juice
½ teaspoon powdered sugar
½ teaspoon salt
¼ teaspoon paprika

Mix ingredients in order given. Put in a glass jar, chill thoroughly and shake well before using.

Cream French Dressing

½ teaspoon salt
¼ teaspoon pepper
3 tablespoons heavy cream
2 tablespoons lemon juice
4 tablespoons olive oil

Mix ingredients and stir until well blended.

Tabasco French Dressing

4 tablespoons olive oil
2 tablespoons lemon juice
1 teaspoon powdered sugar
¼ teaspoon salt
⅛ teaspoon pepper
5 drops Tabasco Sauce

Mix ingredients in order given. Chill and shake vigorously before using.

Columbia French Dressing

1 teaspoon salt
1 teaspoon mustard
½ teaspoon onion juice
6 tablespoons olive oil
1 tablespoon Worcestershire Sauce
2 tablespoons lemon juice

Mix ingredients in a small glass jar, set in a cold place and shake thoroughly before using.

Chutney Dressing

½ teaspoon salt
¼ teaspoon paprika
1 tablespoon vinegar
1 tablespoon lemon juice
4 tablespoons olive oil
⅔ cup Col. Skinner's Chutney

Mix first five ingredients in order given, and when well blended add chutney. Serve on lettuce.

Chiffonade Dressing

2 tablespoons finely chopped parsley	2 hard-boiled eggs finely chopped
2 tablespoons finely chopped red pepper	1 teaspoon salt
	½ teaspoon black pepper
1 teaspoon finely chopped shallot	¼ teaspoon paprika
	5 tablespoons olive oil
2 tablespoons vinegar	

Mix ingredients in order given. Turn into jar or bottle, cover and let stand in ice box until very cold. Shake thoroughly before using as a dressing for lettuce or any salad green.

Mayonnaise Piquante

To one cup Mayonnaise Dressing add two tablespoons, each, olives and pickles, finely chopped.

Mayonnaise à la Connelly

To one cup Mayonnaise Dressing add one-half cup cold boiled rice.

Chutney Mayonnaise

To one cup Mayonnaise Dressing add one and one-half tablespoons chutney, and stir until thoroughly blended.

Denver Cream Salad Dressing

1 tablespoon mustard	2 tablespoons lemon juice
1 teaspoon salt	1 cup heavy cream

Mix mustard and salt and moisten with lemon juice; then add two tablespoons cream. Beat remaining cream until it begins to thicken, then add mixture gradually, while beating constantly, continuing the beating until mixture is stiff enough to hold its shape.

Horseradish Cream Dressing

½ cup heavy cream
3 tablespoons vinegar
¼ teaspoon salt
Few grains pepper
2 tablespoons grated horseradish root

Beat cream until it begins to thicken; then add gradually vinegar, while continuing the beating. When mixture is stiff, add seasonings and fold in grated horseradish.

Fruit Salad Dressing

2 eggs
3 tablespoons melted butter
3 tablespoons lemon juice
½ teaspoon salt
1 cup heavy cream
¼ cup powdered sugar
½ teaspoon celery salt
½ teaspoon vanilla
¼ teaspoon paprika
3 drops onion juice

Beat eggs until very light, and add gradually, while beating constantly, melted butter, lemon juice and salt. Cook over hot water, stirring constantly, until mixture thickens. Cool and add cream, beaten until stiff, and remaining ingredients.

Los Angeles Dressing

Yolks 4 eggs
¼ cup olive oil
1 tablespoon lemon juice
1½ tablespoons vinegar
1 teaspoon salt
1 teaspoon mustard
Few grains cayenne
1 cup heavy cream
1 teaspoon sugar
1½ tablespoons grated horseradish root

Beat yolks of eggs slightly and add oil, lemon juice, vinegar, salt, mustard and cayenne. Cook in double boiler, stirring constantly, until mixture thickens. Chill and add cream, beaten until stiff, sugar and horseradish.

Cream Salad Dressing

¼ teaspoon mustard	2 eggs
⅛ teaspoon salt	2 tablespoons lemon juice
⅛ teaspoon paprika	⅓ cup milk
½ pint heavy cream	

Mix mustard, salt and paprika, and when thoroughly blended, add eggs, slightly beaten, lemon juice and milk. Cook in double boiler, stirring constantly, until mixture thickens. Cool and add cream, beaten until stiff.

Ruthven Salad Cream

½ tablespoon salt	2 eggs yolks
½ tablespoon mustard	3 tablespoons melted butter
¾ tablespoon sugar	¾ cup milk
1 tablespoon flour	¼ cup vinegar

Mix dry ingredients, and when thoroughly blended, add egg yolks, slightly beaten, melted butter, milk and vinegar. Cook in double boiler, stirring constantly, until mixture thickens. Strain and cool.

Waltham Salad Dressing

1 cup sour cream	2 teaspoons salt
1 egg	2 teaspoons sugar
¼ cup vinegar	1 teaspoon mustard
⅛ teaspoon pepper	

To cream add egg, slightly beaten, vinegar and remaining ingredients, thoroughly mixed. Cook in double boiler, stirring constantly, until mixture thickens.

Ohio Salad Dressing

1 tablespoon powdered sugar	1 tablespoon olive oil
2 teaspoons Worcestershire Sauce	½ teaspoon salt
	¼ teaspoon mustard
2 teaspoons Tomato Catsup	Few grains cayenne
1½ tablespoons vinegar	3 drops Tabasco Sauce
1½ tablespoons lemon juice	

Mix ingredients and stir until well blended.

Indian Salad Dressing

Yolks 2 hard-boiled eggs	½ cup olive oil
¾ teaspoon salt	1 tablespoon red pepper, finely chopped
½ teaspoon powdered sugar	
¼ teaspoon paprika	1 tablespoon green pepper, finely chopped
Few grains cayenne	
Few grains white pepper	1 tablespoon pickled beets, cut in small cubes
1 tablespoon lemon juice	
2 tablespoons vinegar	1 teaspoon finely chopped parsley

Force egg yolks through a strainer and add salt, sugar, paprika, cayenne, white pepper, lemon juice, vinegar and olive oil. Shake thoroughly and add remaining ingredients.

Carlton Salad Dressing

¾ cup Mayonnaise Dressing	1½ teaspoons powdered sugar
	¼ teaspoon Worcestershire Sauce
2 tablespoons tomato purée	
½ tablespoon lemon juice	½ teaspoon A. I. Sauce

Mix ingredients in order given.

To obtain tomato purée drain one-half can tomatoes, put in saucepan, bring to the boiling point and let simmer until reduced one-half. Force through a fine strainer, return to saucepan and let simmer (having an asbestos cover under saucepan) until thick in consistency.

Astoria Salad Dressing

¼ cup Mayonnaise Dressing
¼ cup French Dressing
2 tablespoons Tomato Catsup
½ tablespoon finely chopped green pepper
3 drops Tabasco Sauce

Add French Dressing slowly to Mayonnaise Dressing, stirring constantly; then add remaining ingredients.

CHAPTER XXI

ENTRÉES

Pear Condé

Put one-half teaspoon salt and one cup boiling water in double boiler, place on range, and add, gradually, one-half cup well-washed rice, stirring with a fork to prevent adhering to boiler. Boil five minutes, cover, place over under part of boiler and steam until kernels have absorbed water. Then add one and one-half cups milk and continue the steaming until kernels are soft. Add three tablespoons sugar and the yolks of three eggs, slightly beaten. Mound on a flat dish in conical shape and place on rice halves of preserved pears, cooked in their own syrup, to which one-third cup sugar has been added, until soft. Sprinkle all with finely chopped Canton ginger.

Peach Compote, Peach Sauce

2 cups milk	Whites 2 eggs
½ cup farina	6 peaches
¼ cup sugar	3 tablespoons water
½ teaspoon salt	6 tablespoons sugar

Scald milk and add farina gradually, while stirring constantly. When mixture thickens, add sugar and salt and cook in double boiler twenty minutes;

then add whites of eggs, beaten until stiff. Turn into a slightly buttered shallow pan and keep in a warm place until serving time. Remove skin from peaches, put in saucepan and add water and sugar; cover and cook slowly until fruit is soft. Cut farina in squares, put a peach on each square and pour over all:

Peach Sauce. — Dilute one-half tablespoon cornstarch with one tablespoon cold water. Add to syrup remaining in saucepan, bring to the boiling point and let boil two minutes; then pour slowly, while stirring constantly, over the yolks of two eggs, beaten until thick and lemon-colored. Add two teaspoons lemon juice and a few grains salt.

Cheese and Pepper Croquettes

Wipe small Bell peppers, place in pan, put in hot oven and turn occasionally, until skins blister. Take from oven, remove skins, make a lengthwise slit in each and take out seeds. Fill with Cheese Filling, dip in crumbs, egg and crumbs, fry in deep fat and drain on brown paper.

Cheese Filling. — Melt one and one-half tablespoons butter, add two tablespoons flour and stir until well blended; then add one-third cup milk and bring to the boiling point. Add one-fourth cup grated Gruyère cheese and one egg, slightly beaten. As soon as cheese melts remove from fire and fold in one-half cup small cubes of soft mild cheese. Season with one-half teaspoon salt and a few grains, each, of pepper and cayenne.

Scallops en Brochette. — *Page* 223.

Cutlets of Ham Alexandria. — *Page* 234

CHICKEN À LA KING. — *Page 228.*

CHICKEN AND MUSHROOM TIMBALES. — *Page 230*

Cheese Custard Timbales, Bread Sauce

4 eggs	3 tablespoons grated cheese
¾ cup cold water	½ teaspoon salt
⅛ cup heavy cream	⅛ teaspoon pepper
2½ tablespoons melted butter	Few grains cayenne
	Few drops onion juice

Beat eggs slightly and add remaining ingredients. Strain into buttered individual moulds, set in pan of hot water and bake until firm. Remove to hot serving dish, pour around Bread Sauce (see p. 155) and garnish with parsley.

Eggs en Surprise

Cut stale bread in two-inch slices and then in circular or elliptical shapes. Remove centres, leaving cases. Fry in deep fat until delicately browned and drain on brown paper. Half fill cases thus made with Creamed Asparagus tips. French poach six eggs, coat with egg (slightly beaten and diluted with one tablespoon cold water), roll in bread crumbs to which has been added Parmesan cheese (allowing two tablespoons cheese to three-fourths cup crumbs) and fry one minute in very hot deep fat. Drain and arrange in croustades. Garnish with parsley.

Chaudfroid Eggs Alexandria

French poach six eggs, trim into shape and let cool. Melt one tablespoon butter, add one tablespoon flour and stir until well blended; then pour on gradually, while stirring constantly, one cup chicken stock. Bring to the boiling point and add one-fourth teaspoon salt, one-eighth teaspoon pepper, a few grains cayenne and one tablespoon granulated gelatine. Coat eggs with sauce and when sauce has become firm, place each egg in a puff paste case made of correct size. Garnish with thin slices of truffle cut in fancy shapes, and around each pipe a border of caviare butter.

Stuffed Mushroom Caps

Wipe, peel and remove centres from six large mushroom caps. Cook two tablespoons, each, chopped mushrooms, bread crumbs, chopped, lean, cooked ham and finely chopped onion, and one teaspoon, each, Parmesan cheese and finely chopped parsley with three tablespoons butter, three minutes. Moisten with one-fourth cup tomato sauce and season with salt, pepper and cayenne. Stuff prepared caps with mixture and sprinkle with one-third cup bread crumbs mixed with one and one-half tablespoons Parmesan cheese. Arrange in pan, surround with three-fourths cup tomato sauce and bake in a hot oven twenty minutes. Remove to six rounds of sautéd bread, cut somewhat larger than caps, and pour around sauce remaining in pan. Garnish with parsley.

Shrimps, Louisiana Style

2 tablespoons butter
1 teaspoon chopped onion
⅔ cup canned shrimps
⅔ cup hot boiled rice
⅜ cup heavy cream
½ teaspoon salt
¼ teaspoon celery salt
Few grains cayenne
3 tablespoons tomato sauce

Cook butter with onion five minutes, stirring constantly. Add shrimps, broken in pieces, rice and heavy cream. When thoroughly heated, add salt, celery salt, cayenne and tomato sauce. Turn on a hot serving dish and garnish with puff paste crescents and parsley.

Scallops en Brochette

Clean scallops, put in saucepan and cook until they begin to shrivel. Drain and dry on a towel. Alternate scallops and pieces of thinly sliced bacon on skewers, allowing four scallops and five pieces bacon to each skewer. Balance skewers in upright position by putting through cubes of bread placed on rack in dripping pan and bake in a hot oven until bacon is crisp. Arrange on serving dish and garnish with lemon and parsley.

Scallops à la Newburg

1 pint scallops	1 teaspoon lemon juice
3 tablespoons butter	1 teaspoon flour
½ teaspoon salt	½ cup thin cream
Few grains cayenne	2 egg yolks
2 tablespoons Sherry wine	

Put scallops in omelet pan and cook until they begin to shrivel; drain thoroughly, cut in halves, and cook in two tablespoons butter three minutes. Add salt, cayenne and lemon juice and cook one minute.

Melt remaining butter, add flour and stir until

blended; then pour on gradually, while stirring constantly, cream. Bring to the boiling point and add egg yolks, slightly beaten, scallops and wine.

Oyster and Shrimp Newburg

1 pint oysters	2 egg yolks
1 can shrimps	½ teaspoon salt
¼ cup Sherry	Nutmeg
¼ cup butter	Paprika ⎫ few grains each
1½ tablespoons flour	Cayenne ⎭
1 cup cream	2 tablespoons brandy

Wash and parboil oysters and drain from their liquor. Clean and break shrimps in small pieces. Mix oysters and shrimps, add wine, cover and let stand one hour. Put in blazer, add butter and cook five minutes. Sprinkle with flour and cook two minutes. Add three-fourths cup cream and when mixture has thickened, add egg yolks, slightly beaten and diluted with remaining cream; then add seasonings and serve on toast or in puff paste shells.

Oyster Crabs, Béarnaise

Wash and pick over one pint oyster crabs. Put in saucepan, place on range, and add one-half cup Sherry wine, one tablespoon butter, one-half teaspoon salt and one-fourth teaspoon paprika. Light Sherry and let burn two minutes. Turn on serving dish, pour over Béarnaise Sauce II (see p. 158) and garnish with puff paste points.

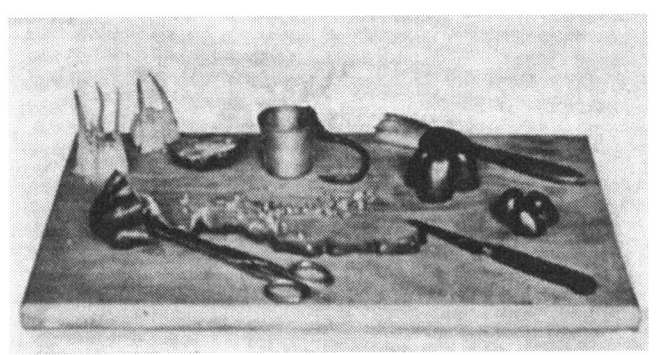

LINING OF MOULD FOR TRAYMORE TIMBALES.—*Page* 231

TRAYMORE TIMBALES.—*Page* 231.

LOBSTER BOATS. — *Page 225*.

CRAB AND MUSHROOM VOL-AU-VENT. — *Page 233*

Hampden Halibut en Coquilles

½ cup cold flaked halibut	½ teaspoon salt
3 tablespoons butter	⅛ teaspoon paprika
1½ tablespoons flour	Few grains cayenne
1½ tablespoons cornstarch	⅛ cup canned mushrooms
⅛ cup fish stock	Whites 2 eggs
⅛ cup mushroom liquor	¼ cup grated cheese
⅛ cup cream	⅛ teaspoon paprika
Yolks 2 eggs	Few grains salt

Melt butter, add flour and stir until well blended; then pour on gradually, while stirring constantly, fish stock, mushroom liquor and cream. Bring to the boiling point and add egg yolks, slightly beaten, salt, pepper and paprika; then add flaked fish and mushrooms cut in thin slices. Fill buttered shells with mixture, cover with whites of eggs, beaten until stiff, mixed with cheese and seasoned with paprika and salt. Sprinkle with more cheese and bake until well browned.

Lobster Boats

2 tablespoons butter	Few grains soda
1 tablespoon chopped onion	Salt
⅔ cup hot boiled rice	Celery salt
1¼ cups lobster dice	Cayenne
¼ cup Tomato Sauce	½ cup heavy cream

Cook butter with onion five minutes, stirring constantly. Add lobster, rice and cream. When heated, add Tomato Sauce (to which soda has been added) and season highly with salt, celery salt and cayenne.

Fill pastry boats with mixture, garnish with tail pieces and tips of lobster claws and pour around Tomato Sauce. Insert sails made of rice paper and small wooden skewers, covering skewers with thin white cardboard (which will keep in place if simply folded over).

Éclairs of Chicken Mayonnaise

¼ cup butter	2 eggs
½ cup boiling water	1 cup cold cooked chicken,
½ cup flour	cut in small cubes
⅓ cup Mayonnaise Dressing	

Put butter and water in saucepan and place on range; when boiling point is reached, add flour (all at once) and stir until mixture is well blended and leaves sides of pan. Remove from fire and add eggs, one at a time, beating vigorously between the additions. Shape on a buttered sheet, three and one-half inches long by one and one-half inches wide, and bake in a moderate oven twenty-five minutes. Cool, split and fill with chicken mixed with mayonnaise.

Chicken Croquettes, Macedoine

3 tablespoons butter	Yolks 3 eggs
1 shallot, finely chopped	1 cup cold cooked chicken,
¼ cup flour	cut in dice
1 teaspoon salt	½ cup boiled ham, cut in
¼ teaspoon paprika	dice
⅛ teaspoon pepper	¼ cup mushrooms, cut in
Few gratings nutmeg	small pieces
1 cup chicken stock	1 tablespoon Madeira wine

Melt butter, add shallot and cook three minutes, stirring constantly. Add flour, mixed with seasonings, and stir until well blended; then pour on gradually, while stirring constantly, chicken stock. Bring to the boiling point, and add remaining ingredients, except wine, and cook five minutes. Add wine and spread on a plate to cool. Shape, roll in flour, eggs and crumbs, fry in deep fat and drain on brown paper. Mound in centre of heated flat dish and surround with hot seasoned vegetables, including peas, small carrot cubes, and cauliflower flowerets. Garnish with parsley.

Macedoine Loaf

½ tablespoon butter
½ tablespoon flour
½ cup milk
½ cup bread crumbs
Yolks 2 eggs
1 cup cooked macaroni
½ cup cold cooked chicken
½ cup mushroom caps
1 tablespoon canned pimiento
½ cup heavy cream
1½ teaspoons salt
1 teaspoon parsley, finely chopped
Whites 2 eggs

Melt butter, add flour and stir until well blended; then pour on gradually, while stirring constantly, milk. Bring to the boiling point and add bread crumbs, egg yolks, beaten until thick and lemon-colored, macaroni cut in one-half-inch pieces, chicken and mushroom caps, cut in strips, pimiento, cut in small pieces, cream, beaten until stiff, salt and parsley. Stir until thoroughly mixed and fold in whites of eggs, beaten until stiff. Turn into a mould lined with buttered paper, cover with buttered paper and bake until firm. Remove from mould to hot serving dish and garnish with parsley. Serve with tomato or white sauce, to which sautéd sliced mushroom caps have been added.

Chicken à la King

1½ tablespoons chicken fat	1 cup cold boiled fowl, cut in strips
1 tablespoon cornstarch	
½ cup chicken stock	½ cup sautéd sliced mushroom caps
½ cup milk	
¼ cup cream	¼ cup canned pimientoes, cut in strips
½ teaspoon salt	
2 tablespoons butter	Yolk 1 egg

Melt chicken fat, add cornstarch and stir until well blended; then pour on gradually, while stirring constantly, stock, milk and cream. Bring to the boiling point and add salt, butter bit by bit, fowl, mushroom caps and pimientoes. Again bring to the boiling point and add egg yolk, slightly beaten.

Chop Suey

Remove the breast meat from an uncooked chicken and cut in strips one inch long. Melt one tablespoon butter, add chicken meat and cook two minutes; then add three-fourths cup celery, cut in thin slices crosswise, one onion, peeled and sliced, and six mushroom caps cut in slices. Cook five minutes and add one cup chicken stock, one-half teaspoon sugar, two teaspoons Shoyu Sauce, one-half green

Sweetbreads à la Root. — *Page* 128

Sweetbreads Monroe. — *Page* 129.

PEAR CONDÉ, COMPOTE OF RICE. — *Page* 219

WALDORF SWEETBREADS. — *Page* 130.

ENTRÉES

pepper (from which seeds have been removed), cut in thin strips, and one teaspoon cornstarch, diluted with two tablespoons cold water. Bring to the boiling point and let simmer three minutes.

Veal Timbales

1½ cups cold cooked veal	Few grains paprika
Yolks 3 eggs	Whites 3 eggs
½ cup heavy cream	1 cup white sauce
⅛ cup white wine	1½ tablespoons
½ teaspoon salt	chopped truffle

Force remnants of veal through a meat chopper; repeat. Pound in a mortar, adding gradually the yolks of eggs, slightly beaten; then add cream, wine, seasonings, and cut and fold in whites of eggs beaten until stiff.

Butter individual timbale moulds and fill one-fourth full of white sauce, to which truffles have been added; then fill with chicken mixture. Set moulds in pan of hot water, cover with buttered paper and bake until firm. Remove from moulds to hot serving dish, when sauce will run down sides of timbales. For the white sauce melt three tablespoons butter, add three tablespoons flour and pour on gradually, while stirring constantly, one cup milk. Bring to the boiling point and season with one-fourth teaspoon salt and a few grains pepper.

Chicken Réchauffé

Make same as Veal Timbales, using chicken in place of veal, chicken stock in place of white wine, and chopped red or green pepper in place of truffles.

Chicken and Mushroom Timbales

Garnish bottom of buttered timbale moulds with thin slices of truffle, cut in fancy shapes. Line moulds with Chicken Forcemeat II (see The Boston Cooking-School Cook Book, p. 150). Fill centres with creamed mushrooms and cover with forcemeat. Set in pan of hot water, cover with buttered paper and bake until firm. Remove to serving dish, pour around one cup cream sauce, to which has been added one tablespoon Madeira wine, and garnish with sprigs of parsley.

Chicken and Liver Timbales

1 cup chopped cooked chicken	1 teaspoon salt
½ cup chopped cooked chicken livers	¼ teaspoon paprika
	⅛ teaspoon salt
Yolks 3 eggs	½ cup heavy cream
3 tablespoons white wine	Whites 3 eggs

Mix chicken and livers and pound in a mortar, adding gradually yolks of eggs slightly beaten, and white wine. When thoroughly blended, add seasonings, heavy cream, beaten until stiff, and whites of eggs, beaten until stiff. Turn into buttered timbale moulds, set in pan of hot water, cover with buttered paper and bake until firm.

Remove from moulds and arrange around Creamed Mushrooms (see p. 170) to which has been added one tablespoon Sherry wine.

Ham Timbales

1 cup stale bread crumbs	½ teaspoon salt
1 cup milk	⅛ teaspoon pepper
4 tablespoons butter	Whites 2 eggs
1 cup chopped cooked ham	2 hard-boiled eggs

Cook bread crumbs and milk until of the consistency of a smooth paste. Add butter, ham, salt and pepper; then cut and fold in whites of eggs, beaten until stiff. Fill buttered individual moulds two-thirds full of mixture. Set in pan of hot water, cover with buttered paper and bake in a moderate oven until firm, the time required being about twenty minutes. Turn on a hot serving dish and garnish with slices of hard-boiled eggs and sprigs of parsley.

Traymore Timbales

Cut a slice from the stem end of parboiled green peppers and remove seeds; then cut in thin strips, by working around and around the pepper, using the scissors. Line the sides of buttered timbale moulds with the pepper, by coiling it around and around, and fill with the following mixture: Peel and chop mushroom caps; there should be one-fourth cup. Add one tablespoon butter and one tablespoon flour, and stir until well blended; then pour on gradually one-fourth cup cream. Bring to the boiling point, beat in the yolks of two eggs, one at a time, and fold in the whites of two eggs, beaten until stiff. Season with one-half teaspoon salt, one-eighth teaspoon pepper and a few grains paprika.

Place timbales in pan of hot water, cover with buttered paper and bake until firm. Remove to serving dish on circular pieces of sautéd bread, garnish top of each with a sautéd mushroom cap and pour around

Traymore Sauce. — Melt two tablespoons butter, add two tablespoons flour and stir until well blended; then pour on gradually, while stirring constantly, one-half cup, each, chicken stock and cream. Bring to the boiling point and add one-half teaspoon beef extract, one-half teaspoon salt and a few grains pepper.

Salmon Mayonnaise

3 slices salmon	1 sprig parsley
Cold water	1 teaspoon salt
½ bay leaf	¼ teaspoon pepper
2 cloves	¼ cup vinegar
2 slices lemon	¼ cup white wine
1 small sliced onion	1 cup Mayonnaise Dressing
6 slices carrot	1 teaspoon granulated gelatine
½ tablespoon cold water	

Wipe salmon cut in two-inch slices (each weighing two-thirds pound), put in a pan, cover with cold water and add seasonings. Let stand two or three hours; then cook slowly on top of range until fish is tender. Take from pan, remove skin and bones, and press, using the hands, to keep in shape. Cool and cover with one cup Mayonnaise Dressing, to which has been added one-half teaspoon granulated gelatine soaked in one teaspoon cold water.

ENTRÉES 233

Garnish with thin slices of truffle, cut in fancy shapes.

English Patties

1 cup cold cooked chicken, cut in ¼ inch cubes
6 mushroom caps
½ truffle
2 tablespoons butter
2 tablespoons flour
1 cup chicken stock
½ teaspoon salt
⅛ teaspoon cayenne
⅛ teaspoon grated nutmeg
1 tablespoon Sherry wine
1 egg
1 tablespoon cream

To chicken add mushroom caps, peeled and cut in cubes, truffle, cut in small pieces, and butter. Cook five minutes, stirring almost constantly; then add flour and when well blended, pour on chicken stock and let simmer ten minutes. Season with salt, cayenne, nutmeg and Sherry. Beat egg slightly, dilute with cream and add. When thoroughly heated, fill six patty cases with mixture, arrange on serving dish and garnish with parsley.

Crab and Mushroom Vol-au-Vent

Melt three tablespoons butter, add three tablespoons flour and stir until well blended; then pour on gradually, while stirring constantly, one cup chicken stock and one-half cup cream. Bring to the boiling point and add one and one-half cups crab meat and the caps from one-half pound mushrooms, cut in strips and sautéd in butter. As soon as thoroughly heated, add one-half cup grated Parmesan cheese, three tablespoons Sherry wine, one-half teaspoon salt and one-eighth teaspoon, each, pepper and paprika. Fill vol-au-vent with mixture. Adjust cover and garnish with sprigs of parsley.

Ham Mousse, Epicurean Sauce

1 tablespoon granulated gelatine	1 teaspoon mixed mustard
	Few grains cayenne
½ cup hot water	½ cup heavy cream
2 cups chopped, cold boiled ham	

Dissolve gelatine in hot water and add to ham, which has been pounded in a mortar. Season with mustard and cayenne, add cream beaten until stiff, and turn into a mould, first dipped in cold water. Chill, remove from mould, garnish with parsley and serve with Epicurean Sauce (see p. 156).

Cutlets of Ham, Alexandria

½ pound lean raw ham	½ cup heavy cream
4 eggs whites	Few gratings nutmeg
⅛ teaspoon pepper	Allemande Sauce
Asparagus tips	

Finely chop ham, add the unbeaten egg whites and mix to a smooth paste. Rub through a sieve, add seasonings and cream a little at a time. Fill slightly buttered cutlet moulds, set in pan, surround with hot water, cover with buttered paper and bake until firm. Remove to hot serving dish, coat with Allemande Sauce and garnish with buttered hot asparagus tips and parsley.

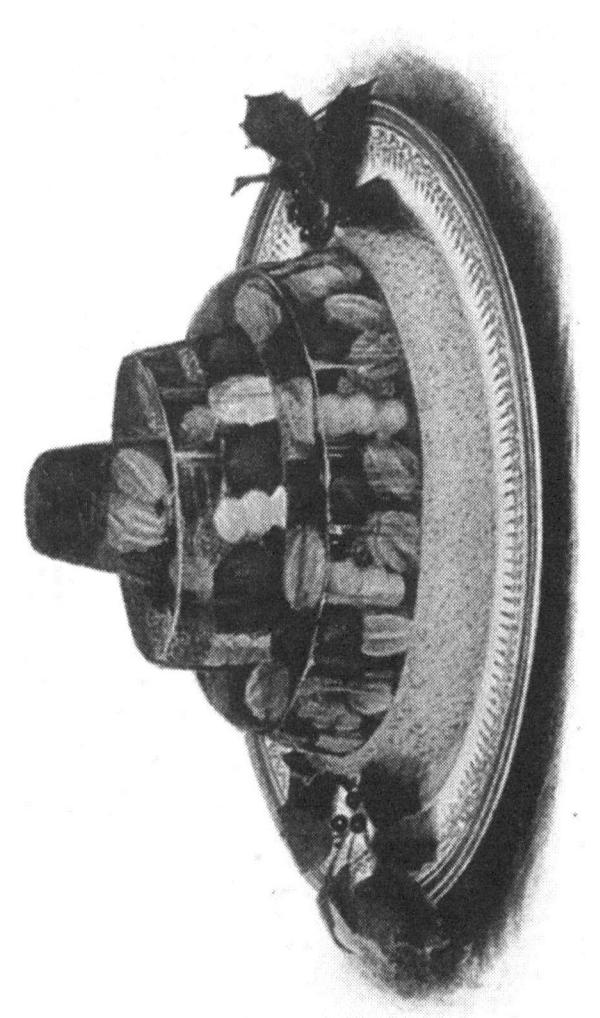

MACEDOINE IN ASPIC.—*Page* 239

Shrimp Patties

1½ tablespoons butter	¼ teaspoon paprika
1½ tablespoons flour	Few gratings nutmeg
¾ cup cream	1 cup shrimps
¼ teaspoon salt	¼ cup walnut meats
¼ teaspoon celery salt	½ teaspoon Orange Curaçoa

Melt butter, add flour and stir until well blended; then add cream gradually while stirring constantly. Bring to boiling point and add salt, celery salt, paprika, nutmeg and shrimps, cut in halves. Again bring to boiling point and add walnut meats, broken in pieces, and orange curaçoa. Reheat patty shells and fill with mixture.

Epicurean Bouchées

⅛ pound mushroom caps	¼ teaspoon paprika
1 dozen frogs' legs	½ cup Sherry wine
½ pound crab meat	1⅛ cups cream
2 tablespoons melted butter	1 tablespoon cornstarch
2 teaspoons salt	1 tablespoon cold water
Yolk 1 egg	

Clean and peel mushroom caps, cut in one-fourth-inch strips crosswise, and sauté in butter three minutes. Clean and steam frogs' legs until tender, then add crab meat, butter, salt, paprika and Sherry wine. Cover and let stand thirty minutes. Put on range and cook five minutes. Pour off one-half wine and add mushrooms. Scald cream in double boiler; dilute cornstarch with cold water, add gradually to scalded cream and cook ten minutes, stirring constantly until mixture thickens and afterwards occasionally; then add yolk of egg, slightly beaten.

Add to first mixture, reheat and season highly with salt and cayenne. Fill bouchée cases with mixture or serve with puff paste points.

Sweetbread and Mushroom Patties

Parboil one sweetbread, cool and cut in one-fourth-inch pieces. Clean and peel ten large mushrooms and cut in pieces. Put in a small pan and add one tablespoon butter, one teaspoon lemon juice, one-fourth teaspoon salt and a few grains pepper. Cover and cook fifteen minutes, stirring occasionally. Melt two tablespoons butter, add four tablespoons flour and stir until well blended; then pour on gradually, while stirring constantly, one cup chicken or brown stock. Bring to the boiling point, add sweetbreads, mushrooms and one tablespoon heavy cream. Again bring to the boiling point and season with one-half teaspoon salt and a few grains, each, pepper and paprika. Line patty-pans with puff paste, fill with mixture, cover with pastry tops, brush over with white of egg, slightly beaten, and bake in a moderate oven twenty-five minutes. Serve at once.

Huntington Sweetbreads

Parboil one pair sweetbreads, cool, trim and lard upper surface. Clean and peel twelve mushroom caps and cook in two tablespoons butter two minutes. Add one-fourth cup Sherry wine and cook five minutes.

Wash one-half cup butter, put in a mortar with

ENTRÉES 237

three tablespoons mashed, boiled sweet potatoes, one-half teaspoon finely cut chives, and one shallot and one clove garlic, each, finely chopped. Work until thoroughly blended; then rub through a sieve. Season with salt and paprika. Cut bread in one-third-inch slices, cut in rounds, toast on one side and spread untoasted sides with prepared butter. Put in four individual baking dishes, over each put a piece of sweetbread, over sweetbread arrange mushroom caps and spread with remaining butter. Pour around heavy cream, allowing two tablespoons to each portion. Put on glass covers and bake in a moderate oven eight minutes.

Glazed Sweetbread Lucullus

Trim sweetbread and parboil in Sherry wine until plump, the time required being about one-half hour. Keep covered during the cooking, turning twice. Cool and cut in pieces. Put one and one-half tablespoons butter in frying pan, and when melted add one-half teaspoon beef extract. Cook sweetbread in mixture until glazed, turning frequently. Drain canned artichoke bottoms and reheat; then arrange on circular pieces of sautéd bread. Place pieces of sweetbread on each and pour around Lucullus Sauce made by adding one cup chopped sautéd mushrooms to one cup tomato sauce.

Macedoine in Aspic

Put three cans tomatoes (quart capacity) in stewpan and bring to the boiling point. Turn into a purée strainer and force through most of the pulp. Add one and one-half teaspoons onion juice, one and one-half tablespoons salt, one-half cup Sherry wine and a few grains cayenne. Soak two packages granulated gelatine in one cup cold water and add to mixture when cool. Clear, using the white and shell of three eggs; then strain through four thicknesses of cheese-cloth, placed over a fine strainer, and add one-third cup Sherry wine. Cut cold boiled corned tongue in one-inch strips; there should be one and one-third cups. Peel sixteen small tomatoes, by rubbing over the entire surface with the dull edge of a knife, until skins may be easily taken off. Finely chop the breast meat of a raw chicken and force through a meat chopper; there should be three-fourths cup. Pound in a mortar and add gradually whites two eggs and one-half pint heavy cream. Season highly with salt and cayenne and a slight grating of nutmeg; then force through a fine strainer. Shape mixture with a pastry bag and tube on buttered paper, making quenelles. Invert paper into a kettle of boiling salted water (when forms will slip off at once) and cook five minutes. Remove with skimmer and drain on cheese-cloth. Turn an elliptical mound two inches high of cold cooked hominy on a serving dish and spread sides with parsley butter.

Fill an elliptical-shaped border mould with tongue, tomatoes, chicken quenelles and aspic. Fill a charlotte russe mould that will just fit into border mould

MOULDED FISH IN ASPIC. — *Page* 239

DRESSED CUCUMBER. — *Page* 195.

PREPARATION OF STUFFED SMOKED TONGUE. — *Page* 241

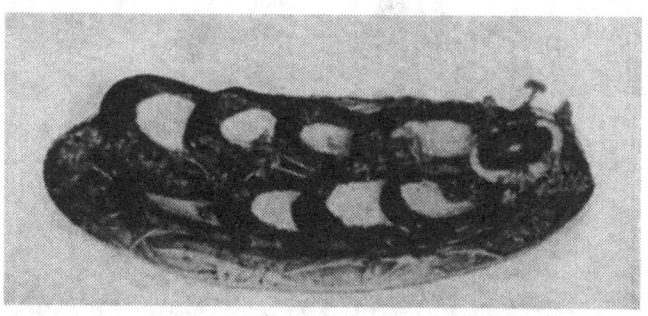

SLICED STUFFED SMOKED TONGUE. — *Page* 241.

after same fashion. Fill a muffin tin in same fashion. When thoroughly chilled, turn contents of border mould on hominy, fill space with thick shaped slice of bread, put contents of charlotte russe mould on top and surround with contents of muffin tin. Garnish with spray of holly and serve with Mayonnaise à la Connelly (see p. 214).

If insides of moulds are rubbed very sparingly with olive oil, there will be no trouble in removing the contents.

Moulded Fish in Aspic

Wipe a slice of halibut, remove skin and bones and force fish through a meat chopper; there should be three-fourths pound. Melt three-fourths tablespoon butter, add one tablespoon flour and stir until well blended; then pour on gradually, while stirring constantly, one-third cup fish stock. Bring to the boiling point, add fish and pound in a mortar until thoroughly blended. Add two whole eggs and three egg yolks, two teaspoons salt and one-fourth teaspoon pepper. When well mixed, add one-half cup heavy cream. Garnish a buttered fish mould with truffle, cut in slices, then in strips to represent tail and fins, and small crescent shapes to represent scales. During the process of garnishing, the pieces of truffle, after being placed, should be frequently sprinkled with some of the liquid drained from truffles, otherwise they will become dry and curl. It is desirable after a portion is completed to cover it with a piece of cheese-cloth, wrung out of cold water, for the same reason.

Fill moulds with fish forcemeat, set in pan of hot water, cover with buttered paper and bake until fish is firm to the touch. Remove from mould, cool and put in a mould of aspic. Chill and remove from mould to serving dish. Garnish with watercress and cucumber ribbons.

Fish Aspic. — To two and one-half quarts cold water add two pounds halibut (cut from nape), wiped and cut in small pieces. Add liquor drained from one quart canned tomatoes, one onion stuck with three cloves, three-fourths teaspoon peppercorns, one-eighth teaspoon celery salt, two allspice berries and one-fourth cup white wine. Cover, bring slowly to the boiling point and let simmer two hours. Strain, cool and add three-fourths tablespoon salt, one-fourth teaspoon pepper and two tablespoons lemon juice. Soak eight tablespoons granulated gelatine in one-fourth cup cold water, add to stock and clear. To each quart of cleared stock add three tablespoons white wine and two teaspoons tarragon vinegar.

Lobster in Aspic

Wipe and cut one pound halibut (cut from nape) in small pieces. Put in stewpan, add body bones and meat contained therein of two one-and-one-half-pound lobsters, three pints cold water, bring gradually to the boiling point and let simmer one and one-half hours. Strain; there should be one quart fish stock. Cook two tablespoons, each, chopped carrot, onion, and celery, two sprigs parsley, bit of bay leaf and one and one-half teaspoons peppercorns with one cup white wine eight minutes. Strain, add to fish stock and season with salt, cayenne and lemon juice. Cool and add one box granulated gelatine (which has been soaked in one-fourth cup cold water thirty minutes) and whites two eggs. Put on range and stir constantly until boiling point is reached. Remove to back of range and let simmer ten minutes. Strain through several thicknesses of cheese-cloth, placed over a fine wire strainer.

Remove meat from lobsters, cut in pieces, and marinate with a French Dressing, substituting lemon juice for vinegar. Place individual moulds in pan of ice water, cover bottoms with jelly mixture and when firm garnish with tough claw meat of lobster, and truffle, cut in fancy shapes. Cover with jelly mixture and when firm, fill with lobster meat, mixed with some of the jelly mixture, just as it is ready to set. Chill thoroughly, remove from moulds, place on lettuce leaves and serve with Mayonnaise Dressing.

Stuffed Smoked Tongue

Wash a smoked tongue, put in kettle, cover with cold water, bring slowly to the boiling point, cover and let simmer until meat is tender, and cool in water in which it has been cooked. Cut off root, then thick slice, and scoop out centre, leaving a wall one-half inch in thickness; fill cavity with forcemeat, replace thick slice and fasten with small wooden skewers. Tie in cheese-cloth and steam from forty-five to sixty minutes. Remove from cheesecloth, take off skin, brush over with aspic jelly, chill thoroughly, cut in slices crosswise, arrange overlapping one another, lengthwise of platter, and garnish with parsley and slice of lemon.

Tongue and Chicken Forcemeat.—Chop the breast of a raw chicken, pound in a mortar, and add gradually the whites of two eggs and work until smooth. Then add gradually cup heavy cream and one-fourth cup tongue, removed from centre, forced through a purée strainer. Season highly with salt, cayenne and Sherry wine.

Boned Turkey

Singe, remove pinfeathers, head, neck, tendons, feet and legs to second joint and cut off wings close to body of a small, plump turkey; then bone (for directions see The Boston Cooking-School Cook Book, p. 24). Remove and set aside dark meat, cut breast in slices and arrange in a layer of uniform thickness over body skin. Turn in small pieces of leg and wing skin remaining. Spread with forcemeat, draw body skin over forcemeat and sew into shape. If turkey is allowed to stand before being spread with forcemeat, it must be covered with a double thickness of cheese-cloth, wrung out of cold

Boned Turkey.—*Page* 242.

Slices of Boned Turkey and Cubes of Garnished Aspic.—*Page* 243

water. Tie in a double thickness of cheese-cloth. Put bones and dark meat in kettle, pour over two quarts water, bring to the boiling point and steam prepared turkey (over stock thus made) until tender; the time required being about two hours. Remove, drain thoroughly and let stand fifteen minutes. Take off cloth and sew securely and tightly in cheese-cloth wrung out of cold water.

Put between two boards, place a weight on top and let stand in a cold place. Take from cheese-cloth and pour over the following sauce: Melt one tablespoon butter, add one and one-half tablespoons flour and stir until well blended; then pour on gradually, while stirring constantly, one-half cup chicken stock. Bring to the boiling point and add one-half teaspoon salt, one-eighth teaspoon pepper, one-half teaspoon lemon juice, one egg yolk, slightly beaten and diluted with one tablespoon cream and one teaspoon granulated gelatine, dissolved in one tablespoon hot water. Let stand until mixture begins to thicken, before pouring over turkey. Garnish with truffles, cut in fancy shapes, and brush over with melted aspic jelly. Place on serving dish, surround with crisp, small lettuce leaves and cubes of aspic jelly, garnished with parsley and pimiento butter, forced through a pastry bag and tube.

Forcemeat. — Force one and one-half pounds, each, raw lean veal and meat cut from fresh fat pork chops through a meat chopper; then force through a purée strainer.

Cook one-half cup Sherry wine with four shallots, peeled and cut in pieces, four sprigs parsley and one-fourth teaspoon dried tarragon leaves, until reduced one-half. Strain through cheese-cloth and add to meat; then add yolks two eggs, slightly beaten, one cup smoked tongue, cut in one-half-inch cubes, one-half cup blanched pistachio nuts, cut in pieces, four truffles, cut in pieces, one tablespoon truffle liquor and one cup one-half-inch cubes larding pork, parboiled two minutes, drained and thoroughly chilled. Season with one tablespoon salt, one-eighth teaspoon cayenne, one-half teaspoon grated nutmeg, one-half teaspoon allspice and two teaspoons rum.

Chicken Mousse

1 cup hot chicken stock	1 tablespoon cold water
Yolks 3 eggs	½ cup cold cooked chicken (white meat)
¼ teaspoon salt	½ cup blanched almonds
¼ teaspoon paprika	1 cup heavy cream
1 tablespoon granulated gelatine	Few grains cayenne

Beat egg yolks slightly, add salt and paprika, and pour over, gradually, chicken stock. Cook over hot water until mixture thickens, add gelatine soaked in cold water and, when dissolved, strain and add to chicken and almonds, finely chopped, pounded, and forced through a sieve. Season highly with salt and cayenne. Put in ice water and stir until mixture thickens, then fold in cream, beaten until stiff. Turn into mould and chill. Remove from mould and garnish with Sauterne Jelly (see The Boston Cooking School Cook Book, p. 420).

CHAPTER XXII

HOT PUDDINGS

Emergency Puddings

1 cup bread flour	2 tablespoons baking powder
½ teaspoon salt	Milk
	Canned peaches

MIX and sift flour, salt and baking powder and moisten to a soft dough with milk, the amount required being about one-third cup. Drop a tablespoonful in each buttered individual mould, add a small section cut from a canned peach, cover with another tablespoon dough and steam ten minutes. Sections of other canned fruits or raspberry or blackberry jam may be used in place of peaches. Serve with any pudding sauce.

Broiled Oranges on Toast

Pare oranges, cut in one-half-inch slices and remove seeds. Brush over with melted butter, place in a buttered broiler and broil over a clear fire five minutes. Remove to circular pieces of sautéd bread and sprinkle with grated sweet chocolate. Serve with whipped cream, sweetened and flavored with vanilla.

Snow Eggs

White 1 egg
1 tablespoon powdered sugar
⅛ teaspoon cornstarch
Egg yolk

Beat egg white until stiff and add gradually, while beating constantly, powdered sugar and cornstarch. Butter a tablespoon, cover bowl of spoon with mixture, make a depression in the centre and fill cavity with mixture, to which has been added enough yolk of egg (beaten until thick and lemon-colored) to give color. Cover with white mixture, having the spoon well rounded. Repeat until the mixture is used. Cook in a blazer containing boiling water, placed over hot water pan also containing boiling water, and cook six minutes, turning once during the cooking. Cover bottom of dish with strawberry preserve, arrange eggs on preserve and pour around Orange Sauce (see p. 258).

Apple Canapés, Cream Sabayon Sauce

Cut bread in one-third-inch slices, shape with a round cutter and sauté in butter until delicately browned. Pare and cut apples in halves; then remove cores, thus making cavities. Sauté apples in butter, cavity side down, in a covered pan. When apples are half done, turn, fill cavities with sugar and continue the cooking until apples are soft. Place on prepared bread and serve with Cream Sabayon Sauce I (see p. 263).

Apricot Sandwiches, Roxbury Sauce

1 egg	2 tablespoons sugar
Yolks 2 eggs	¾ cup milk
¼ teaspoon salt	Slices of stale bread

Cut stale bread (preferably baker's) in one-fourth-inch slices. Remove crusts and cut slices in halves crosswise. Beat egg and egg yolks slightly, add salt, sugar and milk and strain into a shallow dish. Soak bread in mixture until soft, then sauté in butter. Spread one-half the pieces with apricot marmalade, cover with remaining pieces and serve with Roxbury Sauce (see p. 259).

Dresden Sandwiches, Sherry Sauce

3 eggs	1 cup milk
½ teaspoon salt	6 slices stale bread,
2 tablespoons sugar	⅛ inch thick
Jam or marmalade	

Beat eggs slightly, add salt, sugar and milk, and when well blended, strain into a shallow dish. Remove crusts from bread and cut slices in halves, crosswise. Soak bread in custard mixture until soft. Cook in a buttered, hot frying pan. Brown on one side, turn and brown other side. Spread half the pieces with any jam or marmalade that may be at hand and cover with the remaining pieces. Serve hot with Sherry Sauce (see p. 260).

Rhubarb Tapioca Pudding

⅔ cup pearl tapioca	3 cups rhubarb
1¼ cups boiling water	1⅛ cups sugar
⅜ teaspoon salt	

Soak tapioca in cold water to cover over night or several hours. Drain, put in double boiler, add boiling water and salt and cook until tapioca has absorbed water. Peel rhubarb, cut in three-fourths-inch pieces crosswise, and sprinkle with sugar. Add to tapioca and cook until tapioca is transparent and rhubarb is soft. Turn into a fancy dish and serve with sugar and thin cream.

Fruit Tapioca

½ cup pearl tapioca
2½ cups cold water
¾ teaspoon salt
1 inch stick cinnamon
1 tumbler currant jelly

¼ cup sherry wine
Almonds
Seeded raisins ⎫
Citron ⎬ ¼ cup each
Sugar ⎭

Soak tapioca in cold water over night or several hours. Cook in same water in double boiler with salt and cinnamon until transparent. Remove from range and add currant jelly, Sherry wine, almonds (blanched and shredded), raisins (cut in pieces) and citron (cut in thin slices). Sweeten to taste. Turn into a serving dish, cool slightly, and serve with thin cream.

Lemon Cream Rice

½ cup rice
3 cups milk
½ cup sugar
Grated rind of ¾ lemon
1⅛ tablespoons lemon
    juice

¾ teaspoon salt
Yolks 2 eggs
Whites 2 eggs
2 tablespoons powdered
    sugar
¼ teaspoon lemon extract

Pick over rice, cover with cold water and let soak over night. Drain, put in double boiler, add milk and cook until rice is soft. Add sugar, lemon rind, lemon juice, salt and egg yolks, slightly beaten. Cook until mixture thickens, turn into a buttered pudding dish and cool. Beat whites of eggs until stiff and add gradually powdered sugar and lemon extract. Cover top of pudding with meringue and bake in a moderate oven just long enough to brown meringue. Serve with or without Strawberry Sauce (see p. 257).

Club Indian Pudding

1 quart scalded milk	1 teaspoon salt
5 tablespoons granulated Indian meal	¾ teaspoon cinnamon
	½ teaspoon ginger
2 tablespoons butter	2 eggs
1 cup molasses	1 cup cold milk

Add meal gradually while stirring constantly, to scalded milk and cook in double boiler fifteen minutes; then add butter, molasses, seasonings and eggs, well beaten. Turn into a buttered pudding dish and pour on cold milk. Bake in a moderate oven one hour. Serve with or without vanilla ice cream.

Squash Pudding

2½ cups steamed and strained squash	1 teaspoon salt
	¾ teaspoon cinnamon
½ cup sugar	2 eggs
2¼ cups milk	

Mix sugar, salt and cinnamon and add to squash; then add eggs, slightly beaten, and milk. Turn into a buttered pudding dish and bake in a moderate oven until firm. Cool slightly before serving.

Sally's Bread Pudding

2 cups stale bread crumbs	Few gratings nutmeg
1 quart scalded milk	¼ teaspoon soda
Yolks 4 eggs	2 teaspoons hot water
2 tablespoons melted butter	Whites 4 eggs

Pour milk over bread crumbs, cover and let stand fifteen minutes. Add yolks of eggs, well beaten, butter, nutmeg and soda, dissolved in water; then fold in whites of eggs, beaten until stiff. Turn into a buttered pudding dish and bake in a moderate oven forty-five minutes. Serve hot with Roxbury Sauce.

This pudding is excellent served cold with a fruit sauce.

Caramel Bread Pudding

4 cups milk	2 eggs
½ cup sugar	⅔ cup sugar
2 cups stale bread crumbs	½ teaspoon salt
1 teaspoon vanilla	

Caramelize one-half cup sugar and add to milk which has been scalded in double boiler. When caramel has dissolved, add bread crumbs and let soak thirty minutes. Beat eggs slightly, add two-thirds cup sugar, salt and vanilla. Add to first mixture, turn into a buttered pudding dish and bake in a moderate oven one hour. Serve with whipped cream sweetened and flavored with vanilla.

Banana Pudding

1 cup stale sponge cake crumbs	¼ teaspoon salt
2 cups milk	1 tablespoon brandy
½ cup banana pulp	1 teaspoon vanilla
¼ cup sugar	3 eggs

Scald milk, pour over cake crumbs, cover, let stand one-half hour and rub through a sieve. Add banana, which has been rubbed through a sieve, sugar, salt, brandy, vanilla and eggs, slightly beaten. Turn into buttered individual moulds, set in pan of hot water and bake until firm. Remove from oven, let stand five minutes, turn out and serve with Cream Sabayon Sauce I (see p. 263).

Roxbury Pudding, Hot Chocolate Sauce

½ cup butter	2½ cups flour
1 cup sugar	3½ teaspoons baking powder
½ cup milk	Few grains salt
	Whites 4 eggs

Work butter until creamy and add sugar gradually, while beating constantly; then add milk, flour mixed and sifted with baking powder, salt and whites of eggs, beaten until stiff. Turn into six well-buttered half-pound baking powder tins, adjust covers, which should also be buttered, and put on trivet in kettle containing boiling water, allowing water to come only half-way up around mould. Cover closely and steam one hour, adding, as needed, more boiling water, never having the water reach a lower temperature than the boiling point.

Remove from mould and serve with Hot Chocolate Sauce (see p. 257).

Steamed Ginger Sponge

½ cup butter	3 teaspoons baking powder
2 tablespoons sugar	¼ teaspoon salt
2 eggs	¼ cup Canton ginger, cut
1 cup milk	in small pieces
2½ cups flour	1 tablespoon ginger syrup

Cream butter and add sugar gradually and eggs, well beaten; then add milk alternately with flour, mixed and sifted with baking powder and salt. Add ginger and ginger syrup and turn into a buttered mould. Steam one and three-fourths hours. Remove from mould and serve with half-pint bottle heavy cream, beaten until stiff and sweetened with four tablespoons powdered sugar and flavored with two tablespoons ginger syrup.

Orange Cream Sponge.

3 tablespoons butter	4 eggs
¼ cup flour	¼ cup sugar
1 cup scalded milk	1 tablespoon orange juice
1 teaspoon grated orange rind	

Melt butter, add flour and stir until well blended; then pour on milk gradually, while stirring constantly, and bring to the boiling point. Add orange juice and grated rind to yolks of eggs and beat until thick and lemon-colored; then add sugar, continuing the beating. Combine mixtures and fold in whites of eggs, beaten until stiff and dry. Turn into a buttered melon mould and steam thirty-five minutes. Serve with Orange Sauce (see The Boston Cooking-School Cook Book, p. 407) or Creamy Sauce, flavored with juice and grated rind of orange.

Raisin Puff

½ cup butter	2¼ cups flour
2 tablespoons sugar	2 teaspoons baking powder
2 eggs	¼ teaspoon salt
1 cup milk	1 cup raisins

Cream butter, add sugar gradually and eggs, well beaten; then add milk alternately with two cups flour, mixed and sifted with baking powder and salt. Seed and chop raisins, dredge with remaining flour and add to mixture. Turn into a buttered mould, adjust cover and steam one and one-half hours. Remove to hot serving dish and serve with whipped cream, sweetened and flavored with grated nutmeg.

New England Pudding

8 common crackers	1 cup brown sugar
Butter	1 teaspoon salt
1 quart scalded milk	1 teaspoon cinnamon
3 eggs	½ teaspoon grated nutmeg
3 egg yolks	1½ cups seeded raisins
1 cup thin cream	

Split crackers and spread with butter, using two teaspoons to each half cracker. Arrange alternate layers of crackers and raisins (which have been cooked in a very small quantity of boiling water until plump) in a buttered pudding dish. Pour over scalded milk, cover and let stand one hour. Beat egg and egg yolks and add sugar, salt and spices and cream. Pour over first mixture and bake in a slow oven two and one-half hours. Serve with a hard or liquid sauce.

Honeycomb Pudding

1 cup sugar	½ cup butter
1 cup flour	½ cup lukewarm milk
1 cup molasses	1 teaspoon soda
4 eggs	

Mix sugar and flour, then add molasses. Melt butter in milk and add soda. Combine mixtures, beat thoroughly and add egg, well beaten. Turn into a buttered baking dish and bake in a moderate oven. Serve with Florodora Sauce.

Almond Pudding

4 tablespoons butter	1½ cups flour
⅛ cup sugar	½ teaspoon soda
½ cup molasses	¼ teaspoon cinnamon
2 eggs	¾ cup almonds, blanched
½ cup milk	and roasted
¼ teaspoon salt	

Cream butter, add sugar gradually, molasses and eggs, well beaten. Mix and sift dry ingredients and add alternately with milk to first mixture; then add almonds, finely chopped. Turn into buttered mould and steam two and one-half hours, never allowing water to go below the boiling point. Serve with whipped cream, sweetened and flavored with vanilla.

Snow Eggs. — *Page* 246.

Sterling Fruit Pudding. — *Page* 255

Irish Plum Pudding. — *Page 255.*

Irish Plum Pudding Steamed in Ring Mould and Garnished for Christmas. — *Page 255.*

Sterling Fruit Pudding

1 cup suet	1 cup raisins
2⅔ cups stale bread crumbs	¾ cup currants
	⅛ cup flour
1 cup grated raw carrot	1½ teaspoon salt
Yolks 4 eggs	1 teaspoon cinnamon
1⅛ cups brown sugar	½ teaspoon grated nutmeg
Grated rind 1 lemon	¼ teaspoon cloves
1 tablespoon vinegar	Whites 4 eggs

Work suet until creamy, using the hand, and add bread crumbs and carrot. Beat egg yolks until light and add gradually, while beating constantly, sugar. Combine mixtures and add lemon rind and vinegar. Mix raisins, seeded and cut in pieces, with currants and dredge with flour, mixed and sifted with salt and spices. Add to mixture with whites of eggs, beaten until stiff. Turn into a buttered mould garnished with citron (cut in thin slices, then in fancy shapes), and adjust cover. Steam three and one-half hours. Serve with Mousselaine Brandy Sauce.

Irish Plum Pudding

2½ cups stale bread crumbs	4 eggs
	½ pound raisins
1 cup milk	½ pound citron
½ pound beef suet	½ pound currants
⅓ cup sugar	3 tablespoons flour
½ cup maple syrup	2 teaspoons baking powder
1½ teaspoons salt	⅛ cup brandy

Put bread crumbs in double boiler, add milk and cook until milk is scalded. Chop suet and work with the hands until creamy; then add sugar gradually, while working constantly. Add maple syrup, salt, eggs well beaten, and raisins stoned and cut in pieces, citron cut in thin strips, and currants mixed and dredged with flour mixed with baking powder; then add brandy. Turn into a buttered mould, cover and steam twenty-four hours. It may be steamed twelve hours one day and twelve hours the next. Re-heat in steamer for serving; the time required being about one and one-fourth hours. Turn on a hot serving dish, insert sparkers and garnish with holly (if used at Christmas dinner) and Brandy Sauce (see p. 262); also accompany with Yankee Sauce (see p. 259).

CHAPTER XXIII

PUDDING SAUCES

Hot Chocolate Sauce

1 square unsweetened chocolate	⅛ cup boiling water
1 tablespoon melted butter	1 cup sugar
½ teaspoon vanilla	

Melt chocolate in saucepan, placed in larger saucepan of boiling water. Add butter and when thoroughly blended, pour on gradually, while stirring constantly, boiling water; then add sugar. Bring to the boiling point and let boil fourteen minutes. Cool slightly and flavor with vanilla.

Raspberry Sauce

½ cup butter	1½ cups confectioners' sugar
¼ cup Raspberry Syrup	

Cream the butter and add sugar gradually while stirring and beating constantly; then add Raspberry Syrup (see p. 398) slowly (at first drop by drop) to prevent a separation. Pile on a dish and chill. Serve with Sally's Bread Pudding, Cottage Pudding, boiled rice, etc.

Strawberry Sauce

⅛ cup butter	1 cup confectioners' sugar
⅔ cup strawberries	

Cream butter and add sugar gradually while stirring constantly. Wash, hull and drain berries; add to first mixture one at a time, beating between each addition until well blended. If these directions are not followed, sauce will have a curdled appearance.

Orange Sauce

Grated rind ½ lemon
Juice ½ lemon
½ cup orange juice
⅛ cup sugar
Few grains salt
Yolks 2 eggs
Whites 2 eggs
½ tablespoon apricot brandy

Mix grated rind, fruit juices, sugar, salt and egg yolks, beaten slightly. Put on range and stir constantly until mixture thickens. Add gradually, while beating constantly, to whites of eggs, beaten until stiff. Cool and flavor with brandy.

Sea Foam Sauce

2 tablespoons butter
2 tablespoons flour
½ cup sugar
White 1 egg
Yolk 1 egg
½ cup water
1 teaspoon vanilla

Cream butter and add flour, mixed with sugar, gradually, while stirring constantly; then add egg yolk, well beaten; water and vanilla. Cook in double boiler until mixture thickens, stirring constantly at first, and afterwards occasionally. Cool and just before sending to table add egg white, beaten until stiff.

Roxbury Sauce

Yolk 1 egg
1 cup powdered sugar
½ cup scalded milk
1 teaspoon cornstarch
⅛ teaspoon salt
½ teaspoon vanilla
1 tablespoon lemon juice
Grated rind ¼ lemon
White 1 egg

Beat egg yolk until thick and lemon-colored and add three-fourths of sugar gradually, while beating constantly. Mix remaining sugar with cornstarch and salt and pour on, gradually, scalded milk. Cook in double boiler ten minutes, stirring constantly, until mixture thickens and afterwards occasionally. Combine mixtures, add flavorings and egg white, beaten until stiff.

Cambridge Sauce

⅓ cup butter
1 cup powdered sugar
2 teaspoons flour
1¼ tablespoons cold water
½ cup boiling water
3 tablespoons wine

Cream butter and add sugar, gradually, while beating constantly. Dilute flour with cold water, add gradually to boiling water and let boil five minutes. Cool and just before serving, combine mixtures and add wine.

Yankee Sauce

Cream one-half cup butter, and add gradually, while beating constantly, one cup powdered sugar. Dilute one tablespoon cornstarch with two and one-half tablespoons cold water and add gradually to one cup boiling water, placed in saucepan on range.

Again bring to the boiling point and let boil until liquid is clear. Combine mixtures, stirring briskly, and flavor with one teaspoon vinegar and three tablespoons Sherry wine. Especially good with Steamed Berry Pudding.

Monroe Sauce

2 cups brown sugar	4 tablespoons butter
⅔ cup boiling water	4 tablespoons Sherry wine
4 tablespoons cold water	1 teaspoon vanilla
2 teaspoons cornstarch	Slight grating nutmeg

Few grains salt

Make a syrup by boiling sugar and water twelve minutes. Add cold water to cornstarch and stir until smooth; then add gradually, while stirring constantly, to syrup and let simmer forty minutes. Add butter, wine, vanilla, nutmeg and salt and serve at once.

Sherry Sauce I

Mix thoroughly one-half cup sugar and one tablespoon cornstarch; then pour on gradually, while stirring constantly, one cup boiling water. Bring to the boiling point and let simmer three minutes. Remove from range, add a few grains salt, two tablespoons butter, bit by bit, and one tablespoon Sherry wine.

Sherry Sauce II

Whites 2 eggs	1 tablespoon apricot
⅔ cup powdered sugar	marmalade

¼ cup Sherry wine

FANCY CUTTERS, PANS AND MOULDS

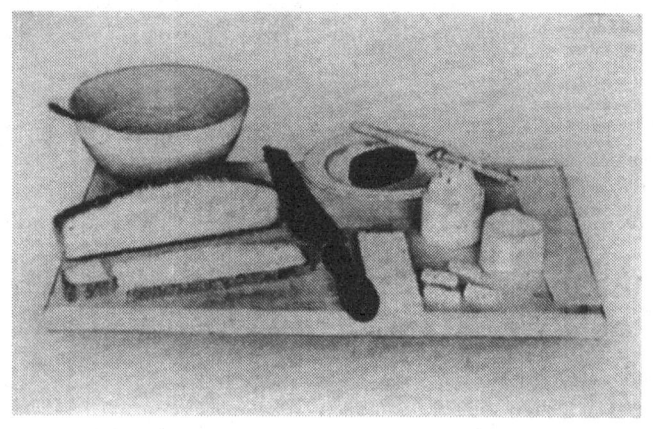

CHARLOTTE RUSSE IN THE MAKING. — *Page 276*

CHARLOTTE RUSSE. — *Page 276.*

Beat whites of eggs until stiff. Add sugar gradually, continuing the beating, then add marmalade and Sherry wine.

San Monica Sauce

1 tablespoon butter	Yolk 1 egg
1 tablespoon flour	1 banana
¼ cup sugar	Few grains salt
½ cup milk	½ cup heavy cream

Cream butter, add flour and stir until well blended; then add sugar gradually. Scald milk, add mixture and stir constantly until thickened. Add egg yolk slightly beaten and cook three minutes; then add banana, skinned, scraped and forced through a strainer. Chill and add salt and cream, beaten until stiff.

Denver Sauce

¼ cup butter	2 tablespoons coffee infusion
1 cup powdered sugar	2 teaspoons breakfast cocoa
1 teaspoon vanilla	

Cream butter and add sugar gradually, while beating constantly; then add coffee, drop by drop, cocoa and vanilla.

Dearborn Sauce

½ cup butter	1½ tablespoons Sherry wine
1 cup brown sugar	2 teaspoons brandy
2 tablespoons cream	Few grains salt

Cream butter and add sugar, gradually, while beating constantly. Add cream, and wine and brandy, drop by drop, to prevent a separation; then add salt.

Brandy Sauce

Work one-half cup butter until very creamy, and add gradually, while beating constantly, one and one-third cups powdered sugar; then add two tablespoons of brandy, at first, drop by drop. Force through a pastry bag and tube on thin slices of lemon, from which seeds have been removed, and sprinkle with chopped pistachio nuts.

Peach Brandy Sauce

½ cup butter	⅓ teaspoon salt
1 cup powdered sugar	½ cup heavy cream
Whites 2 eggs	2 tablespoons Peach Brandy

Cream butter and add sugar gradually, while beating constantly; then add whites of eggs, beaten until stiff, and salt. Place over hot water and stir constantly until mixture is heated. Remove from range and add cream, beaten until stiff, and brandy.

Florodora Sauce

White 1 egg	¾ cup heavy cream
¾ cup powdered sugar	2 tablespoons Madeira wine
Yolk 1 egg	Few grains salt

Beat egg white until stiff and add, gradually, while beating constantly, sugar; then add egg yolk, beaten until thick and lemon-colored, cream beaten until stiff, wine and salt.

White Wine Sauce

½ cup sugar	Yolks 2 eggs
½ tablespoon cornstarch	1 cup white wine
Grated rind ½ lemon	Few grains salt
Juice ½ lemon	Whites 2 eggs

Mix sugar and cornstarch and add lemon rind and juice, yolks of eggs, slightly beaten, wine and salt. Place saucepan containing mixture on range and stir constantly until the boiling point is reached. Remove from range and add whites of eggs, beaten until stiff.

Cream Sabayon Sauce I

Yolks 2 eggs	½ cup cream
1 tablespoon sugar	1 teaspoon Apricot brandy

Add sugar to egg yolks and beat until light. Heat cream to boiling point and pour slowly, while beating constantly, on egg yolks. Add brandy and cook, stirring constantly, three minutes. Strain and serve.

Cream Sabayon Sauce II

½ cup milk	2 tablespoons Sherry wine
½ cup cream	½ teaspoon vanilla
Yolks 2 eggs	Few grains salt
2 tablespoons sugar	Whites 2 eggs

Scald milk and cream in double boiler. Beat yolks of eggs until thick and add sugar. Pour milk and cream gradually, while beating constantly, on egg mixture and cook in double boiler until mixture thickens. Add wine, vanilla and salt and pour over whites of eggs, beaten until stiff.

Brandy Mousselaine Sauce

Yolks 4 eggs
1 cup powdered sugar
2 tablespoons brandy

1 cup heavy cream
1 teaspoon vanilla
Few grains salt

Beat yolks of eggs until light and add gradually, while stirring constantly, sugar and brandy. Cook over range five minutes, stirring constantly. Set pan containing mixture in larger pan of ice water and beat until cold; then add cream, beaten until stiff, vanilla and salt.

Dewey Sauce

1 cup sugar
¼ cup water
Yolks 2 eggs

2 tablespoons rum
1 teaspoon curaçoa
Red coloring

Put sugar and water in saucepan, bring to boiling point and let boil until a thin syrup is formed. Pour slowly on the well beaten yolks of eggs and cook, stirring constantly, until mixture thickens slightly. Color red, cool slightly, add flavorings and stir slightly. Serve with vanilla ice cream.

CHAPTER XXIV

COLD DESSERTS

Berkshire Cornstarch Pudding

2 squares unsweetened chocolate	3 tablespoons cornstarch
2 cups milk	¼ teaspoon salt
¼ cup sugar	¼ cup milk
½ teaspoon vanilla	

Put chocolate and two cups milk in double boiler. Mix sugar, cornstarch and salt and when well blended, pour on gradually one-fourth cup milk. Add to milk which has scalded with chocolate and cook fifteen minutes, stirring constantly until mixture thickens and afterwards occasionally. Add flavoring and turn into a serving dish. Chill and serve with or without sugar and cream.

Jordan Pudding

2 cups boiling water	5 tablespoons cornstarch
¾ cup sugar	¼ cup cold water
¼ teaspoon salt	Whites 2 eggs
⅛ cup lemon juice	

Add sugar and salt to boiling water. Dilute cornstarch with cold water and combine mixtures. Bring to the boiling point, stirring constantly, and let boil five minutes; then add whites of eggs, beaten until stiff, and lemon juice. Turn into a mould, first dipped in cold water, and chill.

Remove from mould and serve with Custard Sauce.

Fig Custard

1 quart milk	½ pound figs
2 tablespoons cornstarch	¼ cup boiling water
¾ cup sugar	¼ cup sugar
¼ teaspoon salt	1½ tablespoons lemon juice
Yolks 3 eggs	Whites 3 eggs
3 tablespoons powdered sugar	

Scald milk. Mix cornstarch, sugar and salt. Pour on gradually scalded milk and cook in double boiler ten minutes. Add egg yolks, slightly beaten, and cook three minutes.

Cut figs in small pieces, put in double boiler, add water, sugar and two-thirds lemon juice and cook until figs are soft. Combine mixtures and cool; then turn into serving dish. Beat whites of eggs until stiff and add powdered sugar gradually, while beating constantly; then add remaining lemon juice. Pile by spoonfuls over pudding, just as sending to table. This meringue, to be at its best, cannot stand long.

Orange Cream

4 tablespoons cornstarch	Yolks 2 eggs
½ cup cold milk	2 tablespoons sugar
3½ cups scalded milk	½ teaspoon salt
½ teaspoon orange extract	

Mix cornstarch with cold milk, add gradually to scalded milk and cook in a double boiler fifteen minutes, stirring constantly until mixture thickens and afterwards occasionally. Beat yolks of eggs and add sugar and salt. Add to first mixture and cook three minutes. Turn into a serving dish, sprinkle with two tablespoons granulated sugar, cover and let stand until cold. Cover with a meringue and surround with a border of sections of orange. Serve with thin cream.

For the meringue beat the whites two eggs until stiff, and add gradually, while beating constantly, two tablespoons powdered sugar, one-half teaspoon vanilla and a few grains salt. Poach by heaping tablespoonfuls in boiling water.

Baked French Custard

1 pint thin cream	2 tablespoons sugar
Whites 3 eggs	½ teaspoon vanilla
¼ teaspoon salt	

Heat cream in double boiler. Beat whites of eggs until stiff and add sugar, vanilla and salt. Add mixture to cream and beat, using an egg beater. Turn into buttered cups, set in pan of hot water and bake until firm. Chill thoroughly, remove from moulds and serve with sugar and cream.

Danish Custard

⅔ cup sugar, caramelized	1 quart milk
¼ cup sugar	½ teaspoon salt
5 eggs	1 teaspoon vanilla

Put two-thirds cup sugar in agate pudding dish, place on hot part of range and stir constantly until sugar is melted and a syrup of light brown color is formed; then set pan at once in larger pan of cold water to stop the cooking and let stand about one minute, turning the pan to allow the caramel to coat sides as well as bottom. Beat eggs slightly, add plain sugar, milk, salt and vanilla and strain into pan lined with caramel. Set in pan of hot water and bake until firm, which may be determined by running a silver knife through custard. If knife comes out clean, custard is done. During the baking, do not allow the water surrounding the mould to reach the boiling point, or custard will whey. Chill and turn on a glass serving dish

Ginger Custard

Canton ginger	½ cup sugar
4 eggs	¼ teaspoon salt
2 cups milk	2 tablespoons rum

Cut Canton ginger in thin strips and use for garnishing sides of buttered individual moulds. Beat eggs slightly, add sugar, milk and seasonings and strain into moulds. Set in pan of hot water and bake until firm. Chill thoroughly and remove from moulds to serving dish.

Prune Pudding

¼ pound prunes	½ cup sugar
Whites 4 eggs	

Wash and pick over prunes. Put in a saucepan, cover with cold water and soak two hours. Cook in same water until soft, when water should be nearly evaporated. Remove stones and cut prunes in small pieces; then sprinkle with sugar. Beat whites of eggs until stiff and add prunes gradually. Pour into a slightly buttered pudding dish and bake in a moderate oven twenty-five minutes. Chill and serve with Custard Sauce or whipped cream, sweetened and flavored.

Cold Chocolate Bread Pudding

1 cup soft stale bread crumbs	2 cups milk
1½ squares unsweetened chocolate	Yolks 3 eggs
	2 tablespoons butter
1 cup sugar	¼ teaspoon salt
½ teaspoon vanilla	

Add bread, chocolate and sugar to cold milk, reserving one-half cup. Put in double boiler and let cook until a smooth paste is formed. Beat yolks of eggs until light, add reserved milk, butter and salt and stir into hot mixture. Cook until mixture thickens, then add vanilla. Turn in a buttered pudding dish and bake in a moderate oven twenty minutes. Cool slightly, cover with meringue and bake in a moderate oven eight minutes. Serve very cold.

For the meringue beat the whites of three eggs until stiff and add, gradually, one-fourth cup powdered sugar, continuing the beating; then cut and fold in one-fourth cup powdered sugar and add one-half teaspoon vanilla.

Lemon Jelly

1½ cups cold water	1 tablespoon granulated
1 cup sugar	gelatine
4 cloves	2 tablespoons cold water
½-inch piece stick cinnamon	¼ cup lemon juice
	Few grains salt

Put water, sugar, cloves and cinnamon in saucepan, place on range, stir until sugar has dissolved and bring to boiling point. Add gelatine which has soaked in cold water five minutes. Stir until gelatine has dissolved; then add lemon juice and salt. Strain into a mould, first dipped in cold water, and chill thoroughly.

Pineapple Jelly

2 cups boiling water	2 tablespoons granulated
½ cup sugar	gelatine
1 cup pineapple juice	2 tablespoons cold water
3 tablespoons lemon juice	1⅓ cups pineapple cubes

Pour water over sugar and when sugar has dissolved, add gelatine soaked in cold water five minutes; then add juice drained from canned pineapple and lemon juice and strain. When mixture begins to thicken, add canned pineapple, cut in one-half-inch cubes. Turn into a mould, first dipped in cold water, and chill thoroughly.

Keswick Pudding

¾ cup sugar	Few grains salt
1 cup boiling water	1¼ tablespoons granulated
Yolks 3 eggs	gelatine
¼ cup sugar	¼ cup cold water
¼ cup lemon juice	

Dissolve sugar in water and again bring to the boiling point. Beat yolks of eggs slightly and add sugar and salt. Pour on gradually the boiling syrup and cook, stirring constantly, until mixture thickens; then add gelatine, soaked in cold water, and lemon juice. Strain, set in ice water and stir until mixture begins to thicken. Turn into a mould, first dipped in cold water. Remove from mould and garnish with whipped cream, sweetened and flavored with vanilla.

Newport Pudding

- 1 cup boiling water
- 1 cup sugar
- 1 tablespoon granulated gelatine
- ¼ cup cold water
- Whites 3 eggs
- ¾ tablespoon Sauterne
- 1½ tablespoons Sherry
- Green coloring
- Red coloring

Put sugar in small saucepan, pour over boiling water, set on range, bring to boiling point and let boil three minutes. Remove from range and add gelatine which has soaked in cold water fifteen minutes. Beat until mixture begins to stiffen; then add whites of eggs, beaten until stiff, and continue the beating twenty minutes. Divide the mixture into thirds. To first third add Sauterne, to second third add one-half the Sherry and color pink; to remaining third add remaining Sherry and color green. Arrange in layers in a fancy mould, first dipped in cold water, first the pink, then the white, then the green.

Chill thoroughly, remove from mould and serve with thin cream.

Coffee Sponge

2 tablespoons granulated gelatine	2 cups strong boiled coffee
¼ cup cold water	¾ cup sugar
	Whites 3 eggs

Few grains salt

Soak gelatine in cold water and add to hot coffee; then add sugar. Strain into pan, set in larger pan of ice water, cool slightly, then beat, using a wire whisk, until quite stiff. Add whites of eggs, beaten until stiff, and continue the beating until mixture will hold its shape. Turn into a mould, first dipped in cold water. Chill thoroughly, remove from mould and serve with sugar and thin cream.

French Macaroon Cream

1 tablespoon granulated gelatine	Yolks 3 eggs
3 tablespoons cold water	½ cup sugar
2 cups milk	¼ teaspoon salt
1 square unsweetened chocolate	Whites 3 eggs
	⅔ cup macaroons, dried and rolled

1 teaspoon vanilla

Soak gelatine in cold water. Scald milk with chocolate and add egg yolks, beaten and mixed with sugar and salt. Stir constantly until mixture thickens, remove from range and add egg whites, beaten until stiff, macaroons and vanilla. Turn into individual moulds, first dipped in cold water, and chill thoroughly.

Jelly Panachée. — *Page* 279.

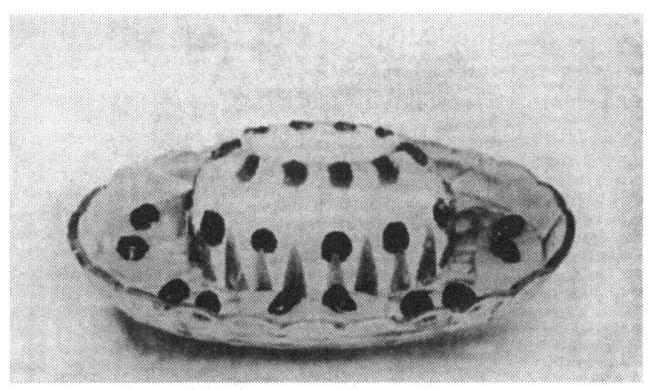

Cold Pineapple Soufflé. — *Page* 273

MACEDOINE OF FRUIT. — *Page* 279.

JELLIED FRUIT, MOULDED. — *Page* 278

Cherry Moss

1 tablespoon granulated gelatine	1½ cups dark red canned cherries
¼ cup cold water	½ cup cherry juice
¼ cup boiling water	Whites 2 eggs |//
Few grains salt	

Soak gelatine in cold water, dissolve in boiling water and add cherries (stoned and cut in halves) and cherry juice. When mixture begins to thicken, add whites of eggs, beaten until stiff, and salt. Turn into a slightly oiled mould and chill. Remove from mould to serving dish and garnish with whipped cream (sweetened and flavored with vanilla) and sprinkle with Jordan almonds, blanched, shredded and roasted, or chopped pistachio nut meats.

Cold Pineapple Soufflé

Yolks 3 eggs	½ cup pineapple syrup
Grated rind 1 lemon	1 tablespoon granulated gelatine
Juice 1 lemon	
½ cup sugar	⅛ cup cold water
Few grains salt	½ cup heavy cream
⅔ cup canned sliced pineapple	Whites 3 eggs

Beat egg yolks slightly and add grated rind, lemon juice, sugar and salt. Cook over hot water, stirring constantly until mixture thickens. Remove from range and add gelatine which has soaked in water five minutes and pineapple. When mixture begins to thicken, add cream, beaten until stiff, and egg whites, beaten until stiff. Turn into a mould, garnished with pieces of canned sliced pineapple and candied cherries, and chill thoroughly. Remove from mould to chilled serving dish and garnish with half slices of canned pineapple and candied cherries. The garnish may be omitted if a simpler desert is desired.

Pineapple Pyramids

1 can sliced pineapple	3 tablespoons granulated
1 cup pineapple juice	gelatine
2 tablespoons lemon juice	¼ cup cold water
¼ cup sugar	1½ cups thin cream
Few grains salt	1 cup heavy cream
1 glass Red Bar-le-duc currants	

Drain canned pineapple from syrup. Finely chop fruit and again drain. To fruit pulp add pineapple juice, lemon juice, sugar, salt and gelatine, which has been allowed to soak in water fifteen minutes. Heat mixture until gelatine has dissolved. Remove from range, set in pan of cold water and when mixture begins to thicken, fold in whip from thin cream and when well mixed, add heavy cream, beaten until stiff, and currants. Turn into a slightly oiled mould and chill thoroughly.

St. Valentine's Pudding

1 can sliced pineapple	Fruit red
⅔ cup sugar	1 cup heavy cream
⅛ cup Sauterne wine	½ cup marrons
Few grains salt	⅛ cup English walnut meats
2¾ tablespoons granulated gelatine	½ lb. marshmallows
	2 tablespoons powdered sugar
3 tablespoons cold water	Sherry wine
½ teaspoonful vanilla	

Drain pineapple and to syrup add sugar, five slices chopped pineapple and one cup cold water. Bring slowly to the boiling point, remove to back of range, and let stand one hour; then strain through cheese-cloth; there should be two cups syrup. Soak gelatine in cold water, dissolve in hot syrup, add Sauterne wine and salt and color with fruit red. Place a heart-shaped mould in pan containing ice water and pour in mixture to one-half inch in depth. When firm place a smaller heart-shaped mould (containing ice water) on jelly, leaving a space of uniform width. Add jelly mixture a little at a time, and cool between the additions, until space is full. When firm remove smaller mould and fill space with the following mixture thoroughly chilled. Beat cream until stiff and add one-half cup pineapple cubes (cut from sliced pineapple), marrons broken in pieces, English walnut meats, broken in pieces, marshmallows cut in strips, powdered sugar, sherry wine to taste and vanilla. Let stand one hour. Remove from mould to serving dish and surround with pink spun sugar.

Peach Cabinet Pudding

1 can peaches
⅓ cup powdered sugar
2 tablespoons Sherry wine
1 tablespoon brandy
2 cups milk
Yolks 3 eggs

Whites 3 eggs
¼ cup sugar
⅛ teaspoon salt
1½ tablespoons granulated gelatine
2 tablespoons cold water

Drain peaches, cut in quarters, sprinkle with powdered sugar and pour over Sherry and brandy. Make a custard of milk, egg yolks, sugar and salt, and just before removing from fire add gelatine soaked in cold water. Strain and when slightly cooled add liquor drained from peaches. Stir until mixture begins to thicken, then add whites of eggs beaten stiff. Line a mould with peaches, pour in custard and chill.

Grape Juice Soufflé

2 tablespoons granulated gelatine	1 pint grape juice
	Whites 4 eggs
¾ cup heavy cream	

Put gelatine in grape juice and heat in double boiler until gelatine has dissolved. Strain into bowl, set bowl in saucepan of ice water and when mixture begins to thicken, fold in whites of eggs, beaten until stiff. Half fill individual moulds (first dipped in cold water) with mixture. To remainder add cream, beaten until stiff. Fill moulds with cream mixture and chill. Remove from moulds to serving dish and garnish with whipped cream, sweetened and delicately flavored with vanilla.

Charlotte Russe

1¼ cups milk	¼ cup cold water
Yolks 2 eggs	½ pint heavy cream
2 tablespoons sugar	3 tablespoons powdered sugar
Few grains salt	¾ teaspoon vanilla
1¼ tablespoons granulated gelatine	Sponge cake
	Whites 2 eggs

Scald milk and add gradually to eggs, slightly beaten and mixed with sugar and salt. Cook over hot water, stirring constantly, until mixture thickens, then add gelatine, soaked in cold water. Strain and add whites of eggs, beaten until stiff. Set pan in larger pan of ice water and stir, scraping from bottom and sides of pan, until mixture begins to thicken. Then add cream, beaten until stiff and mixed with sugar and vanilla. Line round paper cases with strips of sponge cake, using muffin rings to keep cases in shape. Fill with cream and chill. Remove from cases and garnish tops with four narrow strips of cakes, radiating from centre, and garnish centre with a cube of jelly.

Coffee Charlotte Baskets

Bake sponge cake mixture in buttered gem pans. Cool, remove centres and fill with coffee cream. Garnish tops with whipped cream, sweetened and flavored with vanilla and brandy, and insert strips of angelica to represent handles.

Coffee Cream. — Scald one and one-half cups milk with two and one-half tablespoons ground coffee and strain. Mix thoroughly one-half cup sugar, one-fourth cup flour and one-eighth teaspoon salt. Pour on gradually, while stirring constantly, the scalded milk. Add yolks two eggs, slightly beaten. Return mixture to double boiler and cook fifteen minutes. Cool, add one-third cup English walnut meats, cut in pieces, and one-half teaspoon vanilla.

St. Regis Pudding

½ cup boiling water	1½ tablespoons granulated gelatine
½ cup sugar	¼ cup cold water
½ cup Sherry wine	⅓ cup seedless raisins
½ cup apricot syrup	¼ cup brandy
½ tablespoon lemon juice	⅔ cup canned apricots, cut in pieces
Few grains salt	

Bring water and sugar to boiling point and let boil one minute. Add Sherry wine, apricot syrup, lemon juice, salt and gelatine, soaked in cold water. To raisins add brandy and cook in double boiler until raisins are plump. Add to jelly mixture with apricots cut in small pieces. Turn into a mould, chill thoroughly, remove from mould and serve with or without whipped cream, sweetened and flavored with vanilla.

Fruit Moulded in Jelly

5 tablespoons granulated gelatine	⅔ cup orange juice
1 cup cold water	⅓ cup lemon juice
2 cups boiling water	Few grains salt
1⅛ cups sugar	½ can peaches
1⅛ cups peach syrup	1 quart box strawberries
1 cup Sherry	1 banana
	⅔ cup seeded raisins

Soak gelatine in cold water, dissolve in boiling water and add sugar, fruit juices, wine and salt. Brush over inside of a large fancy mould with olive oil, then wipe over with a piece of tissue paper. Put in pan of ice water and pour in just enough of mixture to cover top ornamentations. When firm, put in each ornament a strawberry, blossom end down; add mixture to cover strawberries and let stand until set. Cut banana in slices, crosswise, shape with small round cutter and arrange a row around strawberry which is in centre of mould. Add more jelly mixture to keep banana in place and let set. To remaining jelly mixture add peaches cut in pieces and raisins (cooked until plump in a small quantity of boiling water drained and cooled). Fill mould with mixture and chill. Remove to serving dish and garnish with remaining strawberries with hulls left on. This is a large receipt to be used for receptions.

Macedoine of Fruit

3½ tablespoons granulated gelatine
½ cup cold water
1 cup boiling water
1¼ cups sugar
1¼ cups peach syrup
¾ cup Sherry
½ cup orange juice
2 tablespoons lemon juice
Few grains salt
Canned peaches
Stewed prunes
Blanched Jordan almonds
Glacéd cherries

Follow directions as given in Fruit Moulded in Jelly.

Jelly Panaché

Cut jelly roll in one-half-inch slices. Line a charlotte russe mould with slices and fill with Strawberry Bavarian Cream.

Jelly Roll. — Beat the yolks of four eggs until thick

and lemon-colored and add three tablespoons cold water; then add gradually, while beating constantly, one cup sugar and beat. Put one and one-half tablespoons cornstarch in cup and fill cup with flour. Mix and sift one and one-fourth teaspoons baking powder and one-fourth teaspoon salt and add to first mixture; then add whites of four eggs, beaten until stiff, and one teaspoon lemon extract. Turn into a buttered dripping pan and bake in a moderate oven. Remove from pan to cloth dredged with confectioners' sugar. Spread with currant jelly, which has been beaten with a silver fork until of the right consistency to spread evenly. Trim off sides and ends with a sharp knife and roll as quickly as possible.

Strawberry Bavarian Cream. — Soak one and one-half tablespoons granulated gelatine in one-fourth cup cold water and dissolve in one-third cup boiling water. Add one cup syrup drained from canned strawberries and more sugar if not sweet enough; then color pink. Set bowl containing mixture in pan of ice water and stir until mixture begins to thicken; then fold in whip from one pint heavy cream beaten until stiff.

CHAPTER XXV

FROZEN DESSERTS

Ices, Ice Creams, etc.

Lemon Ice

½ cup cut sugar
4 lemons
1 cup hot water
2 cups cold water
¾ cup granulated sugar

RUB entire surface of cut sugar over rind of lemons, which have been washed and wiped until dry. Pour over sugar the juice expressed from the lemons (of which there should be one-half cup) and hot water. When sugar is dissolved, add cold water and granulated sugar. Strain and freeze.

Crême de Menthe Ice

To one-half the recipe for Lemon Ice add two tablespoons Crême de Menthe cordial and freeze.

Raspberry Ice

2 cups raspberry juice
2 cups water
Sugar
Lemon juice

To juice drained from canned raspberries add water; then add sugar to sweeten and lemon juice to taste. Freeze, pack in salt and ice and let stand one hour.

Grape Fruit Frappé

1 quart water	2½ cups grape fruit juice
2½ cups sugar	⅔ cup orange juice
Rind ½ orange	3 tablespoons lemon juice
Rind ½ lemon	½ cup Forbidden Fruit Cordial

Put water, sugar and the cuttings from the yellow part of the rind in saucepan. Bring to boiling point and let boil three minutes. Strain, cool and add remaining ingredients. Freeze to a mush and serve in tall glasses.

Club Punch

3 cups water	1 cup pineapple juice
2½ cups sugar	1 cup candied fruit
1 cup lemon juice	¼ cup rum
1 cup orange juice	¼ cup brandy

Put sugar and water in saucepan, bring to the boiling point and let boil ten minutes. Remove from range, add fruit juices, cool, and strain. Cut candied fruits in small pieces, using equal parts of cherries, pineapple, apricot, and plums. Add liquors, cover and let stand one hour. Freeze mixture to the consistency of mush, add soaked candied fruits and continue the freezing. Serve in punch glasses.

Orange Cream Sherbet I

1¼ cups sugar	1½ cups milk
1½ cups orange juice	1½ cups thin cream
Few grains salt	

Mix sugar and orange juice and add gradually milk and cream. then salt. Freeze and serve.

UTENSILS FOR FREEZING

STANDISH PUDDING. — *Page* 287.

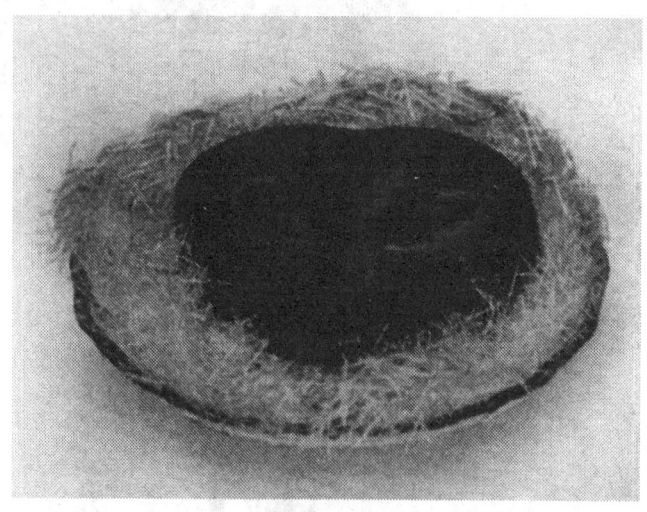

ST. VALENTINE'S PUDDING. — *Page* 274

Orange Cream Sherbet II

2 cups boiling water	1½ cups orange juice
1½ cups sugar	1 pint heavy cream
Grated rind 2 oranges	½ cup sugar
1 cup lemon juice	2 eggs

Few grains salt

Dissolve sugar in boiling water, add orange rind, lemon juice and orange juice. Turn into freezer and freeze to a mush. Beat cream until stiff and add sugar and salt. Separate yolks from whites of eggs, beat yolks until thick and lemon-colored and whites until stiff and add to cream. Turn into frozen mixture and continue the freezing.

Lemon Cream Sherbet

1½ cups sugar	2 cups milk
¾ cup lemon juice	2 cups thin cream

Few grains salt

Mix sugar and lemon juice and add gradually milk and cream, then salt. Freeze and serve.

Coffee Ice Cream

2 cups scalded milk	1 cup sugar
⅓ cup ground coffee	1 egg
1 tablespoon flour	⅛ teaspoon salt

1 quart thin cream

Scald milk with coffee. Mix flour and sugar, add egg, slightly beaten, and milk, gradually. Cook over hot water twenty minutes, stirring constantly at first and afterwards occasionally. Cool, add cream and strain through a double thickness of cheese-cloth, placed over a fine sieve. Freeze, using three pints finely crushed ice to one pint rock salt.

Prune Ice Cream

1 cup prunes	4 tablespoons lemon juice
1½ cups cold water	1¼ cups heavy cream
1 cup sugar	⅛ teaspoon salt

Pick over prunes and soak over night in cold water. Cook in same water until soft, remove stones and put fruit pulp through a purée strainer. Add sugar, lemon juice, salt and heavy cream, beaten until stiff; then freeze.

Strawberry Ice Cream I

1 quart strawberries	1½ cups milk
1 cup sugar	Whites 4 eggs
1½ cups heavy cream	⅛ teaspoon salt

Wash, pick over, hull and mash berries. Sprinkle with sugar, cover and let stand several hours; then squeeze through a double thickness of cheese-cloth. Mix cream, milk, whites of eggs, beaten until stiff, and salt. Freeze to a mush, using three parts finely crushed ice to one part rock salt. Add fruit juice and continue the freezing. If the fruit is acid more sugar may be necessary.

Quince Ice Cream

Make same as Strawberry Ice Cream I, using one-half cup quince purée in place of strawberries and adding one-half cup quince syrup drained from canned quince and one-half tablespoon lemon juice. To obtain quince purée, drain canned quince and force through a purée strainer.

Strawberry Ice Cream II

3 cups thin cream	Sugar
Syrup from canned strawberries	Few grains salt
Red coloring	

To cream add syrup drained from canned strawberries to flavor, sugar to sweeten, and salt; then color a delicate pink. Freeze, using three parts finely crushed ice to one part rock salt.

Normandy Ice Cream

2 cups sugar	1 pint heavy cream
½ cup water	4 tablespoons Maraschino
Yolks 6 eggs	1 teaspoon vanilla
Few grains salt	

Put sugar and water in saucepan, bring to boiling point and let boil until syrup will spin a thread when dropped from tip of spoon. Pour gradually, while beating constantly, on yolks of eggs, well beaten. Cool, add cream, beaten until stiff, and remaining ingredients. Freeze and serve in glasses with Marshmallow Sauce.

Marshmallow Sauce

¼ pound marshmallows	1 cup confectioners' sugar
¼ cup boiling water	

Cut marshmallows in pieces and melt in double boiler. Dissolve sugar in boiling water, add to marshmallows and stir until thoroughly blended. Turn into a bowl and cool before serving. A delicious accompaniment to chocolate or coffee ice cream.

Marshmallow Ice Cream

1 cup sugar	Whites 3 eggs
¼ cup water	1 tablespoon vanilla
½ pound marshmallows	1⅛ cups heavy cream

Put sugar and water in saucepan, bring to boiling point and let boil until syrup will spin a thread when dropped from tip of spoon. Add marshmallows, cut in halves, and when partially melted beat, using an egg beater, until mixture is smooth. Pour gradually, while beating constantly, on whites of eggs, beaten until stiff, and beat until cold; then add vanilla and cream, beaten until stiff. Freeze, using three parts finely crushed ice to one part rock salt.

Praline Ice Cream

½ cup sugar	½ cup sugar
⅜ cup chopped pecan nut meats	Few grains salt
2 cups scalded milk	1 cup heavy cream
Yolks 3 eggs	¾ tablespoon vanilla

Put one-half cup sugar in small omelet pan and stir constantly, until caramelized. Add nut meats and turn into a slightly buttered tin. Cool, pound and pass through a strainer. Make a custard of milk, egg yolks, remaining sugar and salt. Add prepared nuts and cool; then add cream, beaten until stiff, and vanilla and freeze.

Montrose Pudding. — *Page 288.*

Strawberry Ice Cream en Surprise. — *Page 293*

LIGHTED ICE CREAM. — *Page 294.*

MACAROON BASKET FILLED WITH ICE CREAM. — *Page 371*

Henri Apricot Ice Cream

1 can apricots	¼ cup lemon juice
1½ cups orange juice	Few grains salt
1 cup sugar	

Drain apricots and force fruit through a purée strainer. To syrup add fruit juices and salt, and sweeten to taste; then add apricot purée. Freeze, using three parts finely crushed ice to one part rock salt, and mould in one-half-pound baking powder boxes. Pack in salt and ice and let stand one and one-half hours. Remove from moulds, cut in slices for serving, and garnish with Praline Ice Cream.

Standish Pudding

1 quart box strawberries	1 pint heavy cream
1 cup granulated sugar	½ cup powdered sugar
1 cup water	½ tablespoon vanilla
Lemon juice	⅜ cup rolled dried macaroons

Pick over strawberries, sprinkle with granulated sugar, cover and let stand two hours. Mash, squeeze through a double thickness of cheese-cloth and add water and lemon juice to taste. Turn mixture into a brick mould. Beat cream until stiff and add powdered sugar, vanilla and rolled macaroons. Pour over fruit mixture to overflow mould. Cover with buttered paper (buttered side up), adjust cover, pack in rock salt and finely crushed ice, using equal parts, and let stand three hours. Remove from mould to chilled serving dish and garnish with Spun Sugar (see The Boston Cooking-School Cook Book, p. 548).

Montrose Pudding

Line a melon mould with Lemon Ice, fill with Maraschino Cream, cover with buttered paper, adjust cover, pack in salt and ice, using one part salt to two parts ice, and let stand three hours. Remove to serving dish and garnish with Maraschino Cream, forced through a pastry bag and tube, crystallized mint leaves and glacéd cherries.

Lemon Ice. — Make a syrup by boiling four cups water and two cups sugar five minutes. Add three-fourths cup lemon juice, cool, strain and freeze.

Maraschino Cream. — Beat one pint heavy cream until stiff. Add one-half cup powdered sugar, two tablespoons Maraschino Cordial and a few grains salt.

Glacé Hélène

Line a mould with vanilla ice cream and fill with the following mixture: Beat one pint heavy cream until stiff and add one-half cup powdered sugar, one jar red Bar-le-duc Currants, one teaspoon vanilla and one cup canned pineapple, cut in small cubes, and soaked in one tablespoon Kirsch one hour. Cover with ice cream to overflow mould. Adjust cover, pack in salt and ice, using equal parts, and let stand two hours.

Bombe Mousselaine

Line a mould with strawberry ice and fill with the following mixture: Beat one cup heavy cream until stiff and add three-fourths cup powdered sugar, one cup strawberry purée, one tablespoon Kirsch and two teaspoons vanilla. Cover with strawberry ice to overflow mould, adjust cover, pack in salt and ice, using equal parts, and let stand two hours. To obtain strawberry purée force fresh strawberries through a purée strainer. Remove to chilled serving dish and garnish with whipped cream, sweetened and flavored with vanilla, and fresh selected strawberries.

Bombe Suprême

2 cups water	1½ cups orange juice
1 cup sugar	1½ cups grape fruit
Few gratings orange rind	1 tablespoon lemon juice
Yolks 4 eggs	1½ cups heavy cream
1 tablespoon granulated gelatine	½ cup powdered sugar
	Few grains salt
3 tablespoons cold water	¾ tablespoon Maraschino

Put water, sugar and grated rind in saucepan, bring to the boiling point, add yolks of eggs, slightly beaten, and boil one minute. Remove from range and add gelatine, soaked in cold water. Strain, cool, add fruit juices and freeze. Line a two-qaurt melon mould with frozen mixture and fill with cream, beaten until stiff, sweetened and flavored. Cover with buttered paper, adjust cover, pack in salt and ice and let stand two and one-half hours. Remove from mould to serving dish and garnish with red Bar-le-duc Currants and pistachio nuts.

Coffee Caramel Parfait

1 cup milk	½ cup sugar
2 tablespoons ground coffee	¼ teaspoon salt
½ cup caramelized sugar	3 cups cream
Yolks 3 eggs	1 teaspoon vanilla

Scald milk with coffee and add caramelized sugar and yolks of eggs, slightly beaten, and mixed with sugar and salt. Cook until mixture thickens, stirring constantly; strain and cool. Add cream and vanilla and freeze. Line moulds with mixture, fill cavities with Sherry Cream, cover, pack in salt and ice, using equal parts, and let stand two hours. Remove from moulds and roll in Jordan almonds, blanched, shredded and browned in oven. Arrange on a serving dish and surround with spun sugar.

Sherry Cream.—Beat one cup heavy cream until stiff and add one-fourth cup powdered sugar, two tablespoons Sherry wine, one-half teaspoon almond extract and a few grains salt.

Strawberry Parfait Amour

Part I

1 quart box strawberries	½ cup water
2 cups sugar	Whites 3 eggs
1 pint heavy cream	

Wash, pick over, hull and mash berries. Sprinkle with one-half the sugar, cover and let stand several hours; then force through a fine strainer. Put remaining sugar in saucepan, add water, bring to boiling point and let boil until mixture will spin a thread when dropped from tip of spoon. Pour syrup gradually, while beating constantly, on whites of eggs, beaten until stiff. Cool and fold in cream, beaten until stiff. Freeze strawberry juice to a mush, add cream mixture and continue the freezing.

Part II

1 pint heavy cream	1½ teaspoons vanilla
½ cup powdered sugar	¾ cup brittle
¾ cup Jordan almonds	Few grains salt

Beat cream until stiff and add sugar, almonds (blanched, roasted in a slow oven and chopped), brittle (broken in small pieces) and salt. Turn into a border or ring mould, cover with buttered paper, adjust cover, pack in salt and ice, using two parts finely crushed ice to one part rock salt, and let stand three hours.

Remove Part II from mould to chilled serving dish, pile Part I in centre and garnish with one or two crystallized pink California roses. Such roses may be bought of large city, fancy grocers or confectioners.

For brittle put three-fourths cup sugar in small omelet pan, place on range and stir constantly, until reduced to a syrup. Pour into a hot dripping pan, allowing syrup to barely cover bottom of pan. Cool, remove from pan, and roll fine.

Marron Plombière
Part I

2 cups scalded milk	⅛ teaspoon salt
¾ cup sugar	2 cups thin cream
Yolks 5 eggs	2 tablespoons brandy
1 tablespoon vanilla	

Make a custard of first four ingredients; strain, cool, add cream and freeze to a mush. Add brandy and vanilla and finish the freezing.

Part II

½ tablespoon granulated gelatine	1 teaspoon vanilla
2 tablespoons cold water	A few grains salt
¼ cup scalded cream	10 brandied marrons
⅛ cup powdered sugar	¼ cup Sultana raisins
2¼ cups thin cream	5 macaroons
	1½ tablespoons brandy

Soak gelatine in cold water, dissolve in scalded cream and add powdered sugar. Set in pan of ice water and stir until mixture begins to thicken; then add the whip from cream, vanilla, salt, marrons, broken in pieces, Sultana raisins and macaroons (broken in pieces), soaked in brandy one hour.

Line a mould with Part I and fill with Part II. Cover, pack in rock salt and finely crushed ice, using equal parts, and let stand two and one-half hours.

New Year's Bomb
Part I

1½ cups milk	⅛ teaspoon salt
5 eggs	2½ cups cream
¾ cup sugar	1½ tablespoons vanilla

Make a custard of milk, eggs, sugar and salt. Strain, cool and add cream and vanilla. Freeze and line a melon mould with mixture.

Part II

1 cup sugar	3 tablespoons cold water
2 cups cream	⅛ cup Jordan almonds
¾ tablespoon granulated gelatine	¼ cup powdered sugar
	1 teaspoon vanilla
⅛ teaspoon salt	

Put sugar in small saucepan or omelet pan, place on hot part of range and stir constantly until melted and of the color of maple syrup. Care must be taken to prevent sugar from adhering to sides or bottom of pan. Turn caramelized sugar into a dripping pan, cool and roll. Beat cream until stiff and add gelatine, soaked in cold water (then heated over hot water until gelatine has dissolved), caramelized sugar, almonds (blanched, roasted in a hot oven until brown, and chopped), powdered sugar, vanilla and salt. Fill lined mould with Part II, adjust cover, pack in salt and ice and let stand three hours.

Strawberry Ice Cream en Surprise

Beat whites of four eggs until stiff and add gradually, while beating constantly, two-thirds cup sugar, continuing the beating until mixture will hold its shape; then cut and fold in one-third cup sugar and flavor with one-half teaspoon vanilla. Brush over a pasteboard box (of correct size to cover a three-pint brick mould) with a piece of tissue paper dipped in olive oil. Cover box with mixture forced through a pastry bag and large rose tube in parallel rows, lengthwise. Place on tin sheet and bake in a slow oven fifty minutes. Remove case from box, cool and put over a three-pint brick of strawberry ice cream, on a chilled serving dish. Garnish with a crystallized pink California rose. Cut in slices, crosswise, for serving.

Lighted Ice Cream

2 cups scalded milk
½ cup sugar
Yolks 6 eggs
¼ teaspoon salt
2 cups thin cream
Canned quinces
½ cup quince syrup
3 tablespoons orange Curaçoa
1 teaspoon Kirsch
½ teaspoon rum

Make a custard of first four ingredients, strain and cool. Drain canned quince and force some of the pulp through a purée strainer; there should be two-thirds cup pulp. Add to custard, cream, quince pulp and remaining ingredients. Freeze and fill one-pound baking powder boxes, pack in salt and ice and let stand two hours. Color cold water violet. Set fancy ring mould in pail on bed of rock salt and finely crushed ice (using equal parts) and fill mould with the colored water. Add salt and ice until it comes nearly to top of mould and let stand until ice is nearly melted. If by this time water is not sufficiently frozen to form a shell, repack. Invert ice shell and drain off water. Put on a folded napkin on serving dish and surround with slices cut from

Grape Fruit Cocktail with Mint Balls   *Page* 295

Coupe Caruso. — *Page 297*

mould of ice cream, sprinkled with candied violets. Have ready a circular piece of cardboard of correct size to fit ring mould. Cut down three small candles, melt bottoms and place at regular intervals on cardboard. Light candles just before sending to table. The effect is heightened when the room is darkened.

Chantilly Mousse

1 pint heavy cream	Few grains salt
½ cup powdered sugar	10 drops Hudnut's essence of violet
2 cups meringues, broken in pieces	

Beat cream until stiff, using a Dover egg beater. Remove beater and add remaining ingredients. Turn into a mould, filling to overflowing, adjust cover, pack in finely crushed ice and rock salt (using equal parts) and let stand four hours. Remove to serving dish and garnish with candied violets and angelica.

Grape Fruit Cocktail with Mint Balls

Remove pulp from grape fruit and cut sections in pieces. Sprinkle with powdered sugar and chill in ice box. Serve in double cocktail glasses and garnish each with three small balls made of Crême de Menthe Ice (see p. 281) and three green leaves.

Coupe Moquin

Make an orange ice mixture (see The Boston Cooking-School Cook Book, p. 435) and freeze to a mush;

then add two tablespoons Crême de Menthe cordial and continue the freezing. Serve in champagne or coupe glasses and garnish with Bar-le-duc Currants, candied orange peel and fresh mint leaves.

Hamburg Grape Coupe

Beat yolks of seven eggs until thick and add three-fourths cup sugar, one-eighth teaspoon salt, one quart thin cream and three tablespoons Sherry wine. Freeze and fill coupe glasses two-thirds full of mixture and pipe Lemon Ice around edge, by forcing through a pastry bag and tube. Fill cavity with Hamburg grapes from which skins and seeds have been removed.

Coupe Majestic

Remove pulp from oranges in sections, allowing three sections to each coupe, as well as one teaspoon Bar-le-duc Currants and two-thirds teaspoon Kirsch. Put prepared fruit in coupe glasses, cover with Orange Ice Cream (see The Boston Cooking-School Cook Book, p. 445) and cover ice cream with Orange Ice (see The Boston Cooking-School Cook Book, p. 435), colored pink. Make a depression in centre of Orange Ice and fill with whipped cream, to which is added Bar-le-duc Currants. Pour over each coupe one-half teaspoon Kirsch.

Pineapple Coupe

Mix one half-cup, each, shredded pineapple and sections of oranges, cut in pieces, and one-fourth cup

Malaga grapes (from which skin and seeds have been removed), cut in halves. Pour over two tablespoons Sherry wine and add two tablespoons powdered sugar and a few grains salt. Cover and let stand in ice box until thoroughly chilled.

Arrange fruit in eight coupe glasses, cover with Vanilla Ice Cream (see The Boston Cooking-School Cook Book, p. 442), slightly piled in centre, and garnish with five triangular pieces of candied pineapple, five circular pieces of angelica, and a glacéd cherry.

Coupe Suzanne

Remove apricots from can and cut in small pieces. To syrup add one-half cup sugar, bring to the boiling point and let simmer three minutes; add apricots and continue the boiling until syrup is thick and apricots are very soft. Half fill coupe, champagne or frappé glasses with vanilla ice cream, put one tablespoon prepared apricots in each, cover with ice cream, and garnish with red Bar-le-duc jam.

Coupe Caruso

Put in coupe glasses one tablespoon, each, shredded pineapple and thin strips of apple, soaked in rum. Fill glasses with Strawberry and Pistachio Ice Cream, using equal parts, having the dividing line between the two kinds extend up and down through centre of glass. Spread evenly on top and garnish with diamond-shaped pieces of angelica and one-half a glacéd cherry.

Coupe Louisiana

Mix two-thirds cup, each, fresh shredded pineapple and strawberries, cut in quarters. Sprinkle with one-fourth cup powdered sugar and pour over one-half tablespoon Maraschino. Cover and let stand in cold place two hours. Put mixture in eight coupe glasses, cover fruit with Orange Ice, colored pink (see The Boston Cooking-School Cook Book, p. 435). Cover ice with Strawberry Ice Cream and garnish top of each with a small cream cake filled with whipped cream, sweetened and flavored with vanilla, and covered with Confectioners' Frosting (see The Boston Cooking-School Cook Book, p. 527), colored pink.

Cognac Pear Coupe

Drain canned pears from syrup and to syrup add one-half cup sugar and a few grains salt. Bring to the boiling point and let simmer fifteen minutes. Add two tablespoons brandy and eight whole pears. Place on back of range and let stand ten minutes; then drain. Cut remaining pears in small pieces; there should be one cup. Add one-half slice canned pineapple, cut in small pieces, and two tablespoons Maraschino cherries, cut in quarters, and pour over one tablespoon brandy and one-fourth cup pineapple syrup. Arrange fruit in eight coupe glasses, cover with Vanilla Ice Cream, place whole pears in centre and garnish with whipped cream, sweetened and

Parfait Amour. — *Page* 300

Cognac Pear Coupe. — *Page* 298.

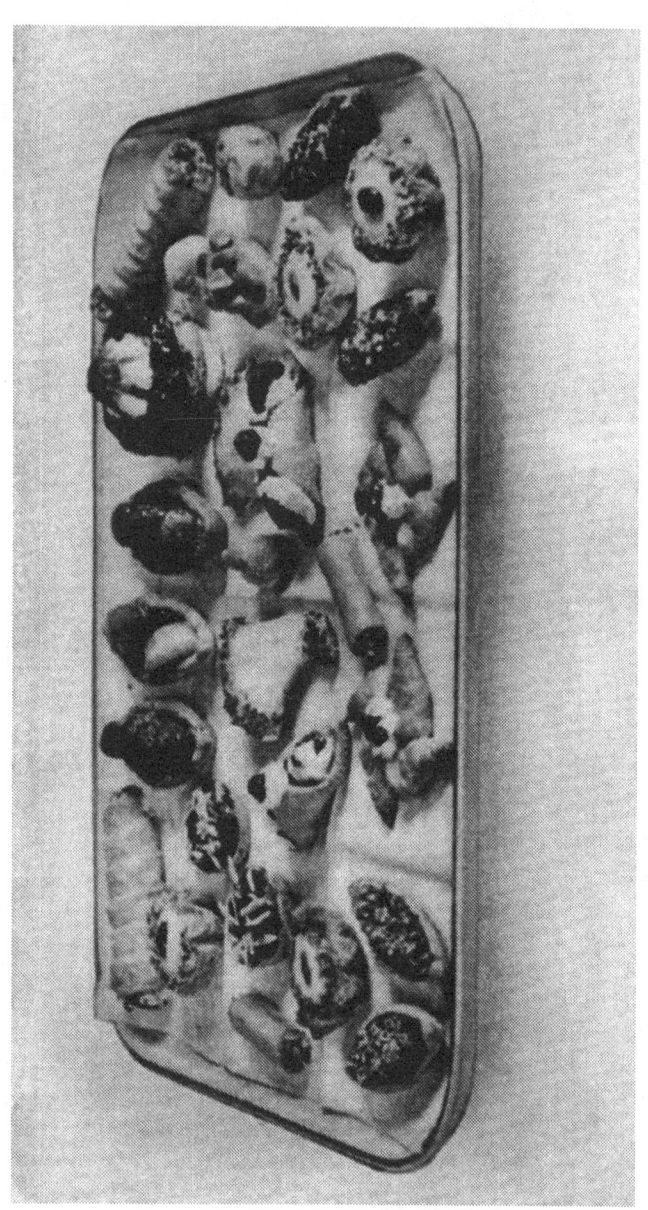

A Tray of Pastry Novelties

flavored with vanilla and forced through a pastry bag and tube.

Chocolate Mint Coupe

Put a layer of Chocolate Ice Cream in coupe glass, cover with a layer of Mint Cream, and cover mint cream with a layer of chocolate ice cream. Garnish each with a glacéd mint paste.

Chocolate Ice Cream. — Put one-half pound sweet chocolate in double boiler, add two cups cold milk and cook over hot water until thick and smooth; the time required being about fifteen minutes. Beat four eggs and add one cup sugar; then add one cup thin cream, one tablespoon, each, vanilla and brandy and one-eighth teaspoon salt. Combine mixtures, strain and freeze.

Mint Cream. — Mix one cup heavy cream, one cup milk, one-half cup sugar and five tablespoons Crême de Menthe; then color green and freeze.

Plombière Charlotte

Turn contents one can peaches into a saucepan, add one-third cup sugar and a few grains salt, bring to the boiling point and let simmer until syrup is thick. Cut fruit in small pieces, pour over two tablespoons brandy and chill. Put one tablespoon prepared fruit in each coupe glass, cover with Junket Ice Cream (see The Boston Cooking-School Cook Book, p. 448) and arrange four halves of lady fingers at equal distances on top. Fill spaces with heavy cream, whipped, sweetened and flavored with brandy and vanilla in combination. Garnish top of each with a glacéd cherry.

Frozen Orange Whip

1 cup sugar	¼ cup orange juice
⅔ cup water	1 pint heavy cream
Grated rind 2 oranges	2 oranges

Boil sugar and water until syrup will thread when dropped from tip of spoon. Add grated rind and orange juice, cover and keep warm one hour; then cool. Beat cream until stiff and add, gradually, the orange syrup. Cut oranges in halves, crosswise, and remove pulp and separate into small pieces. Pour juice from the two oranges into a brick mould; then put in alternate layers of cream and orange pulp until mould is filled to overflowing. Adjust cover, pack in salt and ice, using equal parts, and let stand two hours.

Parfait Amour

4 cups water	Grated rind 2 oranges
2 cups sugar	Granadine
2 cups orange juice	Kirsch
¼ cup lemon juice	Brandy

Mix water and sugar, bring to the boiling point and let boil one minute. Add fruit juices and grated rind; cool, strain and freeze. Serve in tall coupe glasses, make a depression in each one, using the handle of a wooden spoon, and fill each cavity with one teaspoon granadine, one teaspoon Kirsch and one-half teaspoon brandy. By adding the liquors in this order their difference in specific gravity will cause them to appear in three distinct layers.

Pineapple Marquise

2 cups sugar	Few grains salt
2 cups water	1 pint heavy cream
2 cups pineapple juice	1 cup pineapple purée
Juice 1 lemon	¼ cup powdered sugar
¼ cup Swiss Kirsch	1 teaspoon vanilla

Make a syrup by boiling sugar and water two minutes, add pineapple juice, lemon juice, Kirsch and salt, and freeze, using equal parts of finely crushed ice and rock salt. Just before serving add remaining ingredients. Serve in coupe or champagne glasses. To obtain pineapple purée, force canned pineapple through a purée strainer.

Armandine Punch

1 can peaches	⅓ cup prunes
¾ cup sugar	⅓ cup Maraschino cherries
1½ cups water	⅓ cup white canned cherries
Few grains salt	¼ cup brandy
Whites 5 eggs	Heavy cream
1 tablespoon lemon juice	Powdered sugar
¼ cup rum	Red coloring
⅓ cup raisins	Peach extract

Add sugar to peaches, bring to the boiling point and let simmer thirty minutes; then rub through a sieve. Add water, salt, egg whites, unbeaten, and lemon juice. Freeze to a mush and add rum, raisins, seeded and cut in pieces, prunes, stoned and cut in pieces, Maraschino cherries, cut in halves, and canned cherries, cut in halves, soaked in brandy over night or for several hours; then freeze until of the right consistency.

Serve in coupe glasses and pour over each two tablespoons heavy cream, colored pink, sweetened and flavored with peach extract.

Pistachio Parfait

1 cup sugar	1 pint heavy cream
¼ cup water	Green coloring
Whites 3 eggs	½ cup finely chopped
1 tablespoon vanilla	pistachio nuts
1 teaspoon almond extract	Whipped cream

Boil sugar and water until syrup will thread when dropped from tip of spoon. Pour slowly, while stirring constantly, on the beaten whites of eggs, and continue the beating until mixture is cold; then add flavoring. Color cream a delicate green and beat until stiff. Add to first mixture with nut meats. Freeze, using three pints finely crushed ice to one pint rock salt, and serve in glasses. Garnish top with whipped cream, sweetened and flavored with vanilla, and sprinkle with chopped pistachio nuts.

Marron Parfait

1 cup sugar	1 cup marrons, cut in pieces
¼ cup water	1 tablespoon rum
Yolks 6 eggs	1 pint heavy cream
	2 teaspoons vanilla

Mock Mince Pie. — *Page* 306

Chocolate Custard Pie

Put sugar and water in saucepan; bring to the boiling point and let boil five minutes. Pour syrup gradually, while beating constantly, on yolks of eggs, beaten until thick, and cook over hot water, stirring constantly until mixture thickens. Remove from fire and beat until cold. Add marrons, which have soaked in rum one-half hour, cream beaten until stiff and vanilla.

Turn into moulds, adjust covers, pack in salt and ice (using equal parts) and let stand four hours. Remove to chilled serving dish and garnish with whipped cream (sweetened and flavored) and marrons.

CHAPTER XXVI

PASTRY AND PIES

Family Paste

MIX and sift two cups pastry flour with one and one-half teaspoons salt and work in two-thirds cup lard, using the tips of the fingers. Moisten with one-half cup cold water and toss two-thirds of the mixture on a slightly floured board. Pat and roll in rectangular shape, spread with one tablespoon lard and dredge with flour. Cut in thirds, lengthwise; pile strips one on top of another. Fold in halves and then in quarters. Again pat and roll out, spread, dredge and fold as before. Cut in halves, turn over, having cut edges come on top. Pat and roll each piece to fit top of pie, and pat and roll reserved third for two undercrusts.

Oscar's Paste

2⅔ cups pastry flour
¾ cup cold water
¾ cup washed butter
2 tablespoons lard

Put two cups flour in bowl, add gradually cold water and beat until smooth. Put one-third cup flour on board or cloth, turn mixture from bowl on flour. Put two-thirds washed butter mixed with lard in centre of mixture, draw mixture over butter, sprinkle top generously with some of the remaining one-third flour and pat and fold four times. Again sprinkle with flour and pat and roll in long rectangular shape. Spread with remaining butter, dredge with flour and fold from ends towards centre, making three layers. Pat, roll and again fold; repeat three times.

Puff Paste (by Measurement)

I

1½ cups bread flour, once sifted
1 cup washed butter

II

1 cup bread flour, once sifted
½ cup pastry flour, once sifted
1 cup washed butter

Either I or II gives the correct ingredients by measure for the making of puff paste. These have been worked out at the request of many pupils who often do not have family scales or if they do have them, find they do not always weigh correctly or are carelessly used. Follow directions for the making in The Boston Cooking-School Cook Book, p. 461.

Irish Puff Paste

2 cups bread flour   2 cups butter
Cold water

Put flour in bowl and add butter, separated into small pieces. Moisten to a dough with water and toss on a slightly floured board or cloth. Pound, using the rolling pin, until butter is thoroughly incorporated throughout the mixture. If butter becomes so soft that the handling is difficult, put on ice to chill. When thoroughly blended, pat, roll, shape and bake.

Cataldi's Puff Paste

1 pound pastry flour	Yolk 1 egg
2 tablespoons lemon juice	Cold water
½ teaspoon salt	1 pound washed butter

Put flour, once sifted, in bowl, make a depression in centre, pour in lemon juice and add yolk of egg and salt; then add cold water to make a dough. Toss on a floured cloth, knead, cover and let stand five minutes. Pat, roll out and fold in washed butter, same as puff paste (see The Boston Cooking-School Cook Book, p. 461).

Mock Mince Pie Meat

3 pints chopped apples	1 teaspoon clove
3 pints chopped green tomatoes	¾ teaspoon allspice
4 cups brown sugar	¾ teaspoon mace
1⅓ cups vinegar	¾ teaspoon pepper
3 cups raisins	2 teaspoons salt
3 teaspoons cinnamon	¾ cup butter

Mix apples with tomatoes and drain. Add remaining ingredients, except butter, bring gradually to the boiling point, and let simmer three hours, then add butter. Turn into glass jars as soon as made.

Banana Pie

1 cup scalded milk	¼ cup thin cream or top milk
⅓ cup sugar	¾ tablespoon lemon juice
2⅔ tablespoons flour	1 large banana
⅛ teaspoon salt	Whites 2 eggs
Yolks 2 eggs	2 tablespoons powdered sugar

¼ teaspoon lemon extract

Mix sugar, flour and salt, and add egg yolks, slightly beaten. Pour on scalded milk gradually, while stirring constantly, and cook in double boiler fifteen minutes, stirring constantly until mixture thickens, and afterwards occasionally. Cool and add cream, lemon juice and banana, peeled, scraped and cut in one-eighth-inch slices. Chill thoroughly and turn into a pastry pie case (see The Boston Cooking-School Cook Book, p. 466).

Just before serving beat whites of eggs until stiff, add sugar, gradually, and lemon juice. Spread evenly over pie and put under gas flame to cook until delicately browned.

Marlborough Pie

3 apples	Grated rind ½ lemon
⅓ cup butter	1½ tablespoons lemon juice
⅓ cup sugar	1½ tablespoons Sherry wine
3 eggs, slightly beaten	Few grains salt

Wipe, pare, core and steam three apples; then rub through a fine sieve and add remaining ingredients. Line a pie-plate with paste, put on rim and turn in mixture. Bake in a moderate oven until firm. Garnish top lattice fashion with Meringue II (see The Boston Cooking-School Cook Book, p. 480) forced through a pastry bag and round tube, then pipe a border around edge. Ornament with diamond-shaped pieces and cubes of currant or crab apple jelly, as shown in illustration.

Rhubarb and Raisin Pie

Line a plate with plain paste and fill with two cups rhubarb, cut in one-quarter-inch pieces. Sprinkle with one cup sugar and one-half cup raisins, seeded and cut in halves. Cover with crust and bake in a moderate oven forty-five minutes.

Pumpkin Pie

1½ cups steamed and strained pumpkin	½ teaspoon ginger
⅜ cup brown sugar	½ teaspoon salt
1 teaspoon cinnamon	2 eggs
	1½ cups milk
½ cup cream	

Mix sugar, spices and salt and add pumpkin, eggs, slightly beaten, and milk and cream, gradually. Bake in one crust, cool and serve with

Brandy Sauce.—Cream one-fourth cup butter and add gradually, while beating constantly, one and one-fourth cups brown sugar and two tablespoons brandy; then add yolks two eggs, well beaten, and one-half cup milk. Cook over hot water, stirring constantly, until mixture thickens. Pour mixture gradually, while beating constantly, on whites of two eggs beaten until stiff.

Chocolate Custard Pie

1⅛ cups milk	1½ teaspoons butter
2 tablespoons grated chocolate	2 egg yolks
	3½ teaspoons cornstarch
½ cup sugar	½ teaspoon vanilla

Scald one cup milk with grated chocolate, sugar and butter. Add egg yolks, slightly beaten, and cornstarch, diluted with remaining milk, and cook ten minutes, stirring constantly until mixture thickens and afterwards occasionally; then add vanilla. Fill a pastry pie case with mixture, cover with Meringue II (see The Boston Cooking-School Cook Book, p. 480), forced through a pastry bag and tube, and bake until firm and delicately browned.

Butter Scotch Pie

Roll paste to one-fourth inch in thickness, cut three circles nine inches in diameter, prick, place on a tin sheet and bake in a hot oven. Put between layers Butter Scotch Filling and cover top with meringue.

Butter Scotch Filling. — Cream four tablespoons butter and add gradually six tablespoons flour; then add three-fourths cup brown sugar, mixed with two eggs slightly beaten, and one-half teaspoon salt. Scald two cups milk, add three teaspoons caramel syrup and add gradually to mixture. Return to double boiler and cook fifteen minutes, stirring constantly until mixture thickens and afterwards occasionally. Caramel syrup is made by caramelizing one-half cup sugar, adding one-third cup boiling water and letting boil until a thick syrup is formed.

Meringue. — Beat whites three eggs until stiff, and add gradually, while beating constantly, three tablespoons brown sugar and a few grains salt;

then cut and fold in two tablespoons powdered sugar.

Frangipan Cream Pie

Roll paste to one-fourth-inch thickness and cut three circular pieces, nine inches in diameter. Place on a tin sheet, prick with a fork and bake in a hot oven. Put together with Frangipan Cream (see p. 346) and dust top with powdered sugar.

Devonshire Pie

Roll paste one-quarter inch in thickness, cut three circles nine inches in diameter and prick with a fork. From one of the pieces cut a circle seven and one-half inches in diameter, leaving a one and one-half inch ring. Place on a tin sheet and bake in a hot oven. Put cream filling between pieces, place ring on top, and fill space with fresh strawberries, sweetened to taste. Garnish or not, as desired, with whipped cream, sweetened and flavored with vanilla.

Apple Flawn

Wipe, pare, quarter, core and thinly slice four apples. Put in saucepan with one tablespoon butter, three tablespoons powdered sugar, grated rind one-fourth lemon, and one-inch-piece stick cinnamon. Cook, stirring constantly, until reduced to a thick purée; then remove cinnamon. Add one-third the measure of apricot purée and season with one-half tablespoon Apricot Brandy, a few grains salt and more sugar if needed.

Wipe and pare three selected apples, cut in eighths, lengthwise, and remove cores. Make a syrup by boiling one cup sugar and one cup water ten minutes. Add one teaspoon vanilla and one-half the pieces of apple. Cook slowly until apples are soft and clear. Remove from syrup and coat each piece with some of the syrup. To remaining syrup add one-fourth cup boiling water and color red. Bring to the boiling point, add remaining apples and cook and coat. Fill pie pastry shell with first mixture and garnish top with alternate sections of prepared apples, working from outside towards centre.

CHAPTER XXVII

PASTRY DESSERTS

Apple Dumplings

ROLL Plain Paste (see The Boston Cooking-School Cook Book, p. 463), or Family Paste very thin and cut in squares. Pare and core eight medium-sized apples and place an apple on each square. Fill cavities with sugar and add a few grains, each, of cinnamon and nutmeg and a bit of butter. Wet edges of pastry with white of egg and fold points over apples. Place in dripping pan and pour around one cup boiling water, to which have been added one-half cup sugar, one-fourth cup butter and one-half teaspoon cinnamon. Bake in a hot oven until apples are soft. Before removing from oven, brush over with white of egg and sprinkle with sugar. Serve with Creamy Sauce I (see The Boston Cooking-School Cook Book, p. 408).

Pastry Stars

Roll puff paste to one-eighth inch in thickness and cut in three-inch squares. Make a one and one-half inch cut from four corners on diagonal of squares and fold alternate corners to centre in such a way as to make star shapes. Arrange on a tin sheet and bake in a hot oven. Cool, press down centres and fill with any conserve.

Nut Pastry Sticks

Roll plain paste to one-fourth inch in thickness and cut in strips five inches long by one inch wide, using a pastry jagger. Arrange on a tin sheet and bake in a hot oven. Cool slightly, brush over with white of one egg, slightly beaten and diluted with one teaspoon cold water. Sprinkle generously with chopped pecan nut meats, return to oven and bake two minutes.

Swedish Tea Circles

Roll Oscar's Paste (see p. 304) to one-third inch in thickness and spread generously with chopped blanched Jordan almonds, mixed with sugar, using one-half as much sugar as nut meats. Pat and roll to one-eighth inch in thickness and shape with a small circular cutter, first dipped in flour. Arrange on a tin sheet and bake in a hot oven eight minutes.

Nut Pastry Rolls

Roll paste to one-eighth inch in thickness and cut in pieces five by three inches. Spread with jelly, which has been beaten with a fork until of right consistency to spread, sprinkle with chopped pecan nut meats, and roll each piece separately like a jelly roll. Place on a tin sheet, having end of rolls nearest sheet, which keeps them in better shape. Bake in a hot oven.

Marguerite Squares

Pat and roll puff paste to one-eighth inch in thickness and cut in two-inch squares. Arrange on a tin sheet and bake until delicately browned. Cool slightly, spread with Marguerite Frosting, having it come nearly to edge of pastry, and return to oven to finish the baking. Arrange on plate covered with a lace paper doily.

Marguerite Frosting. — Put one and one-half cups sugar in a small saucepan, pour over one-half cup water, bring to the boiling point and let boil until syrup will spin a long thread when dropped from tip of spoon or tines of fork. Remove to back of range and add twelve marshmallows, cut in eighths. Pour gradually, while beating constantly, on whites of two eggs, beaten until stiff, and as soon as thoroughly blended add one-fourth cup shredded cocoanut, one-third cup currants or Sultana raisins and one-fourth teaspoon vanilla. If one is carrying out a color scheme, color as desired.

Pineapple Tartlets

Roll paste to one-quarter inch in thickness. Line patty pans with paste, prick, fill two-thirds full of rice or barley and bake in a hot oven until delicately browned. Mix three-quarters cup sugar and two tablespoons flour. Pour on gradually, while stirring constantly, one-half cup water, bring to the boiling point and let boil five minutes. Add one-half can shredded pineapple, yolks two eggs, slightly beaten, and one-quarter teaspoon salt. Fill pastry cases with pineapple mixture, cover with meringue and bake in a moderate oven until meringue is set and delicately browned.

Pineapple Circles

Put one can sliced pineapple in saucepan, add one-third cup sugar, bring to the boiling point and let simmer until fruit is soft. Roll paste to one-fourth inch in thickness, cut in circles, same size as pineapple slices, arrange on tin sheet, prick and bake in a hot oven ten minutes. Put together in pairs with White Mountain Cream Filling (see p. 345). Place a slice of pineapple on each and garnish centres with halves of candied cherries.

Amsterdam Pastry Novelties

Roll paste to one-fourth inch in thickness and cut in pieces six inches by two inches. Sprinkle ends with sugar mixed with cinnamon (using three parts sugar to one part cinnamon) and roll toward centre twice. Prick unrolled part with a fork, place on a tin sheet and bake in a hot oven. Spread unrolled sections with currant jelly, which has been beaten with a fork until of right consistency to spread evenly. Over jelly arrange one-inch sections of canned peaches. If peaches are not soft, cook in their own syrup, to which a small quantity of sugar has been added.

Mont Blanc

Pat and roll puff or Oscar's Paste to one-eighth inch in thickness and cut in three pieces twelve by three inches. Place on tin sheet, prick and bake in a hot oven. Cut each piece in quarters crosswise, using a sharp knife. Arrange four in square shape on serving dish, leaving a small space between each. Cover with fresh, or canned fruit; cover fruit with pastry squares and pastry squares again with fruit; repeat. Spread sides with whipped cream, sweetened and flavored with vanilla, and garnish with whipped cream, forced through a pastry bag and tube, and chopped pistachio nuts.

Peach Pralines

Roll paste to one-eighth inch in thickness and cut in eight rounds of correct size to cover inverted, circular individual tins. Cover tins with paste, prick several times and bake until delicately browned. Remove from pans, put two tablespoons Praline Cream (see p. 346) in each, on cream place one-half a canned peach, poached in its syrup, cover with meringue and bake until delicately browned.

St. Valentine's Hearts

Roll paste to one-fourth inch in thickness, shape with a heart-shaped cutter, first dipped in flour, place on a tin sheet and bake until delicately browned. Split, fill with orange marmalade, cover tops with

DEVONSHIRE PIE. — *Page* 310

MONT BLANC. — *Page* 316.

Keswick Gingerbread. — *Page 319*

Nut Oatmeal Cookies. — *Page 321*

orange frosting and sprinkle around edge a border of chopped, candied orange peel. Arrange on a plate covered with a heart-shaped lace paper doily.

Cocoanut Fluffs

Roll paste to one-fourth inch in thickness, cover inverted individual round tins, prick, place on tin sheet and bake in a hot oven. Cut circular pieces to fit top of tins and bake. Fill cakes with cocoanut mixture and cover with tops. For the mixture soak one-half cup shredded cocoanut in one-fourth cup milk one hour. Heat in double boiler and add gradually, while stirring constantly, one-half tablespoon cornstarch, diluted with one tablespoon cold water, and cook fifteen minutes, stirring constantly, until mixture thickens, and afterwards occasionally. Scald one-half cup milk and add one egg yolk mixed with one-fourth cup sugar, one tablespoon flour and one-eighth teaspoon salt. Cook fifteen minutes, stirring constantly, until mixture thickens, and afterwards occasionally. Add one tablespoon butter, cocoanut mixture, and one-half teaspoon vanilla; then fold in the white of one egg, beaten until stiff.

Venetian Boats

Roll puff paste to one-eighth inch in thickness and line small boat-shaped tins. Prick and half fill with spice cake mixture; sprinkle with chopped pecan nut meats, put on a tin sheet and bake in a hot oven.

For the spice cake mixture,—cream one-fourth cup butter and add one-fourth cup brown sugar gradually, while beating constantly; then add yolks two eggs, beaten until thick, one-fourth cup, each, molasses and milk and one and one-eighth cups flour, mixed and sifted with one-fourth teaspoon each soda and clove, one-eighth teaspoon grated nutmeg, a few grains cayenne and a few gratings from the rind of a lemon.

CHAPTER XXVIII

GINGERBREADS, COOKIES, AND WAFERS

Marshmallow Gingerbread

½ cup shortening	1¾ teaspoons soda
1 cup molasses	1 teaspoon salt
1 egg	1 teaspoon ginger
2⅛ cups flour	1 cup sour milk
Marshmallows	

MELT shortening (chicken fat may be used to excellent advantage) and add molasses, egg, well beaten, flour mixed and sifted with soda, salt and ginger and sour milk. Beat vigorously, turn into a buttered and floured dripping pan and bake in a moderate oven twenty-five minutes. Remove from pan, cut in halves, crosswise, and put marshmallows between layers. Put in oven and let stand three minutes. Remove to serving dish, cool slightly, cut in squares and serve with whipped cream, sweetened and flavored with vanilla.

Keswick Gingerbread

¼ pound butter	¼ pound brown sugar
¼ pound flour	½ teaspoon ginger
1 ounce candied lemon peel	

Work butter into flour, using the hands, and when well mixed, add sugar, ginger, and lemon peel, cut in small pieces, mixing with the hands. Press into a buttered pan two and one-half inches in thickness, using the back of the hand, and sprinkle with one-half cup of the mixture which has been reserved for the purpose. Bake in a moderate oven, cut in squares and let stand until cold; then remove from pan.

Shubert Gingerbread

2 cups bread flour
½ cup butter
½ cup sugar
1 egg
½ cup sour milk
½ teaspoon soda
½ teaspoon ginger
½ teaspoon grated nutmeg
¼ teaspoon cinnamon

Work flour and butter together, using the hands, until thoroughly mixed; then add sugar and again work together until crumbly, using the hands. Reserve one cup of the mixture as crumbs and to the remainder add egg, well beaten, and sour milk, mixed with soda and spices. Butter a shallow cake pan and sprinkle evenly with one-half of the reserved crumbs. Spread over the batter, sprinkle with remaining crumbs and bake in a moderate oven. Cut in squares or finger-shaped pieces while still hot, and remove from pan.

Sour Cream Molasses Cookies

¾ cup lard
¾ cup brown sugar
¾ cup molasses
2 eggs
¾ cup sour cream
1 tablespoon soda
1 tablespoon salt
½ tablespoon ginger
Flour

Work lard and sugar together until creamy; then add molasses, eggs, well beaten, sour cream, mixed

PEANUT BARS. — *Page* 321.

PEANUT MACAROONS. — *Page* 323

MARSHMALLOW TEAS READY FOR OVEN. — *Page* 324

MARSHMALLOW TEAS. — *Page* 324.

with soda, salt and ginger, and flour, to make a soft dough. Put in ice box or cold place to chill. Pat and roll to one-half inch in thickness (using one-half the mixture at a time) and shape with a round cutter, first dipped in flour. Put on a buttered sheet and bake in a moderate oven.

Nut Oatmeal Cookies

¼ cup butter	½ cup chopped nut meats
¼ cup lard	1½ cups flour
1 cup sugar	½ teaspoon salt
1 egg	½ teaspoon soda
5 tablespoons milk	¾ teaspoon cinnamon
1¾ cups rolled oats	½ teaspoon clove
½ cup raisins	½ teaspoon allspice

Cream butter and lard together, and add gradually, while beating constantly, sugar; then add egg, well beaten, milk, rolled oats, raisins (seeded and cut in pieces) and nut meats, chopped. Mix and sift flour with remaining ingredients and add to first mixture. Drop from tip of spoon on a buttered sheet, one inch apart, and bake in a moderate oven fifteen minutes.

Peanut Bars

1 quart roasted Spanish peanuts	1 cup brown sugar
White 1 egg	¼ teaspoon salt
½ teaspoon vanilla	

Shell, remove skins and finely chop peanuts. Beat white of egg until stiff and add gradually, while beating constantly, sugar, salt and vanilla. Fold in peanuts, spread mixture in a buttered tin square shallow pan and bake in a slow oven. Cut in bars, using a sharp knife, and remove from pan.

Peanut Wafers

¾ cup butter	½ teaspoon soda
1½ cups light brown sugar	3 tablespoons milk
1 egg	1 quart peanuts
½ teaspoon salt	Flour

Cream butter and add sugar gradually, while beating constantly; then add egg, well beaten, salt, and soda dissolved in milk. Shell, skin and chop peanuts. Add one-half to mixture and flour to roll the quantity required, being about three cups. Put a portion of the mixture on a well-greased and slightly floured tin sheet or inverted dripping pan and pat and roll to one-eighth inch in thickness, then sprinkle with peanuts and bake in a hot oven. Cut in strips one inch by three inches. Repeat until all the mixture is used.

Swedish Nut Wafers

¼ cup shortening	2 tablespoons milk
¾ cup sugar	½ teaspoon salt
1 egg	1 teaspoon baking powder
1⅛ cups flour	1 teaspoon vanilla
⅛ cup chopped nut meats	

Cream the shortening (using butter and lard in equal proportions) and add sugar gradually, while beating constantly; then add egg, well beaten, milk, flour, mixed and sifted, with baking powder and salt and vanilla. Spread evenly on the bottom of a buttered inverted dripping pan, using a case knife, sprinkle with nut meats and mark in strips three-fourths inch wide by four and one-half inches long, and bake in a moderate oven twelve minutes. Cut in strips and shape over a rolling pin. If strips become brittle before the shaping is accomplished, return to oven to reheat, when they are again made pliable.

Peanut Macaroons

White 1 egg	5 tablespoons finely chopped
¼ cup fine granulated	peanuts
sugar	1 teaspoon vanilla

Beat white of egg until stiff and add gradually, while beating constantly, sugar; then add peanuts and vanilla. Drop from tip of spoon on buttered sheet one and one-half inches apart. Garnish each with one-half peanut and bake in a slow oven from twelve to fifteen minutes.

Sultana Sticks

1 cup sugar	½ cup flour
¼ cup melted butter	¼ teaspoon salt
1 egg, unbeaten	¼ teaspoon vanilla
2 squares melted chocolate	¼ cup Sultana raisins
¼ cup chopped English walnut meats	

Mix ingredients in order given. Line a seven-inch square pan with paraffine paper, put in mixture, spread evenly and bake in a slow oven. Remove from pan, take off paper and cut at once in bars three and one-half by one and three-quarters inches.

Chocolate Nut Bars

Whites 6 eggs
14 ounces powdered sugar
3 ounces unsweetened chocolate
½ pound Jordan almonds

Beat egg whites until stiff and add gradually, while beating constantly, sugar; then carefully cut and fold in chocolate which has been melted and slightly cooled and two-thirds of the nut meats, blanched and chopped. Spread mixture one-fourth inch thick in two buttered dripping pans, sprinkle with remaining nuts and bake in a slow oven forty minutes. While warm cut in finger-shaped pieces, using a sharp knife. For serving arrange on a plate covered with a lace paper doily.

Scotch Five o'Clock Teas

¾ pound butter
6 ounces powdered sugar
1 pound bread flour

Cream butter and add gradually, while beating constantly, sugar; then work in the flour, using the hands. Press into a buttered dripping pan to one-half inch in thickness, prick with a fork, at even, frequent intervals and bake in a moderate oven thirty-five minutes. Cool slightly, cut in squares or oblongs and remove from pan.

Marshmallow Teas

Arrange marshmallows on thin unsweetened round wafer crackers, allowing one marshmallow to each

CHOCOLATE WALNUT WAFERS. — *Page* 325

PEANUT WAFERS. — *Page* 322.

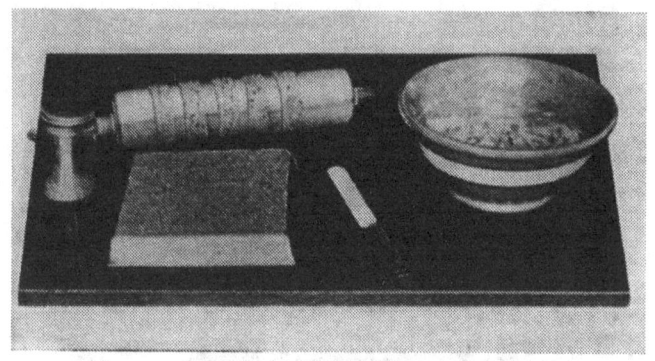

The Rolling of Swedish Nut Wafers. — *Page 322*

Swedish Nut Wafers. — *Page 322.*

cracker. Make a deep impression in the centre of each marshmallow and in each cavity drop one-fourth teaspoon butter. Arrange on a tin sheet and bake until marshmallows spread and nearly cover crackers. Insert one-half a candied cherry in each cavity and arrange on a plate covered with a doily.

Chinese Tea Cakes

¼ cup shortening
1 cup brown sugar
⅛ teaspoon soda
1 tablespoon cold water
½ teaspoon vanilla
1 cup flour

Work shortening until creamy, using equal parts of butter and lard. Add sugar gradually, while beating constantly; then add soda dissolved in water, vanilla and flour. Make into small balls, place on a buttered sheet one and one-half inches apart and bake in a hot oven. This receipt makes twenty-four cakes.

Chocolate Walnut Wafers

½ cup butter
1 cup sugar
2 eggs
2 squares unsweetened chocolate
1 cup chopped walnut meats
¼ teaspoon salt
¼ teaspoon vanilla
⅔ cup flour

Cream butter and add gradually, while beating constantly, sugar; then add eggs, well beaten, chocolate (melted), nut meats, salt, vanilla and flour. Drop from tip of spoon on a buttered sheet, one inch apart, and bake in a moderate oven.

Orange Circles

3 tablespoons butter	Grated rind 1 orange
⅔ cup sugar	Few grains salt
Juice 1 orange	1¾ cups flour

Put butter and grated rind in a bowl and work until creamy, using a wooden spoon. Add sugar gradually, continuing the beating; then add salt and orange juice and flour, a little at a time. Toss on a floured board, pat and roll to one-eighth inch in thickness. Shape with a circular cutter, first dipped in flour, put on a sheet covered with a buttered paper and bake in a moderate oven.

Caraway Seed Cookies

1 cup butter	2 tablespoons milk
1 cup sugar	¼ teaspoon salt
2 eggs	2 cups bread flour
¼ teaspoon soda	1 tablespoon caraway seeds

Cream butter, using the hands, and add gradually, while beating constantly, sugar. Add one egg and beat, still using the hands; then add the other egg and continue the beating. Add soda, dissolved in milk, and remaining ingredients. Toss on a floured cloth and pat and roll to one-fourth inch in thickness. Shape with a small round cutter, first dipped in flour. Arrange on a buttered sheet and bake in a moderate oven.

Chocolate Pâte à Choux Rings

Force cream cake mixture through a pastry bag and tube in ring shapes, three and one-half inches in diameter, on a buttered sheet and bake thirty minutes in a moderate oven. Cool, split and fill with whipped cream, sweetened and flavored with vanilla. Cover with Berkshire Chocolate Frosting (see p. 348) and sprinkle with Jordan almonds, blanched and shredded.

French Meringues

| 2 cups sugar | Whites 5 eggs |
| 1 cup water | 1 teaspoon vanilla |

Put sugar and water in saucepan, bring to the boiling point and let boil until a firm ball may be formed when mixture is tried in cold water. Beat whites of eggs until stiff and add gradually, while beating constantly, the hot syrup. Set saucepan containing mixture in larger saucepan containing ice water, add flavoring and stir five minutes. Cover and let stand fifteen minutes. Shape with a spoon or pastry bag and tube on a buttered sheet, dredged with cornstarch. Bake thirty minutes in a slow oven.

Cinkites

Whites 3 eggs	Grated rind ½ lemon
½ pound granulated sugar	1½ teaspoons cinnamon
½ pound chopped unblanched Jordan almonds	

Beat egg whites to a stiff froth. Mix remaining ingredients and cut and fold into egg whites. Toss on a board dredged with one-fourth cup flour and powdered sugar (using equal parts and mixing thoroughly) and pat and roll to one-fourth inch in thickness. Shape with a small round or fancy cutter, arrange on a slightly buttered sheet and bake in a moderate oven. Spread with Confec-

CHAPTER XXIX

CAKE

Delia's Sponge Cake

Yolks 2 eggs	¼ teaspoon lemon extract
4 tablespoons hot water	Whites 2 eggs
¾ cup sugar	1 cup flour
1¼ teaspoons baking powder	

ADD yolks of eggs to hot water and beat until thick; then add gradually, while beating constantly, sugar and lemon extract. Add whites of eggs, beaten until stiff, and fold in flour, mixed and sifted with baking powder. Turn into a buttered and floured narrow deep cake pan and bake in a moderate oven thirty-five minutes.

Potato Flour Sponge Cake

Yolks 4 eggs	¾ cup potato flour
¾ cup sugar	1 teaspoon baking powder
Whites 4 eggs	¼ teaspoon salt
½ tablespoon lemon juice	

Beat yolks of eggs until thick and lemon-colored and add sugar gradually, while beating constantly; then add whites of eggs, beaten until stiff. Mix and sift dry ingredients and cut and fold into mix-

Gratan Mocha. — *Page* 329

Vienna Cake. — *Page* 329.

BIRTHDAY CAKE FOR A THREE-YEAR-OLD.—*Page* 331

ture. Add lemon juice, turn into a buttered and floured cake pan and bake in a moderate oven thirty minutes.

Gratan Mocha

Bake Cream Sponge Cake mixture (see The Boston Cooking-School Cook Book, p. 501) in two buttered round deep layer cake tins. Put between layers whipped cream, sweetened and flavored with strong coffee. Garnish top with cream, forced through a pastry bag and tube, and glacéd pineapple, cherries and angelica, as shown in illustration.

Vienna Cake

Yolks 4 eggs	Flour
1 cup sugar	1½ teaspoons baking powder
3 tablespoons cold water	¼ teaspoon salt
1½ tablespoons cornstarch	Whites 6 eggs
	1 teaspoon lemon extract

Beat egg yolks until thick and lemon-colored, and add gradually, while beating constantly, sugar; then add water. Put cornstarch in cup and fill cup with flour. Mix and sift with baking powder and salt and add to first mixture; then add egg whites, beaten until stiff, and lemon extract. Turn into a buttered and floured angel cake pan and bake in a moderate oven forty minutes. Remove from pan, cool and cut crosswise, so as to make four layers of equal thickness. Put between the top and bottom layers Mocha Filling, flavored with sweetened chocolate. In the centre and over top and sides of cake, Mocha

Filling, flavored with vanilla. Sprinkle entire frosted surface with Nut Brittle.

Mocha Filling. — Mix one-third cup sugar, one-third cup flour and one-fourth teaspoon salt. When thoroughly blended, add gradually, while stirring constantly, two cups scalded milk and cook in double boiler fifteen minutes, stirring constantly until mixture thickens and afterwards occasionally. Wash one cup butter, add to cooked mixture and let stand until cold; then add one teaspoon vanilla.

Chocolate Mocha Filling. — To one-third Mocha Filling add one ounce melted sweet chocolate.

Nut Brittle. — Blanch and chop Jordan almonds; there should be one-third cup. Put in a small omelet pan with one-third cup sugar, place on range and stir constantly until sugar is well caramelized. Turn into a slightly buttered pan, cool and roll until quite fine.

Silver Sponge Cakes

Whites 5 eggs	½ teaspoon cream-of-tartar
¾ cup sugar	½ cup bread flour
1 teaspoon vanilla	

Beat whites of eggs until stiff and dry and add gradually, while beating constantly, sugar, mixed and sifted with cream-of-tartar. Sift flour into the mixture, add vanilla and cut and fold until blended. Fill buttered individual tins two-thirds full of mixture, sprinkle with powdered sugar and bake in a moderate oven.

Mock Angel Cake

1 cup sugar	⅛ teaspoon salt
1⅛ cups flour	⅔ cup scalded milk
3 teaspoons baking powder	1 teaspoon vanilla
Whites 2 eggs	

Mix and sift first four ingredients four times. Pour on gradually the scalded milk. Fold in whites of eggs, beaten until stiff, and add vanilla. Turn into an unbuttered angel cake pan and bake in a moderate oven forty-five minutes. This is better for being kept twenty-four hours.

White Mountain Angel Cake

1½ cups egg whites	1 cup bread flour
1½ cups sugar	¼ teaspoon salt
1 teaspoon cream-of-tartar	1 teaspoon vanilla

Beat egg whites until stiff, using large egg beater. Remove egg beater and add sugar mixed with cream-of-tartar, gradually, folding in with wooden cake spoon. Cut and fold in flour, mixed with salt, and add flavoring. Turn into an unbuttered angel cake pan, cover and bake in a moderate oven twenty minutes. Remove cover and bake from twenty to twenty-five minutes. Invert pan on wire cake cooler and let stand, when cake should, by its own weight, drop from pan.

Birthday Cake
(For three-year-old)

Make a White Mountain Angel Cake. Cover with Confectioners' Frosting (see The Boston Cooking-

School Cook Book, p. 527) and decorate with citron cut in thin slices and then in shapes, roses made from candied rose leaves, daisies made from small candies, foliage made from citron, dragées and three small candles placed in rose cups (which may be bought of first-class city grocers).

Fruit Cake
(Without butter or eggs)

1 cup sugar	4 teaspoons baking powder
½ cup molasses	½ teaspoon salt
¾ cup milk	1 teaspoon cinnamon
¼ cup coffee infusion	Allspice ⎫
1½ cups entire wheat flour	Clove ⎬ ¼ teaspoon each
½ cup white flour	Mace ⎪
	Grated nutmeg ⎭

1 pound raisins seeded and cut in pieces

Mix sugar, molasses, milk and coffee. Mix and sift dry ingredients, reserving one-fourth cup white flour. Combine mixtures and add raisins, dredged with remaining flour. Turn into a buttered and floured bread pan and bake in a moderate oven fifty minutes.

Grant Cake

½ cup butter	1¼ cups raisins
1 cup sugar	1½ teaspoons soda
1 egg	¾ teaspoon allspice
1 cup sour milk	¾ teaspoon cloves
2¾ cups flour	1½ teaspoon cinnamon

½ teaspoon salt

Cream butter and add sugar gradually, while beating constantly, egg, well beaten, and sour milk. Mix

Raised Loaf Cake. — *Page* 333

Devil's Food Cake. — *Page* 335.

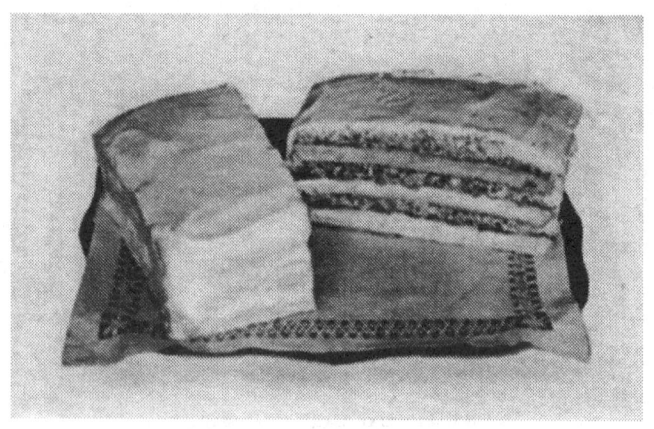

Lady Baltimore Cake.—*Page* 340

Lord Baltimore Cake.—*Page* 341.

and sift two and one-half cups flour with soda, spices and salt and add to first mixture; then add raisins, seeded, cut in pieces and dredged with remaining flour. Turn into a buttered oblong cake pan and bake in a moderate oven fifty minutes.

Raised Loaf Cake

1 cup butter	1 teaspoon cloves
2 cups brown sugar	2 teaspoons soda
2 eggs	1 teaspoon salt
2 cups bread sponge	2 cups raisins
2 teaspoons cinnamon	1 cup flour

Cream butter and add gradually, while beating constantly, sugar; then add eggs, well beaten, bread sponge, spices, soda and salt (mixed and sifted) and raisins, seeded and cut in quarters and mixed with flour. Turn into two buttered and floured oblong pans, cover and let rise three hours and bake in a moderate oven one hour. Remove from pan and cover top with Portsmouth Frosting (see p. 347).

Bread Sponge. — Mix one tablespoon, each, butter, sugar and salt; add one yeast cake, dissolved in one cup lukewarm water and two and one-half cups flour. Cover and let rise until mixture is light.

Potato Flour Cake

2 eggs	1/3 cup potato flour
1 tablespoon cold water	3/4 teaspoon baking powder
1/2 cup sugar	1/4 teaspoon salt
	1/4 teaspoon vanilla

Add water to egg yolks and beat until light. Then add sugar, gradually, while beating constantly.

Mix and sift dry ingredients, combine mixtures and add vanilla, then add whites of eggs beaten until stiff. Turn into a buttered and floured cake pan and bake in a moderate oven twenty-five minutes.

Prize Cake

Yolks 4 eggs	2 cups flour
Whites 2 eggs	2½ teaspoons baking powder
1 cup sugar	½ cup milk
⅛ cup melted butter	

Put egg yolks and whites into a bowl and beat until thick, using a Dover egg beater; then add sugar gradually, while beating constantly. Mix and sift flour and baking powder and add alternately with milk to first mixture; then add one-third cup melted butter. Turn into a buttered and floured shallow cake pan and bake in a moderate oven thirty-five minutes.

This mixture is well adapted for reception cakes. It may be cut into small squares, oblongs, triangles, or any desired shapes, dipped in Oscar's Frosting and decorated with candied fruits, candies or ornamental frosting.

Christmas Cakes

Bake Prize Cake mixture in buttered and floured goldenrod pans. Remove from pans, cool, trim off ends and cut each cake in quarters, crosswise. Spread top of each with Confectioners' Frosting (see The Boston Cooking-School Cook Book, p. 527) and decorate with small leaves, made from Ornamental

Frosting II (see The Boston Cooking-School Cook Book, p. 532), colored green and forced through a bag and tube, and small red candies to represent holly.

Priscilla Cake

½ cup butter	2⅛ cups flour
1½ cups sugar	2¼ teaspoons baking powder
5 eggs	½ cup milk
	1 teaspoon vanilla

Cream butter and add gradually, while beating constantly, sugar; then add eggs well beaten. Mix and sift flour and baking powder and add alternately with milk to first mixture. Beat vigorously two minutes and add flavoring. Turn into a buttered and floured cake pan and bake in a moderate oven forty-five minutes.

Devils' Food Cake

¼ cup butter	1⅛ cups flour
1 cup sugar	3 teaspoons baking powder
2 squares chocolate	½ teaspoon salt
2 eggs	1 teaspoon vanilla
	½ cup milk

Cream butter and add sugar gradually, while beating constantly; then add chocolate, melted, eggs, well beaten, milk, flour, mixed and sifted with baking powder, and salt and vanilla. Turn into a buttered and floured cake pan and bake in a moderate oven forty-five minutes. Cover with Ice Cream Frosting and spread Ice Cream Frosting with a thin layer of melted unsweetened chocolate, using the back of a spoon.

Fudge Cake

1 cup butter	2 cups flour
1 cup sugar	2½ teaspoons baking powder
Yolks 3 eggs	Whites 3 eggs
½ cup milk	2 ounces unsweetened chocolate
	½ teaspoon vanilla

Cream butter and add sugar gradually, while beating constantly; then add yolks of eggs, well beaten. Mix and sift baking powder and flour and add alternately with milk to first mixture. Add whites of eggs, beaten until stiff, chocolate, melted over hot water, and vanilla. Turn into two buttered and floured seven-inch square pans and bake in a moderate oven. Put between and on top Fudge Frosting (see p. 350).

Caramel Potato Cake

½ cup butter	2 teaspoons baking powder
1 cup sugar	½ teaspoon cinnamon
2 eggs	½ teaspoon clove
½ cup milk	½ teaspoon nutmeg
½ cup hot riced potatoes	½ cup grated chocolate
1 cup flour	½ cup chopped nut meats

Cream butter and add gradually, while beating constantly, sugar; then add eggs, well beaten, milk and potatoes. Beat thoroughly and add flour, mixed and sifted with baking powder, and spices, chocolate and nut meats. Turn into a buttered and floured cake pan and bake in a moderate oven fifty-five minutes. Remove from pan and cover with Fudge Frosting (see p. 350).

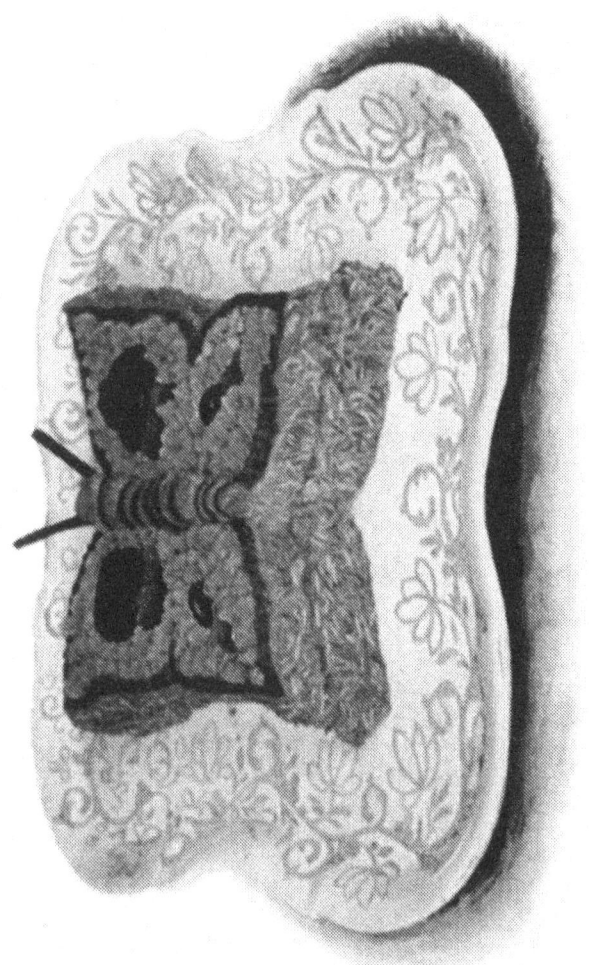

BUTTERFLY CAKE.—*Page* 339

Chocolate Walnut Loaf Cake

⅛ cup butter	⅔ cup brown sugar
1 cup brown sugar	1 cup milk
Yolks 2 eggs	Yolk 1 egg
½ cup milk	1½ cups chopped walnut
2 cups bread flour	meats
1 teaspoon soda	1 cup citron, cut in small
Whites 3 eggs	pieces
4 squares chocolate	2 teaspoons vanilla

Cream butter and add gradually, while beating constantly, one cup sugar; then add yolks two eggs, well beaten, one-half cup milk, flour, mixed and sifted with soda, and whites three eggs, beaten until stiff. Melt chocolate and add two-thirds cup sugar, one cup milk and yolk one egg, slightly beaten. Cook in double boiler, stirring constantly until mixture is smooth. Cool and add to first mixture; then add nut meats, citron and vanilla. Turn into two buttered and floured seven-inch square pans and bake in a moderate oven thirty-five minutes. Remove from pans and cover with white or chocolate frosting.

Gold Cake

½ cup butter (scant)	2 cups flour
1 cup sugar	3 teaspoons baking powder
Yolks 4 eggs	½ cup milk

Cream butter and add gradually, while beating constantly, sugar; then add egg yolks, beaten until thick and lemon-colored. Mix and sift flour and baking powder and add alternately with milk to first mixture. Bake in a buttered shallow pan or layer cake tins, in a moderate oven.

Mrs. Raymond's Gold Cake

½ cup butter	1¾ cups flour
1 cup sugar	3¾ teaspoons baking powder
Yolks 5 eggs	¼ teaspoon salt
1 egg	½ cup milk

Cream butter and add sugar gradually, while beating constantly; then add egg yolks and egg well beaten. Mix and sift dry ingredients and add alternately with milk to first mixture. Turn into a buttered and floured cake tin and bake in a moderate oven forty-five minutes. Remove from pan and cover with Cocoanut Coffee Frosting.

Princeton Orange Cake

½ cup butter	Grated rind 1 orange
1½ cups sugar	1½ cups flour
Yolks 4 eggs	½ cup cornstarch
½ cup orange juice	4 teaspoons baking powder
Whites 4 eggs	

Cream butter and add sugar gradually, while beating constantly. When mixture is creamy, add yolks of eggs, beaten until thick, orange juice and rind, and flour and cornstarch, mixed and sifted with baking powder; then add whites of eggs, beaten until stiff. Turn into buttered and floured individual tins and bake in a moderate oven. Cover tops with Orange Frosting.

Florida Nut Cake

Bake Princeton Orange Cake mixture in a buttered dripping pan, sprinkled generously with chopped walnut meats and sparingly with powdered sugar.

ANNIVERSARY CAKE.—*Page* 343

CHRISTMAS CAKES. — *Page* 334.

ORNAMENTED WEDDING CAKE. — *Page* 344

Remove from pan, cut in halves, crosswise, and put together with Orange Filling, spreading it on the surface, where there are no nuts. Cut in finger-shaped pieces and arrange on a plate covered with a doily.

Butterfly Cake

Turn Prize Cake mixture (see p. 334) into two buttered and floured seven-inch square cake tins and bake in a moderate oven twenty-five minutes. Remove from pans, cool and cut each in the shape of a butterfly. Put layers together with Coffee Butter Frosting. Spread sides with frosting and sprinkle with shredded cocoanut, which has been slightly browned in the oven. Pipe Chocolate Butter Frosting around edge of upper surface. Arrange two halves of glacéd apricots, two halves of glacéd cherries, two crescent-shaped pieces of angelica and two strips of angelica as shown in illustration. Force Coffee Butter Frosting through pastry bag and rose tube around glacéd fruits. Make body of Coffee Butter Frosting, using lady finger tube, and over body arrange a parallel row of Chocolate Butter Frosting. Insert pointed strips of angelica.

Silver Cake

⅔ cup butter
1 cup sugar
½ cup milk
2 cups flour
3 teaspoons baking powder
Whites 4 eggs

Cream butter and add sugar gradually, while beating constantly; then add milk alternately with flour, mixed and sifted with baking powder. Beat whites of eggs until stiff and add to mixture. Turn into a buttered and floured cake pan and bake forty-five minutes in a moderate oven.

White Fruit Cake

⅔ cup butter	1¼ cups powdered sugar
1⅜ cups flour	⅔ cup candied cherries
¼ teaspoon soda	⅓ cup almonds, blanched
½ tablespoon lemon juice	and shredded
Whites 6 eggs	½ cup citron, thinly sliced
1 teaspoon almond extract	

Cream butter, and add gradually flour, mixed and sifted with soda; then add lemon juice. Beat whites of eggs until stiff, add gradually sugar and combine mixtures; then add cherries, cut in pieces, almonds, citron and extract. Bake in a buttered deep cake pan one hour.

Lady Baltimore Cake

1 cup butter	3½ cups flour
2 cups sugar	2 teaspoons baking powder
1 cup milk	1 teaspoon vanilla
Whites 6 eggs	

Cream butter and add sugar gradually, while beating constantly. Mix and sift baking powder and flour and add alternately with milk to first mixture; then add flavoring and cut and fold in whites of eggs, beaten until stiff and dry. Turn into three buttered and floured seven-inch square tins and bake in a moderate oven. Put layers together with Fruit and

Nut Filling and cover top and sides of cake with Fruit and Nut Filling, then with Ice Cream Frosting.

Fruit and Nut Filling

3 cups sugar	1 cup chopped pecan nut meats
1 cup water	
Whites 3 eggs	5 figs, cut in thin strips
1 cup raisins seeded and chopped	1 tablespoon lemon juice
	Few grains salt

Put sugar and water in a smooth graniteware saucepan, bring to the boiling point and let boil until syrup will spin a thread when dropped from tip of spoon. Pour gradually, while beating constantly, on whites of eggs, beaten until stiff, and continue the beating until mixture is of right consistency to spread; then add remaining ingredients. One-half this quantity may be made and used between layers only.

Ice Cream Frosting

2 cups sugar	Whites 2 eggs
1/8 cup water	1/2 teaspoon vanilla

Put sugar and water in smooth graniteware saucepan; bring to the boiling point and let boil until syrup will spin a thread when dropped from tip of spoon. Pour gradually, while beating constantly, on whites of eggs, beaten until stiff (but not dry), and continue the beating until mixture is of right consistency to spread; then add flavoring.

Lord Baltimore Cake

1/2 cup butter	1/2 cup milk
1 cup sugar	1 3/4 cups flour
Yolks 8 eggs	4 teaspoons baking powder
1 1/2 teaspoons vanilla	

Cream butter and add gradually, while beating constantly, sugar; then add yolks of eggs, beaten until thick and lemon-colored, milk, flour, mixed and sifted with baking powder, and vanilla. Turn into three buttered and floured seven-inch square tins and bake in a moderate oven. Put layers together with Lord Baltimore Filling and cover top and side of cake with Ice Cream Frosting; then garnish with halves of candied cherries and diamond-shaped pieces of angelica.

Lord Baltimore Filling.—Make an Ice Cream Frosting (see p. 341) of one and one-half cups sugar, one-half cup water and whites two eggs. When of right consistency to spread, add one-half cup rolled dry macaroons, one-fourth cup, each, chopped pecan nut meats and blanched Jordan almonds, twelve candied cherries, cut in quarters, two teaspoons lemon juice, three teaspoons Sherry wine and one-fourth teaspoon orange extract.

Grandmother's Pound Cake

1 cup butter	5 eggs
1⅔ cups sugar	2 cups flour

Work butter until creamy, using the hand, and add sugar, gradually, while beating constantly; then add eggs one at a time, beating vigorously between the addition of each. When the mixture is of a creamy consistency, fold in the flour and turn into a buttered and floured cake pan. Bake one hour in a slow oven.

ANNIVERSARY CAKE — *Page 343*

Anniversary Cake

Bake Grandmother's Pound Cake mixture in a buttered and floured round pan about seven inches in diameter. Remove from pan, cover with Confectioners' Frosting and decorate as shown in illustration or as one's fancy dictates.

Foliage is best made of citron thinly sliced. The dark-green outside makes attractive leaves, though all may be used to advantage. The little candies for the flowers may sometimes be procured at small shops, though the greatest variety can be bought of a dealer in confectioners' supplies; also the little silver-like dragées, which are so ornamental. The flowers are made on a basis of angelica, cut with a pen-knife into thin shavings, worked with the hands into small balls, then flattened into lozenge shapes, which make a sticky foundation on which the candies may be placed; candied rose leaves and violets may also be used. The cake in the illustration is decorated with daisies and chrysanthemums, goldenrod and forget-me-nots.

The little disks were made of angelica, shaped in half-spheres, dipped in white of egg, and then in the dragées, and the conventional decorations were cut from thin slices of citron.

Birthday Cake

Bake Sponge, Angel or Moonshine cake mixture in an angel cake pan. Remove from pan, cover with Confectioners' Frosting and decorate as shown in illustration, following general directions given under Anniversary Cake.

Ornamented Wedding Cake

Follow recipe for Wedding Cake I or II (see The Boston Cooking-School Cook Book, p. 522). Line a round tin pan twelve inches in diameter with buttered paper, turn in mixture, cover with buttered heavy brown paper (buttered side up) and fasten securely with a string. Steam and bake. Take from pan, remove paper, and let stand until cold. Wrap in cheese-cloth, wrung out of brandy, and store in a cool dry place from one to three months, occasionally sprinkling with brandy. Work one-third pound almond paste with white of one egg until smooth and add one-fourth cup fine granulated sugar. Spread bottom and sides of cake with mixture, put in oven and bake until paste is browned. This prevents frosting from becoming discolored. Cool and spread with a layer of Ornamental Frosting (see p. 353) and let stand until frosting is set.

Ornament by forcing frosting through a pastry bag and tubes or cones made of paper which comes for this purpose and dragées. The doves shown in illustration are shaped on paper, dried and then placed on cake, being held in place by a small quantity of soft frosting.

CHAPTER XXX

CAKE FILLINGS AND FROSTINGS

White Mountain Cream Filling

⅞ cup sugar	1½ cups scalded milk
⅓ cup flour	Yolks 2 eggs
⅛ teaspoon salt	½ cup heavy cream
1 teaspoon vanilla	

MIX sugar, flour and salt and when thoroughly blended, pour on scalded milk. Cook in double boiler fifteen minutes, stirring constantly until mixture thickens and afterwards occasionally. Add egg yolks, slightly beaten, and cook for two minutes. Cool, add cream, beaten until stiff, and flavoring.

Caramel Filling

1½ cups scalded milk	⅛ cup flour
Caramel syrup	1 egg yolk
½ cup sugar	½ teaspoon vanilla

Put one-half cup sugar in a graniteware saucepan or omelet pan, place over hot part of range and stir constantly until melted and of the color of maple syrup. Add one-half of the caramel syrup to scalded milk and when dissolved, pour on gradually to one-half cup sugar thoroughly mixed with flour. Cook twenty minutes, stirring constantly until mixture thickens and afterwards occasionally. Add beaten egg yolk and vanilla.

Praline Cream

To one cup Cream Filling (see The Boston Cooking-School Cook Book, p. 524) add two-thirds cup praline powder. For the powder put one-half cup sugar in a small omelet pan and stir constantly until reduced to a syrup and slightly caramelized; then add two-thirds cup chopped nut meats (preferably blanched Jordan almonds or pecans) and a few grains salt. Turn into a slightly buttered pan, cool, pound and pass through a strainer.

Frangipan Cream

Mix two-thirds cup powdered sugar and one-third cup flour. When thoroughly blended, add yolks of three eggs and one whole egg, slightly beaten, and one-fourth teaspoon salt. Add gradually one cup scalded milk and cook over hot water fifteen minutes, stirring constantly until mixture thickens and afterwards occasionally. Add two tablespoons butter, two tablespoons macaroons (dried and rolled), two-thirds teaspoon vanilla and one-third teaspoon extract of lemon.

Fruit Cream Filling

¾ cup heavy cream
⅛ cup powdered sugar
Few grains salt
3 tablespoons chopped walnut meats
⅓ cup figs
⅓ cup prunes
2 teaspoons lemon juice

Beat cream until stiff and add sugar, salt, nut meats, figs and prunes, cut in very small pieces, and lemon juice.

Orange Filling

1 tablespoon butter	Yolk 1 egg
3 tablespoons powdered sugar	¼ cup orange juice
2 tablespoons flour	Grated rind ¼ orange
⅛ cup sugar	1 teaspoon lemon juice

Wash butter and work until creamy; then add sugar gradually. Mix flour, sugar and egg yolk, slightly beaten. Add orange juice and cook over hot water, stirring constantly, until mixture thickens. Combine mixtures and add grated rind and lemon juice. If the orange juice is sour, it is not necessary to add the lemon juice.

Syracuse Filling

1 cup heavy cream	1 tablespoon hot water
½ cup sugar	6 marshmallows
½ teaspoon granulated gelatine	9 candied cherries
	4 macaroons
1 tablespoon cold water	½ teaspoon vanilla

Beat cream until stiff and add sugar gradually; then add gelatine, soaked in cold water two minutes and dissolved in boiling water. Add marshmallows and cherries, cut in small pieces, macaroons, dried and rolled, and vanilla.

Portsmouth Frosting

2 tablespoons cream	2 teaspoons melted butter
Confectioners' sugar	½ teaspoon vanilla

To cream add sugar until of right consistency to spread; then add butter and vanilla.

Coffee Confectioners' Frosting

2 tablespoons hot coffee infusion	1 teaspoon butter
	½ teaspoon vanilla
Confectioners' sugar	

Melt butter in coffee and add vanilla and confectioners' sugar until mixture is of the right consistency to spread. Vanilla may be omitted.

Berkshire Chocolate Frosting

2 squares chocolate	3 tablespoons boiling water
1 teaspoon butter	Confectioners' sugar
¼ teaspoon vanilla	

Melt chocolate in small saucepan placed over hot water. Add butter and boiling water and stir in sugar, gradually, until mixture is of right consistency to spread; then add flavoring.

Mocha Frosting

⅓ cup butter	1 tablespoon strong, boiled or filtered coffee
1 cup Confectioners' sugar	
¼ cup Jordan almonds	

Wash butter and pat until no water flies. Work until creamy, and add sugar gradually, while beating constantly. As mixture thickens, add coffee, a few drops at a time, keeping the mixture throughout the entire beating of a creamy consistency. Spread on cake and sprinkle with almonds, blanched, shredded and baked in a slow oven until delicately browned.

Cocoa Frosting

Make same as Mocha Frosting, using one and one-half tablespoons breakfast cocoa in place of coffee.

Coffee Butter Frosting

½ cup washed or unsalted butter	1½ cups confectioners' sugar 1½ tablespoons strong coffee infusion

Work butter until creamy and add sugar gradually, while stirring constantly, adding during the process the coffee, a few drops at a time.

Chocolate Butter Frosting

2 tablespoons washed or unsalted butter Confectioners' sugar	1 teaspoon breakfast cocoa ½ tablespoon boiling water ¼ teaspoon vanilla

Work butter until creamy and add sugar gradually, while beating constantly, until mixture is of the right consistency to spread, or force through a pastry bag and tube; then add cocoa, mixed with water and vanilla.

Buttermilk Frosting

Put three-fourths cup buttermilk in a graniteware saucepan, add three-fourths cup sugar, bring to the boiling point and let boil until mixture when tried in cold water forms a soft ball. Remove from range and beat until of right consistency to spread.

Fudge Frosting

2 tablespoons butter	¼ cup milk
1 cup sugar	1 square unsweetened chocolate
½ teaspoon vanilla	

Put butter in saucepan and when melted, add sugar and milk. Bring to the boiling point and let boil ten minutes. Add chocolate and let boil five minutes, taking care that chocolate does not adhere to bottom or sides of pan. Remove from range, add vanilla and beat until of the right consistency to spread.

Fudge Almond Frosting

2 squares unsweetened chocolate	1 cup milk
⅛ cup butter	2 cups sugar
	½ teaspoon vanilla
¼ cup Jordan almonds	

Melt chocolate over hot water and add butter, bit by bit. Stir until butter is melted and add milk gradually, while beating constantly. Bring to the boiling point, add sugar and let boil until mixture will form a very soft ball when tried in cold water; the time required being about twenty minutes. Cool slightly, add vanilla and beat until of the right consistency to spread; then add almonds, blanched and cut in pieces.

Sultana Nut Frosting

2 cups brown sugar	¼ cup sultana raisins
¾ cup heavy cream	¼ cup English walnut meats

Cook sugar and cream in a graniteware saucepan until a soft ball may be formed when mixture is tried in cold water. Turn on a marble slab or large platter, cool, then work until creamy, using a spatula or large wooden spoon. Add raisins and nut meats, cut in small pieces, and spread on cake.

Caramel Frosting

Caramel syrup	1 egg white
1 cup sugar	½ teaspoon vanilla

To caramel syrup remaining from Caramel Filling (see p. 345) add sugar, bring to boiling point and let boil until syrup will spin a thread when dropped from tip of spoons or tines of fork. Pour gradually, while beating constantly, on the beaten white of egg and continue the beating until mixture is stiff enough to spread; then add flavoring.

Chocolate Ice Cream Frosting

Follow recipe for Ice Cream Frosting (see The Boston Cooking-School Cook Book, p. 528). Just before pouring over cake, fold in one square melted unsweetened chocolate.

Orange Frosting

2 cups sugar	Whites 3 eggs
1 cup water	¼ teaspoon tartaric acid
	¼ cup candied orange peel

Boil sugar and water until syrup will thread when dropped from tip of spoon. Pour gradually, while beating constantly, on whites of eggs, beaten until stiff; then add tartaric acid. Continue the beating until of right consistency to spread; then add orange peal cut in thin strips

Quality Frosting

2 cups sugar	15 drops glycerine
3 tablespoons molasses	Few grains salt
½ cup water	⅔ teaspoon vanilla
Whites 2 eggs	⅛ teaspoon lemon extract
1 cup chopped filberts	

Put sugar, molasses and water in saucepan, place on range and stir until sugar has dissolved. Bring to the boiling point and let boil until mixture nearly holds its shape when tried in cold water. Pour syrup slowly, while beating constantly, on whites of eggs, beaten until stiff, and continue the beating until mixture is nearly stiff enough to spread. Set saucepan containing mixture in larger saucepan containing a small quantity of boiling water and cook on range, stirring constantly from bottom and sides of pan until mixture begins to granulate around sides. Remove saucepan containing frosting, add glycerine and beat until of the consistency to spread; then add remaining ingredients. Pour over cake and spread with back of spoon, leaving a rough surface.

Cocoanut Coffee Frosting

1 cup sugar	Whites 2 eggs
½ cup brown sugar	½ cup desiccated cocoanut
½ cup coffee infusion	½ teaspoon vanilla
Few grains salt	

Put sugar and coffee into a saucepan, place on range, bring to the boiling point and let boil until syrup will spin a thread when dropped from tip of spoon. Pour gradually, while beating constantly, on whites of eggs, beaten until stiff, and beat until cool. Set saucepan containing mixture in larger saucepan of boiling water placed on range and cook until mixture becomes slightly granular around sides of pan. Remove from pan of boiling water and beat, using a spoon, until mixture will hold its shape. Then add cocoanut, vanilla and salt. Pour on cake and spread with back of spoon, leaving a rough surface.

Oscar's Frosting

1 tablespoon glucose Confectioners' sugar
½ cup boiling water (scant) ¼ teaspoon Maraschino

Put glucose in saucepan, add boiling water and one-half cup sugar. Stir until well blended; then add one-half cup sugar, and so continue until about six cups of sugar have been used, beating vigorously between the additions. Flavor with maraschino. During the making of this uncooked frosting, the saucepan should be frequently placed in a larger saucepan of boiling water, that mixture may be kept at a uniform lukewarm temperature. To keep the frosting smooth and creamy, the sugar must not be added at too short intervals.

Ornamental Frosting

Whites 3 eggs Confectioners' sugar
¼ teaspoon cream-of-tartar

354   A NEW BOOK OF COOKERY

Put egg whites in large bowl with one-half cup sugar (which has been sifted) and beat vigorously ten minutes; then add another half cup sugar, and beat. Add cream-of-tartar and continue adding sugar and beating until mixture will hold its shape when forced through a bag and tube.

CHAPTER XXXI

CONFECTIONS

Jelly Macaroons

½ pound almond paste   ½ pound powdered sugar
Whites 3 eggs   Jelly
         Confectioners' Frosting

Break paste in pieces, add white of one egg and work with a spatula until well blended; then add sugar and gradually work in remaining whites of eggs. Have ready a tin sheet covered with buttered paper on which is placed, at two and one-half inch intervals, circular pieces of rice paper, one-half inch in diameter. Force mixture, using a pastry bag and small lady finger tube, around pieces of rice paper. Bake fifteen minutes in a slow oven. Remove from paper and fill centres with a small piece of jelly.

Cover jelly with Confectioners' Frosting (see The Boston Cooking-School Cook Book, p. 527), colored red, pink or green.

Salted Filberts

Put one cup filberts in saucepan, cover with boiling water and let stand on range six minutes. Drain and remove skins, which may be best accomplished by the use of a small vegetable knife. Put one-third cup olive oil in omelet pan, and when hot put in one-third of the nuts and fry until delicately browned, stirring constantly. Remove to pan lined with soft paper, taking up as little oil as possible, and sprinkle with salt; repeat until all are fried.

Burnt Almonds

2 cups brown sugar
½ cup boiling water
2 cups blanched Jordan almonds

Put sugar in saucepan, pour over boiling water and place on range. Stir until sugar is dissolved, bring to the boiling point and let boil three minutes. Add almonds and cook, stirring constantly, until nuts are brown and well coated with caramel. Turn on an oiled sieve to drain and cool.

Stuffed Prunes

Remove stones from prunes and dates. Fill cavities made in prunes with prepared dates, shape in original form and roll in sugar.

Devilled Raisins

Remove stems from large selected raisins and cook in hot olive oil until plump. Drain on brown paper and sprinkle with salt and paprika.

Steamed Figs

Steam bag figs until soft. Cool and make in each an incision lengthwise. Stuff with one-half marsh-

THE SALTING OF FILBERTS. — *Page* 355

CHAPIN CHOCOLATE CARAMELS. — *Page* 359.

Raisin Opera Caramels.—*Page* 361

Fudge.—*Page* 363.

mallow and an English walnut meat broken in pieces. Close, press into shape and serve in paper cases.

Knickerbocker Figs

Stuff one-half pound washed figs with Maraschino cherries, cut in halves, and pecan nut meats, broken in pieces, allowing two cherries and five nut meats to each fig. Put two tablespoons sugar, one teaspoon lemon juice and one-half cup Sherry wine in saucepan. Add figs, cover and let simmer until figs are soft. turning and basting several times during the cooking. Drain, cool and serve in individual paper cases.

Popped Corn Balls

3 quarts popped corn	½ cup sugar
1 cup molasses	1 tablespoon butter
½ teaspoon salt	

Pop corn and pick over (discarding kernels that do not pop) and put in large kettle. Melt butter in saucepan and add molasses and sugar. Bring to the boiling point and let boil until mixture will become brittle when tried in cold water. Pour mixture gradually while stirring constantly over corn which has been sprinkled with salt. Shape into balls, using as little pressure as possible.

Stretched Molasses Candy

½ cup butter	1 cup molasses
2 cups sugar	1½ cups boiling water

Put butter in Scotch kettle or saucepan, and when melted add sugar, molasses and water. Bring to the boiling point and let boil, without stirring, until mixture will form a very soft ball that will just keep in shape when tried in cold water. Turn into a buttered dripping pan, and as mixture cools around sides, fold towards centre. When cool enough to handle, pull until porous and light-colored, allowing candy to come in contact with tips of fingers and thumbs, not to be squeezed in the hand.

Cut in small pieces, using large shears or a sharp knife, and arrange on slightly buttered plates to cool. A few drops oil-of-peppermint, clove or cinnamon may be added during the stretching.

Peanut Candy

3 tablespoons butter 2⁄3 cup sugar
2 cups molasses 1 quart peanuts
½ teaspoon salt

Melt butter, add molasses and sugar, bring to the boiling point and let boil until mixture becomes brittle when tried in cold water. Stir in peanuts (shelled, skinned, separated in halves and sprinkled with salt). Turn into a buttered pan, cool slightly and mark in squares.

Walnut Molasses Squares

2 tablespoons butter ⅛ cup sugar
1 cup molasses ½ cup English walnut meats
Few grains salt

Put butter in saucepan and when melted add molasses and sugar. Stir until sugar is dissolved, bring to the boiling point and let boil until mixture is brittle when tried in cold water. During the first of the boiling stirring is unnecessary, but when nearly cooked it should be stirred constantly. Add walnut meats, cut in pieces and sprinkled with salt. Turn into a buttered seven-inch square pan, cool slightly and mark in squares, using a sharp knife.

Butter Taffy

2 cups sugar ¾ cup butter
1 cup water

Melt butter in saucepan and add sugar and water. Bring to the boiling point and let boil, without stirring, until mixture becomes brittle when tried in cold water. Turn into a buttered pan, cool slightly and mark in squares.

Butter Scotch

2 cups brown sugar 1 cup butter
2 teaspoons vinegar 1 cup water
½ tablespoon vanilla

Put ingredients in a smooth graniteware saucepan, bring to the boiling point and let boil, without stirring, until mixture becomes brittle when tried in cold water. Pour into a buttered pan to one-third inch in thickness, cool slightly and mark in squares.

Chapin Chocolate Caramels

3 tablespoons butter 1 cup molasses
¾ cup cream 4 squares unsweetened choco-
1 cup sugar late
½ teaspoon vanilla

Melt butter in a Scotch kettle and add cream, sugar and molasses. Bring to the boiling point and add chocolate, balancing it on a large wooden spoon, that it may melt gradually with no danger of its burning on the kettle. Continue the boiling, stirring occasionally, until a firm ball may be formed when mixture is tried in cold water. Add vanilla and turn into a buttered pan, having the mixture three-fourths inch in depth. When nearly cold, cut in cubes, using scissors or a sharp knife. Wrap in squares of paraffine paper and let stand in a cold place to harden.

Nut Chocolate Caramels

To Chapin Chocolate Caramels add one cup blanched and chopped almonds or chopped English walnut meats, just after taking from fire.

Vanilla Opera Caramels

1 pound confectioners' sugar	$\frac{3}{8}$ cup milk
$\frac{1}{4}$ cup butter	1 teaspoon vanilla

Melt butter in saucepan, add sugar and milk, bring to the boiling point and let boil until mixture, when tried in cold water, will form a soft ball. Remove from range, add vanilla and beat until creamy. Turn into a buttered pan, cool slightly and cut in squares.

Chocolate Opera Caramels

To Vanilla Opera Caramels add two squares unsweetened chocolate after the boiling point is reached.

Nut Opera Caramels

To Vanilla Opera Caramels add one cup chopped English walnut meats as soon as mixture is removed from range.

Smith College Caramels

2½ tablespoons butter	½ cup milk
2 cups brown sugar	4 squares unsweetened
2 tablespoons molasses	chocolate
1 teaspoon vanilla	

Put butter in saucepan and when melted add sugar, molasses and milk. Bring to the boiling point, add chocolate, and stir constantly until chocolate is melted. Let boil until mixture when tried in cold water will form a firm ball. Add vanilla, turn into a buttered tin, cool slightly, and cut in squares.

Raisin Opera Caramels

2 cups light brown sugar	⅞ cup thin cream
½ cup raisins	

Put sugar and cream in saucepan, bring to the boiling point and let boil until a soft ball may be formed when mixture is tried in cold water. Turn on a marble slab or into a large platter, cool slightly and work with a wooden spatula or large wooden spoon until creamy. Add raisins, seeded and cut in pieces and spread evenly in a buttered pan, using the hands, having mixture three-fourths inch in depth. Cool and cut in cubes, using a small knife.

Stretched Chocolate Caramels

2 cups sugar	½ teaspoon glycerine
½ cup boiling water	1½ squares unsweetened
⅛ teaspoon cream-of-tartar	chocolate
2 tablespoons heavy cream	

Put first four ingredients in saucepan, bring to the boiling point and let boil, without stirring, until mixture will become brittle when tried in cold water. When nearly cooked, add cream and chocolate. Turn on a buttered platter, and as edges cool, fold towards centre. As soon as cool enough to handle, pull until glossy, and cut in small pieces, using a knife or scissors. Put in paraffine paper or on slightly buttered plate.

Peanut Penuche

1 tablespoon butter	⅛ cup milk or cream
2 cups brown sugar	¾ cup chopped peanuts
¼ teaspoon salt	1 teaspoon vanilla

Melt butter in saucepan and add sugar and milk or cream. Bring to the boiling point and let boil until mixture will form a soft ball when tried in cold water. Remove from range, beat until creamy and add nut meats sprinkled with salt.

Turn into a buttered pan, cool slightly and cut in squares, using a sharp knife. Walnuts or shredded cocoanut may be used in place of peanuts. If cocoanut is used, add one-half teaspoon vanilla.

Mexican Penuche

2 tablespoons butter	½ cup thin cream
2 cups brown sugar	1 cup chopped walnut meats
½ pound figs cut in pieces	

Make same as Peanut Penuche.

AFTER DINNER MINTS. — *Page 364.*

TURKISH MINT PASTE. — *Page 367.*

MARSHMALLOW MINT BONBONS WITH A VARIETY
OF GARNISHINGS. — *Page* 366

Fudge

3 cups sugar
¾ cup top milk
2½ squares unsweetened chocolate

Put sugar, chocolate, cut in small pieces, and milk in saucepan, and stir constantly until chocolate is melted. Bring to the boiling point and let boil until mixture will form a jelly-like mass when tried in cold water. Pour on a marble slab and work with a spatula until of consistency to knead; then knead, using the hands, until creamy. Put in a slightly buttered pan and press evenly, using the back of the hand. Cool slightly and cut in squares. Fudge made in this way is always more creamy than when beaten.

Peanut Butter Fudge

2 cups sugar
⅜ cup milk
4 tablespoons peanut butter
1 teaspoon vanilla
Few grains salt

Put sugar and milk in saucepan, bring to the boiling point and let boil until a soft ball may be formed when mixture is tried in cold water. Remove from range, add remaining ingredients and beat until creamy. Turn into a buttered pan to three-fourths inch in depth, cool slightly and cut in squares, using a sharp-pointed knife.

Chocolate Marshmallow Fudge

2 cups sugar
1 cup top milk
2 squares unsweetened chocolate
3 tablespoons butter
1 teaspoon vanilla
10 marshmallows

Put sugar, milk and chocolate in saucepan. Heat gradually to the boiling point and let boil until mixture will form a soft ball when tried in cold water. Remove from range, add butter and as soon as butter is melted, beat until creamy. Add vanilla and fold in marshmallows, cut in quarters. Turn into a buttered pan, cool and cut in cubes.

Double Decker

Part I

1 cup brown sugar
½ cup milk
1 cup chopped walnut meats
Few grains salt

Put sugar and milk in saucepan, bring to the boiling point and let boil rapidly, until mixture will form a soft ball when tried in cold water. Remove from range, add nut meats and salt, turn into a buttered tin and cool.

Part II

1 cup white sugar
¼ cup milk
½ square chocolate

Put sugar and milk in saucepan, and bring to the boiling point. Add chocolate and stir until chocolate is melted. Then boil until mixture will form a soft ball when tried in cold water. Remove from range and beat until creamy. Pour over Part I, cool and cut in squares.

After Dinner Mints

3 cups sugar
¼ teaspoon cream-of-tartar
½ cup boiling water
½ tablespoon vinegar
2 drops oil of peppermint

Put ingredients, except peppermint, in saucepan, bring to the boiling point and let boil, without stirring, until mixture will become brittle when tried in cold water. Pour on a buttered large platter. As soon as edges cool, fold towards centre and as soon as mixture can be handled, pull until white, adding the peppermint during the process. Cut in small pieces (using scissors) into a bowl containing powdered sugar. Stir until coated with sugar and put into a glass jar. Cover and let stand from ten to twelve days.

Fondant

2 cups sugar	⅛ teaspoon cream-of-tartar
½ cup boiling water	½ teaspoon glycerine

Put ingredients in smooth graniteware saucepan, stir, place on range and bring to the boiling point. Boil rapidly without stirring until, when tried in cold water, a jelly-like ball may be formed. Pour into a bowl, cool, and stir and beat until white and creamy. Turn on a platter and knead until smooth. Return to bowl, cover with paraffine or oiled paper and let stand twenty-four hours. Heat until melted in dish placed in stewpan containing boiling water. Flavor and color as desired. Fondant may be used for dipping small cakes, frosting larger ones or making confections. If a large quantity is required do not attempt to double recipe, but rather repeat it until the necessary quantity is made.

Dipped Cream Mints

Melt fondant (using once the recipe), and flavor with a few drops oil of peppermint, wintergreen, clove or cinnamon. Stir occasionally, and when cool, turn on marble slab or board, dredged with confectioners' sugar, having mixture about one-fourth inch in thickness. Shape with a small round cutter, cover and let stand over night. In the morning dip in melted fondant, flavored same as mints and colored as desired. For the dipping use a three-tined fork or confectioners' dipper and remove to paraffine paper. During the dipping keep dish containing fondant over saucepan of hot water. It will be necessary to again bring water to boiling if fondant becomes too stiff. If this does not suffice, add a few drops boiling water to fondant.

Marshmallow Mint Bonbons

Cut marshmallows in halves crosswise and flavor with peppermint, by putting a small wooden skewer in a bottle of oil of peppermint, then on the cut surface of the marshmallow. Arrange in layers in a box, cover and let stand over night. In the morning dip in fondant, flavored with a few drops oil of peppermint, and decorate top of each with Oscar's Frosting (see p. 353), forced through a pastry bag and tube. Put in individual paper cases.

Candy Violets

Melt one-half cup fondant, flavor with one drop Violet Essence and color violet. Stir in shredded

DIPPED CREAM MINTS IN THE MAKING. — *Page* 366

DIPPED CREAM MINTS. — *Page* 366.

CANDY BASKET FILLED WITH GLACÉD STRAWBERRIES. — *Page* 370

A BASKET OF HOME-MADE SWEETS FOR CHRISTMAS.

cocoanut, which comes in long pieces (the kind which may be bought in bulk rather than packages), and drop from a two-tined fork on paraffine paper, to represent violets. If Violet Essence is not at hand, substitute a few drops vanilla.

Turkish Delight

1 ounce gelatine	Juice 1 orange
½ cup cold water	Juice 1 lemon
1 pound granulated sugar	1 tablespoon rum
½ cup boiling water	Red coloring
Grated rind 1 orange	½ cup chopped nut meats

Break gelatine in pieces, add cold water, cover and let soak two hours. Put sugar and boiling water in saucepan, bring to the boiling point, add gelatine and let simmer twenty minutes. Add flavorings and coloring, strain, add nut meats and turn into a bread pan (first rinsed with cold water) to one inch in depth. Let stand until cold, remove to board, cut in cubes and roll in confectioners' sugar. The rum and nut meats may be omitted.

Turkish Mint Paste

3 tablespoons granulated gelatine	2 tablespoons lemon juice
½ cup cold water	4 tablespoons Crême de Menthe
2 cups sugar	Few grains salt
½ cup cold water	Green coloring

Soak gelatine in water twenty minutes. Put sugar and water in saucepan, bring to the boiling point, add gelatine and let simmer twenty minutes. Remove from fire, add remaining ingredients and color green. Turn into a pan (first rinsed in cold water) to one inch in thickness. Cool, remove to board, cut in cubes and roll in confectioners' sugar.

Crystal Cups

| 2 pounds sugar | 2 cups boiling water |

¼ teaspoon cream-of-tartar

Put ingredients in a smooth saucepan. Bring to the boiling point and let boil, without stirring, until syrup reaches a temperature of 290° F., using a confectioner's thermometer. As soon as sugar begins to grow granular around sides of pan, wash down with the hand, first dipped in cold water. Set saucepan in larger saucepan containing cold water to instantly stop cooking; then set in a saucepan of boiling water, that syrup may not cool too rapidly.

Brush over a timbale iron with olive oil and wipe with soft paper. Dip into syrup, taking care that syrup covers iron to only two-thirds its depth. Remove from syrup, invert iron and swing in front of an open window. As soon as cup is formed take from iron. Cool iron and repeat.

It is well to have two irons, so that one may cool while the other is being used. If a color scheme is to be carried out, the syrup may be colored as desired, just before shaping.

Arrange cups on a bed of Spun Sugar (see The Boston Cooking-School Cook Book, p. 548) and fill with ice cream. If used for Christmas, garnish with holly.

Crystallized Mint Leaves

Wipe fresh mint leaves, remove from stems and brush each leaf with white of egg, beaten until stiff. Dip in one-third cup granulated sugar flavored with five drops oil of spearmint. Place closely together on a cake rack covered with paraffine paper and let stand in a slow oven until dry. If the leaves are not thoroughly coated, the process may be repeated.

Candied Grape Fruit Peel I

Wipe three grape fruits and remove peel in six sections lengthwise of fruit. Soak over night in one quart cold water to which has been added one tablespoon salt. Drain, put in saucepan, cover with cold water and bring to boiling point; repeat three times and cook in the last water until soft, the time required being about four hours. Drain and cut in strips one-eighth inch wide. Weigh peel and put an equal weight of sugar in saucepan and add one-half cup cold water. Bring to the boiling point, add one-half of the strips, cover and cook until pieces are clear. Remove to plate, taking up as little syrup as possible. Cool, roll each piece separately in powdered sugar and spread on a platter to dry. Proceed in same manner with remaining half. Store in glass jars.

Candied Grape Fruit Peel II

Wipe three grape fruits and remove peel in six sections, lengthwise of fruit; then cut and scrape, using a small vegetable knife, removing almost all of the white portion. Wash in cold water, drain and cut in thin strips lengthwise. Then proceed as in recipe for Candied Grape Fruit Peel I.

Chocolate Dipped Candied Orange Peel

Follow directions for Candied Orange Peel (see The Boston Cooking-School Cook Book, p. 547), leaving on considerable of the white portion. Melt confectioners' dipping chocolate in a small saucepan, placed in a larger saucepan containing boiling water. Dip each piece of candied orange peel separately in chocolate, put on paraffine paper and let stand until cool.

Candy Baskets of Glacé Strawberries

2 cups sugar   1 cup boiling water
⅛ teaspoon cream of tartar

Put ingredients in a smooth saucepan, stir, place on range and heat to boiling point. Boil without stirring until syrup begins to discolor. Remove saucepan from fire, and place in larger pan of cold water to instantly stop boiling. Remove from cold water and place in a saucepan of hot water. Take up small portions at a time, cool and stretch until white, then shape in the form of a basket. It may be necessary to stand near a gas jet or over a hot range while stretching, otherwise the candy may become brittle. Repeat until the number

Crystal Cups in the Making. — *Page* 368

Crystal Cups. — *Page* 368.

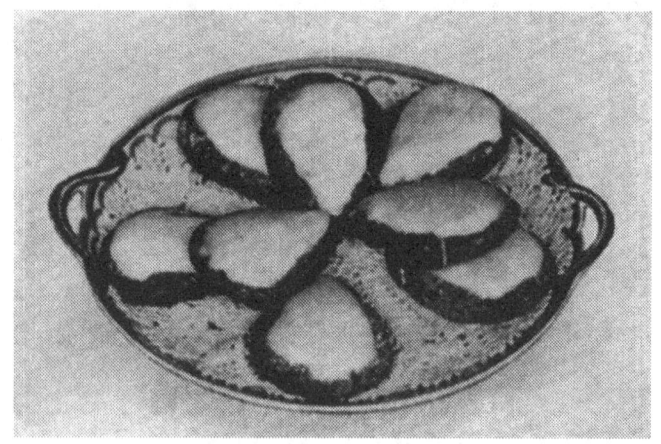

CINKITES. — *Page* 327.

CHOCOLATE DIPPED CANDIED ORANGE PEEL. — *Page* 370.

of baskets required are made. Serve each on a bed of Spun Sugar, and fill with Glacé Strawberries (see The Boston Cooking-School Cook Book, pp. 548 and 547).

Macaroon Baskets filled with Ice Cream and garnished with Whipped Cream

Follow directions for boiling syrup same as given for making Candy Baskets. Dip small macaroons or macaroon drops in syrup at regular intervals close to edge and put two together; when firm add a third macaroon, and so on until a circle is formed large enough for the base of basket. Over these fit another layer of macaroons and over the second layer a third one. Make a handle of stretched candy twisted and adjust same. Arrange basket on plates, fill with ice cream, garnish with whipped cream, sweetened and flavored, and surround with Spun Sugar (see The Boston Cooking-School Cook Book, p. 548).

CHAPTER XXXII

HORS-D'ŒUVRES

Celery with Caviare

WASH, scrape and cut celery stalks in three and one-half inch pieces and curl ends. Spread uncurled portions of grooves with caviare, and arrange each on a small, crisp lettuce leaf, placed on a small fancy plate. Garnish each with a radish, cut to reppresent a tulip. Serve as a first course at a formal dinner or luncheon.

Celery with Roquefort

Wash, scrape and cut celery stalks in two-inch pieces. Work one tablespoon butter until creamy, add two tablespoons Roquefort cheese and stir until thoroughly blended; then season highly with salt and paprika. Spread mixture on inside of celery stalks and serve on bed of chopped ice.

Sardine Cocktail

1 small box sardines	½ teaspoon Tabasco Sauce
½ cup Tomato Catsup	Juice 1 lemon
2 teaspoons Worcestershire Sauce	Salt

Skin and bone sardines and separate in small pieces. Mix catsup, sauce and lemon juice, add sardines and season with salt. Chill thoroughly and serve in scallop shells on a plate of crushed ice.

Danish Canapés

Cut stale bread in one-fourth-inch slices and shape with a round cutter, two and one-half inches in diameter. Toast on one side and spread untoasted side with butter worked until creamy and mixed with chutney, allowing one teaspoon chutney to two tablespoons butter. Garnish with fillets of anchovies, arranged lattice fashion over the top.

Dexter Canapés

Cut stale bread in one-fourth-inch slices, shape with a round cutter, toast on one side, and spread untoasted side with butter worked until creamy and seasoned with anchovy. Cover each with a one-third-inch slice of tomato, spread tomato with mayonnaise dressing, sprinkle with yolk of hard-boiled egg, forced through a potato ricer, and white of hard-boiled egg finely chopped. Garnish around edge with a ring cut from green pepper, and in the centre with a piece of olive and a sprig of parsley.

Laitue Suédoise

Mix one cup finely shredded cabbage, one-half cup finely cut celery, one green pepper (from which seeds have been removed), finely chopped, one-half tablespoon brown sugar, one-half teaspoon salt and one-fourth teaspoon mustard seed. Moisten with French dressing, chill and allow, for each portion, one tablespoon on a small crisp lettuce leaf.

Italian Canapés

Cut stale bread in one-third-inch slices and remove crusts. Cut in finger-shaped pieces and toast on one side. Mix one cup grated Parmesan cheese, two-thirds cup heavy cream, and two tablespoons Madeira wine and season with salt and pepper. Spread untoasted side of bread with mixture, arrange in a pan and bake in a hot oven six minutes. Garnish with sprigs of parsley and serve at once on heated small plates.

St. Valentine's Canapés

Cut bread in one-fourth-inch slices, shape with a heart-shaped cutter and sauté in butter. Drain canned pimiento, dry between towels and shape with a heart-shaped cutter; then sauté in butter. Remove to bread and garnish with a border of finely chopped parsley. Serve hot.

Plaza Canapés

Cut bread in one-third-inch slices, shape in crescent-shaped pieces and sauté in butter until delicately browned. Spread with Anchovy butter and sprinkle one-half the pieces with chopped whites of hard-boiled eggs, sprinkled with paprika; the other half with the yolks of hard-boiled eggs, forced through a sieve. Garnish with sprigs of watercress.

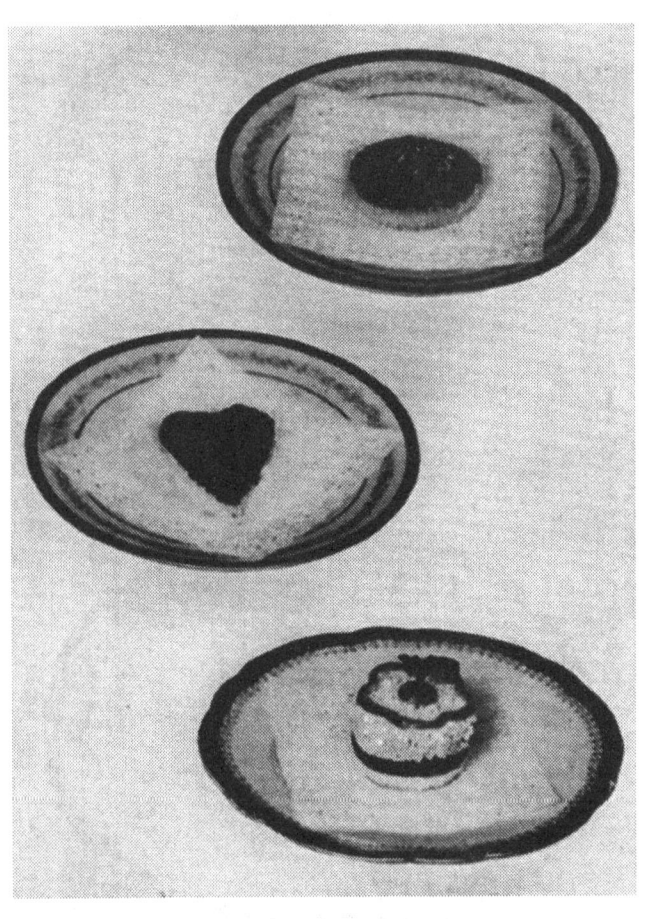

Allen Canapé.   St. Valentine's Canapé.   Dexter Canapé

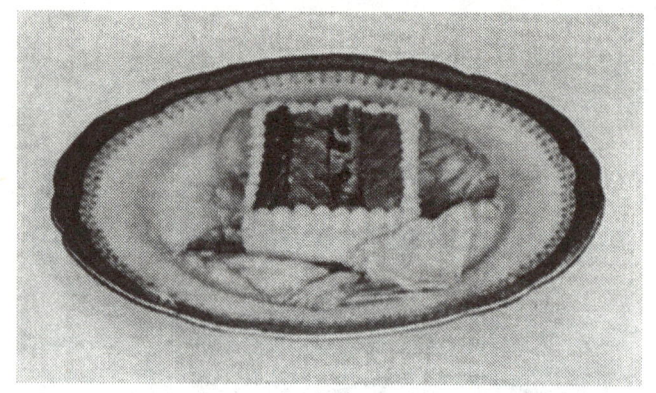

Smoked Fish Canapé. — *Page* 375

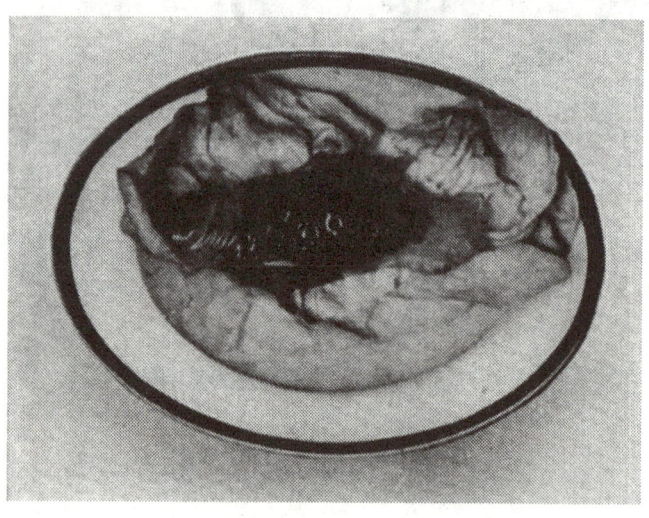

Fish Canapé. — *Page* 376.

Smoked Fish Canapés

Cut stale bread in one-fourth-inch slices, remove crusts and cut in oblongs four by three inches; then sauté in olive oil until delicately browned. Arrange on each, lengthwise, alternate pieces of thinly sliced smoked salmon and smoked herring, using two of each. Pipe around each a border of butter worked until creamy and seasoned with anchovy and lemon juice.

Clam Canapés I

3 dozen clams in shells	1 tablespoon lemon juice
¼ cup water	9 drops Tabasco Sauce
6 mushroom caps	1 teaspoon Sherry wine
2½ tablespoons flour	½ teaspoon evaporated horseradish
2½ tablespoons butter	
⅛ cup clam liquor	1 teaspoon vinegar
3 tablespoons tomato catsup	1 teaspoon salt

Wash clams, changing the water several times. Put in kettle, pour over water, cover and let steam until shells are partially opened. Remove clams from shells, reserving soft portions, and strain liquor through a double thickness of cheese-cloth. Brush, peel and chop mushroom caps. Cook with butter one minute, add flour and then pour on clam liquor. Bring to the boiling point and add catsup, lemon juice, Tabasco Sauce, wine, horseradish mixed with vinegar, salt and soft part of clams. Re-heat and serve on oval-shaped pieces of toast arranged for individual service on small fancy plates.

Clam Canapés II

Cut stale bread in one-third-inch slices, shape in two-and-one-half inch circular pieces and sauté in butter. Spread with paté-de-foie-gras purée. Pipe around edge yolks of hard-boiled eggs, rubbed through a sieve, mixed with creamed butter and seasoned with salt and paprika. Inside of border arrange a ring of white of hard-boiled egg, finely chopped, and sprinkle with finely chopped parsley.

In centre place little neck clams, seasoned with Tomato Catsup, lemon juice, salt, Worcestershire Sauce, Tabasco Sauce and a few gratings horseradish.

Allen Canapés

Cut bread in one-fourth-inch slices and shape with a circular cutter two and one-half inches in diameter. Sauté on one side only, until delicately browned. Spread sides which have not been sautéd with watercress butter and with a pastry bag and tube pipe a border of the butter around circumference. Fill centres with caviare and finely chopped yolks of hard-boiled eggs, used in equal proportions.

Fish Canapés

Remove caviare from can to strainer and pour over hot water to remove some of the oil. Drain thoroughly and season with lemon juice. Brush inside of small fish moulds sparingly with olive oil and put in a shallow pan of crushed ice. Cover bottoms with aspic jelly mixture, made from fish or white stock.

When set, cover body of fish with caviare, and add jelly mixture gradually, by spoonfuls, until moulds are full. Chill thoroughly, remove to crisp lettuce leaves, insert small pieces of truffle to represent eyes, and place on small plates for individual service.

Caviare Rissolettes

Roll puff paste to one-fourth inch in thickness, and shape with a small round cutter, first dipped in flour. Wet edges of one-half the pieces and place in centre of each one teaspoon Russian Caviare seasoned with lemon juice. Cover with remaining pieces and press edges firmly together. Fry in deep fat and drain on brown paper. Arrange for individual service on small plates covered with lace paper doilies. Serve as a first course at a formal dinner.

Butterfly Canapés

Arrange on small serving plate two small crisp heart lettuce leaves, representing wings. Where leaves meet, put one tablespoon thin slices of celery, cut crosswise and moistened with Mayonnaise Dressing. On each side of celery put three-fourths tablespoon Norwegian sardines, separated into flakes. Sprinkle sardines with the chopped white of hard-boiled egg, leaving outer edge of sardine uncovered. Sprinkle celery with yolks of hard-boiled eggs (forced through a strainer) and put a one-half inch band of Mayonnaise Dressing through length of centre. Arrange at regular intervals narrow cross bands of paprika and sprinkle ends with finely chopped parsley.

Washington Canapés

Cut stale bread in one-third-inch slices, shape into rounds two and one-half inches in diameter and toast on one side. Spread untoasted side with butter, worked until creamy, mixed with an equal quantity of grated Parmesan cheese and seasoned with salt and pepper. Cook one finely chopped shallot with one tablespoon butter three minutes. Add two tablespoons flour and stir until well blended; then pour on gradually, while stirring constantly, one cup cream. Bring to the boiling point, add one-half pound crab meat and season with one-half teaspoon salt, one-fourth teaspoon paprika and a few grains black pepper. Spread prepared bread with mixture, rounding slightly, and bake in a hot oven until delicately browned. Garnish with thin strips of red pepper.

Finnan Haddie Canapés

Soak finnan haddie in lukewarm water to cover, set on back of range and let stand until fish may be separated easily into flakes; there should be one cup. Fry one-half tablespoon finely chopped onion and two chopped mushroom caps in three tablespoons butter five minutes. Add two tablespoons flour and pour on gradually, while stirring constantly, two-thirds cup thin cream. As soon as boiling point is reached, add two tablespoons grated cheese, yolks

HORN OF PLENTY CANAPÉ.— *Page 379*

BUTTERFLY CANAPÉ.— *Page 377.*

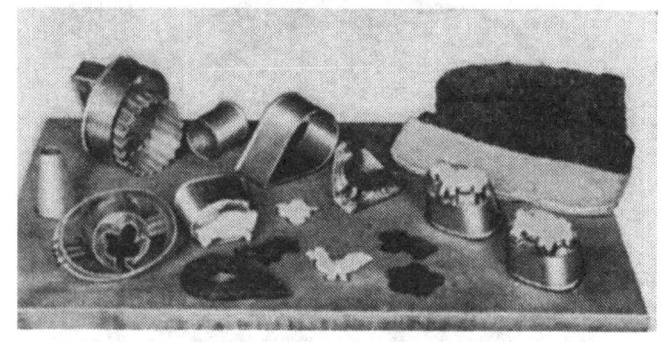

KINDERGARTEN SANDWICHES IN THE MAKING. — *Page* 381

KINDERGARTEN SANDWICHES. — *Page* 381.

of two eggs, slightly beaten, and finnan haddie. Season with salt and cayenne. Cool and pile on circular pieces of toasted bread two inches in diameter. Sprinkle with grated cheese and buttered bread crumbs and bake until crumbs are brown.

Canapés à la Rector

Cut stale bread in one-fourth-inch slices, then in strips three and one-half inches long by one and one-half inches wide. Toast on one side and spread untoasted side with caviare. Divide diagonally into three sections, having two end ones half a square. Sprinkle centre with finely chopped cucumber pickles and ends with finely chopped red pepper. Separate sections with a piece cut from a fillet of anchovy.

Horn of Plenty Canapés

Cut smoked salmon in thin slices, crosswise of fish, and shape in forms of horns of plenty. Fill horns with caviare to which have been added a few drops of lemon juice. Arrange for individual service on elliptical pieces of toasted bread on a plate covered with a lace paper doily.

St. Patrick's Caviare Canapés

Pat and roll puff paste to one-eighth inch in thickness, and shape with small fancy cutter, first dipped in flour; then with a small round cutter (first dipped in flour) make indentation in centres, so a portion may be removed after baking, to admit of filling. Place on a tin sheet and bake in hot oven. Mash yolk of hard-boiled egg, rub through a fine strainer, and add butter to make of right consistency to force through a pastry bag and tube. Season with salt and paprika and garnish edge of pastry forms with mixture, forced through a pastry bag and tube. Color cold water green and fill a small brick mould. Set mould in pail on bed of rock salt and finely crushed ice, using equal parts, and surround with salt and ice nearly to top of mould. Let stand until ice case is formed. Invert to remove water remaining in centre and place mould on a folded napkin on glass dish. Put caviare seasoned with lemon juice in cavity of mould and garnish with large and small clay pipes each tied with green ribbon. Half fill bowls of pipes with alcohol just before sending to table and apply lighted match.

Arrange pastry forms on small plates for individual service and garnish with sprigs of parsley. As soon as alcohol has stopped burning, pass caviare that each guest may fill his case.

CHAPTER XXXIII

SANDWICHES

Kindergarten Sandwiches

REMOVE crusts from a white and graham loaf and cut each in thin slices, lengthwise. Shape with round, round-fluted, elliptical, cutlet-shaped, square or oblong cutters. Spread one-half the pieces generously with butter, which has been worked until creamy. From remaining pieces cut out shapes, using small flower, animal or fancy cutters, and refill cuts thus made with similar cuts of bread of contrasting color. Put together as shown in illustration and wrap in cheese-cloth wrung out of hot water to keep moist until serving time.

Mosaic Sandwiches

Cut three slices each of white and graham bread one-half inch in thickness. Spread a slice of white bread with creamed butter and place a slice of graham on it; spread this with creamed butter and place on it a slice of white bread; repeat this process, beginning with a slice of graham. Put both piles in a cool place under a light weight. When butter has become firm, trim each pile evenly and cut each pile in three one-half-inch slices. Spread these with butter and put together in such a way that a white block will alternate with a graham one. Place again in a cool place under a light weight, and when butter has become perfectly hard cut in thin slices for serving. Arrange on a plate covered with a doily.

Honor Sandwiches

Cut bread in one-fourth-inch slices, spread with pimiento butter and shape with a fancy rectangular cutter. Cover with pieces of bread from which pieces have been removed with a small fancy cutter.

Pimiento Butter.—Cream one-fourth cup butter and add two canned pimientos, which have been forced through a purée strainer. When thoroughly blended, season with one-fourth teaspoon salt.

Toasted Salad Sandwiches

Mash a cream cheese and moisten with French dressing. Cut graham bread in one-fourth-inch slices, spread with cheese mixture and sprinkle with chopped pecan nut meats. Put together in pairs, remove crusts and cut in finger-shaped pieces. Toast, pile log-cabin fashion on a fancy plate and serve as an accompaniment to a dinner salad.

Devilled Sandwiches

Blanch and shred two ounces Jordan almonds; then sauté in enough butter to prevent burning, until delicately browned, stirring constantly. Mix two tablespoons chopped pickles, one tablespoon

Mosaic Sandwiches. — *Page* 381

Honor Sandwiches. — *Page* 382.

HORSERADISH SANDWICHES.—*Page* 389

DREAM SANDWICHES.—*Page* 383.

Worcestershire Sauce, one tablespoon chutney, one-fourth teaspoon salt and a few grains cayenne. Pour over almonds and cook two minutes, stirring constantly. Work a cream cheese until smooth and season with salt and paprika. Spread unsweetened wafer crackers with cheese, sprinkle with nuts and put together in pairs. Arrange on a plate, covered with a doily. A delicious accompaniment to a dinner salad.

Caviare Sandwiches

Cut white bread in thin slices, spread with creamed butter and then with caviare. Sprinkle with lemon juice and cayenne; cover with slices of buttered bread, remove crusts and cut in small finger-shaped pieces.

Dream Sandwiches

Cut stale bread in one-fourth-inch slices; remove crusts and cut in rectangular pieces. Cut mild cheese in slices same size as pieces of bread and sprinkle with salt and cayenne. Put a slice of cheese between each two slices of bread and sauté in butter until delicately browned on one side; then turn and brown other side.

Chicken Cream Sandwiches

¾ cup chopped cold boiled fowl	3 tablespoons flour
	2 tablespoons butter
¼ cup chopped celery	Whites 2 eggs
1 hot boiled onion	½ teaspoon salt
1 cup milk	⅛ teaspoon pepper

Lemon juice

Mix fowl (preferably white meat), celery and onion, forced through a purée strainer, and add milk; then add flour, mixed with butter worked until creamy. Bring to the boiling point and let simmer three minutes; then add whites of eggs, beaten until stiff, and seasonings. Turn into a small mould and let stand in a cold place twelve hours. Remove from mould, cut in slices and put between thin slices of buttered bread. Remove crusts and cut in any desired shape.

Spanish Sandwiches

Put in a mortar and pound to a paste two anchovies, two pickles, one sprig parsley, three tablespoons capers, one teaspoon made mustard, two tablespoons olive oil, two tablespoons vinegar and yolks of two hard-boiled eggs; then season with salt and paprika. Cut bread in thin slices, butter sparingly, spread with mixture and sprinkle with whites of hard-boiled eggs, finely chopped. Cover with slices of buttered bread, remove crusts and cut in fancy shapes.

Fairmont Sandwiches

Cut bread in one-fourth-inch slices. Spread three slices sparingly with butter on both sides, and two slices on but one side. Put between slices layers of finely cut red and green peppers wrung through a cheese-cloth to remove moisture, moistened with Mayonnaise Dressing. There should be two layers of green peppers and one of red. Remove crusts, fold in damp cheese-cloth and press under a weight; then cut in slices for serving, and arrange on a plate covered with a doily.

Sembrich Sandwiches

Cut and spread seven slices bread, same as for Fairmont Sandwiches. Put between slices finely chopped cold boiled ham, moistened with cream and seasoned with salt, mustard and cayenne; finely chopped cold boiled fowl, moistened with Mayonnaise Dressing, and chopped nut meats, moistened with Mayonnaise Dressing: there should be two layers of each filling. Remove crusts, fold in cheese-cloth and press under a weight. Cut in slices and arrange on a bed of crisp lettuce leaves.

Lincoln Sandwiches

Cut brown and white bread in thin slices and spread with butter, which has been worked until creamy. Cut cold boiled tongue and gruyère cheese in thin slices. Put a slice of tongue on white bread, over tongue brown bread, and over brown bread cheese; repeat. Wrap in cheese-cloth, put under a weight and let stand several hours.

For serving cut in thin slices crosswise, and arrange sandwiches overlapping one another, in two parallel rows on a plate covered with a lace paper doily.

German Sandwiches

Cut German Loaf (p. 137) in thin slices and put between thin slices of buttered graham bread.

Royal Sandwiches

½ cup shrimps	½ Bermuda onion
½ cup cooked chicken livers	Salt
½ red pepper	Mayonnaise Dressing

Mix and force through a meat chopper shrimps, livers, pepper (from which seeds have been removed) and onion. Season with salt and moisten with Mayonnaise Dressing. Spread between thin slices of buttered bread, remove crusts and cut in fancy shapes. Arrange on a plate covered with a doily.

East India Sandwiches

Hard cook eggs, separate yolks from whites, mash yolks and finely chop whites. Moisten yolks with Bengal Club Chutney until of the right consistency to spread. Spread thin slices of buttered bread with mixture, sprinkle with chopped whites, cover with thin slices of buttered bread, remove crusts and cut in halves crosswise.

Penobscot Sandwiches

Free cold cooked salmon from skin and bones; there should be one-half cup. Mash and add white of one hard-boiled egg finely chopped and one tablespoon finely chopped cucumber pickle; season with salt and paprika and moisten with Cream Salad Dressing. Mash yolks of two hard-boiled eggs and add one and one-half tablespoons melted butter, one and one-half tablespoons chopped nut meats and a few drops anchovy essence. Re-

Fairmont Sandwiches. — *Page* 384

Egg and Potato Salad. — *Page* 210

BELMONT BAKED APPLES READY FOR THE OVEN. — *Page* 391

BELMONT BAKED APPLES. — *Page* 391.

move crusts from a stale white loaf in four pieces and cut off five one-third-inch slices lengthwise of loaf. Spread three slices, on both sides, with butter worked until creamy, remaining two slices on but one side. Spread two mixtures alternately, between slices of bread, sprinkling egg yolk mixture with finely chopped green pepper. Wrap in paraffine paper or cheese-cloth, place under a light weight and let stand until serving time. Cut in one-third-inch slices crosswise and each slice in halves lengthwise. Arrange overlapping one another on a plate covered with a lace paper doily.

Orange Honey Sandwiches

Spread thin slices of buttered white bread with orange honey. Put together in pairs, remove crusts and cut in fancy shapes. For the orange honey boil one cup sugar with one-fourth cup, each, water and orange juice, until syrup will spin a thread when dropped from tip of spoon. Add one-half cup finely chopped orange peel (from which all white portion has been removed) and one-half teaspoon vanilla. Again bring to the boiling point and cool.

French Prune Sandwiches

Remove stones from French prunes and finely chop. Mix with chopped English walnut meats, allowing seven halves of nut meats to every six prunes. Moisten with a thin syrup (made by boiling one-fourth cup sugar and one-fourth cup water five minutes) and season with salt, paprika and lemon juice. Spread between thin slices of buttered white bread and cut in fancy shapes, using a cutlet cutter.

Jelly Sandwiches

Cut bread in one-third-inch slices, and remove crusts; then toast and cut in halves on the diagonal. Spread with butter and currant jelly (beaten until of the consistency to spread evenly). Sprinkle one-half the pieces with English walnut meats, cover with remaining pieces and arrange for individual service on small hot plates.

Lenox Sandwiches

Work one-fourth cup almond paste until smooth. Add gradually one-fourth cup powdered sugar and a few grains salt; then add three-eighths cup heavy cream. Spread thin slices of buttered bread with mixture, cover with buttered bread, remove crusts and cut in finger-shaped pieces.

Macedoine Sandwiches

¼ cup finely chopped Canton ginger
¼ cup finely chopped pecan nut meats
2 tablespoons finely cut orange pulp
1 tablespoon ginger syrup
1 teaspoon vinegar
Few grains salt
Saltines

Mix ingredients in order given and spread between saltines or thin slices of buttered bread.

Waltham Five o'Clock Tea Sandwiches

Work a cream cheese until of the right consistency to spread. Spread on thin, salted, unsweetened round wafer crackers and cover with halves of marshmallows, cut crosswise, and pulled out with the fingers to about fit crackers. Cover with wafer crackers, arrange on tin sheet and bake until cheese and marshmallows begin to melt.

Horseradish Sandwiches

6 tablespoons butter	1 teaspoon lemon juice
4 tablespoons grated horseradish	Few grains salt.
Pimolas	

Cream butter, add gradually horseradish, lemon juice, and salt. Spread between thin slices of bread, shape with a cutter in form of diamonds and garnish each with a slice cut from a pimola crosswise.

Commonwealth Marmalade Sandwiches

Remove end slice from a loaf of bread. Spread end of loaf evenly with butter which has been creamed. Cut off a thin slice and repeat until the number of slices required are prepared.

Spread with orange marmalade, put together in pairs and press together. Remove crusts and cut in halves crosswise. Put in a pan and bake in a hot oven until delicately browned on both sides, turning once during the browning.

Rochester Chocolate Sandwiches

¼ cup butter	1 square unsweetened chocolate
½ cup sugar	2 tablespoons milk
1 egg	1¼ cups flour
Few grains salt	1 teaspoon baking powder

Cream butter and add gradually, while beating constantly, sugar; then add egg, well beaten, salt, chocolate (melted), milk and flour, mixed and sifted with baking powder. Toss on a slightly floured board, pat and roll as thin as possible. Shape with a small round cutter (first dipped in flour), arrange on a buttered sheet and bake in a moderate oven. Cool and put together with the following mixture: Work a cream cheese until smooth and moisten with cream until of the right consistency to spread; then season highly with salt and paprika.

GRAPE FRUIT À LA RUSSE. — *Page* 392

RECTOR LEAF. — *Page* 393.

CANTELOUPE SUPRÊME. — *Page* 394.

LENOX STRAWBERRIES. — *Page* 394

CHAPTER XXXIV

FRUITS, FRESH, PRESERVED AND CANNED

Belmont Baked Apples

WIPE selected red apples and make two circular cuts through skin, leaving a three-fourths-inch band around apple midway between stem and blossom ends. Put in an earthen or graniteware baking dish, sprinkle generously with sugar and add water to cover bottom of pan. Bake in a hot oven until soft, basting every eight minutes with syrup in pan. Remove to serving dish and pour around syrup.

Baked Apples in Casserole

Wipe, pare and core six medium-sized apples. Put in casserole, add one cup water and one and one-half cups sugar and dredge with flour. Cover and cook in a slow oven one hour. Do not remove cover during the baking.

Apple Ball Sauce

Wipe apples, pare and shape into balls, using a French vegetable cutter; there should be one and one-half cups. Make a syrup by boiling one cup sugar, three-fourths cup water, six cloves and three or four thin shavings from the rind of a lemon, seven minutes. Remove cloves and rind, add one-third of the balls and cook until soft; repeat twice. Cook syrup until reduced one-half and pour over balls.

Stewed Apricots and Prunes

Pick over and wash one-fourth pound each dried apricots and prunes. Put in saucepan, cover with cold water, place on range, bring to the boiling point and drain. Repeat three times; again cover with cold water and add one cup sugar. Again bring to the boiling point and let simmer until soft.

Sautéd Pineapple

Drain canned, sliced pineapple from syrup and dry on a towel. Sauté in butter until delicately browned. Serve around roast turkey or roast chicken.

Pineapple Sauté

Empty a can of sliced pineapple into a shallow graniteware baking pan, not allowing slices to overlap one another. Place on back of range and let simmer two or three hours, when pineapple will be quite clear. Remove to serving dish and garnish centre of each with a glacéd cherry. Serve as an accompaniment to meat or game.

Grape Fruit à la Russe

3 grape fruits	2 tablespoons powdered sugar
⅔ cup sugar	Few grains salt
1 cup heavy cream	½ teaspoon maraschino

Wipe grape fruits, cut in halves, crosswise, and remove seeds and tough portions. Sprinkle with granulated sugar and chill in ice box. Beat cream until stiff and add powdered sugar, salt and maraschino. Pipe a border, by forcing a mixture through a pastry bag and tube, on top of each half in the form of a square. Garnish at each corner with a glacéd cherry. Serve in double cocktail glasses having the larger ones filled with crushed ice.

Grape Fruit Coupe

Remove pulp from grape fruit in sections, cut each section in thirds, sprinkle with sugar and chill in ice box. Arrange six fresh mint leaves at equal distances around inside of each coupe glass, having ends of leaves reach top of glass. Fill with prepared pulp and garnish centre of each with a small sprig of mint.

Rector Leaf

4 grape fruits
½ cup powdered sugar
2 teaspoons orange curaçoa
1 teaspoon lemon juice
1 teaspoon Kirsch
⅛ teaspoon salt

Remove pulp from grape fruit, add remaining ingredients and chill thoroughly. Serve in coupe glasses having six fresh mint leaves arranged lengthwise at equal distances around inside of each glass.

Watermelon Cubes, Sherry Dressing

Cut centre of a thoroughly chilled watermelon into three-fourth-inch cubes and remove seeds. Pour over Sherry Dressing, put in jar and let stand in ice box several hours. Arrange for individual service on green leaves, placed on a fancy plate, allowing seven cubes to each portion. If leaves are not at hand, serve in champagne glasses.

Sherry Dressing. — Mix one-half cup sugar, one-half cup Sherry wine, two tablespoons sloe gin and a few grains salt. Let stand until sugar is dissolved. The sloe gin may be omitted.

Canteloupe Suprême

Wipe canteloupes, cut in halves crosswise, remove seeds and stringy portion and shape into balls, using a French potato ball cutter. Arrange in double coupe or grape fruit glasses (having crushed ice in outer glass), sprinkle with sugar and pour over each one-fourth teaspoon maraschino. If a more elaborate coupe is desired, arrange balls in cases made from halves of orange peel and serve in single glasses.

Lenox Strawberries

Wash, pick over and hull strawberries. Pour over Lenox mixture, chill thoroughly, arrange in glasses and garnish around edge with whipped cream (sweetened and flavored delicately with vanilla) forced through a pastry bag and tube.

For the Lenox mixture, mix juice of one-half orange, four tablespoons sugar and one-fourth teaspoon orange curaçoa, allowing this quantity for each portion.

PASTRY BOATS FILLED WITH FRESH FRUIT.

RHUBARB CONSERVE IN THE MAKING. — *Page* 396

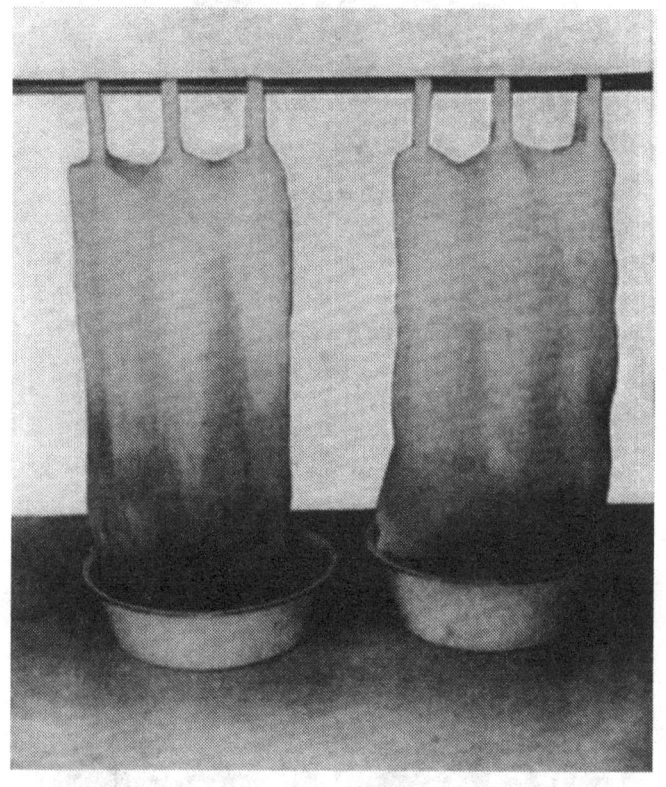

Home-Made Jelly Bags

Claret Strawberries

Prepare and serve strawberries, same as Lenox Strawberries, using claret in place of Lenox mixture.

Lemons Cut for Garnishing

Wash and wipe lemons, and cut in slices crosswise, sections lengthwise, fan-shaped pieces, cups or baskets. Decorate with sprigs of parsley, parsley finely chopped, paprika, canned pimiento (cut in strips or fancy shapes), radishes sliced, or red portion of radishes, chopped or removed and cut in fancy shapes.

Apple Ginger

Wipe, quarter, pare, core and finely chop sour apples; there should be ten cups. Add ten cups sugar, thin shavings from the rind of two lemons, and two two-inch pieces of ginger root. Put in preserving kettle, bring gradually to the boiling point and let simmer, stirring frequently, until apples are transparent, the time required being from two and one-half to three hours. Great care must be taken, otherwise the mixture will burn. It is well to have the kettle placed on an asbestos mat. Turn into a crock or jelly tumblers.

Peach Conserve

1 pound dried skinned peaches
1 quart cold water
1 cup raisins
½ lb. English walnut meats
Juice 1 lemon
Juice 1 orange
1 whole orange
1 lb. sugar

Add cold water to peaches, cover and let stand over night. In the morning add raisins, seeded and cut in pieces, nut meats, cut in pieces, fruit juices, orange, cut in thin slices (removing seeds) and sugar. Bring to boiling point and let simmer one and one-quarter hours, stirring occasionally to prevent burning.

Rhubarb Conserve

4 pounds rhubarb	1 pound seeded raisins
5 pounds sugar	2 oranges
	1 lemon

Wash and peel stalks of rhubarb and cut in one-inch pieces. Put in kettle, sprinkle with sugar and add raisins and grated rind and juice of oranges and lemon. Mix, cover and let stand one-half hour. Place on range, bring to boiling point and let simmer forty-five minutes, stirring almost constantly. Fill jelly glasses with mixture, cool and seal.

Plum Gumbo

| 5 pounds plums | 3 oranges |
| 2 pounds seeded raisins | 5 pounds sugar |

Wipe plums, remove stones and cut in pieces. Force raisins through a meat chopper or chop. Wipe oranges, and cut in thin slices crosswise, removing seeds. Put fruit in preserving kettle, add sugar, bring to boiling point and let simmer until of the consistency of a marmalade. Fill jelly glasses with mixture, cool and seal.

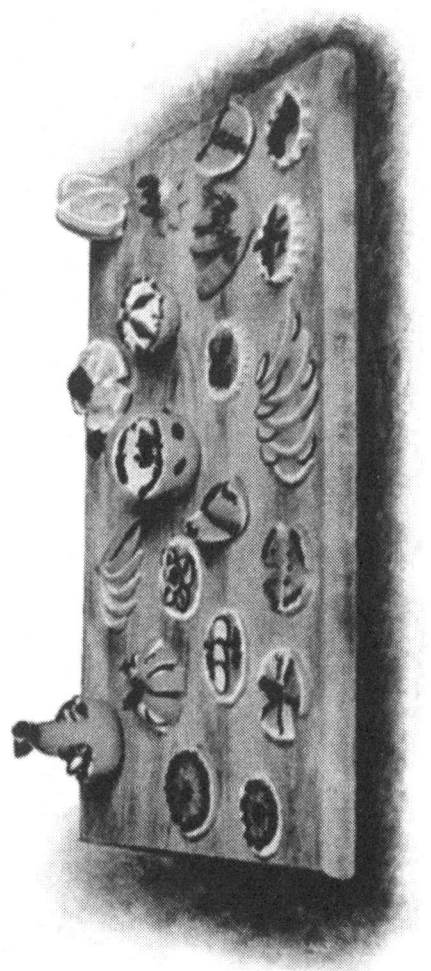

Lemons Cut for Garnishings.—*Page* 395

Cranberry Conserve

1 quart cranberries	¼ lb. seeded raisins
⅔ cup cold water	½ lb. English walnut meats
⅔ cup boiling water	1 orange
1½ lbs. sugar	

Pick over and wash cranberries. Put in saucepan, add cold water, bring to the boiling point and let boil until the skins break. Force through a strainer and add boiling water, seeded raisins, nut meats, broken in small pieces, orange (wiped, thinly sliced, then cut in small pieces, removing seeds) and sugar. Again bring to the boiling point and let simmer twenty minutes.

Spiced Cranberry Jelly

1 quart cranberries	2-inch piece stick cinnamon
1 cup boiling water	24 whole cloves
2 cups sugar	6 allspice berries
⅛ cup cold water	Few grains salt

Pick over and wash berries. Add boiling water and let boil until cranberries are soft. Rub through a sieve and add remaining ingredients, except salt. Again bring to the boiling point and let simmer fifteen minutes. Add salt, turn into a mould and chill.

Cranberry Jelly with Celery

Pick over and wash four cups cranberries. Put in a stewpan and add two cups sugar and one cup boiling water. Bring to the boiling point and let boil twenty minutes; then force through a strainer. When mixture begins to thicken, fold in one and one-half cups celery, cut crosswise of stalks in one-eighth-inch slices. Turn into a mould or moulds and chill. Remove from moulds and garnish with curled celery.

Raspberry Syrup

2 quarts raspberries	1 quart sugar
¾ cup cold water	

Pick over and mash raspberries, sprinkle with sugar, cover and let stand over night. In the morning add water, bring slowly to the boiling point and cook twenty minutes. Force through a double thickness of cheese-cloth, again bring to the boiling point, fill small glass jars to overflow and adjust covers. To use as a foundation for beverages or raspberry ice or for sauces to accompany hot, cold, or frozen desserts.

Orange Marmalade

3 oranges	11 cups cold water
1 lemon	4 pounds sugar

Wipe fruit, cut in halves crosswise; remove seeds and put through a meat chopper. Put in preserving kettle, add water, cover, and let stand twenty-four hours. Place on range, bring to the boiling point and let simmer one and one-half hours. Add sugar and again let stand twenty-four hours. Again bring to the boiling point and let simmer one and one-half hours.

CRANBERRY JELLY WITH CELERY.—*Page* 397

MINT JELLY, CORN RELISH AND PEACH CONSERVE.

Pickled Lime Marmalade

| 12 medium-sized green | 12 selected pickled limes |
| tomatoes | 6 cups sugar |

Wipe tomatoes and drain limes; then force through a meat chopper. Put in saucepan, add sugar, bring to the boiling point and let simmer three hours. Turn into glasses and seal.

Preserved Strawberries

Wash, pick over and hull berries. Put in a preserving kettle and add an equal measure of sugar. Bring to the boiling point and let boil until fruit juice will jell when a teaspoonful is cooled on a saucer. Fill preserving jars and seal.

Mint Jelly

Wipe one peck Porter apples, remove stem and blossom ends and cut in eighths. Put in a graniteware kettle and add two quarts cold water. Cover, bring to the boiling point and let simmer until apples are soft. Mash in same kettle, using a wooden potato masher, and drain through a coarse sieve. Allow juice to drip through several thicknesses of cheese-cloth or a jelly bag. Return juice to saucepan, bring to the boiling point and let boil twenty minutes; then add an equal measure of heated sugar. Again bring to the boiling point and let boil five minutes. Take a large bunch of fresh young mint, wash and bruise some of the leaves slightly, by pressing between the fingers. Hold bunch in hand and pass through and through the syrup, until the desired strength of mint flavor is obtained. This process takes the last three minutes of the cooking. Add two tablespoons lemon juice and color green, using vegetable green paste. Skim and turn into jelly glasses. Put in a sunny window and let stand twenty-four hours. Cover and keep in a cool, dry place.

Rose Geranium Jelly

Follow directions for Mint Jelly, using two or three sprays of rose geranium leaves in place of mint, pink coloring in place of green, and omitting lemon juice.

CHAPTER XXXV

PICKLING

Apple Catsup

WIPE, quarter, pare and core twelve sour apples. Put in a saucepan, cover with boiling water, bring to the boiling point and let simmer until soft, when nearly all the water should be evaporated; then rub through a sieve. To each quart of apple pulp add the following mixture:

Mix one cup sugar, one teaspoon pepper, one teaspoon cloves, one teaspoon mustard, two teaspoons cinnamon and one tablespoon salt; then add two finely chopped onions and two cups cider vinegar. Bring the apple pulp, to which the mixture has been added, to the boiling point and let simmer one hour. Bottle, cork and seal while hot.

Gooseberry Catsup

5 pounds gooseberries	1½ tablespoons cinnamon
4 pounds sugar	1 tablespoon clove
2 cups cider vinegar	1 tablespoon allspice

Pick over, wash and drain gooseberries. Put in kettle and add sugar, vinegar and spices. Bring to boiling point and let simmer two hours. Fill bottles and seal.

Grape Catsup

Pick over, wash, drain and remove stems from grapes. Put in a preserving kettle, add cold water to barely cover, bring to the boiling point and let simmer until fruit is soft; then press through a sieve, discarding skins and seeds. Put ten pounds of the fruit pulp in a preserving kettle and add five pounds sugar, two quarts vinegar, one tablespoon cinnamon, one tablespoon allspice, two tablespoons clove and one grated nutmeg. Bring to the boiling point and let simmer until reduced to the consistency of a catsup. Fill bottles to overflowing, adjust stoppers and seal.

Spiced Rhubarb

2½ pounds rhubarb 　　　⅞ cup vinegar
2 pounds sugar 　　　　 1 teaspoon cinnamon
　　　　½ teaspoon clove

Wipe rhubarb, skin and cut stalks in one-inch pieces. Put in preserve kettle, add remaining ingredients, bring to boiling point and let simmer until of the consistency of a marmalade. Fill jelly glasses with mixture, cool and seal.

Gooseberry Relish

5 cups gooseberries 　　　3 tablespoons ginger
1½ cups raisins 　　　　　3 tablespoons salt
1 onion 　　　　　　　　　¼ teaspoon cayenne
1 cup brown sugar 　　　　1 teaspoon turmeric
3 tablespoons mustard 　　1 quart vinegar

PICKLING 403

Pick over, wash and drain gooseberries. Add raisins (from which seeds have been removed) and onion, peeled and sliced. Chop or force through a meat chopper, put in preserving kettle and add sugar, mustard, ginger, salt, cayenne and turmeric. Pour over vinegar, bring slowly to boiling point and let simmer forty-five minutes. Strain through a coarse sieve, fill bottles with mixture and seal.

Sweet Crabapple Pickle

3 pounds crabapples	1½ teaspoons cloves
2 cups cider vinegar	1½ teaspoons allspice berries
1 cup sugar	1½ teaspoons black pepper
1½ teaspoons ginger	

Wipe crabapples, remove stems and steam until soft. Tie spices in muslin bag, put in preserving kettle, add vinegar, sugar and apples, bring gradually to boiling point and let simmer twenty minutes.

Corn Relish

1½ dozen ears corn	2 cups sugar
1 small cabbage	1 cup flour
1 bunch celery	½ cup salt
4 onions	½ teaspoon mustard
2 green peppers	¼ teaspoon cayenne
2 quarts vinegar	½ teaspoon turmeric

Cut corn from cob. Force cabbage through a meat chopper. Separate celery stalks, remove leaves and chop. Peel onions and cut in thin slices. Wipe peppers and chop. Put vegetables in preserving kettle and pour over one-half of the vinegar.

Mix sugar, flour, salt, mustard, cayenne and turmeric and add remaining vinegar. Combine mixtures, bring to boiling point and let simmer forty minutes. Fill glass jars and seal.

Spiced Celery

6 bunches celery	1 teaspoon mustard
15 tomatoes	1 teaspoon clove
1 red pepper	1 teaspoon allspice
2 cups sugar	1 teaspoon cinnamon
2 tablespoons salt	1 teaspoon celery seed

1½ cups vinegar

Cut off roots and leaves of celery, separate stalks and chop. Wipe, peel and chop tomatoes. Wipe and chop pepper. Mix dry ingredients and add vinegar. Combine mixtures, put in preserving kettle, bring to boiling point and let simmer one and one-half hours. Fill jars to overflow and adjust covers.

Souri

Wipe one peck green tomatoes and cut in thin slices; peel one quart onions and cut in thin slices. Sprinkle alternate layers of tomatoes and onions with one cup salt. Cover and let stand over night. In the morning drain thoroughly, put in a preserving kettle and add four green peppers, finely chopped, six cups brown sugar, six tablespoons celery-seed, six tablespoons mustard-seed and one-half ounce, each, cloves, stick cinnamon and allspice berries tied in a muslin bag. Add vinegar to just cover mixture, bring to the boiling point and let simmer two hours.

This may be given a very fresh taste by adding a small quantity of celery, cut in small pieces, whenever it is served.

Pepper Relish I

12 green bell peppers	3 tablespoons salt
12 red bell peppers	2 cups sugar
3 onions	1 quart vinegar

Wipe peppers, cut in halves lengthwise and remove seeds. Pare onions, add to peppers and force through a meat-chopper. Put in kettle, cover with boiling water and let stand ten minutes; drain, again cover with boiling water, bring to the boiling point and let stand ten minutes. Drain as dry as possible, return to kettle, add remaining ingredients, bring to the boiling point and let simmer fifteen minutes.

Pepper Relish II

1 peck red peppers	2 cups vinegar
2 cups cold water	1 cup brown sugar
1 cup salt	½ cup white mustard seed

Wipe peppers, cut in halves, remove seeds and put through meat chopper. Put in kettle and add water and salt; cover and let stand over night. In the morning drain and pour over vinegar, sugar and mustard seed which have been brought to the boiling point and boiled two minutes. Fill jars to overflow and adjust covers.

Bottled Tomato Sauce

12 large tomatoes	2 onions
3 bunches celery	2 tablespoons salt
4 green peppers	2 tablespoons sugar
3 cups vinegar	

Peel and chop tomatoes and onions, put in kettle and add celery (from which root and leaves have been removed) and peppers, both finely chopped, and remaining ingredients. Bring to boiling point and let simmer one and one-half hours. Fill bottles with mixture, cork and seal.

Chili Sauce

12 medium-sized tomatoes	2 tablespoons salt
4 onions	2 tablespoons celery seed
2 red peppers	¼ cup brown sugar
2 cups vinegar	

Wipe and peel tomatoes and cut in one-fourth-inch slices, crosswise. Put in preserving kettle and add onions, peeled and chopped, peppers, chopped, and remaining ingredients. Bring to the boiling point and let simmer three hours.

Green Sliced Cucumber Pickles
(Uncooked)

2 dozen 6-inch cucumbers	1 cup olive oil
2 quarts boiling water	¼ pound white mustard seed
1½ cups salt	¼ pound black mustard seed
6 cups vinegar	

Wipe and thinly slice cucumbers without paring. Cover with a brine, made of water and salt, and let stand over night.

Drain thoroughly and put in a crock. Mix remaining ingredients and pour over cucumbers. Stir frequently.

Piccalilli

½ bushel green tomatoes	3 pounds brown sugar
½ peck green peppers	2 pounds white mustard seed
½ peck onions	6 ounces stick cinnamon
2 medium-sized cabbages	3 ounces cloves
1½ cups salt	2 ounces allspice berries
Vinegar	

Wash tomatoes and peppers, peel onions and cut cabbages in quarters. Put the vegetables, separately, through a meat-chopper, using a large knife. Sprinkle alternate layers of vegetables with salt, cover and let stand over night. In the morning drain, add sugar, mustard seed and the remaining spices, tied in a bag made of muslin or cheese-cloth. Pour over vinegar just to cover vegetables, bring to the boiling point and let simmer six hours. Remove spice bag, fill glass jars with mixture and adjust covers.

Allerton Pickles

3 pints tomato pulp	4 tablespoons salt
1 cup chopped celery	6 tablespoons sugar
4 tablespoons chopped red pepper	6 tablespoons mustard seed
	1 tablespoon grated nutmeg
4 tablespoons chopped onion	1 teaspoon cinnamon
	½ teaspoon clove
2 cups vinegar	

Wipe, peel and chop ripe tomatoes; there should be three pints. Add remaining ingredients and stir until thoroughly blended. Put in a stone jar and cover. Let stand at least one week before using. This uncooked mixture will keep six months.

Chow Chow

Peel one quart tiny white onions and add one quart small cucumbers, two heads cauliflower, separated into flowerets, and two green peppers, thinly sliced. Cover with brine (allowing one and one-half cups salt to two quarts boiling water) and let stand over night. In the morning drain thoroughly, add fresh brine, bring to the boiling point and let simmer until vegetables are soft, then drain thoroughly. Mix six tablespoons mustard, three tablespoons flour, one tablespoon curry-powder and two-thirds cup sugar. Moisten to a smooth paste with cold vinegar, and add to two and one-half cups vinegar, brought to the boiling point. Cook, stirring constantly at first and afterward occasionally, until mixture thickens; then add drained vegetables and let simmer ten minutes. Store in glass jars.

Petersham Chow Chow

2 quarts green tomatoes	3 quarts water
1 bunch celery	1 cup flour
6 green peppers	8 tablespoons mustard
1 quart button onions	1 tablespoon turmeric
1 cauliflower	1 cup sugar
2 cups salt	5 cups vinegar

Wipe tomatoes and cut in eighths. Scrape celery and cut in three-fourths-inch slices, crosswise. Wipe peppers and cut in pieces. Peel onions, separate cauliflower in flowerets, cover with boiling water, let boil three minutes and drain. Mix tomatoes, celery, peppers, onions and cauliflower and pour over brine, made of salt and water. Let stand over night; in the morning bring to the boiling point in the same brine and let boil until vegetables are tender; then drain. Mix flour, mustard and turmeric and add cold vinegar slowly to make a smooth paste; then add sugar and remaining vinegar. Cook over hot water until mixture thickens, stirring constantly at first and afterwards occasionally. Add drained vegetables to mixture and cook until thoroughly heated.

Mustard Pickles

Wipe four quarts small cucumbers, put in a preserving kettle and add three large cucumbers, cut in pieces, one quart green tomatoes, wiped and cut in slices, four small onions, peeled and cut in slices, four green peppers, wiped and cut in slices, one bunch of celery, chopped, and one cauliflower, separated into flowerets. Add one gallon boiling water, to which has been added one pint salt; cover and let stand over night. In the morning bring to the boiling point and let simmer until the vegetables are tender; then drain. Mix one cup flour, one cup sugar, six tablespoons mustard and one tablespoon turmeric powder; then add slowly, while stirring constantly, enough vinegar to make a paste. Stir into two quarts vinegar, brought to the boiling point, add two tablespoons celery seed, and let boil five minutes. Add the drained vegetables, again bring to the boiling point and let boil fifteen minutes.

Dutch Salad

1 quart green tomatoes	1 small white cabbage
¼ cup salt	2 cauliflowers
2 quarts small pickling cucumbers	9 green peppers
	Boiling water
1 quart small onions	3 tablespoons salt

Dutch Dressing

Wipe and thinly slice tomatoes. Arrange in layers, sprinkling each with salt, cover and let stand over night. In the morning drain thoroughly and chop. Put in a preserving kettle and add cucumbers chopped, cabbage chopped, cauliflowers separated into flowerets and chopped peppers (from which seeds have been removed). Add boiling water to just cover vegetables and salt. Bring to the boiling point and let simmer until vegetables are tender; then drain. Pour over Dutch Dressing and let simmer fifteen minutes. Cool and serve in jars.

Dutch Dressing. — Mix two cups brown sugar, one cup bread flour, one-third cup mustard, one and one-half tablespoons salt and two and one-half tablespoons turmeric. Add gradually, while stirring constantly, two quarts hot vinegar. Bring to the boiling point and let boil until mixture thickens.

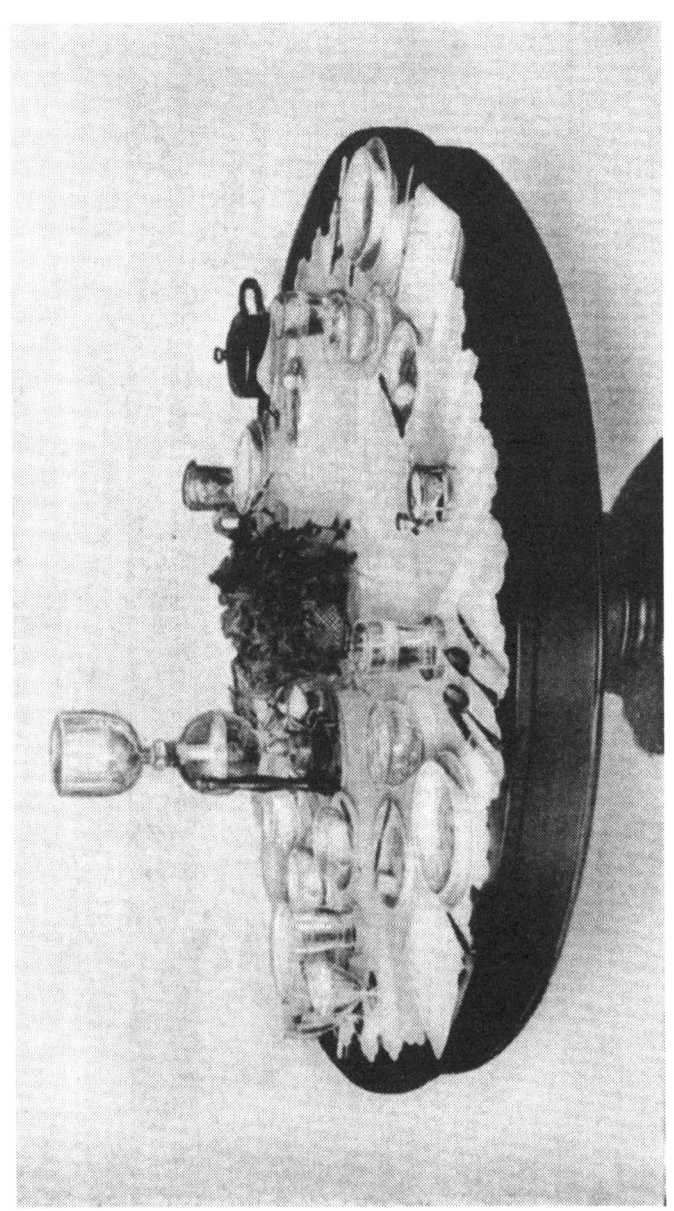

TABLE LAID FOR BREAKFAST.

TABLE LAID FOR LUNCHEON

CHAPTER XXXVI

SUITABLE COMBINATIONS FOR SERVING

Breakfast Menus

Halves of Grape Fruit
Cereal with Sugar and Cream
Corned Beef Tomato Toast à la Bradley
Coffee

Stewed Apricots and Prunes
Cereal with Sugar and Cream
Scrambled Eggs
Golden Corn Cake
Coffee

Oranges
Codfish Cakes
Buttered Toast
Doughnuts
Coffee

Belmont Baked Apples
Cereal with Sugar and Cream
Bacon Curls
Graham Muffins
Coffee

Baked Bananas
Foamy Omelet
Hashed Brown Potatoes
Baking Powder Biscuit
Coffee

Strawberries
Cereal with Sugar and Cream
German Toast
Coffee

Canteloupes
Dried Beef with Cream
Rye Popovers
Coffee

Family Luncheon Menus

Salt Codfish in Cream
Baked Potatoes
Radishes
Luncheon Caraway Cake
Tea

Mock Bisque Soup
Croûtons
Griddle Cakes with Maple Syrup
Tea

Lamb à la Breck
Emergency Biscuit
Raspberry Puffs
Luncheon Cocoa

Macaroni, Virginia Style
Southern Pone
Marshmallow Gingerbread
Milk

Fried Sausages with Apple Rings
Mashed Potatoes
Lemon Cream Rice
Russian Tea

Chicken Salad
Raised Biscuit
Chocolate Ice Cream Sodas
Nut Oatmeal Cookies

Egg Salad
Bread and Butter Sandwiches
Devil's Food Cake
Iced Tea

Buffet-Luncheon Menus

Tomato Bouillon
Crisp Crackers
Olives   Salted Pecans
Chicken à la King   Frosted Ham
Finger Rolls
Glacé Hélène   Cream Sponge Cake
Luncheon Punch

Iced Pimiento Consommé
Macedoine Loaf
Moulded Salmon, Cucumber Sauce
Rasped Rolls
Luncheon Coffee
Orange Ice Cream,   Nut Caramel Cake
   with Crushed Strawberries
Marshmallow Mint Bonbons

Formal Luncheon Menus

Grape Fruit Coupe
Mock Bouillon   Bread Sticks
Tournadoes of Lamb
Savory Potatoes
Glazed Carrots with Peas
Asparagus Salad
Toasted Fromage Rolls
New Year's Bomb   Silver Sponge Cakes
Salted Filberts   Dipped Cream Mints

Table Laid for Dinner

Table Laid for Buffet Luncheon

Manhattan Clam Bisque
Toasted Triangles
Windsor Eggs
Broiled Pompano, Cucumber Hollandaise
Luncheon Rolls
Grape Fruit Jelly Salad
Cream Bread Fingers
Coupe Majestic   Jellied Macaroons
Ginger Fudge

Family Dinner Menus

Celery and Tomato Purée   Imperial Sticks
Iroquois Steak
Potatoes en Casserole
Lettuce and Pimiento Salad, French Dressing
Sally's Bread Pudding, Roxbury Sauce

Onion Soup
Hollenden Halibut
Mashed Potatoes
Templeton Stuffed Peppers
Raisin Puff, Foamy Sauce

Mutton Duck
French Fried Potatoes
Spinach
German Tomato Salad   Cheese Wafers
Fig Custard

Appledore Soup
Crisp Crackers
Smothered Chicken, Swedish Style
Candied Sweet Potatoes
Corn Soufflé
Fruit Tapioca

Potage Longchamps
Kernels of Pork
Savory Potatoes
Glazed Silver Skins
Lettuce and Radish Salad
Cold Pineapple Soufflé

Formal Dinner Menus

Dexter Canapés
Little Neck Clams   Brown Bread Sandwiches
Filippini Consommé   Pulled Bread
Radishes   Salted Almonds
Smelts à la Guaymas
Julienne Potatoes
Dressed Cucumber
Stuffed Mushroom Caps
Larded Stuffed English Partridge,
Cold Orange Sauce
Jarvis Peppers
Carlton Salad
Parfait Amour
Chocolate Dipped Candied Orange Peel
Frozen Cheese Alexandria   Toasted Crackers
Café Noir

SUITABLE COMBINATIONS FOR SERVING 417

Scallop Cocktail
Clear Mushroom Soup   Mock Cassava Bread
Celery   Olives
Stuffed Turbans of Flounder
Delmonico Tomatoes
Devonshire Saddle of Mutton
Lorette Potatoes
Baked Stuffed Egg Plant
Club Punch
Ginger Ale Jelly Salad   Devilled Sandwiches
Montrose Pudding
After Dinner Mints
Liptaner Cheese   Water Crackers
Café Noir

Five o'Clock Tea Menus

Commonwealth Marmalade Sandwiches
Sardine Biscuit
Scotch Five o'Clock Teas
Russian Tea   Hot Marshmallow Chocolate
Turkish Mint Paste

Honor Sandwiches
Marshmallow Teas   Peanut Bars
Hawaiian Five o'Clock Tea   Oriental Punch
Chocolate Fudge

Spanish Sandwiches   Piquante Cheese Crackers
Keswick Gingerbread
Syracuse Tea   Hot Chocolate with Whipped Cream
Raisin Opera Caramels

Fairmont Sandwiches
Cream Wafers   Chocolate Nut Bars
Jamaica Five o'Clock Tea   Card Punch
Knickerbocker Figs

Cinnamon Toast   Pimiento Cheese Wafers
Pastry Stars   Sultana Sticks
Five o'Clock Tea,   Reception Cocoa
   Lemon Cut Sugar   Whipped Cream
Salted Almonds

Sunday Night Supper Menus

Chilaly
Unsweetened Wafer Crackers
Canned Peaches   Mock Angel Cake
Ginger Ale

Bolivia Salad   Celery
Salad Rolls
Frangipan Cream Pie
Pineapple Lemonade

Table Laid for Afternoon Tea

Table Laid for Sunday Night or After Theatre Supper

Manhattan Scallops
Lettuce Sandwiches
Lord Baltimore Cake
Russian Tea

Scalloped Scallops
Pepper Relish
Parker House Rolls
Raised Fruit Loaf
Cocoa with Whipped Cream

Epicurean Finnan Haddie
Brown Bread Sandwiches
Moulded Cheese with Bar-le-Duc Strawberries
Wafer Crackers
Moette Punch

INDEX

AFTER DINNER MINTS, 364.
Afternoon Tea Crackers, 30.
  Doughnuts, 37.
After Theatre Salad, 210.
Allemande Sauce, 154.
Allen Canapés, 376.
Allerton Pickles, 407.
  Salad, 201.
Almond Pudding, 254.
Almonds, Burnt, 356.
Alphonso Potatoes, 184.
Alumni Punch, 11.
Ambassadrice Capon, 142.
Amsterdam Novelties, 315.
Anchovied Stuffed Potatoes, 186.
Angel Cake, Mock, 331.
  White Mountain, 331.
Anniversary Cake, 343.
Apple Ball Sauce, 391.
  Canapés, Cream Sabayon Sauce, 246.
  Catsup, 401.
  Dumplings, 312.
  Flawn, 310.
  Ginger, 395.
Apples, Belmont Baked, 391.
  Baked, in Casserole, 391.
Apricot Sandwiches, Roxbury Sauce, 247.
Apricots and Prunes, Stewed, 392.
Armandine Punch, 301.
Artichokes, French, Vinaigrette Sauce, 161.
  Jerusalem, 161.
Asparagus, Arlington, 161.
  Mousselaine, 162.
  Salad, I, 200.
  Salad, II, 201.
Aspic, Lobster in, 240.
  Macedoine in, 237.
  Moulded Fish in, 239.
  Stuffed Eggs in, 61.
Astoria Salad Dressing, 218.

BACON CURLS, 135.
Baked Blue Fish à la Muisset, 94.
  Egg Plant, 167.
  Egg Plant, Stuffed, 167.
  Eggs with Pimiento Potatoes, 53.
  Halibut, Swedish Style, 88.
  Hominy, Southern Style, 41.
  Larded Liver, Claret Sauce, 116.
  Macaroni with Chipped Beef, 42.
  Macaroni with Peanut Butter, 43.
  Potato Apples, 185.
  Rarebit, 48.
  Shad, Roe Sauce, 97.
Baking Powder Crust, 141.
Banana Pie, 306.
  Pudding, 251.
  Salad, 208.
Bars, Chocolate Nut, 324.
  Peanut, 321.
Bavarian Veal Chops, 125.
Beans, Lima, Fermière, 162.
Beef, 107–119.
  Canadian Meat Pie, 114.
  Cannelon of, 113.
  Casserole of, 115.
  Cold Roast, à la Shapleigh, 116.
  Corned, Tomato Toast à la Bradley, 118.
  Fillet of, à la Newport, 111.
  Fillet of, Larded, 110.
  Hungarian Goulasch, 111.
  Pot Roast, 112.
  Pot Roast, American Style, 112.
  Swedish Meat Balls, 114.

INDEX

Tenderloins à la Wright, 109.
Tournadoes of, 109.
Beefsteak, Iroquois, 107.
Planked Rump, 108.
Planked Sirloin, 109.
Smothered Round, 108.
Steven, 107.
Belmont Baked Apples, 391.
Béarnaise Sauce I, 157.
Sauce II, 158.
Berkshire Chocolate Frosting, 348.
Cornstarch Pudding, 265.
Soup, 65.
Beverages, 5–13.
Birthday Cake, 343.
For three-year-old, 331.
Biscuits, Cheese, 30.
Sardine, 30.
Sultana, 29.
Bisque, Capucine Oyster, 75.
Corinthian Clam, 76.
Corn Mock, 64.
Bread Pudding, Caramel, 250.
Pudding, Cold Chocolate, 269.
Pudding, Sally's, 250.
Pulled, 78.
Sauce, 49.
Southern Spoon Corn, 27.
Swedish Wreaths, 24.
Brioche Cakes, Holland, 20.
Brussels Sprouts with Celery, 162.
with Chestnuts, 165.
Buns, Hot Cross, 23.
Russell, 22.
Burnt Almonds, 356.
Butter Frosting, Chocolate, 349.
Coffee, 349.
Scotch, 359.
Filling, 309.
Pie, 309.
Taffy, 359.
To Measure, 2.
Buttered Eggs à la Roberts, 54.
Butterfly Cake, 339.
Canapés, 377.
Rolls, 17.
Buttermilk Frosting 349.
Griddle Cakes, 34.

Cabbage, Smothered, 163.
Cabinet Pudding, Peach, 275.

Cake, 328–344.
Angel, Mock, 331.
Angel, White Mountain, 331.
Anniversary, 343.
Birthday, 343.
For three-year-old, 331.
Butterfly, 339.
Chocolate Walnut Loaf, 337.
Delia's Sponge, 328.
Devil's Food, 335.
Fillings and Frostings, 345–354.
Florida Nut, 338.
Fruit, 332.
Fudge, 336.
Gold, 337.
Gold, Mrs. Raymond's, 337.
Grandmother's Pound, 342.
Grant, 332.
Gratan Mocha, 329.
Lady Baltimore, 340.
Littleton Spider Corn, 28.
Lord Baltimore, 341.
Potato Caramel, 336.
Potato Flour, 333.
Sponge, 328.
Princeton Orange, 338.
Priscilla, 335.
Prize, 334.
Raised Loaf, 333.
Silver, 339.
Vienna, 329.
Wedding, Ornamented, 344.
White Fruit, 340.
Cakes, Cheese, 59.
Chinese Tea, 325.
Chocolate Nut Bars, 324
Christmas, 334.
Flume Flannel, 21.
Holland Brioche, 20.
Marshmallow Tea, 324.
Meat, 145.
Peanut Bars, 321.
Macaroons, 323.
Sally Lunn Tea, 22.
Scotch Five o'Clock Teas, 324.
Silver Sponge, 330.
Sultana Sticks, 323.
Tea, 21.
Calf's Brains à la York, 118.

Liver à la Beque, 117.
  Baked, Larded, 116.
California French Dressing, 212.
Cambridge Sauce, 259.
Campestris Salad, 206.
Canapés à la Rector, 379.
  Allen, 376.
  Butterfly, 377.
  Clam, I, 375.
  Clam, II, 376.
  Danish, 373.
  Dexter, 373.
  Finnan Haddie, 378.
  Fish, 376.
  Fish, Smoked, 375.
  Horn of Plenty, 379.
  Italian, 374.
  Plaza, 374.
  St. Patrick's Caviare, 379.
  St. Valentine's, 374.
  Washington, 378.
Candied Grape Fruit Peel, I, 369.
  Grape Fruit Peel, II, 369.
  Orange Peel, Chocolate Dipped, 370.
  Sweet Potatoes, 191.
Candy Baskets of Glacé Strawberries, 370.
  Stretched Molasses, 357.
  Peanut, 358.
  Violets, 366.
Cannelon of Beef, 113.
Cantaloupe Suprême, 394.
Capon, Ambassadrice, 142.
Caramel Bread Pudding, 250.
  Filling, 345.
  Frosting, 351.
Caramels, Chapin Chocolate, 359.
  Chocolate, Nut, 360.
  Opera, Chocolate, 360.
  Opera, Nut, 361.
  Opera, Raisin, 361.
  Opera, Vanilla, 360.
  Smith College, 361.
Caraway Seed Cookies, 326.
Card Punch, 8.
Carlton Salad Dressing, 217.
Carrot Timbales, 166.
Carrots, Mint Glazed, with Peas, 166.
Casserole of Beef, 115.
  of Chicken, 139.

Potatoes en, 182.
Squabs en, 148.
Vegetables en, 180.
Cataldi's Puff Paste, 306.
Catsup, Apple, 401.
  Gooseberry, 401.
  Grape, 402.
Caviare Canapés, St. Partick's, 379.
  Rissolettes, 377.
  Sandwiches, 383.
Celery and Tomato Purée, 65.
  Brussels Sprouts with, 162.
  Salad, Bonne Femme, 200.
  Spiced, 404.
  with Caviare, 372.
  with Roquefort, 372.
Cereal, Cheese, and Vegetarian Dishes, 38–52.
Champagne Cup, 12.
  Punch, 13.
Chantilly Mousse, 295.
  Potatoes, 183.
Chard, Swiss, 166.
Charlotte, Plombière, 299.
  Russe, 276.
Cheese and Apple Salad, 206.
  and Pepper Croquettes, 220.
  Biscuits, 30.
  Cakes, 50.
  Crackers, Piquante, 46.
  Croquettes, Wellington, 50.
  Custard, Bread Sauce, 49.
  Custard Timbales, Bread Sauce, 221.
  Frozen, Alexandra, 45.
  Liptaner, 44.
  Moulded, with Bar-le-duc Strawberries, 45.
  Shapleigh Luncheon, 48.
  Soufflé, 49.
  Sticks, Parmesan, 51.
  Walnut Deceits, 46.
Cherry Moss, 273.
  Nut Salad, 205.
Chestnut Soup, Cream, 69.
Chiccory and Celery Salad, 194.
Chicken à la Cadillac, 144.
  à la King, 228.
  and Liver Timbales, 230.

INDEX

and Mushroom Timbales, 230.
Boned Planked, 142.
Cream Sandwiches, 383.
Croquettes, Macedoine, 226.
Delmonico's Devilled, 140.
Eclairs, Mayonnaise, 226.
en Casserole, 139.
Guinea, Larded Breasts of, 149.
Gumbo, 68.
Knickerbocker Suprême of, 143.
Moulded Jellied, 143.
Mousse, 244.
Paprika, 140.
Pie, Country Style, 141.
Réchauffé, 229.
Salad, Mock, 211.
Smothered, Swedish Style, 139.
Chiffonade Dressing, 214.
Chilaly, 47.
Chili Sauce, 406.
Chinese Tea Cakes, 325.
Chocolate Bread Pudding, Cold, 269.
Butter Frosting, 349.
Caramels, Chapin, 359.
Caramels, Nut, 360.
Caramels, Opera, 360.
Caramels, Stretched, 362.
Custard Pie, 308.
Doughnuts, 35.
Egg and Milk Shake, 6.
Hot Marshmallow, 7.
Ice Cream Frosting, 351.
Ice Cream Soda, 7.
Marshmallow Fudge, 363.
Mint Coupe, 299.
Nut Bars, 324.
Pâte à Choux Rings, 326.
Sauce, Hot, 257.
Syrup, 6.
Walnut Loaf Cake, 337.
Walnut Wafers, 325.
Chop Suey, 228.
Chops, Bavarian Veal, 125.
Lamb à la Rector, 122.
Reforme, 120.
Spanish, Truffle Sauce, 120.
Chow Chow, 408.
Christmas Cakes, 334.

Chutney Dressing, 213.
Mayonnaise, 214.
Cincinnati Coffee Bread, 19.
Cinkites, 327.
Cinnamon Toast, 33.
Clam Bisque, Corinthian, 76.
Manhattan, 76.
Canapés I, 375.
Canapés II, 376.
Claret Cup, 12.
Strawberries, 395.
Club Indian Pudding, 249.
Punch, 282.
Cocktail, Grape Fruit, 295.
Oyster, Sherry, 79.
Sardine, 372.
Scallop I, 81.
Scallop II, 81.
Cocoa Egg Nog, 7.
Frosting, 349.
Cocoanut Coffee Frosting, 352.
Fluffs, 317.
Codfish, Gloucester Salt, 104.
Spanish, 105.
Coffee Butter Frosting, 349.
Caramel Parfait, 290.
Charlotte Baskets, 277.
Confectioners' Frosting, 348.
Ice Cream, 283.
Sponge, 272.
Cognac Pear Coupe, 298.
Cold Desserts, 265–280.
Columbia French Dressing, 213.
Compote, Peach, 219.
Condensed Milk Bread, 14.
Condé, Pear, 219.
Confections, 355–371.
After Dinner Mints, 364.
Bonbons, Marshmallow Mint, 366.
Burnt Almonds, 356.
Butter Scotch, 359.
Butter Taffy, 359.
Candy Baskets, 370.
Candy Violets, 366.
Caramels, Chapin Chocolate, 359.
Nut Chocolate, 360.
Opera, Chocolate, 360.
Nut, 361.
Raisin, 361.
Vanilla, 360.
Smith College, 361.

INDEX

Stretched Chocolate, 362.
Corn Balls, Popped, 357.
Crystal Cups, 368.
Crystallized Mint Leaves, 369.
Devilled Raisins, 356.
Dipped Cream Mints, 366.
Double Decker, 364.
Figs, Knickerbocker, 357.
   Steamed, 356.
Fondant, 365.
Fudge, 363.
   Chocolate Marshmallow, 363.
   Peanut Butter, 363.
Macaroon Baskets, 371.
Macaroons, Jelly, 355.
Mints, Cream, Dipped, 366.
Molasses Candy, Stretched, 357.
Molasses Peanut Candy, 358.
Molasses Squares, Walnut, 358.
Penuche, Peanut, 362.
   Mexican, 362.
Popped Corn Balls, 357.
Prunes, Stuffed, 356.
Salted Filberts, 355.
Turkish Delight, 367.
   Mint Paste, 367.
Conserve, Cranberry, 397.
   Peach, 395.
   Rhubarb, 396.
Consommé, Chicken and Oyster, 71.
   Du Barry, 71.
   Filippini, 71.
   Iced Pimiento, 73.
   Japonnaise, 74.
   Montmorency, 72.
   Tillyprone, 73.
Cookies, Caraway Seed, 326.
   Molasses, Sour Cream, 320.
   Oatmeal, Nut, 321.
Corn Bread, Southern Spoon, 27.
   Cake, Littleton Spider, 28.
       Virginia, 26.
   Escalloped, 166.
   Meal Crisps, 27.
   Mock Bisque Soup, 64.
   Oysters, 167.

Relish, 403.

Sticks, Forest Hall, 27.
Toast, 167.
Corned Beef Tomato Toast à la Bradley, 118.
Coupe, Caruso, 297.
   Chocolate Mint, 299.
   Cognac Pear, 298.
   Grape Fruit, 393.
   Hamburg Grape, 296.
   Louisiana, 298.
   Majestic, 296.
   Moquin, 295.
   Pineapple, 296.
   Rector Leaf, 393.
   Suzanne, 297.
Court Bouillon, 106.
Crab and Mushroom Vol-au-vent, 233.
Crab Meat Mornay, 86.
   Urzini, 86.
Crabapple Pickle, Sweet, 403.
Crabs, Oyster, Béarnaise, 224.
   Ravigôte, 87.
Cracker Stuffing, 151.
Crackers, Afternoon Tea, 30.
   Piquante Cheese, 46.
Cranberry Conserve, 397.
   Jelly, Spiced, 397.
       with Celery, 397.
Cream Bread Fingers, 18.
   French Dressing, 213.
   Sabayon Sauce I, 263.
   Sabayon Sauce II, 263.
   Salad Dressing, 216.
   Wafers, 31.
Crême de Menthe Ice, 281.
Creole Tomatoes, 177.   [220.
Croquettes, Cheese and Pepper,
   Chicken, Macedoine, 226.
   Hominy and Horseradish, 41.
   Little Brahmins, 40.
   Little Ducklings, 41.
   Nut and Potato, 190.
   Potato and Spinach, 190.
       Piedmont, 190.
   Rice, Cheese Sauce, 39.
   Wellington Cheese, 50.
Crossett Rolls, 17.
Croûtons, Hominy, 78.
Crystal Cups, 368.
Crystallized Mint Leaves, 369.
Cucumber Cups, 195.

Dressed, 195.
Hollandaise, 157.
Jelly, 169.
Pickles, 406.

Cup, Champagne, 12.
    Claret, 12.
    Ginger Ale, 11.
    Sauterne, 12.
Cups, Crystal, 368.
    Cucumber, 195.
Currant Loaf Bread, 14.
Custard, Cheese, 49.
    Danish, 267.
    Egg, Bread Sauce, 59.
    Fig, 266.
    French, Baked, 267.
    Ginger, 268.
Cutlets, Egg, 56.
    of Ham, Alexandria, 234.

DANISH CANAPÉS, 373.
    Custard, 267.
Dearborn Sauce, 261.
Deerfoot Potatoes, 187.
    Shirred Eggs, 55.
Delmonico Tomatoes, 178.
Delmonico's Devilled Chicken, 140.
Denver Cream Salad Dressing, 214.
    Sauce, 261.
Desserts, Cold, 265–280.
    Frozen, 281–303. [80.
Devilled Oysters on Half Shells, Raisins, 356.
    Sandwiches, 382.
Devil's Food Cake, 335.
Devonshire Pie, 310.
    Saddle of Mutton, 123.
Dewey Sauce, 264.
Dinner Salad, 202.
Dipped Cream Mints, 366.
Dixie Salad, 200.
Double Decker Candy, 364.
Doughnuts, Afternoon Tea, 37.
    Cheap, 34.
    Chocolate, 35.
    Health Food, 36.
    Raised, 36.
    Sour-milk, 35.
Dream Sandwiches, 383.
Dresden Sandwiches, 247.
Dressed Cucumber, 195.
Dutch Salad, 410.

EASTER SALAD, 201.
East India Sandwiches, 386.
Egg and Milk Shake, 6.
    Pimiento Timbales, 59.
Egg Custards, Bread Sauce, 59.
Egg Cutlets, 56.
Egg Nog, Cocoa, 7.
Egg Plant, Baked Stuffed, 167.
    Turque, 168.
Eggs, 53–63.
    à la Benedict, 54.
    à la Victoria, 59.
    Baked, with Pimiento Potatoes, 53.
    Buttered, à la Roberts, 54.
    Chaudfroid, Alexandria, 221.
    Creamed, with Sardines, 60.
    Cutlets, Alexandria, 234.
    Deerfoot Shirred, 55.
    en Surprise, 221.
    Florentine, 62.
    Florentine, in Casseroles, 55.
    French Poached, 53.
    Jellied French Poached, 62.
    Molet Chasseur, 56.
    Omelet à la Columbia, 57.
    Omelet, Japanese Lobster, 58.
        Savoyarde, 58.
        Soubise, 57.
    Scrambled, New York Style, 54.
    Snow, 246.
    Stuffed in Aspic, 61.
    Windsor, 61.
Emergency Drop Muffins, 25.
    Puddings, 245.
English Dumplings, 33.
    Partridge, Larded Stuffed, 148.
    Patties, 233.
Entrées, 219–245.
    Calf's Brains à la York, 118.
    Chaudfroid Eggs Alexandria, 221.
    Cheese and Pepper Croquettes, 220.
    Cheese Croquettes, Wellington, 50.
    Cheese Custard Timbales, 221.
    Cheese Soufflé, 49.

INDEX 427

Chicken à la Cadillac, 144.
Chicken à la King, 228.
Chicken and Liver Timbales, 230.
Chicken and Mushroom Timbales, 230.
Chicken Croquettes, Macedoine, 226.
Chicken, Éclairs of, Mayonnaise, 226.
Chicken Réchauffé, 229.
Chop Suey, 228.
Crab and Mushroom Vol-au-Vent, 233.
Crab Meat Mornay, 86.
　Urzini, 86.
Cutlets of Fish, Epicurean, 102.
Cutlets of Ham, Alexandria, 234.
Éclairs of Chicken, Mayonnaise, 226.
Eggs en Surprise, 221.
English Patties, 233.
Epicurean Bouchées, 235.
Finnan Haddie, Epicurean, 101.
Game Mousse, Sauce Bigarrade, 149.
Ham Mousse, Epicurean Sauce, 234.
　Timbales, 231.
Hampden Halibut en Coquilles, 225.
Lenox Rarebit, 47.
Lobster Boats, 225.
　in Aspic, 240.
Lobster, Planked Live, 85.
　Spanish, in Casseroles, 84.
Macedoine in Aspic, 237.
　Loaf, 227.
Mock Sweetbreads, 131.
Moulded Fish in Aspic, 239.
Mushroom Caps Stuffed, 222.
Oyster and Shrimp Newburg, 224.
Oyster Crabs, Béarnaise, 224.
Oysters Devilled on Half Shells, 80.
　Louisiane, 80.
　Norfolk, 79.
Peach Compote, 219.

Pear Condé, 219.
Salmon Mayonnaise, 232.
Salmon Soufflé, Spanish Sauce, 105.
Scalloped Scallops, 83.
Scallops à la Newburg, 223.
　Bresloise, 83.
　en Brochette, 223.
Shrimps, Louisiana, 222.
Sweetbread and Mushroom Patties, 236.
Sweetbread, Glazed, Lucullus, 237.
Sweetbreads à la Root, 128.
Sweetbreads, Huntington, 236.
　Monroe, 129.
　South Park, 129.
　Waldorf, 130.
Traymore Timbales, 231.
Tongue, Stuffed Smoked, 241.
Turkey, Boned, 242.
Veal Timbales, 229.
Epicurean Bouchées, 235.
　Finnan Haddie, 101.
　Fish Cutlets, 102.
　Sauce, 156.

FAIRMONT SANDWICHES, 384.
Family Paste, 304.
Fats, to Measure, 2.
Fig Custard, 266.
Figs, Knickerbocker, 357.
　Steamed, 356.
　Stuffed, 47.
Filberts, Salted, 355.
Fillet of Beef à la Newport, 111.
　Larded, 110.
Fillets of Flounder in Paper Cases, 95.
　Halibut à la Hollanden, 91.
　Halibut, Moulded, Rolled, 98.
　Lamb, Sautéd, 121.
　Sole, Marguery, 96.
　　St. Malo, 95.
Finnan Haddie, Caledonian Style, 100.
　Canapés, 378.
　Epicurean, 101.
　Savory, 101.
Filling, Butter Scotch, 309.
　Caramel, 345.

INDEX

Chocolate Mocha, 330.
Frangipan Cream, 346.
Fruit and Nut, 341.
Fruit Cream, 346.
Mocha, 330.
Orange, 347.
Praline Cream, 346.
Syracuse, 347.
White Mountain Cream, 345.
Fish, 79–106.
  Canapés, 376.
  Moulded in Aspic, 239.
Fisherman's Haddock, 87.
Five o'Clock Tea, Hawaiian, 5.
  Jamaica, 6.
  Lemon Cut Sugar for, 5.
  Orange Cut Sugar for, 5.
  Syracuse, 6.
Flemish Beauty Salad, 202.
Florentine Eggs, 55.
Florida Nut Cake, 338.
Florodora Sauce, 262.
Flounder, Stuffed Turbans of, 94.
Flume Flannel Cakes, 21.
Fondant, 365.
Forcemeat, Halibut, 99.
  Salmon, 99.
  Tongue and Chicken, 242.
Fort Lincoln, 133.
Frangipan Cream, 346.
  Cream Pie, 310.
Frappé, Grape Fruit, 282.
French Artichokes, Vinaigrette Sauce, 161.
  Meringues, 327.
  Prune Sandwiches, 387.
Fricandeau of Liver, 117.
Fried Bread, 20.
  Potato Curls, 187.
    Dots, 188.
  Potatoes, Bourgoyne, 189.
    French, 187.
  Salt Pork, Country Style, 134.
  Scallops à la Huntington, 84.
  Smelts, Britannia, 103.
Frosted Ham, 136.
Frostings, Berkshire Chocolate, 348.
  Buttermilk, 349.
  Caramel, 351.
  Chocolate Butter, 349.
    Ice Cream, 351.
  Cocoa, 349.
  Cocoanut Coffee, 352.
  Coffee Butter, 349.
    Confectioners', 348.
  Fudge, 350.
    Almond, 350.
  Ice Cream, 341.
  Mocha, 348.
  Orange, 351.
  Ornamental, 353.
  Oscars', 353.
  Portsmouth, 347.
  Quality, 352.
  Sultana Nut, 350.
Frozen Cheese Alexandra, 45.
  Desserts, 281–303.
  Orange Whip, 300.
Fruit and Ginger Ale Salad, 209.
  Cake, 332.
  Cake, White, 340.
  Cream Filling, 346.
  Juice, Iced, 8.
  Punch with Whipped Cream, 10.
  Salad Dressing, 215.
  Tapioca, 248.
Fruits, Fresh, Preserved and Canned, 391–401.
Fudge, 363.
  Almond Frosting, 350.
  Cake, 336.
  Chocolate Marshmallow, 363.
  Frosting, 350.
  Peanut Butter, 363.

GAME, 146–150.
  Mousse, 149.
Gems, Rye Breakfast, 26.
Geranium, Rose, Jelly, 400.
German Caraway Bread, 15.
  Loaf, 137.
  Punch, 9.
  Sandwiches, 385.
  Tomato Salad, 197.
Ginger Ale and Fruit Salad, 209.
  Cup, 11.
Gingerbread, Cookies and Wafers, 319–327.
  Keswick, 319.
  Marshmallow, 319.
  Shubert, 320.
Ginger Custards, 368.

INDEX

Sponge, Steamed, 252.
Glacé Hélène, 288.
Glazed Sweetbread Lucullus, 237.
Gloucester Salt Codfish, 104.
Gold Cake, 337.
  Mrs. Raymond's, 337.
Good Luck Salad, 194.
Gooseberry Catsup, 401.
  Relish, 402.
Graham Bread, Quick, 31.
  Raised Loaf, 15.
Grandmother's Pound Cake, 342.
Grant Cake, 332.
Grape Fruit à la Russe, 392.
  Coupe, 393.
  Frappé, 282.
  Jelly Salad, 207.
  Peel, Candied, 369.
Gratan Mocha, 329.
Griddlecakes, Buttermilk, 34.
Guinea Chicken, Larded Breasts of, 149.

HADDOCK À LA METROPOLE, 92.
  Baked Stuffed, à la Preston, 93.
  Fisherman's, 87.
Halibut à la Suisse, 89.
  Baked, Swedish Style, 88.
  Fillets of, à la Hollanden, 91.
  Fillets of, Rolled and Moulded, 98.
  Forcemeat, 99.
  Hampden en Coquilles, 225.
  Huntington, Sauce Verte, 92.
  Loomis, 90.
  Petite, Lobster Sauce, 97.
  Shattuck, 89.
  Veronique, 89.
Ham à la Van Voast, 135.
  Cutlets of, Alexandria, 234.
  Frosted, 136.
  Mousse, Epicurean Sauce, 234.
  Roast, Cider Sauce, 136.
  Timbales, 231.
Hamburg Grape Coupe, 296.
Hawaiian Five o'Clock Tea, 5.
Health Food Doughnuts, 36.
Heliofolis Salad, 199.
Henri Apricot Ice Cream, 287.
Hollandaise, Cucumber, 157.

Horseradish, 156.
  Mock, 156.
Holland Brioche Cakes, 20.
Hominy and Horseradish Croquettes, 41.
  Baked, Southern Style, 41.
  Croûtons, 78
Honeycomb Pudding, 254.
Honor Sandwiches, 382.
Horn of Plenty Canapés, 379.
Hors-d'Œuvres, 372–380.
Horseradish Cream Dressing, 215.
  Hollandaise, 156.
Hot Chocolate Sauce, 257.
  Cross Buns, 23.
  Marshmallow Chocolate, 7.
  Puddings, 245–256.
Hungarian Goulasch, 111.
Huntington Halibut, 92.
  Salad I, 197.
  Salad II, 207.
  Sweetbreads, 236.

ICE CREAM, Chocolate, 299.
  Coffee, 283.
  Frosting, 341.
    Chocolate, 351.
  Henri Apricot, 287.
  Lighted, 294.
  Marshmallow, 286.
  Mint, 299.
  Normandy, 285.
  Praline, 286.
  Prune, 284.
  Quince, 284.
  Soda, Chocolate, 7.
  Strawberry I, 284.
  Strawberry II, 285.
  Strawberry en Surprise, 293.
Ice Creams with Ices.
  Bombe Mousselaine, 288.
    New Year's, 292.
    Suprême, 289.
    with Mint Balls, 295.
  Coupe Caruso, 297.
    Chocolate Mint, 299.
    Cognac Pear, 298.
    Grape Fruit, 393.
    Hamburg Grape, 296.
    Louisiana, 298.
    Majestic, 296.
    Moquin, 295.
    Pineapple, 296.

INDEX

Suzanne, 297.
Frozen Orange Whip, 300.
Glacé Hélène, 288.
Marron Plombière, 292.
Mousse Chantilly, 295.
Parfait Amour Strawberry, 290.
  Caramel, Coffee, 290.
  Marron, 302.
  Pistachio, 302.
Pineapple Marquise, 301.
Pudding, Montrose, 288.
  Standish, 287.
Sherbet, Lemon Cream, 283.
  Orange Cream I, 282.
  Orange Cream II, 283.
Iced Fruit Juice, 8.
  Pimiento Consommé, 73.
Ices, Armandine Punch, 301.
  Club Punch, 282.
  Crême de Menthe, 281.
  Grape Fruit Frappé, 282.
  Lemon, 281.
  Parfait Amour, 300.
  Plombière Charlotte, 299.
  Raspberry, 281.
Indian Pudding, Club, 249.
  Salad, 198.
  Salad Dressing, 217.
Ingredients, Measuring, 1.
  to Beat, 4.
  to Combine, 3.
  to Cut and Fold, 4.
  to Stir, 4.
Irish Plum Pudding, 255.
  Puff Paste, 305.
Iroquois Steak, 107.
Italian Canapés, 374.
  Spaghetti, 43.

JAMAICA FIVE O'CLOCK TEA, 6.
Japanese Lobster Omelet, 58.
Japonnaise Consommé, 74.
Jarvis Stuffed Peppers, 172.
Jellied Chicken, Moulded, 143.
  French Poached Egg, 62.
  Vegetable Ring, 181.
Jelly, Cranberry Spiced, 397.
  Cranberry with Celery, 397.
  Cucumber, 169.
  Fruit Moulded in, 278.
  Grape Fruit, 207.
  Lemon, 270.
  Macaroons, 355.
  Mint, 399.

Panaché, 279.
  Rose Geranium, 400.
  Sandwiches, 388.
Jerusalem Artichokes, 161.
Joplin Stuffed Tomato Salad 198.
Jordan Pudding, 265.
Julep, Pineapple, 10.

KERNELS OF LAMB, Currant Mint Sauce, 121.
  of Pork, 132.
Keswick Gingerbread, 319.
  Pudding, 270.
Kindergarten Sandwiches, 381.
Knickerbocker Figs, 357.
  Suprême of Chicken, 143.

LADY BALTIMORE CAKE, 340.
Lakewood Salad, 204.
Laitue Suédoise, 373.
Lamb à la Breck, 124.
Lamb and Mutton, 120–125.
Lamb Chops à la Rector, 122.
  Chops, Reforme, 120.
  Chops, Spanish, Truffle Sauce, 120.
  Kernels of, Currant Mint Sauce, 121.
  Rechauffé, 123.
  Roast, Cold, Family Style, 124.
  Sautéd Fillets of, 121.
  Tournadoes of, 121.
Larded Breasts of Guinea Chicken, 149.
  Stuffed English Partridge, 148.
Lemon Cream Rice, 248.
  Sherbet, 283.
  Cut Sugar, 5.
  Ice, 281.
Lemons Cut for Garnishing, 395.
Lenox Rarebit, 47.
  Sandwiches, 394.
Lettuce and Pimiento Salad, 194.
Lighted Ice Cream, 294.
Lima Beans, Fermière, 162.
Lincoln Sandwiches, 385.
Liptaner Cheese, 44.
Little Brahmins, 40.
  Ducklings, 41.
  Roast Pig, 133.
Littleton Spider Corn Cake, 28.

INDEX   431

Liquids, to Measure, 3.
Liver, Baked Larded, Claret Sauce, 116.
    Calf's, à la Madame Beque, 117.
    Fricandeau of, 117.
Loaf, Chocolate Walnut Cake, 337.
    Currant, 14.
    Family White, 14.
    German, 137.
    Macedoine, 227.
    Miss Daniel's Meat, 137.
    Pecan Nut, 52.
    Raised, Graham, 15.
Lobster Boats, 225.
    in Aspic, 240.
    How to boil, 84.
    Live, Planked, 85.
    Live, Planked, with Oysters, 85.
    Spanish, in Casseroles, 84.
Loin of Veal, Allemande, 127.
Lord Baltimore Cake, 341.
Lorrette Potatoes, 188.
Los Angeles Fruit Salad, 208.
Luncheon Caraway Bread, 32.
    Cheese, Shapleigh, 48.
    Coffee, 6.
    Punch, 8.

MACARONI, Baked with Chipped Beef, 42.
    Baked with Peanut Butter, 43.
    Virginia Style, 42.
Macaroon French Cream, 272.
Macaroons, Jelly, 355.
    Peanut, 323.
Macedoine in Aspic, 237.
    Loaf, 227.
    of Fruit, 279.
    Sandwiches, 388.
Manhattan Clam Bisque, 76.
    Muffins, 25.
Marguerite Squares, 314.
Marlborough Pie, 307.
Marmalade, Orange, 398.
    Pickled Lime, 399.
Marron Parfait, 302.
    Plombière, 292.
Marshmallow, Hot Chocolate, 7.
    Gingerbread, 319.
    Ice Cream, 286.
    Mint Bonbons, 366.
    Sauce, 285.
    Teas, 324.
Martinique French Dressing, 212.
    Potatoes, 185.
Mayonnaise à la Connelly, 214.
    Chutney, 214.
    of Oysters, 79.
    Piquante, 214.
Meat and Fish Sauces, 154–160.
Meat Balls, Swedish, 114.
    Cakes, 145.
    Loaf, Miss Daniel's, 137.
Menus, 411–419.
Meringues, French, 327.
Mexican Penuche, 362.
Mince Pie Meat, Mock, 306.
Mint Glazed Carrots with Peas, 164.
    Jelly, 399.
    Leaves, Crystallized, 369.
Mints, After Dinner, 364.
    Creamed, Dipped, 366.
Mocha Filling, 330.
    Frosting, 348.
Mock Angel Cake, 331.
    Bouillon, 64.
    Cassava Bread, 77.
    Chicken Salad, 211.
    Hollandaise Sauce, 156.
    Mince Pie Meat, 306.
    Sausages, 52.
    Sweetbreads, 131.
    Turtle Soup, 74.
Moette Punch, 9.
Molasses Candy, Stretched, 357.
Molasses Cookies, Sour Cream, 320.
Monroe Sauce, 260.
Mont Blanc, 316.
Montrose Pudding, 288.
Moquin Salad, 208.
Moravian Bread, 19.
Moulded Cheese with Bar-le-duc Strawberries, 45.
    Fish in Aspic, 239.
    Jellied Chicken, 143.
    Rolled Fillets of Halibut, 98.
    Spinach, 175.
Mounded Spinach on Artichoke Bottoms, 176.
Mousse, Chantilly, 295.
    Game, Sauce Bigarrade, 149.
    Ham, Epicurean Sauce, 234.

INDEX

Mousselaine Sauce, 158.
Mousselaine Sauce, Brandy, 264.
Muffins, Bran, 29.
    Emergency Drop, 25.
    Manhattan, 25.
    Oatmeal, 26.
    Tea, 25.
Mushroom and Tomato Toast, 171.
    Caps, Stuffed, 222.
    Soup, Clear, 68.
Mushrooms, Creamed, 168.
Mustard Pickles, 409.
Mutton, Devonshire Saddle of, 123.
    Duck, 122.

NAPOLI SPAGHETTI, 44.
New England Pudding, 253.
    Stuffing, 151.
New Vanderbilt Salad, 208.
New Year's Bomb, 292.
Newport Pudding, 271.
Norfolk Oysters, 79.
Normandy Ice Cream, 285.
Nugget Salad, 196.
Nut and Potato Croquettes, 190.
    Brittle, 330.
    Chocolate Caramels, 360.
    Loaf, Pecan, 52.
    Oatmeal Cookies, 321.
    Opera Caramels, 361.
    Pastry Rolls, 313.
        Sticks, 313.
    Wafers, Swedish, 322.
Nymph Aurora, 70.

OATMEAL MUFFINS, 26.
    Nut Cookies, 321.
Ohio Salad Dressing, 217.
Omelet à la Columbia, 57.
    Lobster, Japanese, 58.
    Savoyarde, 58.
    Soubise, 57.
Onion Farci, 170.
    Soufflé, 169.
    Soup, 66.
Onions, Silver Skin, 169.
Opera Chocolate Caramels, 360.
    Nut Caramels, 361.
    Raisin Caramels, 361.
    Vanilla Caramels, 360.
Orange Cake, Princeton, 338.
    Circles, 326.
    Cream, 266.
        Sherbet I, 282.
        Sherbet II, 283.
        Sponge, 252.
    Cut Sugar, 5.
    Filling, 347.
    Frosting, 351.
    Honey Sandwiches, 387.
    Marmalade, 398.
    Peel, Candied, Chocolate Dipped, 370.
    Sauce, Cold, 160.
    Whip, Frozen, 300.
Oranges, Broiled, on Toast, 245.
Oriental Punch, 9.
Ornamental Frosting, 353.
Ornamented Wedding Cake, 344.
Oscar's Frosting, 353.
    Paste, 304.
Oyster and Shrimp Newburg, 224.
    Cocktail, Sherry, 79.
    Crabs, Béarnaise, 224.
    Stuffing, 152.
Oyster Plant with Fine Herbs, 171.
Oysters, Bisque of, Capucine, 75.

    Devilled, on Half Shells, 80.
    Louisiane, 80.
    Mayonnaise of, 79.
    Norfolk, 79.

PANACHÉ JELLY, 279.
    Vegetable, 181.

Parched Rice with Tomato Sauce, 38.
Parfait, Coffee Caramel, 290.
    Marron, 302.
    Pistachio, 302.
Parfait Amour, 300.
    Strawberry, 290.
Parisian Grape Fruit Salad, 203.
Parmesan Cheese Sticks, 51.
Parsnips, Sautéd, 171.
Partridge, English Stuffed and Larded, 148.
Paste, Cataldi's Puff, 306.
    Family, 304.
    Irish Puff, 305.
    Oscar's, 304.
    Puff, by Measurement, 305.
Pastry and Pies, 304–311.

INDEX 433

Pastry Desserts, 312–318.
    Amsterdam Novelties, 315.
    Cocoanut Fluffs, 317.
    Marguerite Squares, 314.
    Mont Blanc, 316.
    Nut Rolls, 313.
        Sticks, 313.
    Peach Pralines, 316.
    Pineapple Circles, 315.
        Tartlets, 314.
    Stars, 312.
    St. Valentine's Hearts, 316.
    Swedish Tea Circles, 313.
    Venetian Boats, 317.
Patties, English, 233.
    Shrimp, 235.
    Sweetbread and Mushroom, 236.
Pea Roast, 51.
Peach Brandy Sauce, 262.
    Cabinet Pudding, 275.
    Compote, 219.
    Conserve, 395.
    Sauce, 220.
Peanut Bars, 321.
    Butter Fudge, 363.
    Candy, 358.
    Macaroons, 323.
    Penuche, 362.
    Wafers, 322.
Pear Condé, 219.
Pecan Nut Loaf, 52.
Penobscot Sandwiches, 386.
Penuche, Mexican, 362.
    Peanut, 362.
Pepper Relish I, 405.
Pepper Relish II, 405.
Peppers, Stuffed, Jarvis, 174.
    Templeton, 175.
    with Fresh Green Corn, 171.
Petersham Chow Chow, 408.
Petite Halibut, Lobster Sauce, 97.
Piccalilli, 407.
Pickle, Sweet Crabapple, 403.
Pickled Lime Marmalade, 399.
Pickles, Allerton, 407.
    Chow Chow, 408.
    Cucumber, Green Sliced, 406.
    Dutch Salad, 410.
    Mustard, 409.
    Petersham Chow Chow, 408.

Piccalilli, 407.
    Souri, 404.
Pickling, 401–410.
Pie, Apple Flawn, 310.
    Banana, 306.
    Butter Scotch, 309.
    Canadian Meat, 114.
    Chicken, Country Style, 141.
    Chocolate Custard, 308.
    Devonshire, 310.
    Frangipan Cream, 310.
    Marlborough, 307.
    Mock Mince, 306.
    Pigeon, 147.
    Pumpkin, 308.
    Rhubarb and Raisin, 308.
Pigeon Pie, 147.
Pimiento Bisque, 68.
    Butter, 382.
    Cheese Wafers, 46.
    Consommé, Iced, 73.
Pineapple Circles, 315.
    Coupe, 296.
    Jelly, 270.
    Julep, 10.
    Marquise, 301.
    Pyramids, 274.
    Sautéd, 392.
    Soufflé, Cold, 273.
    Tartlets, 314.
Piquante, Cheese Crackers, 46.
    Mayonnaise, 214.
Planked Boned Chicken, 142.
    Live Lobster, 85.
        with Oysters, 85.
    Smelts, 104.
    Steak, Rump, 108.
        Sirloin, 109.
Plaza Canapés, 374.
Plombière Charlotte, 299.
Plum Gumbo, 396.
Poinsettia Salad, 197.
Pomme Fondante, 183.
Pompano, Broiled, 88.
Popovers, Rye, 29.
Popped Corn Balls, 357.
Porcupine Salad, 199.
Pork, 132–138.
    Fort Lincoln, 133.
    German Loaf, 137.
    Kernels of, 132.
    Little Roast Pig, 133.
    Roast Crown of. 132.

INDEX

Salt Fried, Country Style, 134.
Portsmouth Frosting, 347.
Port Wine Sauce, 146.
Potage Longchamps, 69.
Potato and Egg Salad, 210.
    Caramel Cake, 336.
    Flour Cake, 333
    Flour Sponge Cake, 328.
    Stuffing, 153.
Potatoes, 182–193.
    à la Goldenrod, 184.
    à la Suisse, 186.
    Alphonso, 184.
    Anchovied Stuffed, 186.
    Apples, Baked, 185.
    Brulé, Sweet, 191.
    Candied Sweet, 191.
    Chantilly, 183.
    Creamed Sweet, Club House Style, 191.
    Croquettes, Piedmont, 190.
        Potato and Nut, 190.
        Potato and Spinach, 190.
    Deerfoot, 187.
    en Casserole, 182.
    Flambant, Sweet, 192.
    French Fried, 187.
    Fried Bourgoyne, 189.
        Curls, 187.
        Dots, 188.
    Lorrette, 188.
    Martinique, 185.
    Moulds, 185.
    Pittsburg, 183.
    Pomme Fondante, 183.
    Princess, 188.
    Rissolée, 189.
    Sautéd Sweet, with Rum, 192.
    Savory, 182.
    Scalloped Sweet, with Apples, 192.
    Spanish, 182.
    Sultan, 189.
Pot Roast, 112.
    American Style, 112.
Poultry, 139–145.
Praline Cream, 346.
    Ice Cream, 286.
Preserved Strawberries, 399.
Princess Potatoes, 188.
Princeton Orange Cake, 338.
Prize Cake, 334.

Prune Ice Cream, 284.
    Pudding, 268.
Prunes, Stuffed, 356.
Pudding, Almond, 254.
    Apple Canapés, 246.
    Apricot Sandwiches, 247.
    Banana, 251.
    Caramel Bread, 250.
    Club Indian, 249.
    Dresden Sandwiches, 247.
    Emergency, 245.
    Fruit Tapioca, 248.
    Ginger Sponge, 252.
    Honeycomb, 254.
    Irish Plum, 255.
    Lemon Cream Rice, 248.
    Orange Cream Sponge, 252
    Raisin Puff, 253.
    Rhubarb Tapioca, 247.
    Roxbury, 251.
    Sally's Bread, 250.
    Snow Eggs, 246.
    Squash, 249.
    Sterling Fruit, 255.
Pudding Sauces, 257–264.
Puddings, Hot, 245–256.
Puff Paste (by Measurement) 305.
    Cataldi's, 306.
    Irish, 305.
Pulled Bread, 78.
Pumpkin Pie, 308.
Punch, Alumni, 11.
    Armandine, 301.
    Card, 8.
    Champagne, 13.
    Club, 282.
    Fruit with Whipped Cream 10.
    German, 9.
    Luncheon, 8.
    Moette, 9.
    Oriental, 9.
    Pineapple Julep, 10.
    Siberian, 10.

Quail, Sautéd, à la Moquin, 148
Quality Frosting, 352.
Quick Bread, Muffins and Doughnuts, 25–37.
    Graham Bread, 31.
    Pecan Nut Loaf, 52.
Quince Ice Cream, 284.

Rabbit à la Southern, 147.
Raised Bread Mixtures, 14–24.

INDEX 435

Doughnuts, 36.
   Loaf Cake, 333.
Raisin Opera Caramels, 361.
   Puff, 253.
Raisins, Devilled, 356.
Rarebit, Baked, 48.
   Lenox, 47.
Raspberry Ice, 281.
   Sauce, 257.
   Syrup, 398.
Rasped Rolls, 16.
Reception Rolls, 15.
Rector, Canapés à la, 379.
   Leaf, 393.
   Potatoes, 187.
   Salad, 196.
Red Wine French Dressing, 212.
Rhubarb and Raisin Pie, 308.
   Conserve, 396.
   Spiced, 402.
   Tapioca Pudding, 247.
Rice Croquettes, Cheese Sauce, 39.
   Fried, 39.
   Parched, with Tomato Sauce, 38.
Rissolettes, Caviare, 377.
Roast Crown of Pork, 132.
   Ham, Cider Sauce, 136.
Rochester Chocolate Sandwiches, 390.
   Salad, 206.
Roe Sauce, 159.
Roll, Jelly, 279.
Rolls, Butterfly, 17.
   Crossett, 17.
   Nut Pastry, 313.
   Rasped, 16.
   Reception, 15.
   Toasted Fromage, 45.
Romaine Salad, 202.
Rosalie Salad, 205.
Rose Geranium Jelly, 400.
Roxbury Pudding, 251.
   Sauce, 259.
Royal Sandwiches, 386.
Runnymede Salad, 209.
Russell Buns, 22.
Ruthven Salad Cream, 216.
Rye Breakfast Gems, 26.
   Popovers, 29.

SABAYON SAUCE, Cream I, 263.
   Cream II, 263.

Saddle of Mutton, Devonshire, 123.
Salad, After Theatre, 210.
   Allerton, 201.
   Asparagus I, 200.
   Asparagus II, 201.
   Banana, 208.
   Campestris, 206.
   Carlton, 196.
   Celery, Bonne Femme, 200.
   Cheese and Apple, 206.
   Cherry Nut, 205.
   Chiccory and Celery, 194.
   Cucumber Cups, 195.
   Cucumber, Dressed, 195.
   Dinner, 202.
   Dixie, 200.
   Dutch, 410.
   Easter, 201.
   Flemish Beauty, 202.
   Fruit and Ginger Ale, 209.
   German Tomato, 197.
   Good Luck, 194.
   Grape Fruit Jelly, 207.
   Heliofolis, 199.
   Huntington, 197.
   Indian, 198.
   Joplin Stuffed Tomato, 198.
   Lakewood, 204.
   Lettuce and Pimiento, 194.
   Los Angeles Fruit, 208.
   Mock Chicken, 211.
   Moquin, 204.
   Moquin, 208.
   New Vanderbilt, 208.
   Nugget, 196.
   Parisian Grape Fruit, 203.
   Peanut, 203.
   Poinsettia, 197.
   Porcupine, 199.
   Potato and Egg, 210.
   Rector, 196.
   Rochester, 206.
   Romaine, 202.
   Rosalie, 205.
   Runnymede, 209.
   Shad Roe, 211.
   Spring, 198.
   Strawberry, 205.
   Touraine Fruit, 203.
Salad Dressing, Astoria, 218.
   Carlton, 217.
   Chiffonade, 214.
   Chutney, 213.
   Cream, 216.

INDEX

Denver Cream, 214.
French, Breslin, 212.
    California, 212.
    Columbia, 213.
    Cream, 213.
    Martinique, 212.
    Red Wine, 212.
    Tabasco, 213.
Fruit, 215.
Horseradish, 215.
Indian, 217.
Los Angeles, 215.
Mayonnaise à la Connelly, 214.
    Chutney, 214.
    Piquante, 214.
Ohio, 217.
Ruthven Cream, 216.
Waltham, 216.
Salad Dressings, 212–218.
Salads, 194–211.
Salmon Forcemeat, 99.
    Mayonnaise, 232.
    Soufflé, 105.
    Spiced, 105.
Salt Codfish, Gloucester, 104.
Salted Filberts, 355.
Salt Pork, Fried, Country Style, 134.
Samp, 38.
Sandwiches, 381–390.
    Apricot, 247.
    Caviare, 383.
    Chicken Cream, 383.
    Commonwealth Marmalade, 389.
    Devilled, 382.
    Dream, 383.
    Dresden, 247.
    East India, 386.
    Fairmont, 384.
    French Prune, 387.
    German, 385.
    Honor, 382.
    Horseradish, 389.
    Jelly, 388.
    Kindergarten, 381.
    Lenox, 388.
    Lincoln, 385.
    Macedoine, 388.
    Mosaic, 381.
    Orange Honey, 387.
    Penobscot, 386.
    Rochester Chocolate, 390.
    Royal, 386.
    Sembrich, 385.
    Spanish, 384.
    Toasted Salad, 382.
    Waltham Five o'Clock Tea, 389.
San Monica Sauce, 261.
Sardine Biscuits, 30.
    Cocktail, 372.
Sardines, Creamed Eggs with, 60.
Sauce, Allemande, 154.
    Béarnaise I, 157.
    Béarnaise II, 158.
    Bigarrade, 150.
    Bread, 49.
    Brown Mushroom, 127.
    Brown Nut, 155.
    Chili, 406.
    Cider, 160.
    Claret, 116.
    Cold Orange, 148.
    Cucumber Hollandaise, 157.
    Currant Mint, 121.
    Devonshire, 159.
    English Fish, 99.
    Epicurean, 156.
    Guaymas, 159.
    Horseradish Hollandaise, 156.
    Lobster, 97.
    Madeira, 110.
    Mock Hollandaise, 156.
    Mousselaine, 158.
    Port Wine, 146.
    Remoulade, 63.
    Roe, 159.
    Spanish, 154.
    Tomato, Bottled, 406.
    Traymore, 232.
    Truffle, 120.
    Vinaigrette, 159.
    Waldorf, 155.
    Windsor, 61.
Sauces, Meat and Fish, 154–160.
Sauces, Pudding, 257–264.
    Brandy, 262.
    Cambridge, 259.
    Dearborn, 261.
    Denver, 261.
    Florodora, 262.
    Hot Chocolate, 257.
    Monroe, 260.
    Mousselaine, Brandy, 264.
    Orange, 258.

INDEX 437

Peach, 230.
Peach Brandy, 262.
Raspberry, 257.
Roxbury, 259.
Sabayon Cream I, 263.
Sabayon Cream II, 263.
San Monica, 261.
Sea Foam, 258.
Sherry I, 260.
Sherry II, 260.
Strawberry, 257.
White Wine, 263.
Yankee, 259.
Sausage Stuffing, 153.
Sausages à la Maître d'Hôtel, 137.
Sautéd Fillets of Lamb, 121.
 Parsnips, 173.
 Pineapple, 392.
 Quail à la Moquin, 148.
 Sweet Potatoes with Rum, 192.
Sauterne Cup, 12.
Savory Finnan Haddie, 101.
 Potatoes, 182.
Savoyarde Omelet, 58.
Scallop Cocktail I, 81.
Scallop Cocktail II, 81.
Scalloped Scallops, 83.
 Sweet Potatoes with Apples, 192.
Scallops à la Newburg, 223.
 Bresloise, 83.
 en Brochette, 223.
 Fried à la Huntington, 84.
 Samoset, 82.
 Savoy, 82.
Scrambled Eggs, New York Style, 54.
Scotch Five o'Clock Teas, 324.
Sea Foam Sauce, 258.
Sembrich Sandwiches, 385.
Shad, Baked, 97.
Shad Roe Salad, 211.
Shapleigh Luncheon Cheese, 48.
Shattuck Halibut, 89.
Sherbet, Lemon Cream, 283.
 Orange Cream I, 282.
 Orange Cream II, 283.
Sherry Oyster Cocktail, 79.
 Sauce I, 260.
 Sauce II, 260.
Shrimp and Oyster Newburg, 224.
 Patties, 235.

Shrimps, Louisiana, 222.
Shubert Gingerbread, 320.
Siberian Punch, 10.
Silver Cake, 339.
 Skins, Creamed, 171.
 Sponge Cakes, 330.
Smelts à la Guaymas, 105.
 au Beurre Noir, 102.
 Fried, Britannia, 103.
 Planked, 104.
 Veronique, 103.
Smith College Caramels, 361.
Smoked Fish Canapés, 375.
 Chicken, Swedish Style 139.
 Round Steak, 108.
Snow Eggs, 246.
Sole, Fillets of, Marguery, 96.
 St. Malo, 95.
Soufflé, Cheese, 49.
 Corn, 168.
 Grape Juice, 276.
 Onion, 171.
 Pineapple, Cold, 273.
 Salmon, 105.
 Squash, 177.
 Tomato, Neapolitan, 179.
Soup, Berkshire, 65.
 Bisque, Corinthian Clam, 76.
  Manhattan Clam, 76.
  Mock Corn, 64.
  of Oysters, Capucine, 75.
  Pimiento, 68.
  Veal Tomato, 67.
 Bouillon, Mock, 64.
 Celery and Tomato Purée, 65.
 Chestnut, Cream, 69.
 Chicken Gumbo, 68.
 Consommé, Chicken and Oyster, 71.
  Dubarry, 71.
  Filippini, 71.
  Iced Pimiento, 73.
  Japonnaise, 74.
  Montmorency, 72.
  Tillyprone, 73.
 French Tomato, 66.
 Mock Turtle, 74.
 Mushroom, Clear, 68.
 Nymph Aurora, 70.
 Onion, 66.

Potage Longchamps, 69.
   Southdown, 67.
   Watercress, Cream of, 70.
Soup Accompaniments, 77–78.
Soups, 64–77.
Sour Cream Molasses Cookies, 320.
Souri, 404.
Sour-milk Doughnuts, 35.
Southdown Soup, 67.
Southern Pone, 28.
Southern Spoon Corn Bread, 27.
South Park Sweetbreads, 129.
Spaghetti, Italian, 43.
   Napoli, 44.
Spanish Codfish, 105.
   Lamb Chops, 120.
   Lobster in Casseroles, 84.
   Potatoes, 182.
   Sauce, 154.
Spiced Celery, 404.
   Cranberry Jelly, 397.
   Rhubarb, 402.
   Salmon, 105.
Spider Corn Cake, Littleton, 28.
Spinach, Moulded, 175.
   Mounded on Artichoke Bottoms, 176.
   Soubrics of, 176.
Sponge Cake, Delia's, 328.
   Potato Flour, 328.
Spring Salad, 198.
Squabs en Casserole, 148.
Squash Pudding, 249.
   Soufflé, 177.
Standish Pudding, 287.
Steamed Figs, 356.
   Ginger Sponge, 252.
Sterling Fruit Pudding, 255.
Steven Steak, 107.
Stewed Apricots and Prunes, 392.
Sticks, Forest Hall Corn, 27.
   Nut Pastry, 313.
   Parmesan Cheese, 51.
   Sultana, 323.
St. Patrick's Caviare Canapés, 379.
Strawberries, Claret, 395.
   Lenox, 394.
   Preserved, 399.
Strawberry Ice Cream I, 284.
   Ice Cream II, 285.
      en Surprise, 293.
   Parfait Amour, 290.

   Salad, 205.
   Sauce, 257.
St. Regis Pudding, 278.
Stretched Chocolate Caramels, 362.
   Molasses Candy, 357.
Stuffed Baked Haddock à la Preston, 93.
   Cushion of Veal, 126.
   Eggs in Aspic, 61.
   Figs, 47.
   Mushroom Caps, 222.
   Peppers, Jarvis, 172.
      Templeton, 175.
   Prunes, 356.
   Smoked Tongue, 241.
   Tomatoes, 178.
   Turbans of Flounder, 94.
Stuffing, Bread and Celery, 152.
   Cracker, 151.
   Fall River, 151.
   New England, 151.
   Oyster, 152.
   Potato, 153.
   Sausage, 153.
   Swedish, 152.
Stuffings for Game and Poultry, 151–153.
St. Valentine's Canapés, 374.
   Hearts, 316.
Sugar, Lemon Cut, 5.
   Orange Cut, 5.
Suitable Combinations for Serving, 411–419.
Sultana Biscuits, 29.
   Nut Frosting, 350.
   Sticks, 323.
Sultan Potatoes, 189.
Suzanne, Coupe, 297.
Swedish Meat Balls, 114.
   Stuffing, 152.
   Tea Circles, 313.
   Wreaths, 24.
Sweetbread and Mushroom Patties, 236.
Sweetbreads à la Root, 128.
   Glazed, Lucullus, 237.
   Huntington, 236.
   Mock, 131.
   Monroe, 129.
   South Park, 129.
   Waldorf, 130.
Sweet Potato Waffles, 33.
Syracuse Filling, 347.

INDEX 439

Five o'Clock Tea, 6.
Syrup, Chocolate, 6.
    Raspberry, 398.

TABASCO FRENCH DRESSING, 213.
Taffy, Butter, 359.
Tapioca, Fruit, 248.
    Garnish for Consommé, 78.
    Rhubarb, Pudding, 247.
Tea, Hawaiian Five o'Clock, 5.
    Jamaica Five o'Clock, 6.
    Syracuse Five o'Clock, 6.
Tea Cakes, 21.
    Chinese, 325.
    Sally Lunn, 22.
Tea Muffins, 25.
Teas, Marshmallow, 324.
    Scotch Five o'Clock, 324.
    Waltham, 389.
Templeton Stuffed Peppers, 175.
Timbales, Carrot, 166.
    Cheese Custard, 221.
    Chicken and Liver, 230.
    Chicken and Mushroom, 230.
    Egg and Pimiento, 59.
    Ham, 231.
    Traymore, 231.
    Veal, 229.

To Measure Dry Ingredients, 2.
Toast, Cinnamon, 33.

    Corned Beef Tomato, à la Bradley, 118.
    Mushroom and Tomato, 173.
Toasted Fromage Rolls, 45.
    Salad Sandwiches, 382.
    Triangles, 77.
Tomato Salad, German, 197.
    Joplin Stuffed, 198.
    Sauce, Bottled, 406.
    Soup, French, 66.
Tomatoes, Broiled, 177.
    Creole, 177.
    Delmonico, 178.
    Soufflé of, Neapolitan Style, 179.
    Stuffed, 178.
    Virginia Style, 180.
    Liquids, 3.
Tongue and Chicken Forcemeat, 242.
    Stuffed Smoked, 241.
Touraine Fruit Salad, 203.
Tournadoes of Beef, 109.
    of Lamb, 121.
Traymore Timbales, 231.
Truffle Sauce, 154.
Turkey, Boned, 242.
    Tetrazzini, 145.
Turkish Delight, 367.
    Mint Paste, 367.
Turnip Cones, 180.

URZINI, Crab Meat, 86.

VANILLA OPERA CARAMELS, 360.
Veal and Sweetbreads, 125–131.
Veal Chops, Bavarian, 125.
    Holstein, 126.
    Loin of, Allemande, 127.
    Stuffed Cushion of, 126.
    Timbales, 229.
    Tomato Bisque, 67.
Vegetable Panachée, 181.
    Ring, Jellied, 181.
Vegetables, 161–181.
    en Casserole, 180.
Venetian Boats, 317.
Venison Steak, Port Wine Sauce, 146.
Vinaigrette Sauce, 159.
Virginia Corn Cake, 26.
Vol-au-Vent, Crab and Mushroom, 233.

WAFERS, Chocolate Walnut, 325.
    Cream, 31.
    Peanut, 322.
    Pimiento Cheese, 46.
    Swedish Nut, 322.
Waffles, Sweet Potato, 33.
Waldorf Sauce, 155.
    Sweetbreads, 130.
Walnut Deceits, 46.
    Molasses Squares, 358.
Waltham Five o'Clock Tea Sandwiches, 389.
Waltham Salad Dressing, 216.
Washington Canapés, 378.
Watercress Soup, Cream of, 70.

Watermelon Cubes, Sherry Dressing, 393.
Wedding Cake, Ornamented, 344.
Wellington Cheese Croquettes, 50.
White Fruit Cake. 340.

White Mountain Angel Cake 331.
　　Cream Filling, 345.
White Wine Sauce, 263.
Windsor Eggs, 61.

YANKEE SAUCE, 259.

www.ingramcontent.com/pod-product-compliance
Lightning Source LLC
Chambersburg PA
CBHW010929180426
43194CB00045B/2835